Development
as Action in Context

Problem Behavior and Normal Youth Development

Edited by
R. K. Silbereisen, K. Eyferth, and G. Rudinger

With 42 Figures

Springer-Verlag
Berlin Heidelberg New York Tokyo

Professor Dr. RAINER K. SILBEREISEN
Professor Dr. KLAUS EYFERTH

Technical University of Berlin
Department of Psychology
Dovestrasse 1 – 5
D-1000 Berlin 10, West Germany

Professor Dr. GEORG RUDINGER

University of Bonn
Department of Psychology
An der Schlosskirche 1
D-5300 Bonn

ISBN 3-540-13449-2 Springer-Verlag Berlin Heidelberg New York Tokyo
ISBN 0-387-13449-2 Springer-Verlag New York Heidelberg Berlin Tokyo

Library of Congress Cataloging in Publication Data. Main entry under title: Development as action in context. Papers presented at an international conference held in Berlin in May 1983. Includes bibliographies and indexes. 1. Youth – Substance use – Congresses. 2. Adolescence – Congresses. 3. Deviant behavior – Congresses. I. Silbereisen, R. K. (Rainer K.), 1944– . II. Eyferth, K. (Klaus), 1928– . III. Rudinger, Georg, 1942– . HV4999.Y68D48 1986 305.2′35 85-27727 ISBN 0-387-13449-2 (U.S.)

Typesetting, printing and bookbinding: Konrad Triltsch, Graphischer Betrieb, 8700 Würzburg
2126/3130-543210

Preface

Most contributions to this volume originated as papers given at an international conference on Integrative Perspectives on Youth Development held in Berlin (West) in May, 1983. This conference was part of a 6-year longitudinal research program on the causes of substance use among adolescents in Berlin, which is now in its fourth year. The conference title deliberately did not refer to substance use. However, its relevance to an explanation of drug-related problem behavior was made evident to everyone invited to the conference.

The search for integrative perspectives in youth development originated in a dilemma that became obvious during the planning of intensive research on concomitants of substance use. In the methodology for research on youth development, there were two lines of thought that seemed completely unrelated to each other: One line of thought was oriented toward the person, leaving situational aspects aside, while the other concentrated on ecological or situational determinants and thus neglected the aspects of development and internal processes. The integration of both these directions seemed to be an unusually promising approach for any project that aimed to understand changes in the individual within a rapidly changing urban setting. The best way to come closer to a resolution of that dilemma seemed to be an intensive exchange between the American and European scientific communities on this issue.

The decision to publish this book was made during the conference in Berlin and some of the papers presented at that meeting are not included here, in particular. The ecological approach, which produced strong counterarguments during the discussion at the conference, is underrepresented.

We would like to mention those colleagues who reported on their research and contributed to the discussion in Berlin who are not represented in this volume: Helmut Becker, Klaus Hurrelmann, Gerhard Kaminski, Ernst-Dieter Lantermann, Erhard Olbrich, Heinz Walter, and Paul Willis. We also appreciate the many fruitful discussions we had with researchers belonging to the TUdrop group at the Technical University of Berlin.

The editors are obliged to Dr. Thomas Thiekötter and Stephanie Benko of Springer-Verlag, Heidelberg, not only for very supportive cooperation but also for their patience during the last months of editing.

The Deutsche Forschungsgemeinschaft (German Research Council) generously supported the conference, thus helping to make this publication possible. Much of the senior editor's work on this book was supported by a grant (*Akademiestipendium*) from the Deutsche Forschungsgemeinschaft (DFG: Si 296/2-1). Special thanks are due to the staff of the Technical University of Berlin, who supported the conference and have been supporting our research on adolescent development for several years.

The conference and this publication also benefited from the diligent and painstaking assistance of Brenda O'Brien, Mary Grunwald, and Ellen Kunze. Bärbel Kracke, Jan Lambertz, and Anne Fina prepared the subject and author indexes. Finally we want to express our gratitude to Joachim Kamratowski, who masterfully managed the conference organization.

K. EYFERTH, G. RUDINGER, and R. K. SILBEREISEN

Table of Contents

C. Development and Problem Behavior

D. Prospects

List of Contributors

Allerbeck, K. R., Johann-Wolfgang-Goethe-University, Department of Social Sciences, Senckenberganlage 15, D-6000 Frankfurt/Main

Argyle, M., University of Oxford, Department of Experimental Psychology, South Parks Road, Oxford OX1 3UD, United Kingdom

Bentler, P. M., University of California, Department of Psychology, 1282a Franz Hall, Los Angeles, CA 90024, USA

Boehnke, K., Technical University of Berlin, Department of Psychology, Dovestrasse 1 – 5, D-1000 Berlin 10, West Germany

Bronfenbrenner, U., Cornell University, Department of Human Development and Family Studies, Martha Van Rensselaer Hall, Ithaca, NY 14853, USA

Caspi, A., University of North Carolina, Chapel Hill, NC 27514, USA

Dittmann-Kohli, F., Max-Planck-Institute for Human Development and Education, Lentzeallee 94, D-1000 Berlin 33, West Germany

Dreher, E., University of Munich, Institute for Educational Psychology, Geschwister-Scholl-Platz 1, D-8000 München 22

Elder, G. H., Jr., University of North Carolina, Chapel Hill, NC 27514, USA

Eyferth, K., Technical University of Berlin, Department of Psychology, Dovestrasse 1 – 5, D-1000 Berlin 10, West Germany

Hoag, W. J., Johann-Wolfgang-Goethe-University, Department of Social Sciences, Senckenberganlage 15, D-6000 Frankfurt/Main

Jessor, R., University of Colorado, Institute of Behavioral Science, Campus Box 483, Boulder, CO 80309, USA

Kandel, D. B., Columbia University, College of Physicians and Surgeons, Department of Psychiatry, 722 West 168th Street, New York, NY 10032, USA

Labouvie, E. W., Rutgers – The State University of New Jersey, Health and Human Development Project, P.O. Box 788, Piscataway, NJ 08854, USA

Lazarus, R. S., University of California, Department of Psychology, Berkeley, CA 94720, USA

Nguyen, T. van, University of North Carolina, Chapel Hill, NC 27514, USA

Noack, P., Technical University of Berlin, Department of Psychology, Dovestrasse 1 – 5, D-1000 Berlin 10, West Germany

Oerter, R., University of Munich, Institute for Educational Psychology, Geschwister-Scholl-Platz 1, D-8000 München 22

Reykowski, J., Polish Academy of Sciences, Department of Psychology, Pl. Malachowskiego 1, PL-00-063 Warszawa

Rudinger, G., University of Bonn, Institute for Psychology, An der Schlosskirche 1, D-5300 Bonn

Silbereisen, R. K., Technical University of Berlin, Department of Psychology, Dovestrasse 1 – 5, D-1000 Berlin 10, West Germany

Trommsdorff, G., Technical University of Rhine-Westphalia, Eilfschornsteinstrasse 7, D-5100 Aachen

A. Introduction

I. Development as Action in Context

R.K. Silbereisen* & K. Eyferth

Introduction

When in 1982 we started to design a longitudinal study on substance use during adolescence, employing developmental concepts to elucidate that behavior seemed almost truistic. But close scrutiny revealed a fairly consistent "developmental paucity" in the body of literature. Proceeding to the literature on normative development in adolescence, we were struck by another pervasive feature, a kind of isolationism: Either researchers emphasized emerging individual capabilities and behaviors apart from everyday contexts; or they stressed contextual features and their differences, apart from the developing individuals. As Bronfenbrenner (this volume) expressed it, the choice was between development out of context and context without development. Our aim with this introductory chapter and the contributions which follow is to illuminate the contours and features of a developmental perspective appropriate to the study of positive as well as problem behaviors in adolescence.

Action Perspective on Development

The brilliant semiotician and novelist Umberto Eco once remarked ironically, "Unfortunately, a title is already a key to meaning" (Eco, 1984, 10, our translation). But the suggestiveness in bringing together three major psychological constructs, each loaded with meaning, in our title, "Development as action in context", is fully deliberate. We are convinced that young people, in action with their context, create the basis for their own development.

Outline of the Model

Before proceeding, we would like to clarify the three major concepts. Development: There is no single theoretical concept of development, but there are a number of accepted propositions (see Baltes, 1983). Certainly the most basic characteristic of development is the change of entities (traditionally in-

---

* Technical University of Berlin, Department of Psychology, Dovestrasse 1 – 5,
   D-1000 Berlin 10, West Germany

Development as Action in Context
Ed. by R. K. Silbereisen et al.
© Springer-Verlag Berlin Heidelberg 1986

dividuals) as a function of time. Because time *per se* is not a psychological construct, it needs to be specified in terms of influences which are corollary to it, such as age-graded social expectations concerning the course of normative development. Further, development is often viewed as the process whereby earlier, less differentiated behavior forms become hierarchically integrated into newer, more complexly articulated forms. The question of which hypothetical mechanisms most adequately explain development remains a matter of great dispute. The action perspective offers one resolution.

Second, action (Brandtstädter, 1984) must be specified. Crudely expressed, we may say that action is behavior plus something. The term is typically used to conceptualize self-initiated, purposeful behavior — behavior that can be interpreted as a means of achieving certain goals, expressing certain values, or solving certain problems. Free choice (at least partial or subjective) among alternative options, based on beliefs and values, is important. Action, in contrast to involuntary behavior, is constitutively characterized by personal control. It is seen in close relationship with the concept of rules. Some action — games, for instance — is constituted by rules; other action is merely regulated by rules such as legal norms or social expectations. Taking action as a unit of psychological analysis emphasizes the dependence of individual behavior on cultural context.

Context is an abstraction of the multivariate actual environments in which human beings live their lives. The history of changing conceptualizations of these environments (see Bronfenbrenner, this volume) is long; physical, interpersonal, and societal environments, even historical periods provide particular experiences to particular generations and are included in the definition of context.

Bringing these three major elements together, "development as action in context" denotes a model of development that entails two critical issues (Silbereisen, 1985): (a) Development is seen as the outcome of a person's own intentional, goal-oriented action aimed at adjusting individual goals and potentials to contextual demands and opportunities. (b) Such action produces not only change in the individual, but change in the context of development as well. The contextual changes thus induced continually provide opportunities for new action aimed at further development.

Action as we use it requires one further specification. The common understanding in research on self-regulation (Carver & Scheier, 1982) conceptualizes action as being hierarchically organized over long periods of time. Thus, the goal of instigating one's own development in a certain area is located at a high conceptual level, implying an extended future-time perspective. At an intermediate level in the hierarchy, the means employed towards the attainment of developmental goals may consist of lengthy action sequences. At a still lower level, single instrumental acts or biophysiological reactions may help promote the intended development.

Thus, action for development ultimately depends upon rather involuntary behavior. There is a further limitation on self-regulation of development: although individuals purposefully plan their action for development, nobody can conceive of all the possible alternatives or avoid all unintended side-effects. Thus, self-planned development depends to some extent on physical restrictions and psychosocial antecedents that may have originated through developmental mechanism other than action.

In short, the action perspective of development is a useful fiction, a paradigm which helps to clarify and systematize basic concepts and methodologies. Certainly, it does not apply equally to all periods in the life-span or all domains of development. For instance, pursuit of complex strategies to instigate change in particular domains depends on having formed abstract socio-cognitive competencies. These competencies are not part of the routine repertoire until adolescence. On the other hand, we do not wish to imply that action aimed at development is always conscious, deliberate, or rational.

We find "development as action in context" especially apt for describing the processes by which adolescents master the transition to adulthood. This is illustrated by the plasticity of the phenomenon itself: Even the very existence of adolescence as a discrete life-stage is subject to intentional change through social as well as personal control. Keniston (1970) postulated the emergence of a new transitional period in highly industrialized societies; a postadolescence or youth period characterizing young people who may have reached the chronological end of adolescence but who are not deemed adults according to societal expectations. Typically, psychosocial independence is at odds with economic dependence. A main social force controlling this shift in the traditional pattern of adolescence is related to the extension of formal education into mid-twenties. Several recent studies (Fischer, Fischer, Fuchs, & Zinnecker, 1981) have demonstrated that the principal aim of a substantial minority of adolescents is to actively postpone their transition to adulthood and its obligations.

Thus, the adolescents' influence extends not only to individual dimensions, but to a considerable degree over the entire system of transition.

Action Perspective – Cure for What?

The classical view of development was highly influenced by research on childhood, where there was good empirical support for concepts of development that view it as a process unidirectionally and universally oriented toward an end state. The researchers expanded into later periods of the life-span, and the more they emphasized new domains such as social development, the less fruitful the traditional views became as a heuristic for research in change processes.

Several arguments have recently excited debate on appropriate models of development; taken together, these arguments provide independent support for the proposed action perspective on development.

Common to one group of arguments are doubts about continuity and universality of development. Kagan (1984) views connections between distinct developmental topics at different periods in life as only too often a product of a mode of thought which strives to overlook their actual independence. Instead of long-term stability, replacement of old structures by new ones seems to be characteristic of development. The chronology of changes depends on age-specific developmental orientations in the context. These expectations, we may add, mirror the cultural regulation of actions. Research in the "contextualistic paradigm" (Baltes, Reese, & Lipsitt, 1980) emphasized the significance of social contexts, historical cohorts, and cultures for molding specific instead of generalized developmental functions and pattern of development. Change is a cross-product of these interacting and contradicting forces which must be coordinated by active attempts by the developing person. The widely demonstrated influence of life-events brings a chance element into development which may account for discontinuities. Some of these events, though unpredictable for the researcher, reveal a strict goal-orientation on the part of the individual. As Bandura (1982) put it, life-paths may evolve or vanish because the person exposes herself purposively to risks and potentials for development.

We may conclude, then, that all these arguments from the developmentalists' side emphasize the active role of the person in arranging and regulating contexts aimed at development.

There are further arguments from environmental psychology: In reviewing recent research, Russell and Ward (1982) complained of a lack of integration between, for instance, studies on cognitive mapping and space-related behavior. Using goal-oriented action as the basic unit of analysis appeared to them a fruitful alternative. In consequence, they plead for more precise consideration of the time dimension in the relation of person and environment. We believe this suggestion could provide a bridge between environmental and developmental psychology. It is action which links the changing individual and the changing environment.

Functional Equivalence

As was mentioned earlier, the action view of development may be regarded as response to problems in long-term prediction of developmental outcomes. Conceptualizing development in terms of self-regulated action can also refresh the spirit of this perennial issue.

Action aimed at development may pursue a certain goal through quite different behavioral means. Evaluated in accordance with legal norms or social expectation, two alternative behaviors may fall into the distinct classes of positive and problem behaviors. In a sense, a problem behavior such as smoking pot or a positive behavior such as having an independent opinion could both serve (at least subjectively) the same function: demonstrating one's independence. On the other hand, even identical behaviors may represent different plans of action.

Thus, in an action format, the equivalence of behaviors is determined on the basis of the underlying structure of goals and other attributes such as regulating rules, necessary requisites, and so forth (see Argyle, this volume), which are seen as essential for a certain prototype of action. Now, let a considerable period of time pass between two manifestations of such a prototype − and the issue of continuity or discontinuity of developmental processes comes clearly into focus in a novel way.

The Case of Substance Use

In the following, we will exemplify some of the key issues of our argumentation up to now. Our reliance on juvenile problem behaviors, especially substance use, is more than a simple reminder of our own research agenda.

First of all, problem behaviors such as drug use (Kandel & Logan, 1984) or delinquency (Rutter & Giller, 1983) show peculiar trends over the life-span. Typically they are highly prevalent and ubiquitous during adolescence and young adulthood, and decrease sharply later on. In a sense, adolescence seems to be prone to rather short episodes of problem behaviors.

Relying on retrospective longitudinal data from a sample of 1,325 persons, Kandel and Logan (1984) found lifetime prevalences at age 18 of 95% for alcohol, 68% for cigarettes, and 54% for marijuana. Periods of highest alcohol and marijuana use peaked at around age 18 and declined sharply after 21. The figures for highest use at 25 resembled those for about age 16. Stabilization periods for cigarettes and psychoactive drugs, in contrast, extended through the mid-twenties. These findings converge with results of repeated cross-sectional surveys (Fishburne, Abelson, & Cisin, 1980), and with data from prospective longitudinal studies (Jessor, this volume). A developmentalists' attention is attracted by the remarkable coincidence of the age-related change in juvenile substance use with the stereotyped chronology of taking on adult roles such as embarking on an occupational career or settling down and starting a family. The data also mirror the legal regulations of substance use. In general, age-graded behavioral expectations seem to influence the time patterning. Thus, one has to expect a considerable degree of variability in accordance with changes in such expectations.

It is important to note, however, that these data mirror substance use in representative samples of adolescent cohorts, not certain groups at risk. Here, the scheduling in accordance to legal norms and social expectations quite obviously underscores Kagan's (1984) arguments: Early antecedents are hardly specifiable under such circumstances. Instead, it seems more informative to explain interindividual change patterns in terms of either differences in the externally provided time schedule, or in terms of differences in the subjective processing of the sociocultural frame of reference.

There is also clear evidence of historical, cultural, social class, and other context-related differences in initiation, maintenance, and discontinuation of substance use. During the last decade, for instance, girls' annual prevalences for smoking increased dramatically in countries such as the U.S. and West Germany, resembling more and more and in some cases even exceeding those of boys (Johnston, Bachman, & O'Malley, 1982). The historical increase in labor force participation of married women (Cherlin, 1983) and a levelling in the gender-typing of socialization coincides with this cohort-related change in female smoking. Once more, a closer look at the time-patterning of substance use demonstrated its variability dependent on contextual factors. Thus, what proponents of the contextualistic life-span view of development had in mind is also true for adolescent substance use. Furthermore, substance use is notoriously subject to arbitrary influences. The spontaneous remission, after their return to the U.S., of soldiers who had been heavy drug users in Viet Nam (Robins, 1978) is a striking example.

Finally, juvenile substance use seems to be a highly multifacetted phenomenon which provides an excellent example of the notion of functional equivalence. Relying on the results of major longitudinal studies (see Kandel, this volume; Jessor, this volume), Silbereisen and Kastner (1985) differentiated at least six prototypes of action which could be expressed in substance use: Taking substances (a) can represent an instance of excessive and ritualized behaviors, (b) it may indicate a lack of self-control, (c) could serve as a means to deviate purposively from norms, (d) is a specific developmental task, considering that controlled, ceremonial use is positively sanctioned, (e) may express an age-typical life-style, and (f) can indicate attempts to cope with helplessness and stress. Thus, the same behavior at the phenomenological level represents rather different orientations. All or part of these heterogeneously motivated behaviors may come together at a certain period of time, or may follow a certain pattern of sequential emergence over time.

In the present discussion, the intentional deviance issue is an instructive example of what Bandura (1982) had in mind. Young people actively expose themselves to deviant encounters. For instance, they seek out certain peer groups in order to restore their self-esteem which suffered from failures to win acceptance from normative reference groups. This "deviance in defense of self" (Kaplan, 1980) expresses itself in substance use or in other functionally equivalent behaviors, including positive behaviors that also result in a gain of self-esteem.

A last point deserving attention is the fact that many problem behaviors in adolescence, like legal substance use or teenage pregnancy, are not problematic as such, but as a function of timing. Thus, at least in the long run, it is not the behavior but its discordance with age-graded expectations which provides risks as well as offering opportunities.

In sum, substance use in adolescence is exemplary for developmental change processes which benefit from study based on the action perspective of development.

Adaptational Demands in Adolescence

A recurrent topic in the discussion thus far has been the importance of age-graded expectations. The notion of development as action in context requires concepts that express the fact that there are prerequisites which provide a base for the formation of individual, development-related goals.

Developmental Tasks

Although there is no single theory of adolescence (see Lerner & Spanier, 1980) there are a number of proposed normative adaptive demands adolescents typically have to face. We begin with a concept, originally introduced by Havighurst in 1951, which has experienced something of a renaissance in the last several years (Oerter, 1985). As people progress through their lives, they have to master series of "developmental tasks" arising from particular constellations of pressures from physical maturation, sociocultural influences, and individual capabilities and aspirations. Examples for the adolescent period are: accepting one's body, learning a masculine or feminine social role, selecting and preparing for an occupation, achieving emotional independence from parents and other adults, establishing a scale of values and an ethical system to live by. These tasks are seen as laying the groundwork for future developments: ". . . a task, which arises at or about a certain period in the life of the individual, successful achievement of which leads to his (sic) happiness and to success with later tasks, while failure leads to unhappiness in the individual, disapproval by society, and difficulty with later tasks." (Havighurst, 1956, p. 215).

Similar lists of adaptive demands have been provided by diverse researchers on adolescence. Sroufe (1979), for instance, presented "salient developmental issues", while Petersen and Spiga (1982) gave a catalogue of "developmental challenges". Despite differences in terminology, all draw from the collective experience of developmentalists such as Erikson (1968), Vygotsky (1962) and Havighurst (1956).

By using such lists of issues, challenges, or tasks for development, one risks overstating the universality of adaptive demands through time and space. Certainly, these demands themselves undergo change. There may be considerable variation in the particular constellation of pressures on adolescent development – between historical periods, between societies, and among different segments of a society.

Viewing development as accomplishing tasks reminds one of the active part individuals play according to the action perspective. On the other hand, the adaptive demands adolescents usually face are not so explicit and definite as the task conceptualization may make them seem. Instead, dealing with one's own fate in view of developmental tasks resembles what Dörner, Kreuzig, Reither, and Stäudel (1983), in their studies on problem-solving in natural contexts, called "acting under indefiniteness and complexity."

A few examples will illustrate the case: (a) Despite the vagueness of many goals related to becoming an adult, quick and momentous decisions are required, for instance, concerning an occupational opportunity. (b) Moreover, there is usually a multiplicity of interdependent and sometimes contradictory goals to be achieved. Autonomy is a good example; it is widely accepted as a desirable goal but adolescents try to achieve it at home. (c) The young suffer from unfamiliarity with the new reality (but also profit from the novelty, Rheingold, 1985) in which they have to operate. (d) The conditions actually relevant for one's development form a highly complex structure. Even under optimal circumstances nobody can ever gain full insight in an appropriate period of time. (e) A further complication is due to the intransparency of the developmental processes themselves. There are no indicators which unambiguously tell about progress and delay. (f) Change in one determinant of the transition is interwoven with change in all other determinants. Peer group activities, for example, facilitate coping with interpersonal problems, but entail a higher risk of drug initiation. (g) Last but not least, only a fraction of the ever-changing influences is susceptible to the individual's control and intervention. A rapid change in physical appearance, for instance, may seriously interfere with one's self-image. Anorexia nervosa demonstrates that it is possible to gain control, although at the cost of destroying health.

Thus, action for development in adolescence may best be described as solving ill-defined, highly complex problems. In contrast to traditional problem-solving paradigms, however, this action is pursued following a unique, far-reaching temporal pattern, where the actor is usually confronted with interferences from other people. Transition in adolescence implies comprehending and solving "... serials − long enterprises in which individuals act in accordance with extended plans of actions" (Little, 1983, 275).

Coping in Adolescence

In earlier research, developmental tasks or equivalent formulations of development-related normative and idiosyncratic goals (challenges, issues, etc.) were appreciated because they provided a theoretical background for integrating results on, for instance, peer group formation and self-esteem, which were originally gathered according to diverse approaches. In recent studies, however, developmental tasks, understood in a more literal sense, have themselves become objects of research on adolescence. The coping processes through which individuals deal with everyday manifestations of developmental tasks are thereby moved into the focus of research attention.

A leading approach is based on the stress-analogy. Developmental tasks are seen as a set of complex strains extending over time which require adaptation. With this perspective, resolving such tasks comes conceptually close to coping with stressful life events. By "coping", Lazarus and Launier (1978) mean efforts (such as information-seeking, direct action, inhibition of action, and intrapsychic devices) to manage environmental and internal demands, and conflicts among them, which tax or exceed a person's resources. Such strains cannot be studied without reference to the person's cognitive appraisal. The same event may be perceived by different individuals or at different periods of the life-span as challenging or threatening. Furthermore, the implications of the event in terms of coping resources and options conceived are relevant. Thus, people attempt to alter the threatening conditions and to regulate the emotional distress induced by their appraisal of them. As Lazarus (this volume) explains, it is not the major events but a continuing series of irritating, frustrating, and distressing daily hassles that matter most.

If research guided by this approach is to be in accordance with the portrayal of adolescents as facing ill-defined and highly complex problems, one would expect extensive data on appraisal processes and major emphasis on normative, age-graded, everyday manifestations of developmental tasks. As summarized in Seiffge-Krenke's (1984; see also Rutter, 1981) review, this is not the case in the international literature: (a) Very few studies deal at all with adolescents' appraisal processes. According to Moriarty and Toussieng (1976), cognitive styles ("sensors" and "censors") seem to play a role in appraisal. Additional evidence may be seen in Haan's (1977) description of coping in terms of several ego-functions ("attention focusing", etc). (b) Almost all studies deal with non-normative, often critical or even traumatic life events such as teenage motherhood, severe illness, and unemployment. The few studies on everyday strains are mostly related to school stress. Interpersonal conflicts predominate in spontaneously reported hassles (Seiffge-Krenke, 1984).

Research Topics

The coping approach is a promising conceptualization which is expanding into new fields: Labouvie (this volume) transfers it to research on juvenile substance use; and in general, the stress-analogy attracts scholars of developmental psychopathology (Garmezy & Rutter, 1983).

According to our view, the appraisal component is the one which especially merits conceptual differentiation and empirical work. In contrast to coping with distinct life-events, strains related to developmental tasks do not usually emerge without activity on the part of the developing person. By actively scanning a multiplicity of interpersonal sources, adolescents may attempt to extract specific goals and forms of action from an ambiguous set of social expectations, personal aspirations, and biological potentials.

Common to information processing and problem-solving approaches is the assumption of certain knowledge bases (see Dörner et al., 1983). An "epistemic" structure contains information on the features of the environment and the capabilities of the individual, and a "heuristic" structure consists of information about strategies for dealing with problems. A major issue for future research, and one that has been almost totally neglected, is the gathering of information on adolescents' epistemic and heuristic structures in relation to producing their own development.

A related question concerns the sources of such information. Silbereisen and Zank (1984), for instance, found age-related differences in the attributed salience of parents, peers, and heterosexual friends as originators of self-related knowledge.

We do need much more research on the subjective definition of developmental tasks: How do adolescents conceptualize their naive theory on age-graded expectations? Specific information on this topic is provided by Dreher and Oerter (this volume).

Typical of attempts to solve ill-defined, highly complex problems is what may be called formation of goals. Here, we have two issues: First, the question of the embeddedness of certain goals in more general personal attributes such as value-orientations (Silbereisen, Boehnke & Reykowski, this volume), and the influence of future-time perspectives, as demonstrated by Trommsdorff (this volume). Second, the process by which adolescents scan problems and gradually come to more precise, situation-specific and manageable goals. How do the young compensate for partial contradictions; what sequential arrangement of goals do they choose? Recently, Cantor and Kihlstrom (1985) proposed "life-tasks" as a means of studying social intelligence. Departing from the classical view of intelligence, they focused on how young people frame problems and shape solutions to adjust to issues on the personals and cultural agenda in a period of environmental change.

In contrast to Lazarus and Launier (1978), research based on problem-solving models (or "motivated social strategies", Showers and Cantor, 1985) will not restrict itself to a few basic styles of coping. Urgency of goal-attainment in a certain domain is one example of many concepts that might fruitfully be transferred into developmental research.

Contextual Potentials

Contexts do exert influences on adolescent's developmental orientations, either by expressing cultural aging stereotypes, or by providing certain direct or vicarious experiences. Because of the high salience of cultural determinants for development in the action perspective, a variety of interpersonal and higher-order social contexts deserve attention (extended family, neighborhoods, communities, etc., and their changing characteristics over time). Thus, research such as Elder's on families in hard times (this volume) is exemplary for research programs studying development as a joint function of changing individuals and changing contexts.

Under the action perspective, those contexts deliberately chosen by the individual deserve particular attention. Here two issues are salient: First, which contexts do adolescents actively seek out? A broad range of environments to which adolescents expose themselves should be considered – from street corners to computer shops. Second, in what way do experiences and ecounters in these contexts interact or interfere with those of others such as family or school? Contextual transition (Bronfenbrenner, this volume) seems to be one source of development.

Control over Environment

Research on adolescents in their environment is fairly rare. There are some studies on the cognitive organization and emotional evaluation of urban environments (Hart, 1979). There is also research on spatial movement, mostly centered on the issue of home range (Lynch, 1977). Although environmental knowledge and action in the environment relate to each other, the two issues typically have not been linked together theoretically in the past.

Control over persons and control over space become increasingly prominent during the course of adolescence (Laufer & Wolfe, 1977). There is a clear relationship between self-esteem and control. Not to have control over territories such as leisure settings reduces self-esteem and promotes deviance such as vandalism (Russell & Ward, 1982). Hormuth (1984) found that people who moved used the opportunity the new environment affords to facilitate self-concept change.

Relating Context and Individual

Studies on the interaction between person and context through time have derived immense benefit from research paradigms using "ecobehavioral units" as the basis for the analysis. Barker used the behavior-setting concept this way, studying adolescents' participation in public settings such as shops or banks (Schoggen & Barker, 1974). From our perspective, one problem with his approach is the rather passive conceptualization of the individual, who is portrayed as being occupied with fixed patterns of behaviors. The action concept serves as an ecobehavioral unit, and at the same time allows more leeway for individual attributes such as goals and plans (Kaminski, in press).

Starting from a personality research viewpoint, Little (1983) introduced the concept of "personal projects" which were conceived as a set of interrelated acts over extended periods of time. They include active commerce with the environment and are used to attain or maintain a state of affairs as foreseen by the individual. Personal projects include idiosyncratic, subtle intentions ("overcoming fear of meeting new people") as well as highly normative plans ("graduating from university"). Characteristic of his concept is a hypothetical sequence of stages through which projects progress to completion.

What is remarkable is the attempt to describe contexts by their function as requisites in the pursuit of an ordered plan of action whose aim is personal growth. The point of departure is a process model of adaptation to developmental tasks (or "projects" located at a level below superordinate core concerns). The development-related function of an environment is then explained, for instance, in terms of providing the knowledge base or modelling the strategies needed to deal with developmental tasks. Thus, a setting's potential for development may be a function of the degree that complexity is reduced — if complexity and indefiniteness are indeed, as we understand them, major problems in adolescent development.

Of course, this is a very general description. In the chapters by Argyle and by Silbereisen, Noack and Eyferth (this volume) much more detail, and some reservations may be found.

Conclusion

We propose to look at development as action in context. We outlined this model indicating that adolescents, particularly, produce their own task environments to actively shape their development. We reviewed other, similar views that are increasingly being heard. Some of these views are to be found in this volume.

We argued that substance use is an informative and suitable example in dealing with two levels of concepts and research: (a) the person-oriented level, including problems of originating and structuring action; (b) the contextual level, including the adolescents' perspectives on their environment. Studies on substance use that clarify this point make up a considerable part of the following contributions.

Two concepts were discussed that are central to adaptation and development: developmental task and coping strategies. Several of the contributions focus on these concepts.

Finally, we dealt with two contextual aspects: the adolescent's control over his or her environment, and the interdependence between external contextual demands and internal knowledge of contexts. Discussion of these aspects, which has been rather scarce in research until now, is pursued in several chapters.

Throughout the book, the value of integrating person-oriented and contextual aspects will be seen to recur as a *leitmotiv*, a key to better understanding of action for development.

References

Baltes, P. B. (1983) Life-span developmental psychology: Observations on history and theory revisited. In R. M. Lerner (Ed.), *Developmental psychology: Historical and philosophical perspectives.* Hillsdale, N. J.: Erlbaum

Baltes, P. B., Reese, H. W., & Lipsitt, L. P. (1980) Life-span developmental psychology. *Annual Review of Psychology, 31,* 65—100

Bandura, A. (1982) The psychology of chance encounters and life paths. *American Psychologist, 37,* 747—755

Brandtstädter, J. (1984) Personal and social control over development: Some implications of an action perspective in life-span developmental psychology. In P. B. Baltes & O. G. Brim, Jr. (Eds.), *Life-span development and behavior* (Vol. 6). New York: Academic Press

Cantor, N. & Kihlstrom, J. F. (1985) Social intelligence: The cognitive basis of personality. *Review of Personality and Social Psychology, 6*

Carver, C. S. & Scheier, M. F. (1982) Control theory: A useful conceptual framework in personality — social, clinical and health psychology. *Psychological Bulletin, 92,* 11–135

Cherlin, A. (1983) Changing family and household: Contemporary lessons from historical research. *Annual Review of Sociology, 9,* 51—66

Dörner, D., Kreuzig, H. W., Reither, F., & Stäudel, T. (Eds.), (1983) *Lohhausen. Vom Umgang mit Unbestimmtheit und Komplexität.* Bern: Huber

Eco, U. (1983) *Nachschrift zum „Namen der Rose".* München: Hanser.

Erikson, E. H. (1968) *Identity, youth and crisis.* New York: Norton

Fischer, A., Fischer, R., Fuchs, W., & Zinnecker, J. (1981) *Jugend '81.* Hamburg: Jugendwerk der Deutschen Shell

Fishburne, P., Abelson, H., & Cisin, I. (1979) *The national survey on drug abuse: main findings.* Washington, D. C.: U.S. Government Printing Office

Garmezy, N. & Rutter, M. (Eds.), (1983) *Stress, coping and development in children.* New York: McGraw Hill

Haan, N. (1977). *Coping and defending. Processes of self-environment organization.* New York: Academic Press

Hart, R. (1979) *Children's experience of place.* New York: Irvington

Havighurst, R. J. (1956) Research on the developmental task concept. *The School Review, a Journal of Secondary Education, 64,* 215—223

Hormuth, S. (1984) Transitions in commitments to roles and self-concept change: Relocation as a paradigm. In V. Allen & E. van de Vliert (Eds.), *Role transitions: Explorations and explanations.* New York: Plenum

Johnston, L. D., Bachman, J. G., & O'Malley, P. M. (1982) *Student drug use, attitudes and beliefs: National trends 1975–1982.* Rockville: National Institute on Drug Abuse

Kagan, J. (1984) Continuity and change in the opening years of life. In R. N. Emde & R. J. Harmon (Eds.), *Continuities and discontinuites in development.* New York: Plenum

Kaminski, G. (in press) *Ordnung und Variabilität im Alltagsgeschehen: Das Behavior Setting-Konzept in den Sozial- und Verhaltenswissenschaften.* Göttingen: Hogrefe

Kandel, D. B. & Logan, J. A. (1984) Patterns of drug use from adolescence to young adulthood: I. Periods of risk for initiation, continued use, and discontinuation. *American Journal of Public Health, 74,* 660—666

Kaplan, H. B. (1980) *Deviant behavior in defense of self.* New York: Academic Press

Keniston, K. (1970) Youth: A "new" stage of life. *American Scholar, 39,* 631—641

Laufer, R. S. & Wolfe, M. (1977) Privacy as a concept and a social issue: A multidimensional developmental theory. *Journal of Social Issues, 33,* 22—42

Lazarus, R. S. & Launier, R. (1978) Stress-related transactions between person and environment. In L. Pervin & M. Lewis (Eds.), *Perspectives in interactional psychology.* New York: Plenum

Lerner, R. M. & Spanier, G. B. (1980) *Adolescent development.* New York: McGraw-Hill

Little, B. R. (1983) Personal projects: A rationale and method for investigation. *Environment and behavior, 15*, 273–309

Lynch, K. (Ed.) (1977) *Growing up in cities: Studies of the spatial environment of adolescence in Cracow, Melbourne, Mexico City, Salta, Toluca, and Warszawa.* Cambridge, Mass.: MIT Press

Moriarty, A. E. & Toussieng, P. W. (1976) *Adolescent coping.* New York: Grune & Stratton

Oerter, R. (1985) Developmental task through the life-span: A new approach to an old concept. In D. L. Featherman & R. M. Lerner (Eds.), *Life-span development and behavior* (Vol. 7). New York: Academic Press

Petersen, A. G. & Spiga, R. (1982) Adolescence and stress. In L. Goldberger & S. Breznitz (Eds.), *Handbook of stress: Theoretical and clinical aspects.* New York: The Free Press

Rheingold, H. L. (1985) Development as the acquisition of familiarity. *Annual Review of Psychology, 36*, 1–17

Robins, L. N. (1978) The interaction of setting and predisposition in explaining novel behavior: Drug initiation before, in, and after Vietnam. In D. B. Kandel (Ed.), *Longitudinal research on drug use.* Washington: Hemisphere

Russell, J. A. & Ward, L. M. (1982) Environmental psychology. *Annual Review of Psychology, 33*, 651–688

Rutter, M. (1981) Stress, coping and development: Some issues and some questions. *Journal of Child Psychology and Psychiatry, 22*, 323–356

Rutter, M. & Giller, H. (1983) *Juvenile delinquency: Trends and perspectives.* Harmondsworth: Penguin

Schoggen, P. & Barker, R. G. (1974) The ecological psychology of adolescents in an American and an English town. In H. Thomae & T. Endo (Eds.), *The adolescent and his environment: Contributions to an ecology of teen-age behavior.* Basel: Karger

Seiffge-Krenke, I. (1984) *Problembewältigung im Jugendalter.* Habilitationsschrift des Fachbereichs 06 der Justus-Liebig-Universität, Gießen

Showers, C. & Cantor, N. (1985) Social cognition: A look at motivated strategies. In M. Rosenzweig & L. Porter (Eds.), *Annual Review of Psychology, 36*, 275–305

Silbereisen, R. K. (1985) Action theory perspectives in research on social cognition. In M. Freese & J. Sabini (Eds.), *Goal directed behavior: Psychological theory and research on action.* Hillsdale, N. J.: Erlbaum

Silbereisen, R. K. & Kastner, P. (1985) Entwicklungstheoretische Perspektiven für die Prävention des Drogengebrauchs Jugendlicher. In J. Brandtstädter & H. Gräser (Eds.), *Entwicklungsberatung unter dem Aspekt der Lebensspanne.* Göttingen: Hogrefe

Silbereisen, R. K. & Zank, S. (1984) Development of self-related cognitions in adolescence. In R. Schwarzer (ed.), *The self in anxiety, stress and depression. Proceedings of the International Conference held in Berlin, July 27–29, 1983.* Amsterdam: GSP North Holland

Sroufe, L. A. (1979) The coherence of individual development. *American Psychologist, 34*, 834–841

Vygotsky, L. S. (1962) *Thought and language.* Cambridge, Mass.: MIT Press

B. Approaches to Managing Life-Tasks in Adolescence

II. Problem Identification and Definition as Important Aspects of Adolescents' Coping with Normative Life-Tasks

F. DITTMANN-KOHLI*

Objective

The objective of the following presentation is to describe and explain from a transactional perspective a study on adolescents in West German apprenticeship training.[1] This study tried to incorporate both the individual and his environment by investigating behavior in a life-world context, on the one hand, and the representation of these situations and behaviors in adolescents, on the other. The awareness and understanding individuals have of their situation and of the corresponding possibilities for action are seen as a central factor in successful life mastery, whereas, conversely, a lack of understanding of the conditions of action in personally relevant reality domains, that is, one's life world, is believed to increase the probability of failure and disappointment.

The approach to the study of coping as described here (i. e., Lebensbewältigung) is cognitive, as it focuses on problem understanding as a part of the problem-solving process. An understanding of reality is seen as a crucial factor in efficient coping. A cognitive approach to the study of coping is advantageous in that it is relatively easy to develop intervention programs designed to improve the adolescent's understanding of reality, for example, by adapting the school curriculum. It is probably not difficult to include behavioral learning in such programs, thereby increasing the likelihood of successful application of acquired knowledge.

The study was designed in 1976 as a response to the German Education Ministry's funding[2] of conceptual work leading to the development of learning programs aimed at strengthening adolescent's competency in interpersonal and social domains. This was hoped to be a necessary supplement to the exclusive emphasis on training vocational skills typical of appprentices' on-the-job training and the one day per week classroom work required of such trainees.

* Max-Planck-Institut for Human Development and Education, Lentzeallee 94, D-1000 Berlin 33, West Germany.

[1] For a detailed presentation of theory and empirical results of this study see Dittmann-Kohli, Schreiber, & Möller, 1982a.

[2] Additional funding was obtained from the Deutsche Forschungsgemeinschaft for 1978/1979.

Development as Action in Context
Ed. by R. K. Silbereisen et al.
© Springer-Verlag Berlin Heidelberg 1986

Curriculum programs designed to aid in the personal growth of adolescents during apprenticeship training must, in contrast to individualized therapy, be concerned with generally applicable competencies and normative life tasks which are relevant for all members of the target group. Nonnormative events like severe personal and social problems (e. g., drug addiction) are not included in this approach. (However, heavy substance use *may* be a special manifestation of unsuccessful coping which results from an inadequate understanding of reality.)

The study of the cognition and behavior of adolescent apprentices in their ecological context is seen as an important addition to the psychological study of adolescence in general. In Germany, the majority of young people in the age group of 15–19 years undergo apprenticeships. However, there is little psychological research on the topic. This seems to be a problem insofar as the life world (e. g., ecology) and the experiences of apprentices are radically different from those of regular students. In particular, it is the world of work and of the adult which dominates the apprentices' lives and helps to shape their psychological development. Organized work has not been given much consideration as a social and action context in adolescent developmental psychology. This has had consequences for the conceptualization of many issues in the area of adolescent personality development, especially with respect to developmental tasks.

The theoretical framework to be presented centers on understanding of and coping with normative life tasks in a problem-solving perspective. The theoretical framework is then extended to identify objective situations and life-tasks of adolescents, and is presented as a guiding framework for the design and assessment methods of the present study on apprentices' coping with normative developmental life tasks. Finally, results on interpersonal and intrapersonal coping will be reported and discussed.

Relevant Research Traditions

The concepts and ideas used in the present action psychological approach to coping stem from various research traditions and meta-theoretical orientations which can be briefly summarized as follows:

a) In an *active organism* paradigm, in the *living system* model as well as in functionalism the individual is understood as acting upon his environment and himself, thus also producing his own development (Brandtstädter, 1984; Heidbreder, 1933; Kocowski, 1975; Lerner & Busch-Rossnagel, 1981; Reese & Overton, 1970).

b) As is stressed in East European action psychology (e. g., Leontjew, 1979; Tomaszewski, 1978), individuals are located in societal contexts which develop historically.

c) East European action theorists stress the activity concept and discriminate between reactive behavior and intentional activity as two different kinds of behavior. Tasks in the real world are solved by goal-oriented activity (Lompscher & Kossakowski, 1977; Tomaszewski, 1978, 1981). Reality-oriented coping (Haan, 1977; Lazarus, 1980; Lazarus, Averill, & Opton, 1974; Lazarus & Launier, 1978) would also fall into this category as it stresses the centrality of problem solving to coping.

d) Problem-solving and information processing research traditions (Aebli, 1980, 1981; Dörner, 1976; Dörner, Kreuzig, Reither, & Stäudel, 1983; Simon, 1973, 1980; Tuma & Reif, 1980) are considered in harmony with action theory and offer additional useful and well-known concepts.

e) Praxeology and the planning sciences (Gehmacher, 1975; Kirsch, 1977; Musto, 1972; Zieleniewski, 1966) espouse concepts of efficiency, utility, and cost-benefit evaluation used as criteria to judge success or failure in coping.

Coping from Within a Developmental Perspective

In a developmental perspective, coping is of interest in that it may influence the life course and the nature of developmental functions. For instance, coping is comprised of activities which shape one's interpersonal relations, one's career, one's conduct vis à vis oneself, one's use of leisure time, etc. The alternatives which are open to individuals and the effects which can be produced are, of course, limited by the social, psychological, and biological forces acting upon them. For instance, with respect to the environment, sociological research on the life course (Hagestad & Neugarten, 1985) points to the limits within which the individuals can influence their life course. Among others, the fields of clinical psychology and education elucidate the possible range of individual change open for self-development.

In an action-psychological perspective, the concept of individuals as producers of their own development (Lerner & Busch-Rossnagel, 1981) takes the meaning of active and possibly planful self-development (Brandtstädter, 1984; Dittmann-Kohli, 1982). The question of interest here is how well adolescents can act on themselves and on their environment in a growth-inducing way and how they can be taught or helped to achieve such self-development.

The Concept of Coping

In personality models based on the active organism paradigm (Reese & Overton, 1970) or on living system concepts (Tomaszewski, 1978, 1981), the individual can affect changes and control internal and environmental states. An action-psychological perspective of coping also focuses on those aspects of the self and the environment which can potentially be controlled by the individual.

The concept of coping as used here is based on the more general process of action as problem-solving, in the sense of mastering everyday life with its regular and irregular events. Life management and the process of coping occur with respect to both recurring situations and single short- or long-term events. Thus, successful coping in the sense of effective problem-solving is important for good decision-making in career planning as well as in efficient work organization. The term coping is not restricted to repair-type situations or threat (Lazarus, 1980; Lazarus & Launier, 1978; Prystav, 1981). Rather, it is understood as a striving for enhancement of the self, both by maintaining or regaining positive states of affairs as well as by increasing present rewards and developing new goals altogether. Rewards and goal states may be valued because they produce positive feeling or because they are positively evaluated on a cognitive level.

Coping includes reactive and routinized behavior as well as intentional activities or action systems. Both types of behavior can be external as well as internal (for instance, cognitive problem-solving is internal intentional activity). Coping can be more or less effective and life management more or less efficient; the effects of one's actions can be positive or negative with respect to one's present and future development and quality of life. An individual's activities are ineffective if they do not result in the attainment of a given goal or if the goals accomplished have little utility – that is, do not contribute to the overall benefit of the individual. Coping is also considered suboptimal if activities have more negative side effects, or costs, than gains, and if opportunities are not used to one's advantage, because, for instance, they have been overlooked or not understood. In order to assess and evaluate an individual's coping from the perspective of optimization, both the already chosen solution and other possible ways of action have to be taken into account. Coping efficiency can thus be viewed with respect to a criterion of ultimate benefit or maximal utility for the actor. The criterion of utility and efficiency can be applied to internal and external reactive and routinized behaviors, as well as actions.

Speaking in terms of problem-solving theory, one must consider the field of possible operators, that is, possible other solutions in a problem space, as well as the solution chosen by the problem solver, in order to judge coping efficiency. The problem space is here constituted as an action space, the operators as action possibilities, and the solution chosen as the action plan. The implementation of the solution changes, in turn, the social, material, psychological, and other aspects of reality. The concept of action space indicates an action-psychological approach to environment.

Problem Understanding as a Factor in Coping

In problem-solving theory, one differentiates between open and closed tasks. If the task in question has a known solution and readily available means we speak of a closed task; in the event where the desired end state and/or the solution, as well as perhaps the initial state, are not given and have to be defined and invented, we speak of an open task or problem. As Tomaszewski (1978, 1981) has emphasized, the execution of actions or goal-directed activities in everyday life can be understood as the solution of a closed task because it changes an initial undesired state into a desired end state by implementing a readily available solution, that is, the action plan. The planning phase preceding implementation, however, covers an open task, as it involves the identification and definition of a problem (an undesirable state and its related context), the formation of goals, and the design and selection of possible action strategies.

Researchers in the area of problem-solving have not only investigated the solution process in the narrower sense but have also stressed the problem identification and definition processes (e. g., Greeno, 1980; Kozmetsky, 1980; Reif, 1980; Scriven, 1980; Seidel, 1976; Simon, 1973). With respect to complex, uncertain problems, this has been referred to as problem understanding by Simon (1973) and Scriven (1980). They consider problem understanding as the most important part of the solution process as it guides the search for and the choice of solutions. Problem understanding and reality perception is therefore also the central factor in coping with respect to the complex, ill-defined aspects of life management. Transferred to an action-psychological terminology, problem understanding is often denoted as reality perception or understanding of situations, and definition of tasks. In addition to problem identification and definition in a wider reality context, problem understanding includes goal setting, planning, and evaluation. In Lazarus' terminology these are referred to as the primary, secondary, and tertiary appraisal processes (Lazarus & Launier, 1978).

Many of the tasks in private and occupational everyday life need only routinized activities; the term *everyday life* is referring to this fact. The construct "coping with life tasks", as used here, refers to tasks which are open (i. e., are problems), uncertain or ill-defined, complex, dynamic or self-changing, not transparent, and netted with other tasks (Dörner, Kreuzig, Reither & Stäudel, 1983; Simon, 1973). In the case of applying everyday routines, the actor is solving a closed task. However, when he reflects about their efficiency and utility, he tackles a problem. Thus, even everyday routines or habitual activity can be the object of problem-solving activities when questioning their utility or adequacy.

However, what is to be defined as a problem by the researcher must not necessarily be perceived as such by the actor. From the perspective of the researcher, for instance, a problem can exist for the actor with respect to routinized activities or social situations if a practice is violating the actor's own interests without being noticed (Kocowski, 1975). In such cases the actor does not perceive it as a problem situation: Subjectively, there is no problem (Seidel, 1976). For our purposes, therefore, the subjectively perceived problem situation, that is, a felt need or desire to change or retain a certain state of affairs, is not the criterion for speaking of a problem-solving approach to coping with normative life tasks. On the contrary, the lack of awareness of a problem is considered to be a possible reason for suboptimal problem-solving or failure in coping, because one does not search for solutions if the state of affairs seems satisfactory.

Cognitive as well as emotional factors may hinder an individual from adequately understanding the situation and defining the task. For example, psychotherapy and encounter groups are geared towards the improvement of problem understanding by uncovering emotional barriers to reality perception. Psychotherapy as well as everyday observation show that problem understanding is often inadequate because of lack of knowledge, inadequate thinking, and prejudice against talking about private problems. From an overall perspective, real-life coping is an open-ended task, one which is ill-defined, complex and not transparent. There are often no clear-cut solutions, but in many cases it is possible to increase transparency by acquiring knowledge about and concepts useful for understanding of the self and the environment, for task perception, problem identification, and problem definition. It is also possible to develop a system of criteria to evaluate past performances and future plans in terms of a clearer picture of one's needs and values.

Intervention

In late adolescence, individuals may be able to learn facts, conceptions, action strategies, and other techniques which will/can make them better problem solvers. Thus, educational exercises can be devised which would make adolescents more knowledgeable about their personal lives as well as their own activities therein. The quality of problem understanding and reality perception is of importance for successful coping or mastery throughout the life span, but particularly so in youth because youth represents the entry phase to adult life. Intervention is crucial because adolescents can usually be reached by large scale programs while they go to school, but few adults are able to participate regularly in educational or training settings. Reality understanding and problem definition could be made a central issue in large scale intervention programs which could be designed to improve coping in adolescence and adulthood. In contrast to psychotherapy, these programs can reach more than a few individual cases.

In the planning of such intervention strategies, it is necessary to define situation appraisal and reality perception as problem understanding guiding real-life behavior in order to draw on research and theory on problem-solving and the teaching of problem-solving (e. g., Tuma & Reif, 1980). Psychological research in cognitive science and various other fields may be used to design learning activities which foster intellectual means to guide planning and evaluation activities (Gehmacher, 1975); meta-planning principles (Wilensky, 1981) may help to conduct cost-benefit analyses useful in checking the relationship between needs, goals, and action strategies. In addition to research related to cognitive psychology, curriculum research as well as new knowledge gained from clinical uses of a problem-solving approach (Bergold, 1980; Fiedler, 1981; Greif, 1980; Kaiser, 1980; Kommer & Linsenhoff, 1980) can guide efforts to devise such programs.

Life World and Life Tasks

Prior to the construction of such programs aimed at the enhancement of adolescents' reality perception, information about their initial understanding of reality has to be collected. Such data about adolescents' present understanding of reality can then be used as a basis for curriculum development and can also be transformed and used as learning materials stimulating self-reflection, self-evaluation, and exchange of experience. In order to collect valuable information on the understanding of and coping with reality, however, the researcher himself must acquire information about the life world of the group of individuals in question (Bronfenbrenner, 1979; Lewin 1963). Both the life world and the understanding of reality must be broken down into meaningful subunits in which a set of developmental or life tasks can be defined and the corresponding set of subjective problem spaces can be determined. In the following description of a taxonomy of life tasks, a systematic way of arriving at meaningful subunits is offered. This classification system is both contextual (socioecological) and action-psychological (transactional).

Taxonomy of Life Tasks

Two principles have been used to define a set of developmental tasks (i.e., life tasks which are typical for a developmental period) for a target group. The first principle is socio-ecological in nature, the second is action-psychological (Dittmann-Kohli, 1982).

1. The *socio-ecological principle* of defining developmental tasks (see Figure 1a) is based on the fact that any target group is part of a social system, and that the life world of the individuals in that group is located in the social stratification system of society. Therefore, in a first step, the normative world of the members of the target group must be identified. In order to further divide the life world into ecologically meaningful reality domains, the various simultaneous social roles of the individual must be considered. The social institutions in which these roles are played represent spatio-temporal units which are experienced as separate reality domains. These in-

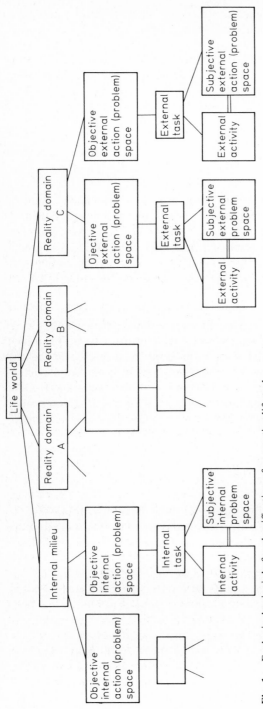

Fig. 1a. Ecological principle for classification of normative life tasks

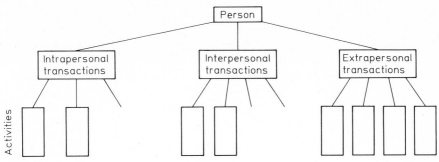

Fig. 1 b. Transactional classification of life tasks

stitutional reality domains, however, are rather broad in that they comprise many different micro-settings (actions spaces, problem spaces) where different kinds of activities are carried out. Such micro-settings or activity centers, as Tomaszewski (1978, 1981) has defined them, represent the ecological basis for defining developmental tasks and corresponding subjective problem spaces.

2. The *transactional classification principle* is behavioral (action-psychological) in nature and is used as a criterion to select those micro-settings or action spaces in the reality domains that are strategically important for the target group members. In other words, the application of this second classification principle is necessary because the tasks in the institutional reality domains must be defined from the perspective of the individual's needs and goals and from the possibilities for action (see Figure 1 b).

This second classification principle comprises *three transactional categories* which have been labelled extra-personal, inter-personal, and intra-personal. The three categories can be seen as three general areas of coping, or of problem understanding and planning, in three classes of micro-settings or objective problem spaces. Each of the three classes of problem spaces has its own set of characteristics which make different demands on human cognition and behavior and partly also involve quite different kinds of needs and possibilities for satisfaction. The extra-personal and the inter-personal categories represent classes of micro-settings which are external to the person. They are located in and pertain to the ecological structure of the outer life world and they are part of the institutional reality domains:

– *The extra-personal category* refers to tasks which consist of instrumental behaviors aimed at possible rewards and goal states in institutional reality domains. The competencies and behaviors needed to pursue these tasks are, for instance, detailed knowledge of institutionally permitted ways of action, and detailed programs (plans) of efficient instrumental behavior.

– *The inter-personal category* refers to tasks resulting from the existence of significant others in various social roles in the institutional reality domains.

– *The intra-personal category* refers to tasks resulting from the fact that individuals can be objects of knowing, thinking, and feeling *to themselves* and that they can control their psychological states and behavior and modify their own personality. The intra-personal category represents the internal milieu of the person who is in turn a highly organized and active system in the environmental system, the life world.

Extra-personal activities refer to instrumental behaviors directed at environmental, institutionally-related goal states. These activities include the kinds of behavior analyzed in the East European work psychology (e. g., Hacker, 1978; Volpert, 1974) and the kinds of behaviors usually used as illustrations in action theory. Such behaviors are directed toward some product or change in the environment, and toward the relationship between person and environment. Such behaviors can be planned because there is a designated goal state, and because discernible activities or action systems exist which can be adopted or organized to produce the desired goals.

Interpersonal activities represent a separate transactional category because the objects of behavior (i. e., other individuals) are in themselves living systems; therefore, the laws of intersystem relations govern their exchange. This includes, in addition to instrumental behavior in favor of the actor's goals, cooperative behavior, communication, and expressive behavior. Social roles and their settings as well as the individual personalities of the actors and the history of their relationship define the action spaces for interpersonal tasks.

The second category thus comprises two major kinds or aspects of interpersonal interaction. The first is instrumental to one or both partner's goals and can be planned in some detail. The second kind of interaction cannot be planned in detail because it is spontaneous and expressive. On a higher level, however, spontaneous behavior can be an intended, and thus planned, component in social episodes and in planful regulation of interpersonal relationships.

The intrapersonal category refers to tasks concerning the self as a direct object of internal (and sometimes external) behavior. The self can be the object of intentional and spontaneous activities in the sense of internalized interpersonal behavior. The self can be the object of perception, understanding, evaluation, feelings, and modification or control. Regarding the last two, the term *intrapersonal coping* has been used to denote cognitive and affective processes directed at controlling internal states, such as those associated with emotional disruption (Lazarus, Averill, & Opton, 1974).

The Target Group and the Study

As was mentioned above, a precondition for the identification of the normative life tasks of the target group is an adequate understanding by the researcher of the sociological and psychological characteristics of the members defining the group, and of the ecological characteristics of the life world. The more such information is taken into account, the easier it is to define the tasks and understand their interrelationships. Adequate understanding of the life world of a target group is necessary to determine the objective tasks or problem spaces which should represent the units of analysis for the assessment of the subjective representation of these tasks in the members of the target group. Sociological information must be collected and other social science data must be used to acquire an understanding of the life world structure of the target group in question (Dittmann-Kohli, Schreiber, & Möller, 1982a).

We shall now turn to *apprentices as a target group* for the study of the life world and task perception of adolescents. Basic decisions on the type of design and methodology were derived from the theoretical framework. As explained earlier, the task perception and reality understanding of adolescents is seen as the important factor for improvement of coping. The kind of data necessary for this purpose does not have to be quantitative. Rather, it is more useful to obtain prototypes of the various ways in which these adolescents interpret their position and situation in various settings, and to obtain descriptions of the types of activities they use to deal with these situations. For the researcher, this material is necessary to understand and evaluate the adolescents' task perception and coping. With respect to the teaching of improved problem-solving, Scriven (1980) has argued that the analysis of students' ways of problem-solving need not be overly detailed and need not demonstrate every single mistake that can be made. Rather, the analysis must show the typical way students deal with the problems in question.

These considerations led to the decision to follow a qualitative design using interview and ethnographic data to investigate the life world and task perceptions of a relatively small group of 20 apprentices representing five typical German trades. The trades selected are among the ten most frequent training vocations (*Ausbildungsberufe*) in Western Germany and represent various sizes of firms and types of work environment for males and females.

Normative Life Tasks During Apprenticeship

The planning of the empirical study on apprentices was based on the classification system of life tasks described above. In order to define the required set of normative tasks for apprentices, considerable effort was necessary to gain an adequate understanding of the life world and social situation of the target group before collecting interview data on a specific sample. On the basis of these preliminary analyses, the following institutional reality domains were considered to be the most important ecological subdivisions of apprentices' life world: *work, school, home,* and *leisure time settings* (see Figure 2). Each of these reality domains were then subdivided into tasks be-

Transactional dimension	External ecological dimensions: institutional reality domains			
	Work	School	Home	Leisure time settings
Interpersonal category	– Superiors – Colleagues	– Teachers – Classmates	– Parents	– Best friend – Peers
Extrapersonal category	– Career – Qualifications – Work activity	– School learning	– Chores	– Leisure time activities

Fig. 2. Taxonomic classification of apprentices' normative life tasks in the interpersonal and extrapersonal domain

longing to the extrapersonal category and into tasks of the interpersonal category.

Extrapersonal Tasks. The *work domain* has been divided into three tasks:

a) Promotion of occupational planning, that is, preparatory activities to find a job after apprenticeship:

b) maximizing the acquisition of vocational qualifications while working in the firm. (This is a critical aspect in many work places because apprentices are often left to themselves and are assigned low-level work where they cannot learn what they need for the final exam;)

c) maintaining a balance between living up to institutional work demands and pressures and maintaining an overall sense of work satisfaction and a manageable work load. This involves good planning and effective organization of the work day as well as efficient work management.

In the other reality domains (i.e., Home, School, Leisure Settings) only one extrapersonal task in each domain has been defined, because these domains are much less demanding of apprentices' time requirements. Each of these tasks is related to the adolescents' main extrapersonal activity in this institution:

d) In the *school domain,* the task is to optimize learning in a part-time vocational training school without putting in too much time and energy;

e) in the *home domain,* the task is defined as the goal to carry out chores and school work in a well-organized, efficient way which leaves enough time for leisure;

f) in the *Leisure time domain* the task was defined as finding out and implementing the most rewarding and stimulating leisure time activities.

Interpersonal Tasks. In order to define the tasks in the interpersonal category, the significant role partners of apprentices have been selected in each of the reality domains. In each case, the task for the adolescent is to develop the best possible relationship with significant other(s). The optimal relationship varies depending on the respective roles [e.g., regarding the amount of instrumental, cooperative, and expressive behavior; with respect to being more or less formalized, and with respect to reciprocity (see Dittmann, 1978)]. The significant others for which interpersonal tasks have been defined for the apprentices are the following:

a) Their superiors in their firm;
b) their colleagues at work;
c) their teachers at school;
d) their classmates at school;
e) their parents at home;
f) their best friends (same sex and/or other), and
g) their peers during leisure time.

Intrapersonal Tasks. With respect to adolescent development, the following two internal action spaces have been differentiated: First, the self-concept as an object of one's cognitive, affective, and evaluative activities; and second, the self as an object of control or change, including self-control and self-modification (in the sense of long-term development). The tasks defined in relation to these intrapersonal problem or action spaces are the following:

a) To understand and effectively evaluate one's cognitively based self-concept;

b) to understand and emotionally accept one's needs and emotions, as well as to control them;

c) to recognize and use the possibilities for self-development and growth.

Method

The appropriate method of assessment to provide a systematic description of subjective task perception and behavior seemed to be the interview combined with content-analysis, based on the concepts developed for the definition of the transactional categories. The interview method used was the open, semistructured interview, supplemented by observational and descriptive data on the work and vocational school settings. Information on the demographic and economic structure of the region and on each of the apprentices' trades was also compiled.

The interviews were designed to give adolescents the opportunity to speak about general aspects of each of the reality domains and more specific aspects of the life tasks. The interview materials were then content-analyzed sentence by sentence in the following way (see Möller & Schreiber, 1978): In the first step, content categories for each life task were defined on the basis of the concepts used in the definition of the transactional categories; the transactional concepts had to be adapted for each reality domain and its corresponding life tasks. In the second step, these content categories were applied to some interviews in an attempt to test their usefulness. After slight reformulation, all interviews were rated by two members of the research team; occasional discrepant ratings were solved by consensus on the basis of theoretical arguments. In a third step, the responses classified in these content categories were then collapsed into one or a few response types to describe the different types of goals, perceptions and evaluations of settings and persons, perceived problems, and action strategies used by these adolescents. This collapsing was done in order to make data more manageable and to observe regularities in the data. These results were used to create prototype descriptions in the form of a script representing adolescents' coping with each of the life tasks in each of the reality domains. The description of the qualitative results of this study thus fills well over 200 pages.

Since the goal of the study was geared to intervention, these descriptions were written in a style suitable also for use by teachers as well as students. Teachers should be able to use such descriptions of adolescents' task perception of problem understanding in their instructional planning designed for improving students' subjective representations of action spaces and their problem definitions, and students should be able to use the descriptions of their peers' coping and life world as discussion materials. In order to make the results more useful for this purpose, the task descriptions were used to prepare case studies on one apprentice in each of the five trades studied. The apprentice selected for a case study was the person for which additional observations in the school and work setting were most comprehensive (Schreiber, 1978). The case studies were added to the task descriptions to offer a coherent picture of the life world and transactions of selected adolescents.

Results

One of the problems in qualitative research is that it is not possible to report the results in their original form. They are simply too voluminous. Therefore, only summary data and interpretations based on the raw materials can be reported. However, there is too little work of this kind done and too few standards hitherto developed so that convenient procedures for summarizing such results are lacking. Consequently, it is very difficult to write such results in a form suitable for journal publications or conference presentations which means such results are not as easily communicated. Nevertheless, an attempt will be made to present summary data on adolescent coping in two of the three transactional categories. These data are meant to show the necessity of differentiated situational specification of psychological concepts like coping or problem understanding.

The results of the present study show large intertask differences in the cognitive level of task definition and in corresponding action strategies, even between those tasks which belong to the same transactional categories. This finding suggests that situation-specific, rather than person-specific, factors bridging broad areas of coping are predominant. In the following example, this is illustrated first for intertask competence differences in the *interpersonal* category, then with respect to intrapersonal tasks.

Many adolescents employed, often with success, flexible strategies in interaction with their parents in order to negotiate later curfews while at the same time maintaining a good overall relationship with them, especially with their mothers. Adolescents were also able to formulate their goals with respect to the kinds of relationships they wanted to have with their parents and felt generally able to control the outcomes (e. g., see their parents as friends and ask their advice if needed).

The ability to perceive desirable interaction possibilities in a social setting was also evident in their relations to classmates and teachers. They grasped strategies like common actions and solidarity as means of influencing the subject matter taught in the classroom. Their relationship to their bosses and colleagues, however, was quite different. With respect to their bosses, passive acceptance of the situation and of the relationship as determined by the boss predominated. Most adolescents were not even able to form goals for these relationships beyond that of expressing the desire that their relationship should be "OK".

Even after $1-2$ years in the firm, the apprentices acquired little insight into the possible motivations, action strategies, and personalities of their superiors. They especially did not seem to be aware of the possibility that interaction between superiors and employees or apprentices can take many forms beyond submission and obedience. Consequently, they seemed to have overlooked the options that were in fact open to them. Such an understanding of the reciprocal nature of the relationship between employee and employer requires the ability to define the situation, initiate behavior, and plan and design strategies which would allow the apprentice to be an active agent in the workplace.

With respect to their colleagues, similar inadequacies in apprentices' understanding was evident. There was little awareness among apprentices for mutual help, common interests, solidarity, and assistance vis à vis their superiors, including the older skilled workers assigned to do on-the-job training. (The latter often have little talent for teaching, so apprentices depend on mutual help to find out about chores and useful work techniques.) The other apprentices and employees in the work place were viewed from a friendly distance; polite interaction or being on superficially good terms was the criterion for evaluation; negative feelings tended to be overlooked or were only admitted unintentionally.

Intrapersonal tasks are, in addition to interpersonal tasks, another example for differences in the level of problem understanding or task perception within the same transactional category. As in the case of interpersonal tasks, one of the intrapersonal tasks was dealt with in a rather efficient way, whereas the others seemed to be an instance of inadequate understanding and of overlooking opportunities for growth and satisfaction. Regarding *effectiveness in dealing with one's emotions*, most adolescents seemed to be skillful in their reactions to their own feelings, including negative emotions. They were cognizant of their feelings and of possible strategies for dealing with them. Furthermore, they appeared not to be defensive – that is, not negating, but accepting their emotions.

With respect to both the desirability and possibility of self-change, however, many apprentices' opinions resembled "premature closure of identity" (Marcia, 1980). Some adolescents felt that they were already the person they wanted to be and/or that, at any rate, change was not possible. They seemed to have settled with the kind of person they were at that point in time for the rest of their lives. At the same time they compared their self-concept to what other people, especially parents and other adults, wanted them to be; they had often not developed explicit personal standards and values for their self-image.

Conclusions

The view is taken here that developmental psychology should not ignore the detailed investigation of life world and person-environment transaction in such important topics as successful coping (i. e., with both self and environment) and the support of self-development during the main developmental phases in human life. The approach used here reflects a view which has also been stressed by Aebli (1980), namely that it is necessary to apply theoretically guided, general psychological constructs to developmental research. It is evident that the differentiation of such general concepts as problem understanding, problem-solving as coping, and action space (problem space) into subsets of life world and behavior of a given age group illustrates the enormous *situational* variability of behavior. Results obtained with differentiated procedures cast further doubt on the hypothesis that nonsituation-specific person variables (like transsituational traits) can explain a major portion of the variance in individual behaviors in real-life settings.

In this context it is interesting to note that adolescents seemed to be more efficient and more autonomous copers in their social relations in family and school than in the work place. Perhaps they are less able to develop a good understanding in social situations which are new and where an altogether different set of problems and activities exist. It is also possible that their efficiency in perceiving social relations is poor in settings where formal authority (with material consequences) is present. In any case, it seems important to assess adolescents' cognitions and external behaviors in the work place, and not only as is usually done in the family and the school.

The above illustrations suggest additional observations. Studies such as this, of adolescents in their real life contexts, make evident that the formulation of *normative life tasks* should *not* be derived from the general idea of adolescents as an age-specific group, but should take into consideration the common life conditions of *specific groups* of adolescents in a specific culture or society. The construct of developmental tasks and of coping strategies should be emphasized with respect to the tasks which real individuals have to fulfill in the real (inner and outer) world.

A similar conclusion pertains to theories of adolescence presupposing that adolescence is a time of crisis or a particularly difficult life period. The notion of "crisis" and of "difficult period" should be redefined as "being faced with a series of difficult inner or outer life tasks or situations." The assumption that adolescents are, in general, faced with more difficult life tasks than, for instance, adults or the elderly, is not warranted and should be restated for particular groups of people living under particular conditions.

References

Aebli, H. (1980) *Denken: Das Ordnen des Tuns. Kognitive Aspekte der Handlungstheorie:* Vol. 1. Stuttgart: Klett-Cotta

Aebli, H. (1981) *Denken: Das Ordnen des Tuns. Denkprozesse:* Vol. 2. Stuttgart: Klett-Cotta

Bergold, J. B. (1980) Handlungstheorie und klinische Psychologie: Eine Einführung in die Thematik des Symposiums. In W. Schulz & M. Hautzinger (Eds.), *Klinische Psychologie und Psychotherapie.* Kongreßbericht Berlin 1980. Tübingen: Deutsche Gesellschaft für Verhaltenstherapie

Brandtstädter, J. (1984) Personal and social control over development: Toward an action perspective in life-span developmental psychology. In P. B. Baltes & O. J. Brim, Jr. (Eds.), *Life-span development and behavior:* Vol. 6. New York: Academic

Bronfenbrenner, U. (1979) *The ecology of human development: Experiments by nature and design.* Cambridge, MA: Harvard University Press

Dittmann, F. (1978) *Soziale Kompetenz in interpersonellen Beziehungen.* (Arbeitsbericht Nr. 8) Konstanz: Universität Konstanz, Zentrum I

Dittmann-Kohli, F. (1982) Theoretische Grundlagen der Analyse von Lebensbewältigung und Umwelt. In F. Dittmann-Kohli, N. Schreiber & F. Möller (Eds.), *Lebenswelt und Lebensbewältigung.* Konstanz: University of Konstanz

Dittmann-Kohli, F., Schreiber, N., & Möller, F. (1982a) Methodik und Ergebnisse einer qualitativen empirischen Studie über Lebenswelt und Lebensbewältigung von Lehrlingen. In F. Dittmann-Kohli, N. Schreiber & F. Möller (Eds.), *Lebenswelt und Lebensbewältigung.* Konstanz: University of Konstanz

Dittmann-Kohli, F., Schreiber, N., & Möller, F. (1982b) *Lebenswelt und Lebensbewältigung.* Konstanz: University of Konstanz

Dörner, D. (1976) *Problemlösen als Informationsverarbeitung.* Stuttgart: Kohlhammer

Dörner, D., Kreuzig, H. W., Reither, F., & Stäudel, T. (Eds.) (1983) *Lohhausen: Vom Umgang mit Unbestimmtheit und Komplexität.* Bern: Huber

Fiedler, P. A. (1981) Verbesserung von Problemlösefähigkeit und Selbstbehandlungskompetenz durch Psychotherapie. In P. A. Fiedler (Ed.), *Psychotherapieziel Selbstbehandlung.* Weinheim: Edition Psychologie im Verlag Chemie

Gehmacher, E. (1975) *Lebensmanagement: Planungswissenschaft für die individuelle Daseinsgestaltung.* Stuttgart: Seewald

Greeno, J. G. (1980) Trends in the theory of knowledge for problem solving. In D. T. Tuma & F. Reif (Eds.), *Problem-solving in education: Issues in teaching and research.* Hillsdale, N. J.: Erlbaum

Greif, S. (1980) Handlungstheorie und kognitive Therapie. In W. Schulz & M. Hautzinger (Eds.), *Klinische Psychologie und Psychotherapie.* Kongreßbericht Berlin 1980. Tübingen: Deutsche Gesellschaft für Verhaltenstherapie

Haan, N. (1977) *Coping and defending: Processes of self-environment organization.* New York: Academic

Hacker, W. (1978) *Allgemeine Arbeits- und Ingenieurpsychologie.* Bern: Huber

Hagestad, G. O. & Neugarten, B. L. Age and the life course (1985). In E. Shanas & R. Binstock (Eds.), *Handbook of aging and the social sciences.* New York: van Nostrand-Reinhold (2nd ed.)

Heidbreder, E. (1933) *Seven psychologies.* Englewood-Cliffs, N. J.: Prentice-Hall

Kaiser, P. (1980) Kompetenztraining zur Bewältigung von Lebenssituationen als Beispiel integrativer Psychotherapie. In W. Schulz & M. Hautzinger (Eds.), *Klinische Psychologie und Psychotherapie.* Kongreßbericht Berlin 1980. Tübingen: Deutsche Gesellschaft für Verhaltentherapie

Kirsch, W. (1977) *Einführung in die Theorie der Entscheidungsprozesse.* Wiesbaden: Gabler

Kocowski, T. (1975) Eine Systemtheorie menschlicher Bedürfnisse und Gesellschaftstechnik. In J. Schmidt (Ed.), *Planvolle Steuerung gesellschaftlichen Handelns.* Opladen: Westdeutscher Verlag

Kommer, D. & Linsenhoff, H. (1980) Zielorientierte Psychotherapie als interaktioneller Problemlöseprozeß: Heuristische Überlegungen zu Problemlösegrundlagen. In W. Schulz & M. Hautzinger (Eds.), *Klinische Psychologie und Psychotherapie.* Kongreßbericht Berlin 1980. Tübingen: Deutsche Gesellschaft für Verhaltenstherapie

Kozmetsky, G. (1980) The significant role of problem solving in education. In D. T. Tuma & F. Reif (Eds.), *Problem solving in education: Issues in teaching and research.* Hillsdale, N. J.: Erlbaum

Lazarus, R. (1980) The stress and coping paradigm. In L. A. Bond & J. C. Rosen (Eds.), *Competence and coping during adulthood.* Hanover, N. H.: University Press of New England

Lazarus, R. S., Averill, J. R., & Opton, E. M. (1974) The psychology of coping: Issues of research and assessment. In G. V. Coelho, D. A. Hamburg & J. E. Adams (Eds.), *Coping and adaptation.* New York: Basic Books

Lazarus, R. S. & Launier, R. (1978) Stress-related transactions between person and environment. In L. Pervin & M. Lewis (Eds.), *Perspectives in interactional psychology.* New York: Plenum Press

Leontjew, A. (1979) *Tätigkeit, Bewußtsein, Persönlichkeit.* Berlin: Volk und Wissen

Lerner, R. M. & Busch-Rossnagel, N. A. (1981) Individuals as producers of their development: Conceptual and empirical bases. In R. M. Lerner & N. A. Busch-Rossnagel (Eds.), *Individuals as producers of their development.* New York: Academic Press

Lewin, K. (1963) *Feldtheorie in den Sozialwissenschaften.* Bern: Huber

Lompscher, J. & Kossakowski, A. (1977) Persönlichkeitsentwicklung in unterschiedlichen Tätigkeitsarten. In A. Kossakowski, H. Kühn, J. Lompscher & G. Rosenfeld (Eds.), *Psychologische Grundlagen der Persönlichkeitsentwicklung im pädagogischen Prozeß.*

Marcia, J. E. (1980) Identity in adolescence. In J. Adelson (Ed.), *Handbook of adolescent psychology.* New York: Wiley

Möller, F. & Schreiber, N. (1978) Struktur und Verfahren der empirischen Untersuchung. (Arbeitsbericht Nr. 5) Konstanz: University of Konstanz, Zentrum I

Musto, S. (1972) *Evaluierung sozialer Entwicklungsprojekte.* Berlin: Hessling

Prystav, G. (1981) Psychologische Copingforschung: Konzeptbildungen, Operationalisierungen, Meßinstrumente. *Diagnostica, 27* (3), 189 – 214

Reese, H. W. & Overton, W. F. (1970) Models of development and theories of development. In L. R. Goulet & P. B. Baltes (Eds.), *Life-span developmental psychology: Research and theory.* New York: Academic Press

Reif, F. (1980) Theoretical and educational concerns with problem solving: Bridging the gaps with human cognitive engineering. In D. T. Tuma & F. Reif (Eds.), *Problem-solving in education: Issues in teaching and research.* Hillsdale, N. J.: Erlbaum

Schreiber, N. (1978) Zur Konstruktion von Fallstudien. (Arbeitsbericht 15). Konstanz: University of Konstanz, Zentrum I

Scriven, M. (1980) Prescriptive and descriptive approaches to problem-solving. In D. T. Tuma & F. Reif (Eds.), *Problem-solving in education: Issues in teaching and research.* Hillsdale, N. J.: Erlbaum

Seidel, R. (1976) *Denken. Psychologische Analyse der Entstehung und Lösung von Problemen.* Frankfurt: Campus

Simon, H. A. (1973) The structure of ill structured problems. *Artificial Intelligence, 4,* 181−201

Simon, H. A. (1980) Problem solving and education. In D. T. Tuma & F. Reif (Eds.), *Problem-solving in education: Issues in teaching and research.* Hillsdale, N. J.: Erlbaum

Tomaszewski, T. (1978) *Tätigkeit und Bewußtsein.* Weinheim: Beltz

Tomaszewski, T. (1981) Struktur, Funktion und Steuerungsmechanismen menschlicher Tätigkeit. In T. Tomaszewski (Ed.), *Zur Psychologie der Tätigkeit.* Berlin: VEB Deutscher Verlag der Wissenschaften

Tuma, D. T. & Reif, F. (1980) *Problem-solving in education: Issues in teaching and research.* Hillsdale, N. J.: Erlbaum

Volpert, W. (1974) *Handlungsstrukturanalyse als Beitrag zur Qualifikationsforschung.* Köln: Pahl-Rugenstein

Wilensky, R. (1981) Meta-planning: Representing and using knowledge about planning in problem-solving and natural language understanding. *Cognitive Science, 5,* 197−233

Zieleniewski, J. (1966) Die Leistungsfähigkeit des Handelns. In K. Alsleben & W. Wehrstedt (Eds.), *Praxeologie.* Quickborn: Schnelle

III. Puzzles in the Study of Daily Hassles [1]

R. S. LAZARUS *

Introduction

Theory and research in psychological stress has shifted from an earlier perspective of environmental inputs or outputs to a relational one. Stress is now
treated as harms, threats and challenges, the quality and intensity of which
depend on personal agendas, resources and vulnerabilities of the person, as
well as on environmental conditions. This implies a knowing person who
construes or appraises the significance of what is happening for his or her
well-being. Such a "paradigm shift" requires a different approach to stress
measurement, one that takes into account the cognitive activity evaluating
the personal significance of transactions, and examines the multiple specific
variables of person and environment that influence the appraisal process.
The need for a different approach to stress measurement has generated research by the Berkeley Stress and Coping Project on what we have called
daily *hassles and uplifts.*

In three previous articles (DeLongis, Coyne, Dakof, Folkman, & Lazarus, 1982; Kanner, Coyne, Schaefer, & Lazarus, 1981; and Lazarus & De-
Longis, 1983), we argued the theoretical and empirical case for daily hassles
as an anroach to stress measurement. Here I propose to examine the problem at a somewhat deeper level, and only touch lightly on what we have reported before.

In the above articles, we noted numerous conceptual, methodological,
and empirical limitations of the life events approach to stress measurement,
pointing, for example, to the overemphasis on change, the failure to consider
the individual significance of events, the person's coping resources and liabilities, and the low explanatory power of life events with respect to health
outcomes. Our effort to measure daily hassles arose from concern about
these limitations, and above all, from a respect for what Lewin (1936, 1951)
and others meant by the person's *psychological situation,* that is, the environment as perceived and reacted to as opposed to the objective en-

* University of California, Department of Psychology, Berkeley, CA 94720, USA
[1] Orginally published in *Journal of Behavioral Medicine,* 1984, vol 7. Printed here by permission.

Development as Action in Context
Ed. by R. K. Silbereisen et al.
© Springer-Verlag Berlin Heidelberg 1986

vironment. This subjective metatheory underlies our emphasis on appraisal and coping and our definition of stress as an inharmonious fit between the person and the environment, one in which the person's resources are taxed or exceeded, forcing the person to struggle, usually in complex ways, to cope.

What Are Hassles and Uplifts?

When the members of the Berkeley Stress and Coping Project constructed the Hassles Scale for a field study begun in 1977, we had not thought through all of the implications of format and wording. Our aim had been to cover the broad ground of relatively minor psychological difficulties of living as sensed by the person rather than to create pure and objective stimulus and response categories. Mixed together are references, implicit or explicit, to environmental inputs, appraisals, and emotional reactions, all brought within the same scale, and usually within the same item. Therefore, the scale includes a mixture of items depicting (1) *environmental events* such as "an inconsiderate smoker" and "unexpected company," (2) disappointing or worrisome *chronic environmental conditions* such as "rising prices of common goods" and "neighborhood deterioration," (3) *ongoing worries or concerns* such as "troubling thoughts about your future" and "job dissatisfactions," and (4) *distressed emotional reactions* such as "being lonely" and "fear of rejection."

How should daily hassles and uplifts be defined? Our approach, consistent with the way we have defined psychological stress in general, is that *daily* hassles are *experiences and conditions of daily living that have been appraised as salient and harmful or threatening to the endorser's well-being.* This is a definition that emphasizes the individual psychological or subjectively experienced situation in the Lewinian sense, and treats hassles as proximal phenomena rather than distal (cf. Jessor, 1981). Even when hassles reflect actual, objectively harmful or threatening events that have occurred, their meanings to the individual lead them to be remembered (because they are salient) and viewed as distressing. As we have argued elsewhere, what makes them harmful or threatening is that they involve demands that tax or exceed the person's resources. Daily uplifts, in contrast, consist of *experiences and conditions of daily living that have been appraised as salient and positive or favorable to the endorser's well-being.* For this reason they give the person a lift, so to speak, and make them feel good − a good night's rest, making a friend, receiving a compliment, and so on.

Occurrences that to some are hassles can be experienced as uplifts by others, and vice versa. Thus, writing a paper can be a distressing chore to some and an exhilarating experience to others. Assessing uplifts as well as hassles seemed to us to offer a fuller picture of the affective bases of daily living, both positive and negative, than was possible by studying hassles alone. Our findings thus far with uplifts, however, have seemed less fruitful than those with hassles, and I shall emphasize the latter more in this presentation.

Hassles, Uplifts, and Health

The feature of our research that has gained the most attention is the relationships we have demonstrated between hassles and uplifts and health-related variables such as morale, psychological symptoms, and somatic health. We found that hassles frequency and intensity, averaged for nine months of separate assessment on the same people, were capable of explaining psychological and somatic health better than life events could, the bivariate relationship to health being quite robust. Hassles and life events were only modestly correlated, and hassles scores added their own unique variance to the relationship, whereas life events scores did not. Thus, some of the explained health variance reflected the overlap between life events and hassles, which we interpreted as evidence that life events alter the day-to-day routines of living and hence its daily hassles; however, many hassles were independent of life events, deriving alternatively from the individual's usual ways of living. It seemed to us that we had found a way to measure stress that supplemented life events measures importantly, and was besides a more effective predictor of health outcomes. Given the self-report nature of both hassles and health measurement, there is always the possibility that the obtained relationships are artifactual. This is of greater concern with psychological symptoms and morale, the outcome variables of the Kanner et al. (1981) study, than with somatic health, the outcome variable of the DeLongis et al. (1982) study. It is also noteworthy that our basic claim about the relationships between hassles and psychological symptoms has already been supported in independent research conducted elsewhere (cf. Monroe, 1983); however, in that study too there is some danger of tautology between the antecedent and outcome measures, though I do not think this is the whole story. The methodological problems inherent in this research are substantial, and a degree of wariness is appropriate.

It is tempting to argue that hassles, as a subjective measure of daily stress, explains health variance because stress impairs health, an assumption that also has fueled extensive research with life events. We presented our original findings with this assumption in mind, though with the usual disclaimers that the obtained correlations − cross-sectional rather than longitudinal − are subject to uncertainty about causal implication. In this regard, we had found hassles frequency scores quite stable over nine months, and our strategy of analysis made them even more stable for purposes of explaining health by aggregating nine months of hassles frequency scores for each subject (cf. Epstein, 1983). Because health status too was quite stable over the nearly one year of its assessment, we had not shown, therefore, that ups and downs in hassles covaried with ups and downs in health status within individuals, but only that people with overall high hassles scores had a poorer health status than people with overall low hassles scores. To demonstrate the functional significance of this relationship, it would also be important to show that ups and downs in hassles or uplifts are associated with ups and downs in health within the same persons (cf. Lazarus, 1978).

Some of our current research efforts are designed to examine the above possibility about within-individual covariation between daily stress and health. However, it is quite likely that some kinds of health outcome are neither very variable nor responsive to stress, whereas others are both. Thus, although blood pressure in nonhypertensives may well bounce up and down with stress-related encounters and their cessation, in well-consolidated hypertensives blood pressure probably is consistently high regardless of circumstances, presumably because of irreversible somatic changes in kidney function that are part of the disorder (Kaplan, 1979). Similarly, disorders such as arthritis, atherosclerosis, Alzheimer's disease, etc., are probably not particularly subject to variation from day to day or week to week. On the other hand, many of the classic so-called psychosomatic disorders such as ulcers, intestinal colitis, allergy, asthma, etc., could be extremely subject to change with stress. And still others, such as bacterial and viral infections, which depend on variations in immune functioning, might also show a strong relationship with stress (e.g., Meyer & Haggerty, 1962), since there is substantial evidence of stress-related effects on immune competency (Ader, 1981). This means that to test the intraindividual covariation between stress and health requires that the global variable of health status be differentiated into the many states and conditions that comprise it, distinguishing thereby those subject to stress effects from those not (cf. Luborsky, Docherty, & Penick, 1973).

It is of course equally plausible that poor health could affect the results in the pattern of hassles or result in higher hassles frequency and intensity, thus reversing the cause-and-effect argument. If people are ailing, especially in the population studied in this research, namely those aged 45 – 64, then it is quite likely that they will experience more hassles; also, high hassles scores were associated with poor overall morale and more psychological symptoms, which could have come about because people with low morale and many distressing psychological symptoms were more likely to interpret the specific facets of the daily grind more negatively than those who feel generally good about their lives. We need not, of course, choose between these two causal alternatives; most likely there is a recursive relationship, in keeping with the tenets of our transactional metatheoretical framework (cf. Coyne & Lazarus, 1980; Lazarus, Coyne, & Folkman, 1982; Lazarus & Launier, 1978).

If, for the moment, we assume that hassles affect health for the worse, then we must consider the possible mechanisms of this causal link. The simplest hypothesis is an additive one, or dose–response relationship, that is, the more hassles occurring in any given time frame, the more there will be bodily disequilibrium in the sense suggested by the Cannon-Selye tradition of stress hormone-induced tissue disturbance (see also Mason, 1970). For certain somatic illnesses to be generated, the conditions producing disequilibrium must be chronic and probably extended over a considerable period of time. Since our subjects' hassles scores were averaged over a year and were observed to be fairly stable, this necessary condition of chronic or extended disequilibrium, inferred from a high hassles frequency and/or intensity over nine months, could well have been achieved in our data.

There are, on the other hand, a number of nonadditive possibilities. The simplest is a threshold model, an upper limit of the amount of stress that is tolerable, as in a plimsole line that, when exceeded, causes the ship to founder. This model is also expressed in the aphorism about the straw that breaks the camel's back. We are hard put, however, to identify when the degree of daily stress exceeds the capacity of the physiological and psychological system to operate without damage; we do not know where to draw the line. The placement of this line probably differs from one person to another, and within a person from one time to another. In my view, what surpasses credibility in this simple hypothesis and the additive model as well, and makes it less than promising, is its presumption that all hassles are equal in their capacity to generate disequilibrium or distress. Alternative hypotheses about this mechanism, which I will now discuss, reject this.

It is quite possible that hassles operate selectively on health, which is to say, paraphrasing George Orwell, that some hassles are more equal than others. Such a claim derives from two considerations inherent in our theoretical stance about stress, namely, that hassles vary in meaning and importance, with some capable of either demoting or promoting other hassles in power, perhaps subtracting from, alternatively even dividing or multiplying their destructive effects. These are the powerful hassles that have major significance for a person's long-range values and goals; they may also carry heavy existential freight compared with others. Variations in the power and salience of hassles derive from personal agendas and coping resources and limitations that shape cognitive appraisal of harm, threat and challenge; that is, they create a particular pattern of vulnerability to react with psychological stress in the ordinary transactions of living.

The more a particular hassle has influence beyond the brief encounter, entering into much of the life space, pervading thought and generating emotion, mobilizing sustained coping especially when it is inept, and touching on long-range values, goals and commitments, the more impact it should have on health. This impact will often extend beyond hormonal disruption of cellular function and cause illness by virtue of poor coping decisions (see, for example, Cohen & Lazarus, 1983; Holroyd & Lazarus, 1982) which fail successfully to address the troubled person−environment relationship. For example, failure to act appropriately with respect to health could arise as a result of denial models of coping, or engaging in damaging coping activities involving drugs, alcohol, smoking, over- or undereating, and foolish risk-taking — some of the ways that coping failure can affect the health picture over and above emotion-generated disturbances of tissue function.

The hypothesis that hassles differ in their impact on health and functioning implies a nonlinear, nonadditive relationship among hassles, and between hassles and health. For some hassles to have a subtractive or divisive influence on the capacity of other hassles to disturb, as when a particular problem intrusively takes over attention (Horowitz, 1976, 1982), they would in effect wipe out other hassles in the person's attention or concern. An example might be devastating criticism from one's mentor or peers at work; if the person experiencing this put-down regards it, correctly or incorrectly, as having major significance, it may result in mobilization to deal with the problem and thereby crowd out any or all other potential hassles. Alternatively, the presence of a major, pervasive, and intrusive hassle might even multiply the capacity of other hassles to mobilize or disturb. Thus, when lovers fall out, many other routine hassles such as parking problems, work responsibilities, inclement weather, and bad political news might all gain greatly in their psychological power to mobilize or disturb; everything now seems dour or ugly, and each hassle is enhanced in its influence. In both these alternative models, we see not a linear relationship among hassles, but a tendency for some hassles, more central to important personal agendas, to change the overall pattern and dynamics of stress and to affect health. These four models of the way daily stress might work to affect health outcome represent alternative hypotheses for which there is, as yet, no evidence.

Similar arguments could apply to uplifts, expressed in the question of whether positive experiences make hassles more bearable or buffer their presumed deleterious effects on health. The hypothesis is basically a simple one to test: Do people who have a high hassles score *and* a high uplifts score do better in health, morale, or whatever than those who have high hassles and few if any uplifts? To complete the test one would need also to examine adaptational outcomes in people with low hassles scores and low uplifts compared with those with low hassles scores and high uplifts.

This was the hypothesis about uplifts with which we began. We found that hassles and uplifts were highly correlated; those who reported more hassles also reported more uplifts, a relationship that must be partialled out when comparing hassles and uplifts individually as correlates of health. However, when we made an interactional comparison, we found that uplifts did not add any independent variance to the relationship between hassles and health. We were, in effect, unable to confirm the buffering hypothesis despite its reasonableness and attractiveness.

However, in light of our conceptualization that uplifts reflect the appraised significance of experiences rather than merely the objective world, the idea that uplifts buffer the destructive effects of hassles now seems less persuasive. Older people, for example, endorsed as uplifts more health-related positive experiences than younger ones (see DeLongis & Lazarus, 1982; Lazarus & DeLongis, 1983), a pattern that seemed to depend on older persons' tendencies to expect worsened health. Since getting enough sleep or feeling healthy is less expectable for older people compared with the young, when these good experiences occur they are more likely to be regarded as salient and positive by older persons, whereas when they occur to younger people they are apt to be taken for granted and perhaps not even noticed.

Therefore, perhaps we should not say that the presence of uplifting events buffers the deleterious effects of stress, but rather that what serves as a health preserver is to be able to put a positive light on experiences, or to have agendas and expectations that allow for the experience of uplifts. The issue of buffering then devolves into the question of how one appraises and copes. The same principle may apply, incidentally, to the hypothesis of social supports as buffers; people who are in trouble may be those who believe that they have no one to call upon for help, or who cannot ask for help or accept it when they need to, or lack the skill or foresight to cultivate supportive relationships. Lack of social support may say as much about how people cope as about their social networks and relationships.

The Psychodynamics and Sociodynamics of Hassles and Uplifts

It may be an unimaginative reading of the importance of hassles and uplifts to emphasize their functional relationship to health. Equally if not more important is what hassles-uplifts patterns might tell us about the psychodynamics and sociodynamics of stress, coping, and adaptation. To be clear about this we must consider the individual meaning of hassles and uplifts, and their place in coping and adaptation.

The question of meaning arises most readily in the effort to interpret why a person endorses an item (or pattern of items) as a hassle. We do not follow the usual reasoning, that also lies behind life events checklists, that hassles scores provide merely an inventory of stressful events that have actually taken place. On the contrary, hassles are heavily weighted by appraisals of the significance of what happened, based in large part on individual patterns of beliefs, values and commitments. When subjects endorse a hassle they are indicating not only what happened, but how they appraised and experienced it, which reflects its immediate or long-range significance for their well-being. The wording of the items encourages endorsement of the idea that one is "hassled" sufficiently to find the experience both negative and salient.

To one person a traffic jam, or air pollution, is simply a condition of life to be expected and managed philosophically or with amusement, or negotiated with minimal stress and distress; to another it is evidence of a vexing condition of life, an assault on pressured time, a personal affront, being thwarted. The experience will certainly be remembered and endorsed more readily by the latter person than the former. Life events too are not always best regarded as merely adventitious environmental happenings, since in most instances (e.g., job loss or divorce) there is an unknown but often substantial degree of personal contribution to its occurrence, significance, and salience.

What are some of the promising candidates among the factors contributing to individual differences in the hassles and uplifts that people experience or that are salient enough for them to note and remember? The theory of primary and secondary cognitive appraisal processes in stress and emotion directs us toward some of the obvious possibilities.

Primary appraisal concerns mainly the discrimination between transactions in which there is some personal investment and those that are irrelevant for the person's well-being. The core psychological issue involved in such appraisal is whether there is something *at stake* in an encounter and whether this stake is considered to be in jeopardy. A traffic jam will be far more distressing when a person must get to an important appointment and there is just enough time than when there is plenty of time, or when nothing important will be lost by a delay. If the sense of time urgency is high, for whatever reason, and if being late will endanger an important goal or violate strong internal standards, the person can be said to be vulnerable to stress and distress with respect to being on time. The quality and strength of the emotional reaction to even so common and relatively insignificant an event can inform us, after the fact, about *patterns of commitment* or about idiosyncratic personality characteristics that make the person especially vulnerable. Before the fact, person characteristics may permit prediction of threat appraisals in some people in contexts in which others might not be threatened.

Secondary appraisal concerns *resources and options for coping* with stressful demands and constraints. When the person faces stressful demands, negative beliefs about resources for coping effectively will enhance threat appraisals, and positive beliefs about such resources will dampen them. For some persons, the traffic jam mobilizes efforts − sometimes frantic − to locate alternative routes if they are available, which, when successful, eliminate the threat. Although any thought or act can serve multiple coping function, we have spoken of this latter process as *problem-focused coping* (Folkman & Lazarus, 1980; Lazarus & Folkman, 1984). This sort of coping can also be anticipatory, as in the case of arranging to leave extra time in case a traffic jam or some other impediment materializes on the way to an important appointment.

Even when nothing can be done to alter the realities of the situation, *emotion-focused coping* can also dampen or short-circuit threat. For example, thinking that one can successfully counter the bad impression of being late, realizing that there are later airplane flights, or otherwise depreciating the significance of being late, can neutralize or markedly reduce the stress and distress that would otherwise be entailed. Avoidance of thinking about the distressing possibilities can also help to regulate the emotions that might be generated. The above examples illustrate the role of secondary appraisal and emotion-focused coping as determinants of the experience of hassles. They are also relevant to uplifts because emotion-focused coping can result in thinking positively about bad experiences. In consequence of these cognitive coping processes, the person may not even think of the experience as stressful, or will give a much reduced estimate of their severity when later asked about hassles. Therefore, what will be endorsed as a hassle or uplift by one person will not be by another.

Notice what has been done here analytically. I started with hassles as *antecedents* of appraisal and coping but noted the inadequacies of this stimulus-centered perspective. This led me to view hassles – and uplifts – as *consequences* of appraisal, and these processes are in turn dependent on personal agendas, resources for coping, and coping thoughts and acts. Thus, the causal question has been turned around so that the processes that underlie individual patterns of hassles and uplifts come into focus as the central issue. Such patterns can inform us not only about what is important to the person and hence threatening or challenging, but also about the arenas of human activity in which any given individual or group is vulnerable to stress. A transactional formulation in which all processes are interdependent, each capable of affecting the other in the ordinary flow of experience, can help turn attention toward hassles and uplifts patterns as diagnostic of individual strengths, liabilities, and hence vulnerabilities.

Consider, for example, the person who experiences frequent hassles in dealing with others, as in handling encounters with a supervisor at work. A stimulus or environmental formulation of such stress would implicate only the behavior of the other person. The other person could be hostile, demanding and assaultive, and might provoke nearly anyone, including the person in question. The same facts of stress could be explained, on the other hand, by tendencies in this person to overreact to hostility, or even to imagine assaults; one might draw on hypotheses about sibling rivalries, an overcritical parent, or perhaps a rigid, compulsive style of defending, as sources of vulnerability. Both viewpoints are, in a sense, productive but incomplete. A transactionalist would assume that usually two sets of antecedent variables – one environmental, the other within the person – are operating.

One clue about such vulnerabilities in any given individual is the *quality and intensity of the emotion* generated. A second is the *recurrent or chronic nature of the hassle*. If we study the person's hassles over time we may find, for example, that the same type of hassles keep recurring, a sign that either the environment is fairly constant as a source of stressful demands and/or that the person is bringing to this environment special vulnerabilities. The two possibilities, of environmental or person causation, can probably never be fully disentangled. Still, recurrent hassles should be good candidates for special study to evaluate to what extent the problem lies in the person, to what extent in the environment, and in what respects. Only an in-depth examination of the pattern and experience of hassles can provide insight into the provocations, personal agendas, appraisal characteristics, and coping pattern contributing to recurrent hassles.

How could a conceptualization like this be tackled in research? Our research group has been struggling to develop a workable strategy. It is a difficult and challenging task. Fundamental is a style of research I have referred to elsewhere as ipsative-normative, in which the same persons are examined again and again in different stressful encounters (Lazarus & Folkman, 1984; Lazarus & Launier, 1978). The person is compared with himself or herself (ipsative) and ultimately intraindividual hassles and uplifts patterns are compared across persons with different characteristics (normative). Using in-depth interviews reconstructing some of the most frequent, important, and intense hassles and uplifts, we pay attention to the phases of each encounter, for example, anticipation, confrontation, and outcome, examine the emotions experienced at each phase, and the coping processes employed using our Ways of Coping checklist. For example, with respect to the outcome phase, subjects are asked to tell us what aspects of the encounter were important to them, the outcome in each case, and the emotions and coping thoughts or acts that occurred with respect to each aspect and outcome.

I emphasize here the attempt to delineate the separate aspects of what is usually a complex experience. If a cancer patient is asked, for example, "How did you feel emotionally about your illness?" or "How did you cope with your cancer?", reactions are apt to be reported that commonly defy understanding because we do not learn the specific threats that explain the emotion or to which the coping process is directed (cf. Folkman & Lazarus, 1985). The coping process may be quite different when dealing with an uncertain prognosis, concerns about dying, difficulties created in relationships with family or peers, decisions about whether and what to tell others about the illness, the pain or side effects of treatment, and so on. Similarly, since emotion and coping change as the complex experience unfolds over time, if the inquiry does not specify the time period or stage, it may be difficult to say when it was in the process that the patient is reacting as described. Without such specificity, processes and emotional reactions are aggregated so that it is difficult if not impossible to disentangle them with respect to the eliciting conditions. To truly understand what is happening emotionally and with respect to coping, it is necessary to narrow the focus to a particular time period or to a particular aspect of the experience. The question that must always be clarified is "Coping with what?" (and "angry or sad about what?").

In the research I spoke of, we are concerned mainly with recurrent themes, those that recur in different hassles, themes such as vulnerability to criticism, an insatiable need to be approved or loved, failure to communicate to another person what is wanted or felt, a need to always be in control, resentment about another person's insistence on autonomy, a constant tendency to put others down, self-depreciation, and inability to criticize or complain. Our aim is to discover how such themes, in any given individual, enter into and shape diverse hassles experiences and, perhaps, the coping process.

Meichenbaum and Gilmore (1980) have recently offered a similar view in the context of cognitive-behavior therapy. They describe a client who found himself overly irritated, frustrated and angry in diverse encounters with other people. A search for a common theme revealed that these emotional reactions arose frequently in situations in which he felt an injustice had been perpetrated on others or himself, for example, being short-changed by a waiter. He could also recall having similar feelings and thoughts in the past, remembering that he had watched his immigrant father being unable to stand up for his rights when suffering injustice. The client had developed, in effect, a credo — apparently unverbalized and perhaps unrecognized — that operated as a readiness to believe he was being taken advantage of in a variety of social transactions, and a determination never to allow anyone to do so to him or his family. He would assume hostile intension in the other person too readily and was unwilling to consider a more benign interpretation of a simple error.

Benner's (1984) study of work stress in the Berkeley Stress and Coping Project's middle-aged sample provides another example. A fifty-two-year-old man experienced recurrent, nearly chronic stress on a job he had held for many years. By examining multiple work incidents, it was possible to identify the central theme of this stress; despite much experience at the job and high performance effectiveness, he had a vulnerable personal esteem, which led him to appraise every work demand as a threat. Each such demand was construed inappropriately as a personal test on which he could not afford to make any errors. Despite the fact that he did his job in an exemplary fashion, as judged from objective criteria, commendations he received, and offers of other jobs, every task he undertook, even those of little significance, made him tense and led to compulsive efforts to perform perfectly. His repeated hassles at work were reflections of this lifelong agenda of being tested and evaluated and of compulsive coping, an agenda that gave him little opportunity to feel at ease.

In the clinical case cited by Meichenbaum and Gilmore (1980) above, cognitive appraisal often failed to match the actual circumstances as a result of an intrusive personal agenda. The experience of flooding with anger could not be easily resolved by direct confrontation — a form of problem-focused coping — or by emotion-focused coping that might have regulated the angry feelings. A similar conclusion would apply to the case described by Benner (1984). We cannot understand the hassles patterns of these two people solely on the basis of environmental demands and without reference to the different personal agendas they carried with them into social transactions. By examining recurrent hassles in people systematically, we have an opportunity to discover the stable person properties that make them vulnerable to stress under certain environmental conditions, and the ways coping ineptitudes contribute to the diverse hassles patterns. Such clinically derived understanding about areas of personal vulnerability could be treated as research hypotheses to be tested by making predictions of future hassles for each of the persons so assessed.

The Developmental and Sociodemographic Significance of Hassles Patterns

At this point I would like to direct your attention to some of the implications of what I have been saying about the theory of hassles and uplifts for the theme of this conference, which is concerned with adolescent development and adaptation. The research being reported here is being done with adolescents of different ages, of varying socioeconomic status, and in different countries. This activity encompasses, therefore, both developmental and sociodemographic variables, which have a bearing on hassles and uplifts, or more broadly speaking, on daily stress and positive experiences.

In the research reported earlier, the main source of information was a sample of middle-aged people varying in age from 45 to 64, and who were white, Protestant and Catholic, and moderate in income and education. Additional observations were also made on other samples, one a college student group and the other Canadian health professionals, which permitted a comparative analysis. Three types of hassles were among the top ten in frequency in all three groups: misplacing or losing things, physical appearance, and too many things to do. However, the middle-aged participants were more concerned with economic issues such as rising prices of common goods, property, investments, and taxes; the Canadian professionals were concerned more with the anxieties and high pressure commonly found in professional life, such as too many things to do, not enough time to do the things they needed to do, too many responsibilities, and trouble relaxing; and the college students were particularly troubled by academic and social problems connected with being in school such as wasting time, concerns about meeting high standards, and being lonely. There were also group differences in uplifts, with the middle-aged sample finding more satisfaction in good health (e.g., feeling healthy, getting enough sleep) and family life (e.g., home pleasing to you, spending time with family), whereas college students were uplifted more by hedonic experiences (e.g., having fun, laughing, entertainment, music). The middle-aged and student groups also shared two frequent uplifts, namely, completing a task and relating well with friends.

These comparative observations were made too informally, and were based on too small an N, to more than suggest that hassles and uplifts patterns reflect group differences and that they might have individual diagnostic significance as well. However, we are confident that patterns of hassles and uplifts vary with developmental stage and as a function of sociodemographic variables such as education, income, occupation, ethnicity, and culture. A similar principle applies in the case of life events (Brim & Ryff, 1980; Hultsch & Plemons, 1979). This means that measures of both life events and daily hassles are probably capable of revealing the arenas of psychological stress indigenous to various social groups and environments, within and across societies, and to different developmental periods.

With respect to demographics, one could ask to what extent the hassles and uplifts experienced by youths of West Germany and Berlin overlap and differ from those experienced by comparably aged youths in the United States, Great Britain, or wherever. Similar comparisons could also be made for adolescents of different socioeconomic status, ethnicity, and even neighborhoods. With respect to developmental stages, with sociodemographic variables either controlled or examined as interactive variables, one could determine to what extent hassles and uplifts patterns change systematically with age. In making such comparisons, we must remember that within each group defined by age, stage or sociodemographics, there will always be substantial individual variation (cf. Lazarus & DeLongis, 1983).

The study of daily stress developmentally involves a time line that runs perpendicular to a concern with social and psychological processes such as cognition, emotion, motivation, and social behavior. Yet one must ask, "Development of what?". Stress, coping and adaptation abuts that developmental line importantly at every point in the life course, whether in adolescence or in aging.

The above is descriptive, but what about the theoretical issues I have raised about hassles and uplifts, for example, about whether their mode of operation in adaptational outcomes such as health is linear and additive or, alternatively, works in some more complicated fashion? The additive hypothesis assumes all hassles are equivalent, so that group comparisons can appropriately be made with a simple measure of daily stress in which content is less important than frequency or intensity. If, however, equivalency is rejected, then the content of hassles and uplifts takes on fundamental importance in understanding the dynamics of stress, coping and adaptation, and if evidence favors a nonlinear, nonadditive mechanism with respect to adaptational outcomes, then the patterning of hassles among and within adolescent groups must be examined. For if hassles and uplifts patterns are valuable sources of information at the individual level because they are diagnostic of important psychological characteristics, such as vulnerability to stress and coping strengths and weaknesses, then they will also be useful at the group level for the same reason.

My hunch is that nonadditive, linear hypotheses that force us to be concerned with the content and patterning of daily experienced stress will, by the same token, yield a better understanding of how and why young people, looked at individually or as groups, use drugs, conform or deviate from social rules and values, adapt or fail to adapt, and ultimately will yield better suggestions for interventions to facilitate more effective coping than those based on additive or threshold concepts. Research directed at clarifying the dynamic of stress, coping and adaptation in which hassles and uplifts play a measurement role should have a good payoff in the future for those concerned with psychological development and adaptation over the life course.

References

Ader R. (1981) *Psychoneuroimmunology.* New York: Academic
Benner, P. (1984). *Stress and satisfaction on the job: Work meanings and coping in mid-career men.* New York: Praeger
Brim, O. G., Jr., & Ryff, C. D. (1980) On the properties of life events. In P. B. Baltes & O. G. Brim (eds.), *Life-span development and behavior:* Vol. 3 (pp. 367–388). New York: Academic
Cohen, F. & Lazarus, R. S. (1983) Coping and adaptation in health and illness. In D. Mechanic (Ed.), *Handbook of health and health services* (pp. 608–635). New York: Free Press
Coyne, J. C. & Lazarus, R S. (1980) Cognitive style, stress perception, and coping. In I. L. Kutash & L. B. Schlesinger (Eds.), *Handbook on stress and anxiety: Contemporary knowledge, theory, and treatment* (pp. 144–158). San Francisco: Jossey-Bass
DeLongis, A., Coyne, J. C., Dakof, G., Folkman, S., & Lazarus, R. S. (1982) Relationship of daily hassles, uplifts, and major life events to health status. *Health Psychology, 1,* 119–136
DeLongis, A. & Lazarus, R. S. (1982 August) Hassles, uplifts and health in aging adults: A paradox examined. Paper presented at meetings of American Psychological Association, Washington, D. C.
Epstein, S. (1983) Aggregation and beyond: Some basic issues on the prediction of behavior. *Journal of Personality,* 51, 360–392.
Folkman, S. & Lazarus, R. S. (1980) An analysis of coping in a middle-aged community sample. *Journal of Health and Social Behavior, 21,* 219–239
Folkman, S. & Lazarus, R. S. (1985) If it changes it must be a process: A study of emotion and coping during three stages of a college examination. *Journal of Personality and Social Psychology,* 48, 150–170.
Holroyd, K. A. & Lazarus, R. S. (1982) Stess, coping, and somatic adaptation. In L. Goldberger & S. Breznitz (Eds.), *Handbook of stress: Theoretical and clinical aspects.* (pp. 21–35). New York: Free Press
Horowitz, M. (1976) *Stress response syndromes.* New York: Jason Aronson
Horowitz, M. (1982) Psychological processes induced by illness, injury, and loss. In T. Millon, C. Green, & R. Meagher (Eds.), *Handbook of clinical health psychology* (pp. 53–67). New York: Plenum
Hultsch, D. F. & Plemons, J. K. (1979) Life events and life-span development. In P. Baltes & O. G. Brim (eds.), *Life-span development and behavior:* Vol. 2 (pp.1–36). New York: Academic
Jessor, R. (1981) The perceived environment in psychological theory and research. In D. Magnusson (Ed.), *Toward a psychology of situations: An interactional perspective* (pp. 297–317). Hillsdale, NJ: Erlbaum
Kanner, A. D., Coyne, J. C., Schaefer, C., & Lazarus, R. S. (1981) Comparison of two modes of stress measurement: Daily hassles and uplifts versus major life events. *Journal of Behavioral Medicine, 4,* 1–39
Kaplan, N. M. (1979) The Goldblatt memorial lecture Part II: The role of the kidney in hypertension. *Hypertension, 1,* 456–461
Lazarus, R. S. (1978) A strategy for research on psychological and social factors in hypertension. *Journal of Human Stress, 4,* 35–40
Lazarus, R. S., Coyne, J. C., & Folkman, S. (1982) Cognition, emotion, and motivation: The doctoring of Humpty-Dumpty. In R. W. J. Neufeld (Ed.), *Psychological stress and psychopathology* (pp. 218–239). New York: McGraw-Hill
Lazarus, R. S. & DeLongis, A. (1983). Psychological stress and coping in aging. *American Psychologist, 38,* 245–254
Lazarus, R. S. & Folkman, S. (1984) *Stress, appraisal, and coping.* New York: Springer

Lazarus, R. S. & Launier, R. (1978) Stress-related transactions between person and environment. In L. A. Pervin & M. Lewis (Eds.), *Perspectives in interactional psychology* (pp. 287–327). New York: Plenum

Lewin, K. A. (1936) *Principles of topological psychology.* New York: McGraw-Hill

Lewin, K. A. (1951) Field theory and learning. In D. Cartwright (Ed.), *Field theory in social science: Selected theoretical papers by Kurt Lewin.* New York: Harper

Luborsky, L., Docherty, J. P., & Penick, S. (1973) Onset conditions for psychosomatic symptoms: A comparative review of immediate observation with retrospective research. *Psychosomatic Medicine, 35,* 187–204

Meichenbaum D. & Gilmore J. B. (1980) Resistance: From a cognitive-behavioral perspective. In P. Wachtel (Ed.), Resistance in psychodynamic and behavioral therapy. New York: Plenum

Meyer, R. J. & Haggerty, R. J. (1962) Streptococcal infections in families. *Pediatrics,* April, 539–549

Monroe, S. M. (1983) Major and minor life events as predictors of psychological distress: Further issues and findings. *Journal of Behavioral Medicine, 6,* 189–205

IV. Social Behavior Problems in Adolescence

M. ARGYLE*

Introduction

Adolescence is a very interesting time of life for psychologists, but often very difficult for those involved: adolescents and their families. The difficulties lie mainly in the sphere of social behaviour, and recent developments in the study of interaction have a lot to contribute here. The main practical application is in devising methods of social skills training for adolescents with social difficulties, and in advising parents and others who deal with them on the most effective ways of doing so.

Social Difficulties in Adolescence

Most adolescents find some social situations difficult. Bryant and Trower (1974) surveyed a 10% sample of Oxford undergraduates and found that a high proportion reported moderate or severe difficulty with common social situations, especially 'approaching others' (36%), 'going to dances/discotheques' (35%), and 'going to parties' (26%). These were the figures for second-year students; first-year students reported much higher levels of difficulty. Nine per cent of second-year students reported 'moderate difficulty' or avoidance of six common situations out of thirty and were regarded as suffering from serious social problems (Table 1).

Zimbardo (1977) surveyed large samples of American and other students aged 18 − 21 and found that about 40 per cent considered themselves to be 'shy' now, while very few said that they had never been shy. Many adolescents feel lonely, 15 − 20% feel 'seriously lonely', 55 − 65% 'often feel lonely', girls more often than boys (Brennan, 1982).

Some situations are commonly found most difficult. Furnham and Argyle (1981) surveyed 143 adolescents and young adults, and found the clusters of difficult situations shown in Table 2.

In my experience of social skills training the most common difficulty for young neurotic out-patients is in making friends, or in making friends with the opposite sex. Social situations are found to be difficult when they in-

* University of Oxford, Department of Experimental Psychology, South Parks Road, Oxford OX1 3UD, United Kingdom

Development as Action in Context
Ed. by R. K. Silbereisen et al.
© Springer-Verlag Berlin Heidelberg 1986

Table 1. Percentages of a sample of Oxford students who reported moderate difficulty or worse in thirty situations. (Bryant & Trower, 1974)

Situations	Present time	Year ago
21. Approaching others	36	51
14. Going to dances/discotheques	35	45
25. Taking initiative in conversation	26	44
5. Going to parties	25	42
19. Being with people you don't know well	22	37
8. Going out/opposite sex	21	38
11. Being in a group/opposite sex	21	35
24. Getting to know someone in depth	21	29
29. Talking about self and feelings	19	26
26. Looking at people in the eyes	18	26
22. Making decisions affecting others	17	31
17. Going into a room full of people	17	30
30. People looking at you	16	26
18. Meeting strangers	13	28
16. Being with younger people	13	19
7. Making friends of your own age	11	20
27. Disagreeing/putting forward views	9	23
4. Going into pubs	9	17
9. Being in a group/same sex	9	15
28. People standing/sitting very closely	9	14
10. Being in a group/men and women	8	18
6. Mixing with people at work	8	16
12. Entertaining in your own home	7	19
15. Being with older people	5	8
23. Being with just one other person	4	9
13. Going into restaurants/cafés	3	10
2. Going into shops	1	5
1. Walking down the street	1	4
3. Using public transport	1	3
20. Being with friends	1	1

volve the likelihood of conflict or rejection by others, intimacy, sexual or otherwise, public performances, or complex rules and rituals (Argyle, Furnham, & Graham, 1981).

Adolescents may also make life very difficult for others, as studies of their parents show. Marital happiness reaches its lowest period when the children are adolescents (Figure 1).

The Components of Social Competence

Competent social performance consists of a number of component skills, each of which is important, and some of which may go wrong in a number of

Table 2. Difficult social situation clusters. (Furnham & Argyle, 1981)

Assertiveness

1. Complaining to a neighbour about noisy disturbance
9. Taking an unsatisfactory article back to a shop

Intimacy

2. Taking a peson of the opposite sex out for the first time
4. Visiting a doctor when unwell

Counselling

6. Going round to cheer up a depressed friend
5. Going to a close relative's funeral

Public performance

8. Give short speech
7. Being host at a large party
9. Going for a job interview

Parties etc.

13. Going to a function with many people from a different
    culture
14. Attending a wedding

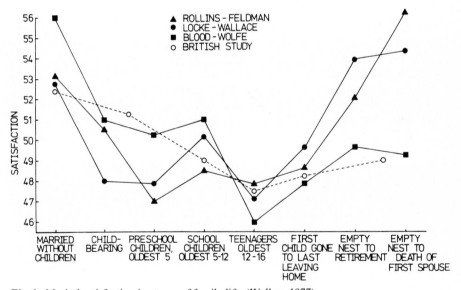

Fig. 1. Marital satisfaction in stages of family life. (Walker, 1977)

different ways. If competent and incompetent performers are compared, for example popular and unpopular adolescents, they are found to differ on some of these components.

Nonverbal Communication (NVC)

When successful and less successful performers of a skill are compared, NVC is always found to be an important area of difference. Trower (1980) found that socially skilled patients looked, smiled, and gestured more than unskilled ones. Romano and Bellack (1980) found that ratings on assertiveness were predictable from smiling and vocal intonation. NVC consists of facial expression, tone of voice, gaze, gesture, postures, physical proximity, and appearance. NVC is important in the communication of emotions and attitudes to other people. A *sender* is in a certain state, or possesses some information; this is *encoded* into a message which is then *decoded* by a *receiver:*

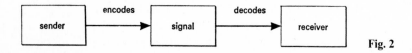

Fig. 2

NV signals are the main ways of communicating attitudes to other people, such as like−dislike, dominant−submissive. In addition there is love, which is a variant of like. These attitudes can be conveyed clearly by NV signals, such as facial expression, tone of voice, and posture. Liking is conveyed by smiling, a friendly tone of voice and so on.

I and my colleagues compared the effect of verbal and nonverbal signals for communicating interpersonal attitudes. Typed messages were prepared indicating that the speaker was superior, equal or inferior; videotapes of a performer counting (1, 2, 3 ...) were made, conveying the same attitudes; the verbal and nonverbal signals were rated by subjects as very similar in superiority, etc. The nine combined signals were presented to further subjects on videotape − superior (verbal), inferior (nonverbal), etc. − and rated for superiority. The variance due to NV cues was about twelve times the variance due to verbal cues in affecting judgements of inferior-superior (Argyle, Salter, Nicholson, Williams, & Burgess, 1970). Some of the results are shown in Figure 3. Similar results were obtained in later experiments with friendly-hostile messages (Argyle, Alkema, & Gilmour, 1972).

The attitudes of others are perceived, then, mainly from their nonverbal behaviour. People can judge with some accuracy when others like them, but are much less accurate in perceiving dislike (Tagiuri, 1958). The reason for this is probably that expressions of dislike are concealed to a large extent and only the more subtle ones remain, such as bodily orientation.

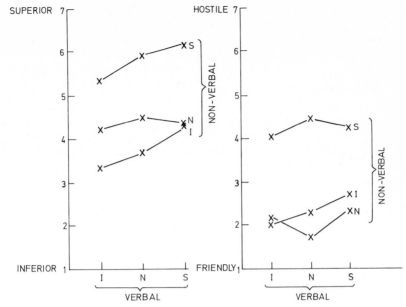

Fig. 3. Effects of inferior, neutral and superior verbal and nonverbal signals on semantic ratings (Argyle, 1969)

NV signals are also the main way of expressing emotions. These can be distinguished from interpersonal attitudes in that emotions are not directed towards others present but are simply states of the individual. The common emotions are anger, depression, happiness, surprise, fear, and disgust/contempt (Ekman, 1982). Fear or anxiety, for example, can be shown by (a) *tone of voice* − breathy, rapid, speech errors; (b) *facial expression* − tense, perspiring, expanded pupils; (c) *posture* − tense and rigid; (d) *gestures* − tense clasping of objects or general bodily activity; (e) *smell* − of perspiration; and (f) *gaze* − short glances, aversion of gaze. Interactors may try to conceal their true emotional condition, but it is difficult to control all these cues, and impossible to control the more autonomic ones. Emotional states can be conveyed by speech ('I am feeling very happy'), but such statements will not be believed unless supported by appropriate NVC, and the NVC can convey the message without the speech.

There are considerable individual differences in the extent to which emotions are expressed. Buck (1979) has shown that there are 'internalizers', who may have high physiological arousal combined with little facial expression, and 'externalizers' who show the opposite; females tend to be externalizers.

It has been found that females are on average more accurate senders. They are also more accurate receivers, but they tend to be "polite" decoders, in that they attend more to the face, rather than, like males, to the voice, which is a less well controlled, "leaky" channel, often expressing emotions which the sender is trying to conceal (Hall, 1979).

Verbal Communication; Conversation

Socially inadequate people are usually very ineffective in the sphere of verbal communication too. They often speak very little, fail to ask questions or to show an interest in others, and fail to produce the kinds of utterances which will be effective in particular situations or sustain conversations. They may be inadequate in the use of NV communication to accompany speech. Trower (1980) found that the main difference in behaviour between socially inadequate and other patients was that the latter talked more.

Conversational sequences are constructed partly out of certain basic building blocks, like the question-answer sequence, and repeated cycles characteristic of the situation. Socially inadequate people are usually very bad conversationalists and this appears to be due to a failure to master some of these basic sequences.

There are several other common two-step sequences such as joke—laugh, complain—sympathise, request—comply. There are a number of two-step sequences which take place not because there is a rule, but as a result of basic psychological processes. For example, there is the powerful effect of reinforcement and there is response-matching, in which one person copies the accent, posture or other aspects of the other's behaviour.

There are also *pro-active* two-step sequences, where one person makes both moves, as in accept—thank, reply—question. Failure to make a pro-active move can stop a conversation.

I shall now discuss sequences of more than two steps. The social skill model which is described later generates a characteristic kind of four-step sequence (Figure 4).

This is a case of asymmetrical interaction with A in charge. A's first move, A_1, produces an unsatisfactory result, B_1, so A modifies his behaviour to A_2, which produces the desired B_2. Note the link $A_1 - A_2$, representing the

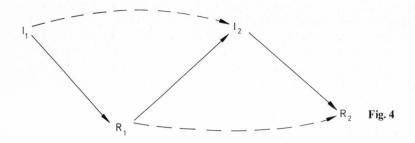

Fig. 4

persistence of A's goal-directed behaviour. The model can be extended to cases where both interactors are pursuing goals simultaneously, as in the following example, from a selection interview:

I_1: How well did you do at physics at school?
R_1: Not very well, I was better at chemistry.
I_2: What were your A-level results?
R_2: I got a C in physics, and an A in chemistry.
I_3: That's very good.

Further complexities of conversational sequences are discussed by Clarke (1983) and Clarke & Argyle (1982).

Rewardingness

One effect of reinforcement is in the control of others' behaviour. If A consistently gives small signs of approval immediately after B produces some form of behaviour, the frequency of that behaviour is rapidly increased (or decreased following disapproval). This is one of the main processes whereby people are able to modify each other's behaviour in the desired direction. Clearly, if people do not give clear, immediate and consistent reinforcements, positive and negative, they will not be able to influence others in this way, and social encounters will be correspondingly more frustrating and difficult for them. This appears to be a common problem with many psychiatric patients who characteristically fail to control or try to over-control others.

Rewardingness also affects popularity. There are a number of different sources of popularity and unpopularity but there is little doubt that being a source of rewards is one of the most important (Rubin, 1973). A person may be rewarding because the interaction with him is enjoyable, for example making love or playing squash; he may be rewarding because he is kind, helpful, interesting, etc. Some people are rewarding just by being attractive or of high status.

An early study of popularity in a girls' borstal found that the popular girls helped other girls, encouraged them, cheered them up, or simply made them feel wanted or accepted. The unpopular girls did not provide rewards in those ways, but tried to extract rewards for themselves by demanding attention, or trying to dominate others, or make them do things for them (Jennings, 1950).

Taking the Role of the Other

There are individual differences in the ability to see another person's point of view, as measured by tests in which subjects are asked to describe situations as perceived by others. Those who are good at it have been found to do better at a number of social tasks (Feffer & Suchotliff, 1966) and to be more altruistic. Meldman (1967) found that psychiatric patients are more egocentric, that is talk about themselves more than controls, and it has been our experience that socially unskilled patients have great difficulty in taking the role of the other. This appears to be a cognitive ability which develops with age (Flavell, 1968), but which may fail to develop properly.

Self-Presentation

When the self is activated, there is heightened physiological arousal, and greater concern with the impression made on others. This can be controlled to some extent by 'self-presentation', that is sending information about the self. This is done partly to sustain self-esteem, and partly for professional purposes. For example, teachers teach more effectively if their pupils think they are well informed. If people tell others how good they are in words, this is regarded as a joke and disbelieved, at least in western cultures. Jones (1964) found that verbal ingratiation is done with subtlety (e.g., drawing attention to assets in unimportant areas). Most self-presentation is done non-verbally: by clothes, hair style, accent, badges, and general style of behaviour. Social class is very clearly signalled in these ways, as is membership of rebellious social groups (Argyle, 1975). Self-presentation is needed in all social skills, but especially in those which require performance in front of an audience, or where it is important to win the confidence of clients.

Physical attractiveness (p.a.) can be regarded as part of self-presentation, since it is partly, even mainly, under an individual's control. Attention to clothes, hair and skin, binding or padding, height of shoes or hat, diet and exercise, facial expression, and posture can do a great deal for p.a. People who are attractive are believed rightly or wrongly, to be superior in all sorts of ways, are liked more, and are treated better (Berscheid & Walster, 1974). The faces of mental patients were less attractive before they became patients and they became less attractive while being patients (Napoleon, Chassin, & Young, 1980).

A normally competent interactor sends mainly NV signals to indicate his role, status or other aspects of his identity. From these signals others know what to expect, including what rewards are likely to be forthcoming, and how to deal with him. Self-presentation can go wrong in a number of ways: (1) bogus claims which are unmasked; (2) being too 'grey', that is sending too little information; (3) sending too much, overdramatizing, as hysterical personalities sometimes do; (4) inappropriate self-presentation, a female research student who looks and sounds like a retired professor.

The Analysis of Social Situations

We saw above that certain situations are often found difficult. Clients for social skills training (SST) usually report difficulty with particular social situations. The traditional trait model supposed that individuals possess a fixed degree of introversion, neuroticism, etc., and that it is displayed consistently in different situations. This model has been abandoned by most psychologists because of an increased awareness of the great effect of the situation on behaviour (e.g., people are more anxious when exposed to physical danger than when asleep in bed), and the amount of person–situation interaction (e.g., person A is more frightened by heights, person B by cows), resulting in low inter-situational consistency (Mischel, 1968).

A number of studies have shown that patients are *less* variable in their behaviour between situations, and that psychotics are less variable than neurotics (e.g., Moos, 1968). This means that the patients are failing to respond appropriately to the requirements of different situations. It suggests that training to deal with different situations may be useful. Furthermore, while some people are socially incompetent in many situations, others find only certain situations difficult. To carry out SST for such people, it has been necessary to analyse the main features of those situations, and to find out where these people are going wrong. Just as a newcomer might be baffled by, say, American football, so might a newcomer be baffled by certain social situations. What does he need to know to be able to perform competently? To understand a new game one needs to know such things as the goals (how to score and win), the moves allowed, the rules, the roles, and the physical setting and equipment. Similar information is needed for a social situation: the goals, rules, roles, physical setting, repertoire of moves, concepts used, and special skills.

We shall now examine some of the main features of situations which need to be taken into account.

Goals and Goal Structure

A number of social psychologists, like Lewin and more recently Pervin (1983), have found goals a useful concept. Also developments in exchange theory, have led us to the study of the benefits received by those who seek or stay in situations and relationships, and the interdependence of participants on one another in this respect.

Our first study was on the goals of social situations. We assumed that people enter social situations because they are motivated to do so, that is, they expect to be able to attain certain goals, which in turn lead to the satisfaction of needs or other drives. Situations have presumably developed as cultural institutions because they satisfy needs in this way. In our analysis of

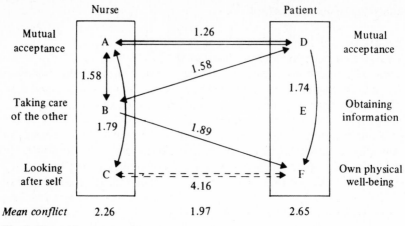

Fig. 5. The goal structure of nursing

situations in terms of their basic features, we considered that the goal structure is the most basic feature, and that all the other features can be explained in terms of the goals and goal structure.

Graham, Argyle, & Furnham (1980) carried out studies of the goals of each participant in common social situations. A total of 133 subjects rated the importance of 21 goals in eight situations. Principal components analyses were carried out for each situation separately with rather similar factors appearing. These were: 1. Own physical well-being, 2. social acceptance, etc., 3. task goals specific to the situation. The three factors for a nurse dealing with a patient are shown on the left-hand side of Figure 5.

We also asked subjects to rate the extent to which each goal was instrumental to, independent of, or interfered with other goals (on a 5-point scale). This showed the amount of conflict vs. instrumentality, and other scales elicited the direction of such relationships; links between goals both within and between persons were found. Figure 4 shows the perceived goal structure for nurse and patients; it can be seen that the nurse's goal of looking after the patient leads to patient's well-being, but that this is in conflict with the nurse's own well-being. We think that this is potentially a powerful method for exploring the conflicts and instrumental links between goals; it is perhaps limited to the goals which subjects are willing to admit to, though in the present study a number of fairly basic and biological goals were reported.

Rules

Rules are one of the main features in our conceptual model of situations, and of relationships. By a rule we mean: behaviour which members of a group believe should, or should not, be performed in some situation, or range of situations. This is based on the notion of appropriateness; when a person breaks a rule he has made a mistake.

The theory we propose is simply this: rules are created and changed in order that situational goals can be attained. It is a familiar psychological principle that an individual person or animal will discover routes to desired goals, either by trial and error or by other forms of problem-solving. We are now proposing an extension to this principle: *groups* of people will find routes to their goals, and these routes will be collective solutions, including the necessary coordination of some behaviours and the exclusion of other behaviours by means of rules. Unless such coordination is achieved group goals will not be attained. Harris (1975) offered an explanation of the Indian rules protecting cows in terms of the value of cow-dung as fertiliser and fuel, of oxen for pulling farm implements, and so on.

We predicted that there would be universal rules which meet the common requirements of all social situations, such as preventing withdrawal and aggression, and making communication possible, and that there would be other rules which meet the requirements of particular kinds of situations — coordinating behaviour so that goals may be attained, guarding against temptations, and helping with common difficulties.

Argyle, Graham, Campbell, & White (1979) carried out two studies using altogether 75 subjects, 25 situations and 124 possible rules, elicited in pilot interviews. The first prediction was that there would be universal rules. A cluster analysis produced a cluster which consisted of the rules which applied to most situations.

We also expected rules which would apply to groups of similar situations. The second cluster for example applied to formal situations. As expected these were rules which guarded against common temptations ("On a first date, one should not touch the other"), and avoided common difficulties ("At a pub, don't leave others to pay"), some of them specific to particular situations ("At the doctor's, make sure that you are clean, and tell him the truth").

Some apparently unruly situations among young people are also rule governed. Some of the rules for fighting among delinquent girls are shown in Table 3. British football hooligans also follow rules. Marsh, Harre, & Rosser (1978) interviewed football hooligans about how to 'put the boot in' and allied matters. In these interviews a number of rules were stated more or less directly by informants: for example, it was not acceptable to injure members of the opposing gang though it was desirable to frighten them or make them look foolish. Failures of social competence among young people are often due to ignorance of the rules of interviews, work situations, or other social occasions.

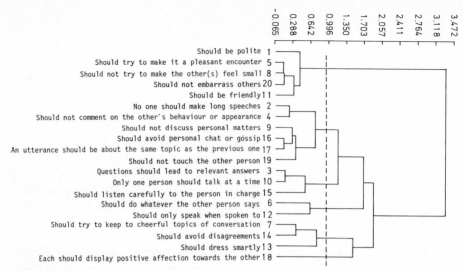

Fig. 6. Clusters of rules for Oxford students

Table 3. Rules for fighting among females. Survey of 251 schoolgirls, borstal girls and prison women. (Campbell, 1980)

1. Should not use a bottle to hit the other person
   schoolgirls 85% (borstal girls 58%)
2. Should not ask friends to call the police
   borstal girls 85%
3. Should not use a handbag to hit the other person
   69%
4. Should not use a knife on the other person
   schoolgirls 89% (borstal girls 52%)
5. Should not report it to the police later
   86%
6. Should not ask friends to join in
   81%
7. Should not tell the school later
   85%
8. It is OK to kick the other person
   borstal girls 78%
9. It is OK to slap the other person
   prison women 85%
10. It is OK to punch the other person
    borstal girls 90%

Repertoire

Every game has a special set of moves, which may be quite distinctive, as in the cases of chess, squash, football, etc. The moves are the steps toward the goals which are allowed in that game. Similar considerations apply to social situations, as is shown by the need to use different category systems for research on doctor—patient communication, psychotherapy, management-union negotiation, and so on (Argyle, Furnham, & Graham, 1981).

The elements of behaviour are also grouped and contrasted differently in different situations, that is, different elements are seen as similar. We carried out a study of the structures of elements, and found that the clusters obtained for different situations had interesting differences, for example, on a date, asking questions about work and private life were grouped together, whereas in a work situation they fell into quite different clusters (Argyle, Graham, & Kreckel, 1982).

In order to perform competently in a social situation it is necessary to know the repertoire, to understand the grouping of elements, and also to be able to perform them in a skilled way. To be able to perform the required moves at cricket or tennis requires a long period of training and practice; the same is true of the moves in making friends and other social skills.

Concepts

In order to behave effectively in any situation people need to possess appropriate concepts. It would not be possible to play cricket without knowing the meaning of *out, over,* etc., or to play chess without knowing what a *queen* is, and what *check* means.

In a social situation an interactor needs categories in order to classify:

1. *Persons:* for example a teacher needs to distinguish between pupils of different intelligence and motivation, since they would need to be handled differently.

2. *Social structure,* that is the relations between those present, in terms of status, role, friendship, etc.

3. *Elements of interaction:* for example between friendly and hostile, and further categories in particular situations.

4. *Relevant objects* of attention: for example parts of the physical environment and task-related objects, such as the pieces at chess.

In addition, people need sufficient cognitive equipment to understand what is happening and to decide how to deal with the situation. A motorist needs to understand something about the workings of cars, and something about local geography. When, for example, he sees a signpost he can then understand where he is, and what direction he should take to reach his goal. In social situations an interactor needs a similar kind of understanding.

Interpreting another's behaviour. He needs to understand why another person is, for example, aggressive, depressed or uncooperative.

Planning his own behaviour. When he has correctly perceived and interpreted another's behaviour, he has to decide how best to proceed. This can be seen in terms of expectancies – he has to know which behaviour will probably have the desired consequences. It also involves understanding, just as a motorist needs to understand engines and maps.

We found that the constructs used to categorize other people varied between situations. Forgas, Argyle and Ginsburg (1979) used multidimensional scaling for ratings of behaviour in four situations. In two of the situations (pub and morning coffee), *evaluation* was found to be the first dimension, followed by *extraversion* and *self-confidence;* in the third situation (a party at the boss's house) the dimensions were *self-confidence, warmth* and *ingratiation.* In the work situation (a seminar), the dimensions were *dominance, creativity* and *supportiveness.* In this experiment it was also found that the perceived structure of the group varied with the situation. For example status was important mainly in the seminar situation; here the senior academics were clearly above the graduate students. At the party there were no dominance differences apart from the position of the host.

People in a number of professions have learnt to categorise others in specialised ways. Policemen are trained to distinguish those who are engaged in illegal behaviour from others; selection interviewers are trained to look for evidence of properties such as stability, achievement motivation, creativity, etc. Doctors, dentists and psychiatrists, all have their category systems for classifying their clients.

Roles

Nearly every situation has two or more different roles. Young people may think it is inauthentic to conform to such roles, or may not realise what they are, (e.g. the role of interviewee has special characteristics).

Roles are interlocked with other features of situations that have been discussed above. The occupant of a particular role has *goals* (e.g., customer versus shopkeeper), can use only part of the repertoire (e.g., umpire vs. bowler), is constrained by certain *rules* which may define the role, occupies a special part of the *physical environment* (e.g., prisoners vs. judge), and is faced by special *difficulties* and requires special *skills* (e.g., performer vs. audience).

Roles fit together to form role systems; they are often complementary. It is impossible to play the role of teacher unless others are prepared to play the role of pupil; doctors need patients, and leaders need followers. In sociology the system of interlocking roles is seen as an enduring social structure. I propose to adopt the same analysis for situational roles.

Roles emerge in situations for several reasons.

1. Groups need leaders (e.g. committees need a chairman); groups are found to be more effective if they have a stable leadership hierarchy, especially for large groups carrying out a task.

2. Cooperative rules, coalitions and subgroups, form when people find that it is in their joint interest to cooperate, to pool their resources.

3. Division of labour in task or problem-solving groups leads to better results since people can specialise.

4. Individuals have different personalities and abilities, and have a need to appear as distinctive individuals. This leads to the selection of different informal roles in groups.

Marsh et al. (1978) reported on the roles they found among football fans at British football grounds. These are: (1) *rowdies,* aged twelve to seventeen, who make the most noise, produce the most violent displays of aggression and wear the most spectacular costumes; (2) *town boys,* aged seventeen to twenty-five, who have graduated from being rowdies, are quieter, dress in a normal way and are deferred to by boys in the other roles; (3) *novices,* younger than the rowdies, set apart from them and keen to join them; (4) *part-time supporters,* a varied group not so fully involved in aggressive displays and despised by the others, (5) *nutters,* extremely aggressive boys who often behave in a crazy way and break the rules accepted by the majority of fans.

Language

Speech style varies a lot between situations. One of the main differences is between formal and informal situations. In formal situations a "high" version is spoken, which is more grammatical and precise, more complex with subordinate clauses, makes more use of nouns and adjectives rather than verbs, adverbs and pronouns, and uses a more upper class accent. The purpose of formal speech is the accurate communication of information or instructions; informal speech is equally or more concerned with sustaining social relationships.

Situations also vary in their technical requirements, and vocabulary varies correspondingly. The vocabularies used by groups of gardeners, doctors, garagemen or physicists are quite distinctive, though they modify their use of technical terms when addressing laymen (Argyle, Furnham, & Graham, 1981). Several studies have shown that groups of criminals develop their own special vocabulary or *argot,* partly with the purpose of preventing outsiders from understanding. Such special vocabularies have been found for professional gamblers, pickpockets, smugglers, drug addicts, prisoners, and others. These argots have been described as *antilanguages,* since they use an alternative vocabulary to that used by 'straight' society, and this has the function of creating and maintaining an alternative social reality (Halliday, 1978). Staples & Robinson (1974), in a study of a Southampton shop, found that formality of address varied with the situation. When speaking to one another in front of customers, employees used title and last name or Sir; address was less formal in the staff canteen and least formal in the street, in a pub or at a staff dance.

Environmental Setting

Most situations take place in special environmental settings: school class-rooms, homes, church, etc. This is the easiest feature of a situation to change. It has been found in Britain that there is more vandalism in lower blocks and deck-access housing (i.e., with long internal corridors) than in accommodation with staircase access and balcony designs. Most damage occurs in semipublic areas.

It is now realised that the vandalism is not entirely due to design features, but also to the high density of children, delinquents, and problem families. Part of the solution to such vandalism is to change the kind of people who live in these buildings. In deck-access buildings in Manchester, problem families were replaced by students; it is often possible to reduce the child density. However, more can be done by modifying the design of buildings. The following steps have been found to be successful: (1) avoid large areas of semipublic impersonal space, (2) avoid dark corners and ensure that parents can see the children's play areas, (3) keep all property occupied, (4) use materials that are very strong, for example armour-plate glass or transparent plastics, and that are difficult to mark, for example glazed tiles, rough bricks, (5) provide all-night floodlighting in certain areas, (6) install a resident caretaker or doorman (Clarke & Mayhew, 1980; Central Policy Review Staff, 1978).

Environmental psychologists sometimes assess situations in purely physical terms. It has been found, for example, that if people meet in a room at a temperature of 93.5 °F, or with four square feet per person, they will like each other less than in a larger and cooler room (Griffit & Veitch, 1971). However, the physical features of the environment work in another way, by their symbolic meaning. A room decorated in red and yellow suggests a warm emotional mood; placing some people at a greater height, as at a high table, suggests dominance; a room with a concrete floor, battered furniture and a bare light bulb suggest prison or interrogation, not love, work, social life or committee meetings. Many situations involve special props; a lecture needs a blackboard and slide projector, while a party needs quite different equipment.

Special Skills

The skills needed in social situations have much in common with those used for motor skills. The social skill model draws attention to a number of anal-

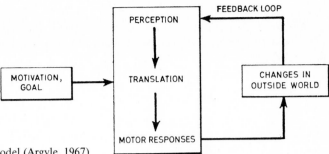

Fig. 7. Motor skill model (Argyle, 1967)

ogies between social performance, and the performance of motor skills like driving a car (see Figure 7). In each case the performer pursues certain goals, makes continuous response to feedback and emits hierarchically-organised motor responses. This model has been heuristically very useful in drawing attention to the importance of feedback, and hence to gaze. It also suggests a number of different ways in which social performances can fail and the training procedures that may be effective, through analogy with motor skills training (Argyle & Kendon, 1967; Argyle, 1969).

The model emphasises the motivation, goals, and plans of interactors. It is postulated that every interactor is trying to achieve some goal, whether he is aware of it or not. These goals may be to get another person to like him, to obtain or convey information, to modify the other's emotional state, and so on. Such goals may be linked to more basic motivational systems. Goals have subgoals: for example a doctor must diagnose the patient's disease before he can treat him. Patterns of response are directed towards goals and subgoals, and have a hierarchical structure – large units of behaviour are composed of smaller ones, and at the lowest levels these are habitual and automatic.

There is another important implication of this line of thought: the moves, or social acts, made in social behaviour are rather different from the actions in a motor skill. Social acts like shaking hands, bidding at an auction sale or asking questions at a seminar are signals with a shared social meaning in a given context. They are like the moves in a game; in any particular game there is a repertoire of possible moves, which is quite different for chess, polo or wrestling; each move has a generally accepted meaning in the context of the game and the move can be made by alternative physical actions.

The social skill model also emphasises feedback processes. A person driving a car sees at once when it is going in the wrong direction, and takes corrective action with the steering wheel. Social interactors do likewise; if another person it talking too much they interrupt, ask closed questions or no questions and look less interested in what he has to say. Feedback requires perception, looking at and listening to the other person. Skilled performance requires the ability to take the appropriate corrective action referred to as *translation* in the model — not everyone knows that open-ended questions make people talk more and closed questions make them talk less. It also depends on a number of two-step sequences of social behaviour whereby certain social acts have reliable effects on another. The social skills which are most effective vary with the situation, and also with culture and social class.

Shure (1981) describes how to train people in a problem-solving approach to difficult social situations, whereby they are encouraged to engage in *means-ends thinking*. Maladjusted adolescents were less able than controls to formulate a step-by-step plan to deal with situations. In the selection interview, various kinds of difficult candidates must be dealt with and interviewers can be taught the special skills needed for each. The translation part of the model often includes complex cognitive structures, including the rules and other features of the immediate situation and knowledge of social processes (Pendleton & Furnham, 1980).

Skilled performance includes the ability to make the individual moves of the repertoire, as prescribed by the rules. However this requires more than knowledge — it requires motor skill, as in the case of sports like tennis, and skills like playing the piano. In social situations there are similar skilled moves, such as those required in public speaking or psychotherapy. Skilled performance also requires mastery of sequences. A motorist can make rapid corrective action if the car goes in the wrong direction or at the wrong speed. An interviewer can take similar corrective action if the answer to one of his questions is not satisfactory (Figure 4).

More complex sequences of interaction may need to be created and controlled, as in the cycles of interaction involved in school teaching (e.g. teacher teaches, asks question, pupil replies). Flanders (1970) observed that much of the skill of teaching consists of the control of such cycles.

Stressful and difficult social situations can be dealt with by mastering the appropriate skills. This will lead to successful performance, avoidance of rejection or other negative reactions from others, and this leads to reduced anxiety. It may however be necessary to control anxiety or other emotional responses, as in public speaking. Similar considerations apply to difficult or dangerous sports, like diving or ski jumping.

The Authenticity Problem

We have emphasised the importance of situations, and the variability of an individual's behaviour between situations. A long series of studies (Endler & Magnusson, 1976) attempted to test trait theory and other models by finding the percentages of variance due to persons (P), situations (S) and P × S interaction. This was done with reported behaviour (e.g., anxiety), and with observed behaviour (e.g., talking, smiling). Typical results were:

Persons	15–30%,
Situations	20–45%,
P × S	30–50%.

However, many adolescents are not aware that situational variability is normal, and think that they or others are being insincere or inauthentic if they change their behaviour to fit into a particular situation. They seem to be "P theorists", and think that traits rather than situations are the proper predictors of behaviour. Snyder (1979) distinguished between high and low self-monitors. High self-monitors watch their behaviour and effects on others carefully, and adjust more to the demands of different situations. Low self-monitors make a point of their genuineness and sincerity, and vary their behaviour less. They are less socially skilled. Many adolescents seem to be low self monitors. We will discuss later some of the relationship skills faced by adolescents.

Social Relationships in Adolescents

Most social behaviour is not with strangers but with friends, siblings, parents, teachers, etc. – with whom there is a social relationship. Many problems of social behaviour arise in connection with establishing or sustaining these relationships. Some of their properties are shown in a study by Wish, Deutsch, & Kaplan (1977) using multidimensional scaling on the judgments of students. Friends and siblings were seen as fairly close and equal, socioemotional and informal. Relations with parents are less close or unequal, and more intense.

We carried out a study of the sources of satisfaction and conflict in different relationships. For adult subjects, relations with adolescent children were seen as a major source of satisfaction, but also as a major source of conflict, especially conflict based on criticism (Figure 8). For the younger subjects, relationships with friends and siblings were intense with high levels of satisfaction and conflict.

Friends

During adolescence friendship is the most important relationship, and a great deal of time is spent with friends, often up to 3 hours per day, with more on the telephone. There are a few close friends (2 – 5) sometimes forming a gang or group, and a wider network with no boundaries.

Between 8 and 10 years there is an important development for many children, to where the child can see the point of view of the other and collaborate for mutual benefit. Children become aware of the needs of others, and will cooperate and reciprocate. They are aware of the possibility of friendship as a permanent bond. This shift in attitude towards friends is of great theoretical interest – it marks the point at which people go beyond concern with receiving rewards (Selman & Jaquette, 1977). The development of cognitive powers and social skills seems to go hand in hand. These older

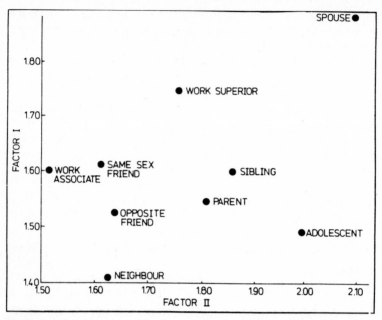

Fig. 8. Relationships plotted on the conflict dimensions. (Argyle & Furnham, 1983)

children understand what friendship is, can see others' point of view, and know the effects of different kinds of behaviour on a relationship. They are acquiring knowledge of social skills.

From 12 years onwards, just before adolescence, children feel the need for a close friend, and are also prepared to allow the other some independence. They are moving towards a very important phase of friendship, where friends help them to become independent of parents, and to acquire further social skills. Friends now come in groups, or networks, and one of the main things they do is to have fun (Fine, 1981).

This is the age at which same-sex friendship is most intense. During adolescence young people are becoming independent of their parents, undergoing physiological changes and having to cope with sexual impulses. The main characteristics of adolescent friendships is their intensity. In fact they are so similar to love that some psychologists have thought that latent homosexuality is present. And when heterosexual relationships are taken up, the same-sex ones decline in intensity. At least we can say that they are a training or preparation for heterosexual intimacy (Kon, 1981).

There is a close connection between the forming of intimate friendships and the establishing of identity. There is some evidence that for girls it is first necessary to have a close relationship, while for boys it is first necessary to establish identity, before a close relationship can be formed (Matteson, 1979). Adolescents choose as close friends people they admire, who they see as similar to their ideal self (the sort of person they would like to be), and they choose friends of the same age as themselves and who are facing similar problems. Great importance is attached to friends being trustworthy at age 15 – 16, and friendships are very exclusive. There is a good deal of anxiety about jealousy and fear of losing friends at this age. Coleman (1974), in a study in London, using a sentence-completion method, found that 15-year-old girls would say, for example, "Often when three people are together . . . there is jealousy, I don't know why." Girls develop a need for a close friendship at an earlier age than boys, and move on to dating sooner. They have a few close friends, where boys have a group (or gang); and pairs of girls are more exclusive. Girls' friendships are like the romantic ideal of a tender relationship, while boys are companions in shared activities.

Friendship is not governed by legal or formal rules in the way that marriage is. But if you ask people what they think friends should or should not do in relation to each other there is a very high level of agreement. What they have in mind presumably is that if such rules are broken then a friendship is likely to break up.

We asked a sample of people to rate the importance of 40 possible rules for friendship: 27 were generally endorsed. These were checked further in other samples by finding which rules distinguished between current and lapsed friends, close and less close friends, and which rules, when broken, were blamed for the collapse of friendship. Using these different criteria, the following rules for friendship appeared to be most important (Table 4).

Table 4. Rules of friendship. (Argyle & Henderson, 1984)

Exchange
13. Seek to repay debts, favours or compliments, no matter how small.
17. Share news of success with the other.
20. Show emotional support.
25. Volunteer help in time of need.
27. Strive to make him/her happy while in each other's company

Intimacy
24. Trust and confide in each other.

Coordination
18. Respect privacy
21. Don't nag.

Third party
10. Don't criticise other in public.
11. Stand up for the other person in their absence.
12. Keep confidences.
23. Be tolerant of each other's friends.
26. Don't be jealous or critical of other relationships.

Loneliness is a common, and very distressing condition. Among adolescents and students it is quite widespread (55% or more say that they often feel lonely). Those who feel lonely also feel depressed, anxious, bored, lacking in self-esteem, shy, self-conscious, and somewhat hostile to others (Peplau & Perlman, 1982). Some people are lonely because they are socially isolated, but it is possible to feel lonely when surrounded by friends and family if the relationships are felt to fall short of the quality desired. In some studies it has been found that lonely people have as many friends as the non-lonely, and are chosen as friends by others, but that there is a lower level of intimacy and self-disclosure (Williams & Solano, 1983). Lonely people are aware of a discrepancy between their social attachments and what they would like; we now know that the problem is primarily that their friendships are not intimate enough.

A number of studies have documented the social skill differences which lead to loneliness, that is not being able to establish friendships of the desired kind. The main findings are that the lonely:

1. engage in less self-disclosure, which in turn leads to less self-disclosure by others, and this hinders the relationship.

2. take less interest in others during interaction – ask fewer questions, refer less to the other, and continue another's topic of conversation less (Jones, Hobbs, & Hockenburg, 1982).

3. are less assertive, more passive.

4. are less rewarding, like and trust others less, have a negative attitude to people.

5. blame their interpersonal failures on an unchangeable lack of social competence in themselves, rather than to lack of effort or use of the wrong strategy, so they are easily discouraged (Anderson, Horowitz, & de Sales, 1983).

6. Lonely and isolated people tend to be deficient in the sending of non-verbal signals, particularly signals of liking via face and voice.

7. Lonely and isolated people, especially in adolescence, may have an inadequate concept of what friendship involves. They do not realise that it requires concern for the other's welfare, together with loyalty and commitment (La Gaipa & Wood, 1981).

Heterosexual Relationships

Adolescence coincides with the onset of romantic and sexual relationships. There is a gradual shift from social life with mixed groups of friends to pairing off, and a shift to more intimate sexual activity. Some do this earlier, some later, others not at all.

Male American students between 19–24 years report an average of five to six affairs or romantic episodes, the women six to seven, but the number of times they say they have been in love is 1.2 and 1.3 respectively (Kephart,

1967). In another study 20% of males and 15% of females that said they fell in love by the fourth date, but 30% of males and 43% of females were unsure whether they were in love by the twentieth date (Kanin, Davidson, & Scheck, 1970).

At what age do people start "falling in love". An early American survey of over 1,000 college students (Kephart, 1967) found that most started dating at 13 years of age. They also report their first "infatuation" at age 13 but their first "love experience" did not occur, for most, till about the age of 17. Girls report first falling in love 5−6 months earlier than boys, and they become infatuated more often. But there is much evidence to show that girls are "cooler" (less impulsive). They are less influenced by physical appearance, they rarely fall in love with men who are younger or of lower social class, and more women than men say that they would marry without love (Cunningham & Antill, 1981). Girls, on the average, have intercourse and engage in other intimate sexual activities at a later age than men.

In our Rules Study, we found the following rules endorsed as the most important ones to apply to the opposite-sex partner in the dating relationship.

As a couple moves from casual to serious dating and to engagement, there is an increase in the level of love. There is also an increase in conflict and negativity from casual to serious dating, which levels off as the couple moves on to engagement. With the increase in conflict which accompanies this change in the relationship, different rules emerge to help in regulating these potential conflict areas. In our study of dating girls, those involved in a single dating relationship thought that it was much more important to show the other partner unconditional positive regard, to look after him when ill, and to show an interest in his daily activities than did girls involved with more than one dating partner. The single partner daters also reported applying the rules differently in practice. They were more likely to be faithful, to

Table 5. Rules for dating. (Argyle & Henderson, 1985)

1. Show mutual trust.
2. Respect privacy.
3. Be willing to compromise.
4. Be emotionally supportive.
5. Keep confidences.
6. Be faithful.
7. Share news of success.
8. Show interest in other's daily activities.
9. Disclose feelings and personal problems.
10. Talk about sex and death.
11. Be tolerant of each other's friends.
12. Stand up for the other in their absence.
13. Ask for personal advice.
14. Don't criticise in public.

ask for personal advice, to show distress or anxiety in front of the other person and to show interest in the partner's daily activities.

Another rule found among groups of American teen-age boys was that it was necessary to check with the group before taking a new girl out in order to avoid fights over girls (Coleman, 1963). The rules about sexual behaviour for dating have been changing fast. Up to about 1939 middle class couples in Britain followed a rule of petting, but no more. In the 1960s surveys found that girls followed the rule of petting if seriously involved, while most of the boys had proceeded to intercourse by the age of 20, especially if they were from the working class. Now there are no generally accepted rules, though many think that intercourse is permissible for engaged or seriously committed couples.

However the skills of courtship are not completely covered by rules. In order to attract members of the opposite sex various strategies may be used: suggesting that one thinks highly of them, doing things for them, agreeing with them, and ascribing attractive characteristics to oneself, directly or indirectly — which can all be described as ingratiation (Jones & Wortman, 1973). One study compared men who were successful and unsuccessful in dating girls. The successful ones were more fluent at quickly saying the right thing, and they agreed more. Their nonverbal behaviour was also different — they smiled and nodded more (Arkowitz, Lichtenstein, McGovern, & Hines, 1975). Nonverbal communication is one of the main ways of signalling sexual interest. Other nonverbal signals here include gaze, pupil dilation (though this is not under voluntary control), proximity and touch, and a state of bodily posture and alertness which signals a high level of arousal (Cook & McHenry, 1978). Attractive males have more dates and more social life, but this is mainly because they are also more assertive and socially competent. Attractive females are *not* more competent than other females: they do not need to be, since men take the initiative (Reis, Wheeler, Spiegel, Kernis, Nezlek, & Perri, 1982).

Relations with Parents

The relationship with children undergoes a major change, and sometimes a temporary breakdown, during adolescence. The child feels increasing urges to break out of a childish, dependent form of attachment to the parents, to one of greater independence and equality. This is less of a problem in primitive cultures where nothing changes very much, but more of a problem in our own where historical changes create a "generation gap" between the ideas and interests of parents and children.

We have seen that the period when the children are adolescents is a bad time for parents (Figure 1, p. 57); it is often a bad time for the children too: self-esteem is lower, and self-consciousness greater at 12 and 13 years than either before or after.

For most adolescents there is some degree of rebellion, if only to establish that they are separate individuals in their own right. For some there is a more serious rebellion, and rejection of the parents, though this is usually temporary. Rebellion is particularly acute among children who are socially mobile, or who have become attached to a deviate peer group; in developing countries adolescents often reject the traditional ways of their parents in favour of modern ideas.

Recent surveys suggest that there is a problem of communication or values for 25 – 30% of adolescents and their parents, but that serious conflict is fairly rare. The nature of these conflicts was explored further by Coleman (1974) in a study in London, using a projective method, in which subjects completed sentences ("When a boy is with his parents. . .") and wrote stories about pictures. On the subject of parents, negative themes were produced by over 90% of adolescents, but the contents were different for boys and girls. Boys reported feelings of frustration – "When a boy is with his parents . . . he is usually chained up". Girls on the other hand reported not feeling themselves when with their parents – "When a girl is with her parents . . . she is not herself . . . she has to behave differently . . . she becomes like them".

We studied sources of conflict in different relationships and found that relationships with adolescent children were seen as high on a factor of conflict based on criticism (II), although they were quite low on the more important general factor (Argyle & Furnham, 1983) (Fig. 8).

For boys the problem was frustration at restraints and demands for greater freedom. This is less important for most girls, because girls were socialised more strongly during childhood to be dependent and obedient, while boys were trained more to be independent. On the other hand boys, as well as girls, have a lot of ambivalence during adolescence: while fighting for more independence they also need parental help and support, and may switch back suddenly into a more dependent relationship.

Just as childhood appeared as a special time of life in the early 19th century, so adolescence emerged as a period between childhood and adulthood in the 20th century. "Teenagers" appeared for the first time during World War II as a special group, with their own clothes and tastes, and postwar parents had to work out how to handle them. The sexual revolution and the drug scene created particularly acute problems for parents of adolescents in the 1960's, but relationships seem to have improved since that time, and there is now less talk of "rebellion", "generation gap", and "identity crisis".

However it should be emphasised that the parent–child relationship is a very strong one, and that after the troubles of adolescence, most children continue to see their parents regularly and to provide major help until the parents' deaths. Adolescence is a temporary disruption of a very powerful bond, perhaps based in part on a concern for shared genes, but due more to the intense closeness of early childhood (Argyle & Henderson, 1985). Nevertheless, experiences in adolescence can have a permanent effect on the development of personality.

Research on the sources of successful identity achievement are informative. Identity achievement is more likely when there has been a good, but not over-close relationship with the parents, "moratorium" when parents have been too authoritarian, "premature foreclosure" when relations have been too close, and "ego-diffusion" when there has been rejection by parents (Bourne, 1978).

We turn now to the parental skills needed for dealing with adolescents. We have seen that this is a period many parents and many children find difficult. The secret lies in continuing those skills that were successful for younger children — warmth, control, and reasonable explanation. The parent now has less power, the child more, and it is necessary for the child to participate more in decisions concerning him or her. Research carried out by Elder (1962, 1963) and others has compared the effects of different parental styles during this period.

1. *Democratic* supervision, is most successful. Here the adolescent contributes freely to discussion of matters relevant to him or her and may make decisions. However the final decision has to be approved by the parents. This style is better than *permissive, equalitarian,* or *authoritarian* styles, in that it is seen as more fair, as less rejecting, and results in greater independence and confidence for the child. The main points of disagreement are often such things as hair styles and time of coming home. Parents need to set limits, but to bear in mind that things might have changed since they were young.

2. *Warm, rewarding,* parental behaviour again has a variety of favourable consequences, including the better achievement of an independent identity, self-confidence, and self-esteem.

3. *Explaining* the reasons for rules and for parental expectations, has similar effects.

Comparisons of the behaviour of the families of normal as compared with disturbed adolescents in laboratory discussions shows that they differ in a number of other respects. In the families of normals there were more jokes and laughter, more cooperation, more information-sharing, and more agreement, though they could also disagree in a friendly way (Riskin & Faunce, 1970).

In our own study of rules, the ten most strongly endorsed rules for parents of adolescents, and for the adolescent children, are shown in Table 6.

Social Skills Training (SST) for Adolescents

SST is being widely used for adolescent and other mental patients. Normal people may be able to find courses on assertiveness or heterosexual skills, and the training for many jobs now includes some SST. The standard procedure now is an elaborated form of role-playing, in which there are three or four main phases.

Table 6. Rules for parents and adolescent children. (Argyle & Henderson, 1985)

Rules for parents
 1. Should respect the other's privacy.
 2. Should give guidance to the child and an example.
 3. Should show affection for the child.
 4. Should encourage the child's ideas.
 5. Should respect the child's own views.
 6. Should be emotionally supportive.
 7. Should not engage in sexual activity with the child.
 8. Should not disclose confidences.
 9. Should not be overly possessive.
10. Should treat the child as a responsible adult.

Rules for adolescent
 1. Should respect the other's privacy.
 2. Should not disclose confidences.
 3. Should not engage in sexual activity with the other.
 4. Should share news of success with the other.
 5. Should be considerate of parent's rights, e.g. noise level, use of telephone and TV.
 6. Should be polite to parents, particularly in company.
 7. Should stand up for the other in their absence.
 8. Should give birthday cards and presents.
 9. Should look the other in the eye during conversation.
10. Should discuss sex and death with parents.

---

1. There is a lecture, discussion, demonstration, tape recording or a film about a particular aspect of the skill. This is particularly important when an unfamiliar skill is being taught or when rather subtle social techniques are used. The demonstration is important: this is known as *modelling*.

2. A problem situation is defined and stooges are produced for trainees to role play with for 7–15 minutes each. The stooges may be carefully trained beforehand to provide various problems, such as talking too much or having elaborate plausible excuses. It is found in microteaching that it is better to use real pupils than other trainee teachers as stooges, although this is a lot more trouble to arrange; the same probably applies to other areas of SST.

3. There is a feedback session, consisting of verbal comments by the trainer, discussion with the other trainees, and playback of audio- or video-tapes. Verbal feedback is used to draw attention constructively and tactfully, to what the trainee was doing wrong and to suggest alternative styles of behaviour. The tape recordings provide clear evidence for the accuracy of what is being said.

4. There is often a fourth phase, in which the role-playing is repeated. In microteaching this is known as *reteaching*.

Role-playing is often carried out in a training laboratory with one-way screen, videocameras, and ear microphones (Figure 9) (Argyle, 1983).

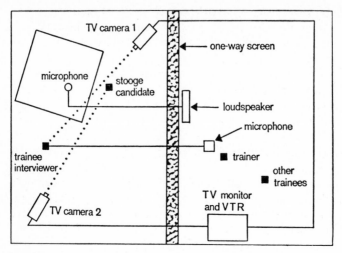

Fig. 9. Laboratory arrangements for interviewer training

While this kind of training has been found to be quite successful, for adolescents and others, in numerous follow-up studies, it is now possible to augment it in several ways as suggested by the research described above.

a) Sending nonverbal signals. Facial expression can be trained using a mirror and later a videotape recorder, taking photographs as models (e.g., from Ekman and Friesen, 1975). Vocal expression can be trained using modelling and playback of audio tape recordings.

b) Perception of nonverbal signals. The Ekman and Friesen photographs can be used to train people to decode facial expression. Trainees can be taught to decode tones of voice by listening to tape recordings of neutral messages produced in different emotional states (Davitz, 1964). In each case it is easy to test the subject, for example by finding out the percentage of recordings which they can decode correctly.

c) Conversational sequences. Samples of the client's conversation are recorded and studied carefully. It is then possible to spot the particular errors being made, for example failure to give a proactive utterance after answering a question, failure to initiate, lack of nonverbal responsiveness.

d) Taking the role of the other. Chandler (1973) succeeded in improving ability to see the other's point of view (and reducing delinquency) by means of exercises in which groups of five young delinquents developed and made video recordings of skits about relevant real-life situations, in which each member of the group played a part.

e) Self-presentation. In addition to the usual role-playing exercises, trainees can be given advice over clothes, hair and other aspects of appearance. Their voices can be trained to produce a more appropriate accent or tone of voice. There is a correlation between physical attractiveness and mental health, and some therapeutic success has been obtained by improving the appearance of patients. The recidivism of male criminals has been reduced by removing tattooing and scars.

f) Focus on situations. SST can focus on the particular situations which are found difficult. A group of trainees work over the rules, difficulties and other features of a situation, are helped to decide on the best skills to use, and then practice these skills in role-playing. Situational analysis has been used in the treatment of obesity and alcoholism, by discovering the situations in which overeating or drinking take place, and finding ways of coping with them.

g) Focus on relationships. This can de done in several ways, for example (i) Teach trainees the appropriate set of rules. (ii) Correct misunderstandings about relationships; we showed that disturbed adolescents often have inadequate and immature concepts of friendship, and may not realise that the relation with parents is very likely to be an enduring one.

References

Anderson, C., Horowitz, L. & de Sales, F. (1983) Attributional style of lonely and depressed people. *Journal of Personality and Social Psychology, 45,* 127–136

Argyle, M. (1969) *Social interaction.* London: Methuen

Argyle, M. (1975) *Bodily communication.* London: Methuen

Argyle, M. (1983) *The psychology of interpersonal behaviour* (4th ed.) Harmondsworth: Penguin

Argyle, M., Alkema, F. & Gilmour, R. (1972) The communication of friendly and hostile attitudes by verbal and non-verbal signals. *European Journal of Social Psychology, 1,* 385–402

Argyle, M. & Furnham, A. (1983) Sources of satisfaction and conflict in long-term relationships. *Journal of Marriage and the Family, 45,* 481–493

Argyle, M., Furnham, A. & Graham, J. A. (1981) *Social Situations.* Cambridge: Cambridge University Press

Argyle, M., Graham, J. A., Campbell, A. & White, P. (1979) The rules of different situations. *New Zealand Psychologist, 8,* 13–22

Argyle, M., Graham, J. A. & Kreckel, M. (1982) The structure of behavioural elements in social and work situations. In M. R. Key (Ed.), *Nonverbal communication today: current research.* The Hague: Mouton

Argyle, M. & Henderson, M. (1985) *The anatomy of relationships.* London: Heinemann

Argyle, M. & Henderson, M. (1984) The rules of friendship. *Journal of Social and Personal Relationships,* I, 211–237

Argyle, M. & Kendon, A. (1967) The experimental analysis of social performance. *Advances in Experimental Social Psychology, 3,* 55–98

Argyle, M., Salter, V., Nicholson, H., Williams, M. & Burgess, P. (1970) The communication of inferior and superior attitudes by verbal and non-verbal signals. *British Journal of Social and Clinical Psychology, 9,* 221–231

Arkowitz, H., Lichtenstein, E., McGovern, K. & Hines, P. (1975) The behavioral assessment of social competence in males. *Behavior Therapy, 6,* 3–13

Berscheid, E. & Walster, E. (1974) Physical attractiveness. *Advances in Experimental Social Psychology, 7,* 158–215

Bourne, E. (1978) The state of research on ego identity – a review. *Journal of Youth and Adolescence, 7,* 223–251, 371–391

Brennan, T. (1982) Loneliness at adolescence. *In* L. A. Peplau and D. Perlman (Eds.) *Loneliness.* New York: Wiley

Bryant, B. & Trower, P. (1974) Social difficulty in a student population. *British Journal of Educational Psychology, 44,* 13–21

Buck, R. (1979) Individual differences in sending accuracy and electrodermal responding: The externalizing–internalizing dimension. In R. Rosenthal (Ed.), *Skill in nonverbal communication.* Cambridge, MA: Oelgeschlager, Gunn and Hain

Campbell, A. (1980) *Female delinquency in social context.* Oxford: Blackwell

Central Policy Review Staff (1978) *Vandalism.* London: H.M.S.O

Chandler, M. J. (1973) Egocentrism and anti-social behavior: the assessment and training of social perspective-training skills. *Developmental Psychology, 9,* 326–332

Clarke, D. D. (1983) *Language and action.* Oxford: Pergamon

Clarke, D. D. & Argyle, M. (1982) Conversation sequences. *In* C. Fraser and K. Scherer (Eds.), *The social psychology of language.* London: Cambridge University Press

Clarke, R. V. G. & Mayhew, P. (Eds.) (1980) *Designing out crime.* London: H.M.S.O

Coleman, J. (1963) *The adolescent society.* Glencoe, Ill.: Free Press

Coleman, J. (1974) *Relationships in adolescence.* London: Routledge and Kegan Paul

Cook, M. & McHenry, R. (1978) *Sexual attraction.* Oxford: Pergamon

Cunningham, J. D. & Antill, J. K. (1981) Love in developing romantic relationships. *In* S. Duck and R. Gilmour (Eds.), *Personality relationships 2: Developing personal relationships.* London: Academic Press

Davitz, J. R. (1964) *The Communication of emotional meaning.* New York: McGraw Hill

Ekman, P. (1982) *Emotion in the human face.* (2nd ed.) Cambridge University Press

Ekman, P. & Friesen, W. V. (1975) *Unmasking the face.* Englewood Cliffs, N. J.: Prentice-Hall

Elder, G. H. (1962) Structural variations in the child rearing relationship. *Sociometry, 25,* 241–262

Elder, G. H. (1963) Parental power legitimation and its effects on the adolescent. *Sociometry, 26,* 50–65

Endler, N. S. & Magnusson, D. (Eds.) (1976) *Interactional psychology and personality,* Washington: Hemisphere

Feffer, M. & Suchotliff, L. (1966) Decentering implications of social interactions. *Journal of Personality and Social Psychology, 4,* 415–422

Fine, G. A. (1981) Friends, impression management and preadolescent behaviour. *In* S. R. Asher and J. Gottman (Eds.) *The development of friendship.* Cambridge: Cambridge University Press

Flanders, N. A. (1970) *Analyzing teaching behavior.* Reading, Mass.: Addison-Wesley

Flavell, J. H. (1968) *The development of role-taking and communication skills in children.* New York: Wiley

Forgas, J., Argyle, M. & Ginsburg, G. P. (1979) Person perception as a function of the interaction episode: the fluctuating structure of an academic group. *Journal of Social Psychology, 109,* 207–222

Furnham, A. & Argyle, M. (1981) Responses of four groups to difficult social situations. *In* Argyle et al. (Eds.), *Social situations.* Cambridge: Cambridge University Press

Graham, J. A., Argyle, M. & Furnham, A. (1980) The goals and goal structure of social situations. *European Journal of Social Psychology, 10,* 345–366

Griffit, W. & Veitch, R. (1971) Hot and crowded: influence of population density and temperature on interpersonal affective behaviour. *Journal of Personality and Social Psychology, 17,* 92–98

Hall, J. A. (1979) Gender, gender roles, and nonverbal communication skills. *In* R. Rosenthal (Ed.) *Skill in nonverbal communication.* Cambridge, Mass.: Oelgeschlager, Gunn and Hain

Halliday, M. A. K. (1978) *Language as social semiotics.* London: Arnold

Harris, M. (1975) *Cows, pigs, wars and witches.* London: Hutchinson

Jennings, H. H. (1950) *Leadership and isolation.* New York: Longmans Green

Jones, E. E. (1964) *Ingratiation: a social psychological analysis.* New York: Appleton-Century-Crofts

Jones, E. E. & Wortman, C. (1973) *Ingratiation: An attributional approach.* Morristown, N. J.: General Learning

Jones, W. H., Hobbs, S. A. & Hockenburg, D. (1982) Loneliness and social skill defects. *Journal of Personality and Social Psychology, 42,* 682−689

Kanin, E. J., Davidson, K. D. & Scheck, S. R. (1970) A research note on male−female differentials in the experience of heterosexual love. *Journal of Sex Research, 6,* 64−72

Kephart, W. M. (1967) Some correlates of romantic love. *Journal of Marriage and the Family, 29,* 470−474

Kon, I. S. (1981) Adolescent friendship: some unanswered questions for future research. *In* S. Duck and R. Gilmour (Eds.) *Personal relationships 3: Personal relationships in disorder.* London: Academic

La Gaipa, J. J. & Wood, H. D. (1981) Friendship in disturbed adolescents. *In* S. Duck and R. Gilmour (Eds.) *Personal relationships 3: Personal relationships in disorder.* London: Academic

Marsh, P., Harre, R. & Rosser, E. (1978) *The rules of disorder.* London: Routledge and Kegan Paul

Matteson, D. (1979) From identity to intimacy: It's not a one way street. In *Symposium on Identity Development.* Groningen: Rijksuniversitat

Meldman, M. J. (1967) Verbal behavior analysis of self-hyperattentionism. *Disorders of the Nervous System. 28,* 469−473

Mischel, W. (1968) *Personality and assessment.* New York: Wiley

Moos, R. H. (1968) Situational analysis of a therapeutic community milieu. *Journal of Abnormal Psychology, 73,* 49−61

Napoleon, T., Chassin, L. & Young, R. D. (1980) A replication and extension of 'Physical attractiveness and mental illness'. *Journal of Abnormal Psychology, 89,* 250−253

Pendleton, D. & Furnham, A. (1980) Skills: a paradigm for applied social psychological research. *In* W. T. Singleton, P. Spurgeon and R. B. Stammers (Eds.) *The analysis of social skill.* New York: Plenum

Peplau, L. A. & Perlman, D. (1982) *Loneliness.* New York: Wiley

Pervin, L. (1983) The stasis and flow of behavior: towards a theory of goals. *Nebraska Symposium on Motivation for 1982.* Lincoln, Nebraska: University of Nebraska Press

Reis, H. T., Wheeler, L., Spiegel, N., Kernis, M. H., Nezlek, J. & Perri, M. (1982) Physical attractiveness in social interaction. II: Why does appearance affect social experience? *Journal of Personality and Social Psychology, 43,* 979−996

Riskin, J. & Faunce, E. E. (1970) Discussion of methodology and substantive findings. *Archives of General Psychiatry, 22,* 527−537

Romano, J. M. & Bellack, A. S. (1980) Social validation of a component model of assertive behaviour. *J. Consulting and Clinical Psychology, 48,* 478−490

Rubin, Z. (1973) *Liking and loving.* New York: Holt, Rinehart and Winston

Selman, R. L. & Jaquette, D. (1977) Stability and oscillation in interpersonal awareness: a clinical-developmental analysis. *Nebraska Symposium on Motivation, 25,* Lincoln, Nebraska: University of Nebraska Press

Shure, M. (1981) A social skills approach to child rearing. *In* M. Argyle (Ed.) *Social skills and health.* London: Methuen

Snyder, M. (1979) Self-monitoring processes. *Advances in Experimental Social Psychology, 12,* 85−128

Staples, L. M. & Robinson, W. P. (1974) Address forms used by members of a department store. *British Journal of Social and Clinical Psychology, 13,* 131−142

Tagiuri, R. (1958) Social preference and its perception. In R. Tagiuri and L. Petrullo (Eds.), *Person perception and interpersonal behavior.* Stanford, Stanford University Press

Trower, P. (1980) Situational analysis of the components and processes of social skilled and unskilled patients. *Journal of Consulting and Clinical Psychology, 48,* 327–339

Williams, J. G. & Solano, C. H. (1983) The social reality of feeling lonely. *Personality and Social Behavior Bulletin, 9,* 237–242

Wish, M., Deutsch, M. & Kaplan, S. J. (1977) Toward an implicit theory of interpersonal communication. *Sociometry, 40,* 234–246

Zimbardo, P. G. (1977) *Shyness.* Reading, Mass.: Addison-Wesley

V. Place for Development: Adolescents, Leisure Settings, and Developmental Tasks[1]

R. K. SILBEREISEN*, P. NOACK, & K. EYFERTH

Introduction

Recent research on adolescent development has increasingly stressed the importance of the adolescents' acting in age-related change of experience and behavior. Adolescents often organize their own development by arranging personal determinants and outer contexts according to their own ideas.

This paradigm reflects recent insights on coping with everyday problems related to development: adolescents apparently try to spread developmental tasks over time ("focusing"), thus keeping the stress at levels they can handle (Coleman, 1980). Further, the paradigm is related to what has been called a trend towards "collective individualization" in sociology (Beck, 1983): during the past several decades, people living in highly industrialized countries have experienced the dissolution of secure traditional ties which are provided by affiliation with a distinct rank or class in society. Major structural changes (e.g., improved educational opportunity, mobility processes, reduced working time) have contributed to the establishment of a social norm prescribing individual responsibility for organizing one's own biography – with all the risks entailed.

This conception of development leads to a particular perspective on adolescent leisure-time activities: leisure time emerges as one aspect of the endeavor to cope incrementally with a series of demands resulting from physical maturation, societal expectations, and individual aspirations. Some classic examples of such developmental tasks faced by adolescents are: learning to accept their bodies; preparing for working life; forming sex-role identities; achieving emotional autonomy vis-à-vis parents; and developing their own value systems (cf. Havighurst, 1948). Such developmental tasks are characterized by long-term goals serving as guidelines for behavior on the biographical level. As a frame of orientation these tasks lead to the definition of

[1] This research was supported in part by a grant ("Akademiestipendium") from the German Research Council (DFG: Si 296/2-1) to R. K. Silbereisen. The Berlin Longitudinal Study on Adolescent Development is supported by grants from the German Research Council (DFG: Si 296/1-1, 2, 3, 4; principal investigators R. K. Silbereisen and K. Eyferth).

* Technical University of Berlin, Department of Psychology, Dovestrasse 1–5, D-1000 Berlin 10, West Germany

Development as Action in Context
Ed. by R. K. Silbereisen et al.
© Springer-Verlag Berlin Heidelberg 1986

goals and recognition of problems on the level of everyday life situations. Leisure-time settings as contexts of everyday life situations can stimulate goal definitions and facilitate or impede attempts at dealing with problems related to development, thus figuring as potential developmental catalysts.

A similar approach has led many researchers to stress the importance of adolescent development of group activities with peers (cf. Oerter, 1982). Payne and Jones (1977), for instance, emphasize the role of peer group experiences in ego-identity development. However, close inspection of the mass of literature reveals a dearth of the kind of empirical studies which one might logically expect to find, namely, longitudinal observations of adolescent behavior in the places where they spend their leisure time.

Keen interest in leisure-time places has so far produced little by way of a concept capable of isolating a place's features and the corresponding actions operating in personality development. Bronfenbrenner (in press) has this deficit in mind when faulting ecologically oriented scholars of socialization for studying mainly "context without development." Likewise, Russell and Ward (1982) plead for more pronounced consideration of the time dimension in the relation of person and environment.

From this state of affairs proceed our efforts to analyze leisure-time places as contexts of development. The analysis takes place as part of the Berlin Longitudinal Study on Adolescent Development, the general design of which relates a prospective longitudinal study of a random population of adolescents to longitudinal assessments in leisure-time places. The unit of analysis is, first, the adolescent (and his or her parents) and second, the setting. In both cases the focus is on development or change over a span of six years.

Settings where adolescents spend their leisure time are proverbially subject to short-lived fashions and tend to change their appearance quickly. Longitudinal assessment reveals that such changes include: attracting a new clientele, diversifying the program offered or renovating the furnishings, as well as providing insight into the interrelation of these components. In our study, however, the main focus is on relating the setting data to the longitudinal data on adolescent development in order to identify the dynamics of mutual influence; changes in a place's attractiveness due to the adolescents' state of development, the adolescents' impact on a setting's features, and the role of experiences gained at a setting in the process of adolescent development.

The following sections are organized according to the major steps of the research strategy underlying the study. Each step is illustrated first by empirical results.

Questionnaire Assessment of Preferred Leisure-Time Places

Precedent to any analysis of leisure-time places as contexts of adolescent development, the places actually frequented must be identified.

The literature on adolescents' leisure time reveals little concerning the whereabouts. Environment-behavior research (cf. Kruse & Arlt, 1984) provides a few clues by way of studies on action space or home range. Van Vliet (1983), for instance, showed that the home range is extended during adolescence, more so for boys than for girls, and more for middle-class youth than for those from lower social strata. But the question of which specific places this age group frequents basically remains unanswered. Insights from leisure-time research undertaken by social scientists (Giegler, 1982) are similarly scarce. The main focus is on leisure-time activities, and no direct conclusion as to where these activities actually occur may be drawn. Yet our focus on the way adolescents deal with developmental tasks requires more knowledge about preferred leisure-time places than about leisure-time activities per se. The fact that an adolescent plays soccer may not be particularly instructive; but whether the activity takes place on inner-city streets or at a sports club could tell something – for example, about the risk of contact with drugs.

Annual assessments in the course of the Berlin Longitudinal Study on Adolescent Development provide the opportunity to specify specific leisure-time places which are frequented by different age groups on a representative basis.

Method

Subjects in the first wave of data assessment, on which the present report is based, were 1,298 adolescents from Berlin (West). They were pupils attending 78 schools (one class per school) which formed a stratified random sample of Berlin schools. The students represent two birth cohorts. At the time of assessment, the average age of the younger group was 11.6 years and that of the older group 14.6 years. The Ss were asked to indicate their preferred leisure-time places including names and exact locations ("What is your favorite place to go to during your leisure time?"). Multiple answers were possible.

Results

A total of 2,806 answers was obtained and grouped according to inductively established categories which, in turn, could be summarized in terms of seven place types: private home, receptive leisure time, unorganized social leisure time, organized social leisure time, street, nature, sports. Table 1 shows the percentages of answers for each place type and some major subcategories according to age and sex.

Among the younger adolescents, places providing for sports top the list by a wide margin; about 40% of the answers fall into this category. In the older group, sports are still most preferred but they comprise only 23% of the answers. The difference stems mainly from a lower interest in swimming pools; the percentage in this subcategory decreases by one half. Private homes (own or friend's places) and street settings follow in second and third

Table 1. Adolescents' preferences for leisure-time places according to age and sex. Column totals add up to 100% each except for rounding

	11:6 years			14:6 years		
	Male	Female	Total	Male	Female	Total
Private home			18.4			22.3
Own home	8.2	10.4		8.4	10.1	
Friend's home	8.4	9.4		10.0	15.9	
Receptive leisure time			7.5			13.2
Cinema	6.4	2.7		8.7	9.1	
Library	0.6	1.5		0.9	1.3	
Other	2.1	1.9		3.8	2.6	
Unorganized social leisure time			1.3			10.5
Disco	0.0	0.6		4.4	6.5	
Pub, café	0.0	0.6		2.8	3.5	
Other	0.0	1.1		1.1	2.6	
Organized social leisure time			4.2			5.4
City-sponsored youth center	1.4	1.0		3.4	2.9	
Church-sponsored youth center	0.6	0.2		0.6	1.0	
Other	0.5	4.5		1.1	1.7	
Street			19.9			19.3
Shopping	2.9	4.8		5.5	11.2	
Residential	6.7	5.8		5.2	5.1	
Other	10.5	9.1		8.4	3.2	
Nature			9.0			6.0
Public park	3.2	4.5		1.4	1.7	
Garden	2.4	3.5		3.4	1.2	
Other	3.0	1.4		2.0	2.3	
Sports			39.7			23.4
Swimming pool	10.0	16.0		4.9	5.2	
Soccer field	17.4	0.6		12.4	0.4	
Other	15.7	20.3		11.8	12.3	

place with approximately 20%. Within street settings, the preference for going to shopping centers and shopping streets is twice as high for girls as for boys. The contrast between the older and the younger group in preference for this subcategory is striking.

For the younger adolescents, nature ranks fourth (approximately 9%), and places providing receptive leisure time (e. g., cinema, library) are fifth, with, for example, boys' preferences for the movies (6%) being twice as high as girls'. Places such as discos, and all places featuring organized leisure activities, are quite plainly at the bottom of the list for this age group. The latter is also true for the older adolescents, with nature being only slightly higher ranked. A middle ranking could be found for places like movie theaters and settings for unorganized leisure time such as discos and cafés.

There is a distinct rise in preference for these kinds of places with age, and there are sex differences, with girls showing more interest.

Summarizing the results, sport locales and private homes can be said to be most preferred as leisure-time settings by both 12- and 15-year-olds. These findings parallel the results on leisure-time activities reported by Kranzhoff and Schmitz-Scherzer (1978). Age and sex differences concerning, for example, discos, correspond to those found by Schilling (1977), who additionally pointed out the importance of swimming pools as leisure-time settings. An interesting finding of the present study is the importance of shopping centers to adolescent leisure-time.

Results reported by Palmonari and Pombeni (1985), who studied adolescents of between 16 and 18 years in Bologna, Italy, suggest that the data collected in Berlin reflect a situation valid at least for Western European cities. Asking Ss to name their favorite places for meeting their peers, the Italian researchers obtained similar distributions for leisure-time places and comparable age and sex differences. The fact that the church figures more prominently as a meeting place than in Berlin tends to increase the credibility of the data.

It must be borne in mind that the results are based solely on adolescents' self-reports in questionnaires. However reliable and differentiated this source may be, it cannot replace the *via regia* in environment-behavior research: analysis of everyday behavior in its everyday contexts. Within the framework of the Berlin Longitudinal Study on Adolescent Development research strategy, the results reported above serve mainly to identify a representative sample of leisure-time places as a basis for more in-depth field analyses.

Field Study of Leisure-Time Places

The first analyses were carried out at shopping centers, discos, and indoor swimming pools in Berlin. The data on which the following is based are taken from assessment at these places.

The choice among the places accessible to the researchers was based on high preference ratings and age-typical differences (see above). Particularly promising as regards the problems in question are those kinds of places which gain or lose attractiveness during the age span under scrutiny. Unlike other everyday contexts of development which are characterized by less avoidable adult expectation pressures, it can be assumed that the decision to frequent these places or not is an expression of age-typical desires. This links the analysis to the research interest in developmental tasks.

The fundamental prerequisite of an environment-behavior analysis is the choice of an appropriate unit of analysis. It was decided to carry out assessments on two levels which are distinguished by the degree of fine-grainedness: "place" and "situation." Those adolescents, for instance, who go to the disco to play video games have little common experience with those who go for the dancing. What both situations have in common is the superordinated features of the place, such as admittance regulations barring certain age groups. Both situation and place are understood as environment-behavioral units which can be characterized by a systematic relation between socio-physical context and occupants' behavior in the same way as Barker's behavioral settings (1968; Saup, 1983).

The places are described in terms of occupants, dominant activities, and spatio-temporal characteristics. For each of those domains, a diversity of variables was assessed, only a few of which are reported in the following[2]. To a varying degree they are all related to adolescents' dealing with developmental tasks. To avoid overestimating the theoretical stringency of these relationships, we prefer to understand the considerations concerning developmental tasks merely as an interpretative framework for the analyses. A direct operationalization of relevant features requires more differentiated ideas on adolescents' coping with developmental tasks than is presently available.

Although the basis ideas go back as far as 1948 to Havighurst's work, only recently have some conceptual and empirical studies been presented (Sroufe & Rutter, 1984; Dreher & Dreher, 1984). These are largely confined to cognitive representation of developmental tasks and their respective changes.

The following are examples of analyses for both kinds of assessment: place and situation.

Situation Profile of Places

Differences among shopping centers, discos, and swimming pools become clear when comparing percentages of adolescent occupants. As was to be expected, systematic assessments of age distributions (Noack & Silbereisen, 1984) revealed that the disco is an almost exclusively adolescent place with adults forming a negligible minority. Swimming pools as well as shopping centers are slightly dominated by occupants older than 18. This contrast suggests that the place types analyzed provide quite different adolescent leisure-time environments, but it tells little about the quality of the differences. Attempting to characterize these places more meaningfully, we examined them for youth-typical situations. Considerations propounded by Argyle, Furnham, and Graham (1981) formed the basis for identifying situations. Situations are understood as clusters of social and physical aspects with a

---

[2] Only findings concerning a small number of variables selected to represent different aspects of the field study are reported; for an overview concerning the whole set of variables assessed see Noack (1985).

pattern of activities (e.g., chatting, laughing, and drinking at a bar) being the central feature. In addition to shared activities and goals, aspects such as a system of roles and rules, as well as the common use of props, time, and space make up a situation.

Method

Data gathered from shopping centers, indoor swimming pools, and discos were analyzed. On the basis of preliminary free observations, several situation types were established for each type of place. The systematic observations reported below were carried out to assess the distributions of these situation types at the six leisure-time places.

For shopping centers, the following situation types were assessed: window shopping, hanging out (spending time with no obvious goals), couples interacting (interaction with girlfriend or boyfriend being central), roughhousing (playful activity involving expressive outbursts of energy), and transition (place used only as a connection or shortcut between two outside points). At the indoor swimming pools, four situation types were distinguished: sports, socializing (social aspect in the foreground), and, again, couple interaction, and roughhousing. The assessments took place on three workdays from early afternoon until closing time. Observers waited at the main entrance and picked out the first individual adolescent or group of adolescents entering after a predetermined time. The adolescent(s) was followed inconspicuously for a period of five minutes. Then it was decided which kind of situation the adolescent(s) participated in, using the previously specified situation-type categories. After noting the situation type, observers returned to the entrance and waited for the next adolescent or group of adolescents to enter.

Situation types relevant at the discos were: dancing, hanging out (using disco like a bar or pub), game playing (billiards, video games or the like), and couple interaction. The mode of assessment had to be slightly altered owing to the peculiarities of the discos and the situation types applying to them: during the first five minutes after entering, for instance, adolescents who will participate in different situation types have to pursue a series of similar activities such as paying the admission charge, lining up to leave their coats at the cloakroom, and finding a place to sit or stand. Moreover, people belonging to one group do not necessarily stay together for the entire time. Thus, instead of directly counting the frequency of situation types, an overall person count was carried out on the total number of adolescents present and on the numbers of adolescents dancing, playing video or other games, and belonging to a couple. On the basis of situation observations providing information concerning the composition of people and activities in the different situation types, the relative frequency of a given situation type could be estimated using the results of the person count.

Using a sample of observations, the mean place-to-place agreement of two independent observers on the situation-type judgements was 90% for shopping centers and swimming pools. At the discos, each overall count was carried out by two independent observers; the average difference in the number of people counted was 8.6% and was independent of the specific activity observed.

Results

A total of 188 situations was observed at shopping centers, 93 at swimming pools, and 277 at discos. Table 2 shows the percentage of the different situation types. Since there were only minor differences within each type of location, the two places belonging to a given place type are summarized in the table.

As may be seen from the table, for all places the expected behavior is at least complemented or even surpassed by other types of activities: at shopping centers, window shopping is predominant, making up about 60% of the situations. Hanging out (24%) and the couple situation (15%), however, are of substantial importance as well. At swimming pools, even sports (34%) is surpassed by a nearly 45% share of socializing situations; 14% of the observed situations were identified as roughhousing. The discos are dominated by a pub-like use which was registered in almost 60% of all cases, whereas dancing attains only some 25% and couple situations little more than 10%.

To overstate the point, it can be said that the inofficial function of shopping centers is amusement; that swimming pools are mainly places for socializing; and that discos offer the comforts of a pub.

The question remains as to whether the observed situation types form steps in a sequence of activities during the stay at a given place, or whether they are characterized by discrete groups of people. Free observations suggest only slight overlaps in participation.

The different situation types may also make up another kind of sequence which corresponds to different age groups; that is, with increase in age, the

Table 2. Situation profile for place types. Column totals add up to 100% each

Situation types	Place types		
	Shopping center	Swimming pool	Disco
Couple	14.4	6.4	12.7
Roughhousing	0.5	14.0	
Hanging out	23.9		57.8
Strolling	59.6		
Transit	1.6		
Sport		34.4	
Socializing		45.2	
Dancing			24.9
Playing video games, etc.			4.6

situation type in which adolescents participate may change. While observations of the different situation types seem to support this interpretation, it is by no means certain that the same people go through a sequence of situation types when frequenting a place over an extended period of time. Clarification of this point requires longitudinal data on the visitors to a place. More detailed questions concerning the use of the preferred leisure-time places have accordingly been included in the questionnaire assessment of the Berlin Longitudinal Study on Adolescent Development. These data will show whether there is a connection between the state of development and the use of a given place.

Although the reported observations are "large-grained," they help to identify those situation types which are important (numerical significance, potentially conflict-prone divergence from the expected behavior or "official program") under the perspective of the issues pursued.

Behavioral Profile of Situation Types

The situation types were analyzed in detail. The emphasis of the investigation was on systematic observations of actual behavior.

Method

For each situation type, eight to twelve randomly selected situations were observed. Roughhousing and transition in the shopping centers, as well as games at the discos were excluded from the analysis because of their rare occurrence (see Table 2). A total of 205 situations was observed. The observation of each single situation lasted 10 minutes. Then a protocol sheet was inconspicuously completed. The observed behaviors were rated on five-point scales which either covered frequency of occurrence ($0 = $ no occurrence; $1 = 1\times$; $2 = 2 - 3\times$; $3 = 4 - 10\times$; $4 = $ more than $10\times$) or duration of behavior ($0 = $ no occurrence; $1 = $ less than 1 minute; $2 = 1 - 4$ minutes; $3 = 4 - 8$ minutes; $4 = $ more than 8 minutes). Based on experience gained in preliminary observations, the scale anchors were chosen with the intention of assuring an appropriate differentiation for all behaviors at different places.

Labels for the behaviors reported below are: chatting, observing others, hanging around, body contact, and meeting people (all places); walking around, cigarette smoking, and drinking alcohol (shopping centers and discos); horsing around and swimming (swimming pools); listening to music and dancing (discos). Table 3 briefly defines these behaviors.

Below, the score of a variable is expressed as the ordinal number (0, 1, 2, 3, 4) of the rating category within which the median of the situations included in the calculations occurs (e.g., 10 situations concerning chatting in couple situations of one shopping center; 60 when couple situations at all places are considered; 200 when all situation types at all places form the basis of the data). This report is confined to descriptive analyses.

Table 3. Definition of observational categories

Label	Place[a]			Description
Chatting	S	P	D	Small talk; relaxed conversation
Observing others	S	P	D	Looking at people not participating in the situation to pick up information on their dress, behavior, etc.
Hanging around	S	P	D	Unfocused stay at a certain part of the place; standing, sitting; no indication of intense involvement
Body contact	S	P	D	Any kind of actual contact of body parts; intimate, aggressive, neutral
Meeting people	S	P	D	New contact to person(s) not participating in the situation; friend(s) or stranger(s)
Running around	S		D	Spatial movement across the place
Cigarette smoking	S		D	Excludes pipe, cigar, or illegal drugs smoking
Drinking alcohol	S		D	Includes beer, wine, and hard liquor
Window shopping	S			Looking at goods displayed in a shop window, showcase, on shelves, etc.
Listening to music			D	Attentive listening, indicated by, e. g., orientation towards the sound source
Dancing			D	Dancing on the dance floor, in the aisles; excludes rhythmic movements while sitting
Horsing around		P		Energetic physical activity such as pushing, mock fighting, etc.
Swimming		P		Swimming proper and use of diving board or start block

[a] S = Shopping center; P = Public indoor swimming pool; D = Disco

Results

Shopping Centers. Table 4 summarizes the behavior scores averaged (median) across 10 situations each. The table shows the results for each shopping center (S 1, S 2) as well as the average for both.

Looking first at contrasts between shopping centers regardless of situation type, the data reveal that correspondences prevail: of 27 comparisons, 17 show no difference; in nine cases the scores differ by only one category, and only once (walking around in couple situations) is there a larger difference. Taking into consideration the higher percentage of walking around at S 1 (see Table 2), the lower predominance of window shopping and the more prominent display of hanging around in hanging out situations as well as more walking around and observing others during the strolling situations can be understood as complementary results. The "informal program" of Shopping Center 1 seems to focus more on diversion and less on trade.

Table 4. Behavior profile for three situation types in two shopping centers (Median frequency or duration during 10-minute observations)

Label	Strolling			Hanging out			Couple		
	S1	S2	Md.	S1	S2	Md.	S1	S2	Md.
Chatting[b]	2	2	2	3	3	3	2	2	2
Observing others[b]	1	0	1	2	2	2	0	0	0
Hanging around[b]	0	0	0	3	2	3	0	0	0
Body contact[b]	0	0	0	1	0	0	3	2	3
Meeting people[a]	0	0	0	0	0	0	0	0	0
Running around[b]	4	3	3	2	2	2	4	2	3
Cigarette smoking[b]	0	0	0	0	1	1	1	0	0
Drinking alcohol[b]	0	0	0	0	0	0	0	0	0
Window shopping[b]	3	3	3	0	1	0	2	3	3
Total situations	10	10	20	10	10	20	10	10	20

[a] 0: no occurrence; 1: $1 \times$; 2: $2–3 \times$; 3: $4–10 \times$; 4: more than $10 \times$
[b] 0: no occurrence; 1: less than 1 minute; 2: 1–4 minutes; 3: 4–8 minutes; 4: more than 8 minutes

Behaviors showing considerably more occurrences which are shared by the three different situation types are: walking around (row total of medians 8) and chatting (7). Turning to contrasts between situations, a clear-cut distinction between hanging out, on one hand, and strolling and couple situations on the other, can be seen: hanging around and window shopping exclude each other (see the opposite directions of scores).

Indoor Swimming Pools. The results obtained at the indoor swimming pools are given in Table 5, separately for each (P1, P2), as well as the average for both.

When compared with the shopping centers, the two swimming pools seem to be more distinct from one another: there are 12 differences in 28 contrasts, eight differing by one category, four by two categories. At S2, sport-oriented activities appear to be more predominant, as can be seen from a lower chatting score in the sport situation and, correspondingly, a higher swimming score in the socializing situation.

Again, most prominent of all behaviors is chatting, with high scores in all situation types and the highest row total of medians (8). It is followed by body contact (6); swimming itself only ranks third (4). The last behavior which is shared by all situation types to some extent is observing others (3).

Discos. Table 6 shows the results from the observations at two discos, separately (D1, D2) and together.

Of 30 comparisons between the two discos, 14 reveal no differences, 12 show differences of one category, and four of two categories. Thus, the two

Table 5. Behavior profile for four situation types in two swimming pools (Median frequency or duration during 10-minute observations)

Label	Socializing			Sports			Roughhousing			Couple		
	S1	S2	Md.	S1	S2	Md.	S1	S2	Md.	S1	S2	Md.
Chatting[b]	2	3	2	2	0	1	3	3	3	3	2	2
Observing others[b]	1	2	2	1	0	0	1	1	1	0	0	0
Hanging around[b]	0	2	1	0	0	0	0	0	0	0	2	0
Body contact[b]	2	1	1	0	0	0	3	2	2	3	3	3
Meeting people[a]	0	0	0	0	0	0	0	0	0	0	0	0
Horsing around[b]	0	0	0	0	0	0	4	3	3	0	0	0
Swimming[b]	0	2	0	3	3	3	0	0	0	1	0	1
Total situations	11	11	22	10	10	20	10	10	20	10	8	18

[a] 0: no occurrence; 1: $1\times$; 2: $2-3\times$; 3: $4-10\times$; 4: more than $10\times$
[b] 0: no occurrence; 1: less than 1 minute; 2: 1–4 minutes; 3: 4–8 minutes; 4: more than 8 minutes

discos present the most distinct differences within the place types analyzed. This is most obvious when looking at the dancing situations: at D1, dancing is characterized by a higher extent of hanging around (and drinking alcohol); at D2 the focus is on listening to music, meeting people, and dancing itself.

The search for dominant features in all three situation types shows chatting (row total of medians 6), and observing others (6) as being overshadowed. Allowing for the fact that body contact appears mainly in couple situations, its significance is comparable to the ones reported above (7).

In addition to the ratings, a methodically independent assessment of the behavioral variable "meeting people" was carried out: contacts with friends and strangers were counted separately according to the sex of the people involved. The identification "friend" or "stranger" was based on greeting rituals observed, as well as on features of expressive behavior indicating prior acquaintance.

A higher frequency of contacts was found at D2. More impressive, however, is the contrast of contacts with friends vs. with strangers. While contact was established with an average of 2.6 friends, there were only 0.3 contacts with strangers − a ratio of almost 9:1. Going to the disco seems to mean socializing with almost closed circles of friends.

Settings' Common Features. Table 7 gives an overview summarizing all situation types at each of the three types of place. The medians are low compared to those in the above tables because the broader basis of calculation included irrelevant situation types. Only behavior variables common to all situation types are reported.

Table 6. Behavior profile for three situation types in two discos (Median frequency or duration during 10-minute observations)

Label	Hanging out			Dancing			Couple		
	D1	D2	Md.	D1	D2	Md.	D1	D2	Md.
Chatting[b]	3	2	2	2	2	2	2	2	2
Observing others[b]	3	2	2	2	2	2	2	1	2
Hanging around[b]	3	3	3	3	1	2	2	0	0
Body contact[b]	1	1	1	2	3	2	3	4	4
Meeting people[a]	0	1	1	0	2	1	1	1	1
Running around[b]	1	1	1	1	1	1	1	0	0
Cigarette smoking[b]	0	1	0	0	0	0	2	1	1
Drinking alcohol[b]	1	0	0	1	0	0	0	0	0
Listening to music[b]	0	0	0	0	2	0	0	0	0
Dancing[b]	0	0	0	2	3	2	0	0	0
Total situations	12	11	23	12	10	22	10	10	20

[a] 0: no occurrence; 1: 1×; 2: 2–3×; 3: 4–10×; 4: more than 10×
[b] 0: no occurrence; 1: less than 1 minute; 2: 1–4 minutes; 3: 4–8 minutes; 4: more than 8 minutes

Table 7. Behavior profile for three place types (Median frequency of duration during 10-minute observations)

Label	Shopping centers	Swimming pools	Discos
Chatting[b]	2	2	2
Observing others[b]	1	2	1
Hanging around[b]	0	2	0
Body contact[b]	1	2	1
Meeting people[a]	0	1	0
Total situations	60	80	65

[a] 0: no occurrence; 1: 1×; 2: 2–3×; 3: 4–10×; 4: more than 10×
[b] 0: no occurrence; 1: less than 1 minute; 2: 1–4 minutes; 3: 4–8 minutes; 4: more than 8 minutes

The general impression is unambiguous: chatting ranks highest, followed by observing others and body contact. Chatting behavior appears to have major importance in all situation types regardless of place.

While body contact only ranks third, its ubiquity is striking. A further independent assessment focusing on body contact was made. Different types of body contact, such as kissing, hugging, and pushing, were counted according to the sex of the people involved. For discos as well as shopping centers, body contact between people of different sex far exceeded same sex contacts (the ratios vary between 4:1 and 10:1). At swimming pools, on the other hand, more body contact with the same sex occurred. Furthermore, body contact at both discos and shopping centers was predominantly tender in nature, whereas at swimming pools, rough contact was observed about four times as often as tender contact. But while type of contact and sex of the people involved generally correspond, this does not mean, for example, that tender body contact between members of the same sex does not occur.

The couple situation is the only one which occurs at all places analyzed. A comparison of the respective columns in Table 4 through 6 shows that whereas couples in discos display hardly more body contact than at swimming pools or shopping centers, they observe others to a far greater extent.

Adolescents' Intention at Discos

The results reported so far are based solely on field observations. We will now consider adolescents' own view of their reasons for frequenting a place.

Our main interest concerning places' functions in development centered on adolescents' statements about their goals; these can be viewed as expressions of reflection on one's development.

Method

At each place, 20 open interviews were carried out (21 at Shopping Center 2). Interviewees were adolescents between ages 11 and 18 who were randomly selected, independent of the selection of adolescents for the observation study (see above). The interviews lasted between 15 and 45 minutes, and were tape-recorded. If the interviewee mentioned goals related to age-typical developmental tasks, the goal or goals they characterized as "most important" at the place was dealt with in more detail.

The interviews were subjected to a content analysis. The categories reported here are labeled in terms of developmental tasks. They were scored if a goal mentioned in the interview could be subsumed under one of the pre-defined developmental tasks (e.g., "I come because of the girls" – romantic contacts; "I come here to see my buddies" – peer group integration). A relatively broad lifestyle theme usually came up in terms either of affinity to some subcultural group, or of aesthetic orientation (music, clothing, make-up, etc.). Other goals mentioned were summarized in a default category.

Results

A total of 155 goals were registered, ranging from 22 at Swimming Pool 1 to 29 at Disco 1. Adolescents occasionally mentioned goals apparently unrelated to developmental tasks (e.g., "killing time"), but only once was such a goal characterized as "most important." This is not all that is surprising. In general, it is difficult to identify goals which do not refer to themes that can

Table 8. Main goals relating to developmental tasks in adolescent self-reports at six places. Multiple responses possible

Developmental Task	Discos		Shopping centers		Swimming pools	
	D1	D2	S1	S2	P1	P2
Romantic contacts	11	15	14	6	0	2
Peer contacts	7	10	2	2	11	9
Lifestyle	10	0	0	0	0	0
Physical maturation	1	0	0	0	11	17
Consumer role	0	0	7	20	0	0
Total	29	25	23	28	22	28
Number of interviews	20	20	20	21	20	20

be related to one of the domains of development. More instructive is the distribution of mentioned goals according to the different places. Table 8 shows the main goals referring to developmental tasks broken down by place.

At both discos, romantic contact was mentioned most often as main goal: 11 times at Disco 1, 15 times at Disco 2. A similar picture is obtained for peer group contact (D1:7; D2:10); but the lifestyle theme is clearly different: interviews at Disco 1 feature lifestyle as a main goal almost as often as romantic contrasts (10); whereas at Disco 2, lifestyle is never mentioned as a main goal.

At the two shopping centers, both romantic contacts and consumer goals figure prominently; the importance adolescents attached to them, however, is virtually reversed at the two places: at Shopping Center 1, 14 adolescents said pursuing romantic contacts was their main goal; at Shopping Center 2, only six mentioned it. At the latter place, the consumer goals were mentioned in each interview (20), but only seven times at Shopping Center 1.

The two swimming pools emerge as more similar to one another: at both places, physical fitness and athletic skills, categorized as being related to physical maturation, are most important (P1:11; P2:17). Contacts to peers are equally important at Swimming Pool 1 (11), whereas these take second place at Swimming Pool 2 (9).

Discussion

The aim of the present report is to elucidate the underlying research paradigm and investigation strategy pursued in the Berlin Longitudinal Study on Adolescent Development. Accordingly, following the summary of results, a major section is devoted to conceptual considerations and one to research prospects.

Summary of Results

Adolescents' leisure-time places are numerous, encompassing shopping centers and school activity rooms, swimming pools and subway stations. Top-ranking in preference for 12- as well as 15-year-olds are private homes and places which provide for sports activities. Shopping centers, discos, and swimming pools show most pronounced popularity differences by age and were thus subjected to more detailed analyses.

Besides situations which conform to a place's official behavior program, all places feature spatial and functional niches accommodating adolescents' intentions to use them "against" the official lines. Examples of such (expressly prohibited) informal functions are hanging out at shopping centers or roughhousing at swimming pools. These results generalize what Willis (1980) described as characteristics of subcultural cliques. Because the sets of participants in different situation types do not seem to overlap, it can be assumed that situation types express differences in the way a place is used rather than steps in a process of adjustment to place-typical practices.

The possibility cannot be ruled out, however, that the participation in different situation types may form steps related to the trajectory of adolescent development. With longitudinal data on the occupants of a given place, a clarification of this question will be within reach. The questionnaire used in the Berlin Longitudinal Study on Adolescent Development has been extended accordingly.

Two representatives of each place type were analyzed; these differ, though not strongly, in several respects: one shopping center shows a more distinct orientation towards "official" goals; the other is characterized rather by diversion. A similar picture is reflected in the swimming pool findings, with one more concentrated on the sport and the other more entertainment-prone. The most pronounced contrasts were found at the discos. At one disco, music and dancing are "taken seriously"; at the other, the boundaries between music and dancing and hanging out are fluid.

In general, the results show that the distinction between two units of analysis, place and situation, is meaningful. As can be seen with the discos, for instance, couple and hanging out situations are almost unspecific with regard to a particular place; dancing, on the other hand, is a situation type which expresses the peculiar style of the disco. The couple situation, which was analyzed for all places, gives some idea of the variety within one situation type: whether at shopping centers, swimming pools, or discos, the extent of body contact hardly differs. At discos, however, couples tend to observe others more often; they seem to be less intimate, less exclusively preoccupied with one another.

Regardless of place and situation type, three youth-typical behaviors are dominant: chatting, observing others, and body contact.

While the importance of chatting and observing others is stressed in the work of other scholars, too (e. g., Dreher & Dreher, 1984; Palmonari & Pombeni, 1985), the widespread occurrence of body contact is striking. More in depth observations revealed that body contact is by no means a uniform phenomenon. The different varieties (same-sex vs. other-sex; tender vs. rough) seem clearly related to types of places. It is uncertain, however, whether these may be but different expressions of a highly prevalent striving for physical closeness which is realized according to the rules and opportunities characterizing a given environment.

Besides observations at leisure-time places, interviews with adolescents were conducted in order to assess their own points of view. It was possible to categorize the adolescents' expectations about going to these places according to age-typical developmental tasks. A disco, for instance, might represent just another hang-out; or it could be the expression of a desire for individuality and one's own lifestyle. The uniformity of intentions expressed does not affect the validity of such statements. There seem to be differences between observed behavior and expressed intentions assessed in the interviews. Contact is more often desired than achieved. Despite the attention devoted to other people, attempts at contact rarely extend beyond the circle of acquaintances. Those who are already friends seem to reinforce this relationship continually. In the observers' field protocols, this phenomenon appeared in the form of greeting rituals. Contact boundaries are nigh on impermeable: if you don't know anybody, tough luck; fat chance of changing that here. However, the high degree of reserve might reflect the peculiar "philosophy" widespread among the staff and clientele of a given disco.

With shopping centers and swimming pools, the goals mentioned reflect a split between the orientation towards the official program of the places and an informal, mostly social program pursued by the adolescents. Whereas some interviewees frequent shopping centers and swimming pools in order to pursue developmental tasks included in the places' particular programs, others are mainly interested in contacts with age-mates. At the swimming pools, socializing tends to involve same-sex peers; at the shopping centers, interest is more in the other sex. The degree to which socializing or the official functions of the place come into the foreground varies notably within both place types.

Towards New Conceptualizations

"Place for development" − the title is intended to convey the role in development of such places as those analyzed. Evidence for the relationship of current experience at leisure-time places on the one hand to various personality characteristics some time (maybe years) later in life, on the other, is still lacking. Consequently, we have confined ourselves to considerations based on plausibility and attempts at a theoretical conceptualization.

If one accepts the adolescents' self-reports as a credible source of information on the reasons for their visits, there is further empirical support for the developmental functions of shopping centers, swimming pools, and discos. Content analyses of the interviews (see Schuhler & Kastner, 1985) suggest that adolescents go to a certain disco, for instance, in order to participate in a certain kind of lifestyle, that is, to adopt it. Taking on a particular lifestyle can be considered a developmental task. From a biographical point of view, then, an instrumental function in the pursuit of development of a lifestyle can be ascribed to frequenting that disco.

Further support results from comparison of our findings from observational studies with current research on the cognitive representation of developmental tasks. Dreher and Dreher (1984) carried out open interviews with adolescents between 15 and 18 years of age. For a diversity of tasks, they asked what the adolescents could do themselves or who/what could help them when approaching a given task. Besides task-specific concepts of coping, there were general ones: for example, forming one's own opinion by drawing upon information from media and behavioral models and evaluating it in interaction with peers.

Their descriptions of "know-how" in self-initiated development agree strikingly with our results from systematic field observations in youth settings (see particularly Table 7): chatting and observing others are the dominant behaviors, independent of place and situation type. Content analyses of our interviews with adolescents (not reported here) lead to the conclusion that chatting and observing others in fact serve to develop one's own opinion (though this is not their only function). These findings suggest that visits to leisure-time settings particularly help adolescents to gather information and establish an orientation, that is, general ways of coping (Dreher & Dreher, 1984).

Finally, a concept is needed to account for the apparent developmental function of leisure-time places. We suggest one dealing with processes of coping with developmental tasks, although theory in this domain is still in the nascent stage (Oerter, 1985). The organization of a biography into sequential and mutually influential developmental tasks is a theoretical abstraction of the ways in which one's development is planned and these plans realized in one's everyday experience. It is the nature of these planning processes to reveal the structure of the problems involved only in the course of their realization. Within this context, Silbereisen and Kastner (1985) interpret ways of coping with developmental tasks as analogous to process strategies for solving complex planning problems as studied by Dörner (Dörner, Kreuzig, Reither, & Stäudel, 1984). Similarly, content and form of goal-directed plans for one's own development ("personal projects") serve as the basic concept of an environment-behavioral psychology of personality in the work of Little (1983).

Some researchers (e. g., Vaillant, 1977; Seiffge-Krenke, 1985) conceptualize coping with developmental tasks in accordance with stress-coping models (Lazarus, see Chapter III). In our opinion, integrating the important issue of developmental action goals and their formation is a promising, maybe even necessary extension of these concepts.

Two advantages of approaching action related to one's development in terms of a problem-solving or planning paradigm are:

a) Models of this type provide a repertoire of concepts which allow formalization of well-known albeit conceptually vague insights in youth psychology. Coleman's focusing theory (1980), for example, postulates that adolescents solve developmental tasks in a stepwise fashion in order to keep the stress bearable. We have tried to establish that the sequence of dealing with developmental tasks is a function of developmental pressure created by the gap between the current and the desired states of development, and of further components defined analogously to problem-solving concepts.

b) Personal prerequisites to development can be formulated such as social skills, or conceptual and affective stress. These are analogous to problem-solving prerequisites. Environmental prerequisites can also be characterized within the framework of this paradigm. The social and physical setting is seen as a "complexity-reducing orientation context" (see Kaminski, 1983, p. 154). Adolescents' behavior shows that orientation in the literal sense of the word, that is, looking around and observing other people and their use of the place, for instance, is one feature common to all places. In accordance with environment-behavioral thought, the basis for this is to be found less in the individual person than in the socio-physical environmental conditions. That was Barker's (1968) intention in postulating the concept of behavior-environment synomorphy.

Prospects

At this point it is necessary to discuss the role of the reported findings and the meaning of the concepts developed as part of the general design of the Berlin Longitudinal Study of Adolescent Development. The strategy is an attempt to overcome a schism characteristic of research on youth: either the development of an individual is investigated within a dispositional approach, or the focus is on environments such as peer groups or city neighborhoods (Bronfenbrenner, see Chapter XV).

Surprisingly, Lewin's (1939) or Muchow's (1935) work relating development to the life-space seems largely to have slipped from memory. Within the Berlin Longitudinal Study on Adolescent Development, the concept of "development as action in context" produced a research strategy characterized by the way in which the development of person and life-space are related: questionnaire assessments concerning leisure-time settings allow for the selection of representative places. Individual observations carried out in the field enable interest-provoking features to be taken into account at the representative level in later data-gathering waves. For example, questions concerning the dominance of different activities at preferred leisure-time places have been included in the annual questionnaire assessment.

It is important that, on both levels, the assessments are longitudinal in nature. While present analyses were confined to comparisons of age groups, changes will be analyzed longitudinally in the future. Further assessments will allow us, in addition to comparing different leisure-time places, to look for changes within a given place across time. The data provide the basis, for instance, for differentiating quantitative increases of the home range and qualitative changes of meeting places according to various contextual conditions, and for relating them to age-correlated changes in personality characteristics.

References

Argyle, M., Furnham, A., & Graham, J. A. (1981) *Social situations.* Cambridge: Cambridge University Press

Barker, R. G. (1968) *Ecological psychology.* Stanford: Stanford University Press

Beck, U. (1983) Jenseits von Stand und Klasse? Soziale Ungleichheiten, gesellschaftliche Individualisierungsprozesse und die Entstehung neuer sozialer Formationen und Identitäten. *Soziale Welt*, Sonderband 2, pp. 35–74

Coleman, J. C. (1980) *The nature of adolescence.* London: Methuen

Dörner, D., Kreuzig, H. W., Reither, F., & Stäudel, T. (Eds.) (1983) *Lohhausen: Vom Umgang mit Unbestimmtheit und Komplexität.* Bern: Huber

Dreher, E. & Dreher, M. (1984) *Developmental tasks in adolescence.* Paper presented at the Inaugural European Conference on Developmental Psychology, Groningen, The Netherlands, August

Giegler, H. (1982) Dimensionen und Determinanten der Freizeit. Eine Bestandsaufnahme der sozialwissenschaftlichen Forschung. *Beiträge zur sozialwissenschaftlichen Forschung*, Bd. 20. Opladen: Westdeutscher Verlag

Havighurst, R. J. (1982) *Developmental tasks and education.* (First edition 1948) New York: Longman

Kaminski, G (1983) Potentielle Beiträge handlungstheoretischer Konzeptionen zur Neuorientierung motivationspsychologischer Perspektiven im Sport. In J. P. Janssen & E. Hahn (Eds.), *Aktivierung, Motivation, Handlung und Coaching im Sport.* Schorndorf: Hofmann

Kranzhoff, U. & Schmitz-Scherzer, R. (1978) Jugend und Freizeit. *Psychologische Praxis*

Kruse, L. & Arlt, R. (1984) *Environment and behavior,* Vol. 1, 2. München: Saur

Lewin, K. (1939) Field theory and experiment in social psychology: Concepts and methods. *American Journal of Sociology, 44,* pp. 868–897

Little, B. R. (1983) Personal projects: A rationale and method for investigation. *Environment and Behavior, 15,* pp. 273–309

Muchow, M. & Muchow, H. H. (1935) *Der Lebensraum des Großstadtkindes.* Hamburg: Riegel

Noack, P. & Silbereisen, R. K. (1984) *Youth-specific leisure-time situations and their impact on adolescent development.* Paper presented at the 8th International Conference on Environment and Human Action, Berlin (West), July 25–29

Oerter, R. (1982) Jugendalter. In R. Oerter & L. Montada (Eds.), *Entwicklungspsychologie.* München: Urban & Schwarzenberg

Oerter, R. (1985) Developmental tasks through the life-span: A new approach to an old concept. In D. L. Featherman & R. M. Lerner (Eds.), *Life-span development and behavior,* Vol. 7. New York: Academic

Palmonari, A. & Pombeni, M. L. (1985) Lo spazio di vita dell'adolescente: Il gruppo dei coetanei nella soluzione dei compiti di sviluppo e nella costruzione dell'identita sociale. Bologna: University of Bologna. Unpublished manuscript

Payne, R. T. & Jones, D. R. W. (1977) Children's landscapes in Huntington Hills, Calgary. In P. Suedfeld (Ed.), *The behavioral basis of design*, Vol. 2. Stroudsburg: Dowden, Hutchinson & Ross

Russell, J. A. & Ward, L. M. (1982) Environmental psychology. *Annual Review of Psychology, 33*, pp. 651−688

Saup, W. (1983) Barkers Behavior Setting-Konzept und seine Weiterentwicklung. *Psychologische Rundschau, 34*, pp. 134−146

Schilling, J. (1977) *Freizeitverhalten Jugendlicher.* Weinheim: Beltz

Schuhler, P. & Kastner, P. (1985) Analyse von Freizeitorten im Berliner Jugendlängsschnitt: Manual Interview. In R. K. Silbereisen & K. Eyferth (Eds.), *Berichte aus der Arbeitsgruppe TUdrop Jugendforschung.* Berlin: Technische Universität

Seiffge-Krenke, I. (1985) Problembewältigung im Jugendalter. Submitted for publication

Silbereisen, R. K. & Eyferth, K. (1983) Jugendentwicklung und Drogen − Zweiter Fortsetzungsantrag an die DFG. In R. K. Silbereisen & K. Eyferth (Eds.), *Berichte aus der Arbeitsgruppe TUdrop Jugendforschung.* Berlin: Technische Universität

Silbereisen, R. K. & Eyferth, K. (1985) Jugendentwicklung und Drogen − Dritter Fortsetzungsantrag an die DFG. In R. K. Silbereisen & K. Eyferth (Eds.), *Berichte aus der Arbeitsgruppe TUdrop Jugendforschung.* Berlin: Technische Universität

Silbereisen, R. K. & Kastner, P. (1985) Entwicklungstheoretische Perspektiven für die Prävention des Drogengebrauchs Jugendlicher. In J. Brandtstädter & H. Gräser (Eds.), *Entwicklungsberatung unter dem Aspekt der Lebensspanne.* Göttingen: Hogrefe

Sroufe, L. A. & Rutter, M. (1984) The domain of developmental psychopathology. *Child Development, 55*, pp. 17−29

Vaillant, G. E. (1977) *Adaptation to life.* Boston: Little, Brown & Company

van Vliet, W. (1983) Exploring the fourth dimension. An examination of the home range of city and suburban teenagers. *Environment and Behavior, 15*, pp. 567−588

Willis, P. (1977) *Learning to labour.* Westmead: Saxon House

VI. Children's and Adolescents' Conceptions of Adulthood: The Changing View of a Crucial Developmental Task

E. DREHER & R. OERTER*

Introduction

Some years ago, Bronfenbrenner defined traditional developmental psychology as "the science of the strange behavior of children in strange situations with strange adults for the briefest possible period of time," (Bronfenbrenner 1979, p. 19). This is no longer true. Individuals now are more often studied in their natural environments, and interactions between the environment and the individual are taken into consideration, even though many features of such studies remain at odds with the requirements of ecological research. However, the ecological approach neglects the cognitive development of the individual to a certain extent; it does not comply with the first part of Bronfenbrenner's definition of human development as the "process through which the growing person acquires a more extended differentiated and valid conception of the environment" (Bronfenbrenner, 1979, p. 25). This process has been examined extensively by another research tradition, that of Piaget and the neo-Piagetians, who tried to describe the construction or reconstruction of the outer world through the individual's cognitive activity. Another approach came from sociology and ethnomethodology (Mehan & Wood, 1975).

Educational research on learning as the process of building a cognitive structure according to the structure of the subject being learned contributed to the view of human development as a process of construction of reality.

Looking for an approach in which both the environmental influences and the individual construction of the surrounding world are taken into account, we find that Havighurst's concept of developmental task (1948/1982) is a fruitful one.

Let us start with Havighurst's definition of a developmental task. "A developmental task is a task which arises at or about a certain period in the life of the individual, successful achievement of which leads to his happiness and to success with later tasks, while failure leads to unhappiness in the individual, disapproval by the society, and difficulties with later tasks" (1948/ 1982, p. 6). Havighurst originally distinguished three sources of de-

* University of Munich, Institute for Educational Psychology, Geschwister-Scholl-Platz 1, D-8000 München 22

Development as Action in Context
Ed. by R. K. Silbereisen et al.
© Springer-Verlag Berlin Heidelberg 1986

velopmental tasks: namely, physical maturation, cultural pressure of society, and personal values and aspirations of the individual "which are part of his personality or self" (1948/1982, p. 8).

The ecological nature of the developmental task becomes clearer in Havighurst's later view that it is "primarily based on biological development and the social expectations that change one's life-span development and give force, direction, and substance to the development of personality" (Havighurst, 1973, p. 2). The idea of developmental task, of course is also a basic concept in Erikson's work − although he does not use the term − and implicitly underlies Neugarten's notion of the life cycle controlled by a system of social age norms (Neugarten & Datan, 1973; Neugarten & Paterson, 1957).

Models of Developmental Tasks

In an earlier work (Oerter, 1978) the concept of developmental task was reformulated to operationalize it for empirical research. Using the three components mentioned above, a single model can be derived to incorporate the assumed dynamics of these components. The model itself can be formulated as a purely quantitative one or as a qualitative one, the latter also including quantitative relationships.

As shown in Figure 1, the individual's development is governed by the field of force of two components that change against each other all the time: the actual developmental status and the sociocultural demands regarding either the present desired developmental level, or − more frequently − the future developmental level. From a very early age, the child actively engages in the developmental process, trying to diminish the distance between his/her actual status and sociocultural expectations. The first step toward active engagement in one's own development entails recognizing and assessing both one's own present developmental status and the developmental demands of the surrounding culture. The next step is to estimate the distance between one's own ability and the sociocultural norms of development to allow one's self to set a developmental goal. The third step in the process includes activities aimed at attainment of the chosen developmental goal. Steps 1 and 2 need cognitive activities: step 3 can only be carried out when overt action is

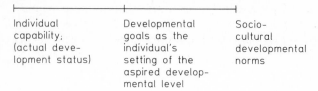

Individual capability; (actual development status)   Developmental goals as the individual's setting of the aspired developmental level   Socio-cultural developmental norms

Fig. 1. A quantitative one-dimensional model of developmental tasks

Fig. 2. A structural model of developmental task

accomplished in addition to cognitive activities. Between step 2 and step 3 there is frequently a mutual influence, leading to a change in the goal that has been set and followed again by adaptive actions.

With reference to a qualitative model of developmental task, Figure 2 shows the same dynamic interplay as Figure 1, but moves from the one-dimensional perspective to a structural perspective. The cultural norms and demands refer to what we call "objective structure" (OS), which is the order of the universe of action possibilities in a given culture. The individual's developmental status is defined as "subjective structure" (SS). The two structures are assumed to be isomorphic, again in consensus with Bronfenbrenner who, as is well known, discerns four environmental systems and relates them to developmental changes in two domains: perception and action. He states: ". . . each of those domains has a structure that is isomorphic with the four levels of the ecological environment" (1979, p. 28).

Although a certain amount of isomorphism between objective and subjective structures is necessary to assure the survival of both the individual and the culture, the discrepancies between the two structures in Figure 2 should also be noted. Moreover, a (certain level of) discrepancy can be identified between segments of the objective structure that provide conceptions of desirable development and the actual developmental status of the individual as the force that drives human development.

Looking more closely at the interaction between the individual and the environment, we see the individual's own activity as an essential component mediating this interplay. This is quite in accordance with the current notion that the individual is the builder (constructor) of his/her own development (Brim & Kagan, 1980; Lerner, 1982; Lerner & Busch-Rossnagel, 1981). If we refer again to the model of developmental task, the individual progressively undertakes the decision of defining and determining the developmental goal. However, this goal is not the product of the subject's independent and uninfluenced thinking, but is, on the contrary, structured according to essential features of the environment (in Figure 2 this is symbolized by arrows leading from regions of the objective structure to the individual's conception of the goal).

Before we turn to empirical research, a last comment seems to be necessary regarding the scope of a developmental task: Havighurst (1948/1982) used the term in a rather general way, listing seven to ten tasks for each of six periods of life. Of course one can think of smaller tasks and also of larger ones. A good example of a more differentiated view is presented in the German Shell Study (Jugendwerk der Deutschen Shell, 1981), in which adolescents are asked at which age they reached or will reach a specific milestone, e. g., earning enough money to live independently, attending a dancing class, leaving the family. On the other hand, one can take into consideration very general tasks, such as becoming adult. We assume that developmental tasks can be conceived as both a horizontal and a vertical system of components, which are both helpful for the individual's coping with the environment and with the demands of the surrounding culture. The horizontal direction can be seen as the expansion of the individual's life space, the vertical direction as an increasing consciousness of goal-directed action in dealing with oneself and the environment.

To summarize the points discussed so far, it turns out that revisiting the concept of developmental task might be quite useful for understanding the developmental process from an ecological perspective, because it also emphasizes development as a process which is governed by general laws. Of course it should always be borne in mind that it can illuminate only some aspects of development and that periods might exist in the individual's life during which active developmental endeavor does not play an essential role.

To test the validity of this concept of developmental task, we conducted several studies.

On the Way to Adulthood: Developmental Tasks in Adolescence

Study 1
About 200 adolescents aged 15—16 years completed a three-part questionnaire, part of which was related to Havighurst's developmental tasks of adolescence.[1] Part 1 asked about the importance of, part 2 about ways of dealing with, and part 3 about the degree of having coped with ten developmental tasks. We controlled for social class, education, and sex.

Hypothesis. We expected the respondents to be highly concerned with most of the presented issues. We also expected a focusing change in dealing with the developmental tasks by analogy with Coleman's focal theory, which

---

[1] As developmental tasks we chose the following ten themes: 1. Achieving new relations with peers of both sexes. 2. Accepting one's physical appearance and physique changes. 3. Achieving a masculine or feminine social role. 4. Achieving physical relations with a partner. 5. Detachment from the parents. 6. Preparing to choose an occupation in line with one's abilities and interests. 7. Development of an idea about your marital partner (wife/husband) and future family. 8. Knowing who you are and what you want. 9. Clarifying one's values and developing an ideology. 10. Developing a perspective on the future and one's goals.

states that adolescents successively cope with problems through changing the focus of their concern. These expectations led us to test samples with small age differences.

Results. We will omit finer details of the study and present only three main results.

1. The majority of the issues presented were perceived as important. Individual differences in the profile of importance within one age group were more related to sex differences than to educational and socioeconomic differences.

2. Age differences accounted for more variance in the perceived level of task accomplishment than sex, education, and social class. Thus, the tasks presented seem to be related primarily to development rather than to specific situational factors. But note that developmental progress remains related to environmental demands.

3. The adolescents said that it was necessary to be actively engaged in dealing with developmental tasks.

On the whole, the study supported the assumption that adolescents are aware of developmental tasks and are consciously active in coping with them.

Study 2

Study 1 revealed that adolescents find it difficult to reach developmental goals. In their comments on the open-ended questions in part 2 of the questionnaire, adolescents frequently mentioned support from their parents as helpful. Thus, the question arose: what contribution could parents make to support their children in coping with developmental tasks? We asked this question of adolescents, young adults, and parents of children who were 13–17 years old. Since not all the data have been analyzed, we refer only to the responses of the young adult sample. Content analyses revealed four main categories of parental support. The first two of them refer to parental personality traits and attitudes and to parent's providing material support, resources, and liberties. The last two include parents' active influence on adolescents' efforts and forms of parent–child interaction stimulating both sides. Unexpectedly, far more statements of young adults fell into the first two categories. Thus, in retrospect, the subjects interpreted effective parental assistance more in terms of considerate emphatic attitudes and of material support (room, money, facilities) than in terms of parents' active influence and even communication. Preliminary results show that adolescents expressed a similar view, while parents responded more in terms of the last two categories, i. e., active influence and interaction.

With respect to the validity of the concept of developmental task, we found that the developmental tasks remained a focus of attention and concern not only for adolescents but also for parents of adolescents and for young adults as well.

Now let us turn to the interesting question of how the individual constructs his/her reality, in terms of the conception of becoming adult as a general developmental task. How, for example, would a child see the task of becoming adult? How would adolescents conceive this task? First of all, we expect that they would not describe the adult primarily in terms of personality traits. Rather, they would emphasize the person—environment interaction in describing both the process of reaching adulthood and the state of the competent adult him/herself, thus painting an ecological picture of human development. Further, we will derive some plausible expectations of how the conceptions of becoming adult would change through different age levels.

The Conceptualization of Adulthood

Study 3
To explore the development of the conceptualization of adulthood as a dimension of reality construction from childhood to adulthood, we carried out a study in which subjects of different ages were each given a semi-structured in-depth interview. The interview contained some questions related to cultural norms of adulthood and other questions about personal developmental goals.

The questions were focused on the following domains:

1. Conceptions about abilities or changes necessary to become adult.

2. Further descriptions about the leading roles of an adult, as worker, family member, and citizen.

3. Questions about subjects' previous personal development: The subjects were asked to describe the progress of their own development in the last few years.

4. Questions about future perspective. Here the developmental goals related to subjects' unique personalities were emphasized.

Subjects included approximately equal numbers of males and females in age groups from 8 to 20. The first sample consisted of 53 subjects. Since German adolescents attend three different types of schools, differences in educational level were taken into account. A content analysis of the taped and transcribed interviews was developed step by step, leading to four main developmental levels in which all subjects could be ranged. The four levels, including their substages, seemed to be a valid characterization of the subjects' knowledge and consciousness.

Before describing these levels in more detail, let us briefly discuss our hypotheses about the developmental direction of conceptions of adulthood. We formulated two general hypotheses.

Hypotheses. First, we expected that there might be a change in conceptualization from superficial features to more deeply structured features. Surface features of adulthood are, for example, overt everyday activities, such as driving a car, smoking cigarettes, having a family, owning a house. Second, we assumed that conceptions of the relationship between the individual and the environment become gradually more sophisticated, showing more clearly at later stages the notion of mutual interdependence, of a dialectical person—environment relationship as an increasing ability of the individual to distance him- or herself from the environment. Following these two dimensions, results can be classified into four main developmental levels.

Results. Levels of Conceptualization of Adulthood

Stage I (Concrete Activities). At ages 8−9 years, children perceived adulthood primarily as being able to perform concrete activities. Those activities were often derived from the children's own experience. Examples: "reading and writing well," "cooking and sewing," and more generally "working well."

Stage II (Personal Involvement in Coping with Everyday Life Problems). Children of 11 and 12 pointed out that the adult is obliged to cope actively with the environment. Progressing along their own ways to adulthood, these subjects made statements such as: "to come through," "to maintain one's self-control," "to cope with other people, otherwise they will do what they want," "to make good decisions." Later, at ages 12−14, the subjects emphasized self-reliance in addition; e. g., to pursue a vocation according to one's own interest. In general, the subjects perceived adults, and themselves as future adults, as struggling with both the social and the physical environment.

Stage III (Autonomy). At this level, it seems necessary to discern between two substages. Stage IIIa can be subtitled control of environment and self; 14- to 16-year-olds clearly reported personal control as being the central goal of adulthood. Coping with life independently, having a mind of one's own, possessing self-assurance, and stability were articulated. Relation between the will and the developmental goal was also voiced. Example: "If you really want to attain a goal, then you'll manage it."

In stage IIIb, autonomy additionally is characterized by a higher degree of reflection on one's uniqueness and self-acceptance. For example, "to accept oneself as one is" was frequently articulated. Generally, subjects at stage III saw themselves as being more detached from their environment than at any other stage. They regarded the autonomous personality as having almost unlimited possibilities within his/her environment.

Stage IV (Reflection on the Relationship Between Individual and Environment [Early Adulthood]). For several reasons the most interesting findings are located at this stage. First of all, it is surprising that there is a conceptualization of adulthood beyond autonomy, since autonomy is the end point of conventional psychological thinking. Consider, for example, concepts like personal control (Kelley, 1967), self-efficacy (Bandura, 1977), and self-realization (Maslow, 1954). At level IV, the subjects recognized their dependence on the surrounding environment. They felt that they could not escape the stamp that culture puts on them. Subjects' reflections on the relations between person and environment fell into three different categories, which will be labeled in the following paragraphs as three different developmental substages.

Substage IVa (Self-Realization Through Partial Inclusion of Structural-Environmental Conditions). At this stage the individual recognizes him/herself as being strongly influenced by the environment but still believes that he/she can realize his/her own goals and ideas. For example, the subjects distinguished explicitly between social roles (family role, vocational role, and political role) and personality. But they believed that they would be able to go beyond the imitation of socially-defined roles by performing them in a personal way.

Substage IVb (Self-Realization Defined as the Partial or Total Negation of the Surrounding Culture). The society and its culture were partially or totally rejected. The subject at this level did not want to live further in his/her society; they particularly did not want to support the culture. These subjects spoke of emigration (e. g., Canada or Australia) or of the establishment of an alternative life-style as means of self-realization.

Substage IVc (Self-Realization as an Attempt to Integrate Conflicting Person—Environment Relations). Subjects in this category endeavor to cope with conflicting relations constructively. Although incompatabilities were recognized more keenly than at a younger age, the subjects tried to cope with this general situation and to engage themselves in society. Some examples: The sharp separation of labor and leisure time was criticized, and more satisfactory relations between work and everyday life were proposed. The dialectics of conformity and individuality were elaborated and ways of integrating both components were developed.

At the end of the description of stage IV we should have a brief look at the form of thinking that underlies this conception of humanity. This seems to be a form of dialectical thinking, which cannot be subordinated to the formal logical operations in the sense of Piaget's theory. Whether dialectical thinking is a higher stage of thinking, as Jürgen Habermas (1971) and others suggest, or whether it is only another form of thinking which is needed for a more appropriate understanding of culture, society, and person—environment relationships, is an open question so far.

Now the findings will be summarized using the ecological notion of person—environment interaction. If we let S stand for subject and E for environment, at stage I there is no clearcut separation between S and E, since

Table 1. The representation of individual–environment relations at four levels of conceptualization

Stage (level)	Description	Representation of subject (S) and environment (E)
I	Concrete activites	$S \rightarrow SE$
II	To engage oneself, to invest personal expenditure	$S \rightarrow S - E$
III a	Autonomy: control	$S \rightarrow S - E$
III b	Autonomy: reflected self-determination	$S \rightarrow SS - E$
IV a	Self-realization through partial inclusion of structural-environmental conditions	$S \rightarrow SS - OS$
IV b	Self-realization through negation of the culture	$S \rightarrow SS - OS$
IV c	Self-realization through integration	$S \rightarrow SS \leftrightarrow OS$

SS, subjective structure; OS, objective structure; $S \rightarrow$ indicates that the S–E-relationship does not exist as an actual relationship but as a representation of the subject

all description used by the subjects refers to S-E units (e. g., performance, actions, skills). At stage II a separation of S and E is clearly present, because S is perceived as coping with E and as investing in E. Stage III a is characterized by further separation of S and E, because S is seen by the subjects as controlling E and as striving for independence from E. At stage III b, self-reflection (symbolized in Table 1 as SS) enters the relationship, enlarging the distance between S and E, because the reflecting subject tends to be more concerned with his/her own personality than with the environment. Actually, S-E interaction is not conceived of as essential for understanding adulthood until stage IV. Substage IV a centers upon SS (subjective structure) and substage IV b upon OS (objective structure), while substage IV c balances both SS and OS. In terms of dialectical thinking, this balance must be seen as an unstable one, since there will never be a final resolution of the conflicting situation and during ongoing development the subject will be confronted with new dialectical relations.

Further Results of Study 3
The availability of independent information on the subjects' environments allows us to relate the interview statements to their ecological background.

Children expressed developmental goals which were connected with their own range of experience. The statements were often unclear unless one knew the life circumstances of the subjects. A second-grade girl repeatedly stressed the goal "to cross the street alone" and "to cope with the traffic". These statements were concerned with going to school — she had to cross a very busy street every day. The real danger had often been stressed by her parents, and this serious daily situation led to her emphasizing coping with traffic as a central developmental task in reaching the status of an adult.

Both the goals and the planning of the steps to become an adult are influenced by the behavior of parents and older siblings, who demonstrate to children how they themselves have become adults. Two examples may illustrate this. A girl wanted to become a mechanic because her brother had this job and was very content with it. A 7-year-old boy developed detailed ideas about the way to become a space explorer. He imagined the career in small steps: mechanic − passing tests − working on the ground − being tested again − working in the crew − tests − training as an astronaut − tests − space explorer. (It should be noted that tests are in fact used widely in West Germany to establish qualifications for occupational advancement). In describing these steps, he stressed the analogies to the career of his father who had moved up from a manual worker to an engineer, and the reasons he gave for his ideas were also guided by the career of his father.

A general environment-related component of the conception of adulthood was the occupation. Adolescents who were serving apprenticeships viewed the occupation as an essential part of their identity, while technical school and high school students mentioned occupation less frequently as an important part of adult life. They actually lived more removed from the life region of work than the apprentices.

In concluding our description of the results of study 3, we would like to stress that the logical structure that implicitly underlies the interview statements and its interpretation as a developmental level is not influenced by specific ecological conditions − social class, educational level and sex − thus providing a logical order of development for the variety of person−environment interaction.

Aspects of Practical Application

The theoretical constructs and the empirical results presented so far may seem to have more academic than practical relevance. But this impression is illusory.

Our results reveal, as just mentioned, a developmental logic that allows us to give the developing individual support in moving toward the next stage. Without neglecting specific ecological influences and interactions, we are able to act as developmentalists have long recommended and as Vygotsky (1964) perhaps formulated best when he defined education as leading of the child to the developmental level that is nearest to his/her own level (zone of proximal development). This idea is of special interest with respect to the transition from stage III to stage IV and that from stage IVa to stage IVc. The practical impact, by the way, was actually obtruded on us. After having finished the interview, many of the subjects were interested in continuing communication about this issue. We discovered the interventional effect of the interview and used it in the following ways, among others.

1. We provided several sessions for subjects who wanted further contact and observed carefully the changes in thinking about person-environment relations.

2. We arranged groups of four to six persons who had completed the interview and had them discuss life in adulthood.

3. We arranged discussion meetings between two groups who had completed the interview. The first group was composed of university freshmen, the second of graduates. Different views of adulthood were still related to age or to time spent at the university. The older group functioned to some extent as teachers of the younger group. On the other hand, the latter served as a sort of mirror for the older group, who recognized their own earlier thinking and the needs they had experienced some years before.

Conclusion

The concept of developmental task was used to describe the individual's voluntary and conscious endeavors on his/her own development from an ecological perspective. Children and adolescents not only perceived developmental tasks on the way to adulthood, but also conceptualized the status of adulthood and the process of becoming adult. Four main stages in conceptualization of adulthood were found, which corresponded roughly to ages ranging from 8−9 years (first level) to adulthood (fourth level). These levels can be ordered theoretically in terms of person-environment relationships, the first level showing no separation between person and environment, and the last level seeming to be a balanced dialectical kind of relationship between individual and environment.

We conclude that the concept of developmental task is fruitful and promising both for a better understanding of the ecological perspective of human development and for the goal-directed enhancement of individuals' development through the life-span.

References

Bandura, A. (1977) Self-efficacy: Toward a unifying theory of behavioral change. *Psychological Review, 2*, 191−215

Brim, O. G. Jr & Kagan, J. (1980) Constancy and change. A view of the issues. In: O. G. Brim, Jr. & J. Kagan (Eds.), *Constancy and change in human development.* Cambridge, Mass.: Harvard University Press

Bronfenbrenner, U. (1979) *The ecology of human development.* Cambridge, Mass.: Harvard University Press

Coleman, J. C. (1980) *The nature of adolescence.* London: Methuen

Habermas, J. (1971) *Knowledge and human interests.* Boston: Beacon

Havighurst, J. (1948/1982) *Developmental tasks and education.* New York: Longman

Havighurst, R. J. (1973) History of developmental psychology: Socialization and personality development through the life-span. In: Baltes, P. B. & Schaie, K. W. (Eds.), *Life-span developmental psychology. Personality and Socialization.* New York: Academic

Jugendwerk der Deutschen Shell (1981) *Jugend '81: Lebensentwürfe, Alltagskulturen, Zu-kunftsbilder.* Hamburg: Author

Kelley, H. H. (1967) Attributional theory in social psychology. In: Levine, D. (Eds.), *Nebraska Symposium on Motivation 1967.* Lincoln, Nebr.: University of Nebraska Press

Lerner, R. M. (1982) Children and adolescents as producers of their own development. *Developmental Review, 2,* 342–370

Lerner, R. M. & Busch-Rossnagel, N. A. (Eds.), (1981) *Individuals as producers of their development. A life-span perspective.* New York: Academic

Maslow, A. H. (1954) *Motivation and personality.* New York: Harper

Mehan, H. & Wood, H. (1975) *The reality of ethnomethodology.* New York: Wiley & Sons.

Neugarten, B. L. & Datan, N. (1973) Sociological perspectives on the life cycle. In: Baltes, P. B. & Schaie, K. W. (Eds.), *Life-span developmental psychology. Personality and Socialization.* New York: Academic

Neugarten, B. L. & Paterson, W. A. (1957) A study of the American age-grade system. In: *Proceedings of the Fourth Congress of the International Association of Gerontology,* Vol. III

Oerter, R. (1978) Zur Dynamik von Entwicklungsaufgaben im menschlichen Lebenslauf. In: Oerter, R (Ed.), *Entwicklung als lebenslanger Prozeß.* Hamburg: Hoffmann & Campe

Vygotsky, L. S. (1964) Denken und Sprechen. Berlin: Akademie

VII. Future Time Orientation and Its Relevance for Development as Action

G. Trommsdorff*

Introduction

Slogans such as "no future" have frequently been used recently to describe the unattractive situation of adolescents who are faced with enormous economic, social, and political problems and insecurities. It should be interesting to study how adolescents themselves anticipate and evaluate their future and which variations may exist among certain groups of adolescents. This should be especially interesting when pursuing the more general question of which function future orientation may have for the development of adolescents. One may assume that the way adolescents anticipate and evaluate their future influences their life planning, decision making, and behavior. One may even hypothesize that adolescents construct their own future according to the future orientation they develop.

Development of Future Orientation

Let us assume that a main developmental task of adolescents is to establish a concept of self identity. This includes subjective theories about one's present but also about one's future self — including wishes, hopes, expectations, and plans for the attainment of one's goals in the future. In the pluralistic value system of our society, adolescents are offered conflicting goals to strive for; clear value priorities are not explicated, and adolescents have to find out themselves which way of life is best for them. Such variety of goals and life styles may create insecurity, especially when criteria for decision making are missing.

Adolescents have to face this insecurity not only with respect to the formation of their present and future self identity but also with respect to their future environment: They cannot develop clear expectations about where they will be living, with whom they will interact, what kind of tasks and responsibilities they will have to fulfill. How will they develop a future orientation? What qualities does their future orientation have? Having this general question in mind, I will first explain the concept of future orientation, then I will briefly discuss some studies on the development and on the be-

* Technical University of Rhine-Westphalia, Eilfschornsteinstrasse 7, D-5100 Aachen

Development as Action in Context
Ed. by R. K. Silbereisen et al.
© Springer-Verlag Berlin Heidelberg 1986

havioral relevance of future orientation which are of some interest for research on substance use in adolescence.

Conceptualization of Future Orientation

In our own studies, we departed from Lewin's (1948; 1965) notion that future orientation is one aspect of time perspective, encompassing goals, aspirations, fears, and hopes for the near and distant future. Following the tradition of expectation-x-value-theories (Atkinson, 1964; Vroom, 1964; Heckhausen, 1980; Gjesme, 1981) we have conceptualized future orientation as a complex cognitive-motivational phenomenon: the *anticipation and evaluation of the future self in interaction with the environment* (Trommsdorff, 1983).

In its *motivational and affective* quality, future orientation is related to the satisfaction of subjective needs; it includes approach and avoidance tendencies and can be described as more optimistic or pessimistic, or as more positive or negative. The motivational and affective aspects of future orientation are interrelated with the person's value and goal system and with cognitive schemata about the self and the environment. These are activated according to the situational context and the thematic content of the relevant anticipations. The *cognitive aspects* of future orientation can be described according to the structure of anticipations. These can be more or less extended, differentiated, precise, coherent, and/or realistic. Furthermore, the future may seem to be more or less controllable, and one's future orientation may rather focus on external or internal causes of future events.

Before future orientation is transformed into life planning, decision making, and behavior, further variables come into play: the relevance of goals embedded into one's future orientation, judgments of self competence and environmental conditions in the present and in the future, heuristic competence in problem solving, readiness to tolerate frustrations, to delay immediate fulfillment of one's needs, and flexibility in restructuring one's goals in case of nonattainability. Since these factors are not necessarily stable person variables, the situational context, which may activate one or the other factor, has also to be taken into consideration. Since systematic studies on the development of future orientation (taking into account the interrelations with these further cognitive and motivational variables) have not yet been carried out, we have to restrict ourselves to studies which may clarify *some* developmental conditions of future orientation. Here, I will focus on four factors relevant for this question: 1. impact of situational demands; 2. processes of cognitive maturation; 3. impact of social learning in family, school or work; and 4. interaction processes.

1. Impact of Situational Demands

The structure of one's future orientation depends, first of all, on the cognitive representation of present and future situations. If fewer instrumental activities are necessary to achieve one's goals, one's future orientation will be structured less complexly. Or, if goals in the distant future seem difficult to attain, it may be more reasonable to structure one's future orientation in terms of available rewards in the near future. This should be the case for rather deprived groups of adolescents.

As we know from studies on economically disadvantaged groups, their future orientation is indeed more directed to events in the near future, as compared to the more extended future orientation of more privileged adolescents (see LeShan, 1952, and Brock & Del Giudice, 1963, for a comparison of lower and middle class children; Shannon, 1976, for children from minority as compared to majority groups). In the same line, adolescents from a lower as compared to a higher social class structure their future less complexly in most domains of life (Lamm, Schmidt, & Trommsdorff, 1976). A rather short or more extended future orientation (and related preferences for delay of gratification) thus can be interpreted as a realistic appraisal of, and coping with, the given social setting.

The situation-specific character of future orientation may be dramatically demonstrated by the impact of situational variables in real life situations such as institutionalization. In our studies on imprisoned juvenile delinquents and army draftees at different times of their institutionalization, as compared with noninstitutionalized delinquent and nondelinquent adolescents, we were able to observe enormous differences between these groups (Trommsdorff & Lamm, 1980). The future orientation of institutionalized adolescents (delinquents and draftees) was dominated by the event of their discharge, and changed with approaching time of release, increasingly including events related to the time of discharge. Their future orientation was filled with anticipations of problems and events after release.

The situation-specific structure of the person's future orientation thus may function as a problem-oriented approach to realistically prepare for certain events in the future. But future orientation is not only a situation-specific phenomenon. It develops in relation to other person variables in early childhood, partly determined by processes of cognitive development and partly influenced by external social learning conditions, which produce a future orientation with more or less stable characteristics. The stability of a person's future orientation can be seen from our results on the striking similarities between adolescents and adults sharing the same social (educational and occupational) background (Trommsdorff, 1983).

2. Cognitive Maturation

Following Piaget (1946, 1966), the development of time concepts is part of the child's general cognitive development. Formal operational intelligence enables the child to anticipate future events and to think in terms of future consequences. Along this line, empirical data show that children and adolescents learn to structure their future more complexly with increasing age and related cognitive maturation. They increase the extension of their time perspective into the future (Klineberg, 1967; Shannon, 1975); they become more realistic (Klineberg, 1967; Trommsdorff, Burger, Füchsle, & Lamm, 1978a), and they learn to take into account specific causes of future events.

3. Impact of Social Learning

Besides endogenous processes of cognitive maturation which are an important precondition for the development of future orientation, learning experiences in family, school or work influence the development of future orientation in its cognitive, affective, and motivational aspects. Several studies on adolescents from different social class, different ethnic and cultural background, and different educational level, clearly demonstrate significant effects of the social environment on the development of future orientation (for a summary, see Trommsdorff, 1983).

Motivational and Cognitive Factors Related to Social Roles. Adolescents' education influences their level of aspiration, goal setting, and anticipation of instrumental activities necessary for achieving these goals. The more relevant goals are then structured in a more differentiated way. However, adolescents from higher educational background need not necessarily structure their future more complexly. Cognitive training, but also motivational stimulation is important for the development of their future orientation. In several of our studies we were able to show that differences in future orientation of adolescents from different educational levels are not only related to differences in cognitive ability and intelligence. For example, adolescents from lower as compared to higher educational level structured their future more differentiatedly in certain areas, such as occupation (Trommsdorff, Lamm, & Schmidt, 1978b). Likewise, Bouffard (1981) has shown for African adolescents that schooling alone is no necessary condition for an extended future orientation.

As an example for the impact of social roles let us have a closer look at the longitudinal study on adolescents from different educational levels (Trommsdorff et al., 1978b). All adolescents went to school at the time of the first measurement; nine months later, one group, the former grammar school pupils, had already started to work, while the other group of high school pupils still went to school. During the period of time from the first to the second measurement, the lower educated adolescents (grammar school) had considerably changed in their future orientation. They now structured the occupational domain of their future much more precisely than before – and more precisely than the more educated students. Furthermore, they increased their belief in internal control of the future: At the first point of measurement, their belief in internal control of the future had been lower than that of high school students. These results support our assumption that motivational factors related to social roles can influence the structure of one's future orientation.

Another example for the impact of social roles on future orientation may be taken from our studies comparing the future orientation of female and male adolescents. A general finding in all of these studies was that significant differences occurred with respect to the thematic content of females' and males' future orientation (Trommsdorff & Lamm, 1975; Lamm et al., 1976; Trommsdorff et al., 1978 a, b; Trommsdorff, Burger, & Füchsle, 1980). In accordance with the traditional sex role, females, especially those from lower social levels, were more likely than males to focus their hopes and fears on the family domain. Their future orientation clearly was also directed towards the attainment of occupational goals, but was extended only to goals in the rather near future (Lamm et al., 1976). Independent of educational and social level, females generally anticipated more problems in the family and occupational domain than males (Trommsdorff et al., 1980). Furthermore, in most studies we found a more profound belief in external control of the future for females than for males (for a summary see Trommsdorff, Burger, & Füchsle, 1982; Trommsdorff, 1983).

These results support the hypothesis that females as compared to males have to deal more with conflicting role expectations, and have experienced less success, which is necessary to believe in one's own competence and positive environmental responsiveness. The general finding of these and other studies is that sex roles and related social and cognitive-motivational learning clearly influence adolescents' future orientation.

Impact of Child-Rearing Practices. In order to study the functions of specific learning conditions for the development of future orientation in more detail, we may refer to studies on child-rearing practices and their effects on the development of self concept, belief in one's own abilities, trust in one's environment, self control, and delay abilities (Rotter, 1966; Mischel, 1974; Stapf, Herrmann, Stapf, & Stäcker, 1972). In line with the theorizing in these studies, we assumed that the experience of parental acceptance would foster a positive, self-assured future orientation in the child. As a matter of fact, we were able to show for adolescents from different age groups that persons who perceived their parents as loving and supporting had a more trusting, hopeful, and positive future orientation, believed more in personal control of their future, and were more willing to delay gratifications (Trommsdorff et al., 1978 a).

To summarize: In several studies, the impact of cognitive development, formal cognitive learning, but also of social settings, roles, and related learning experiences on the development of a rather stable future orientation has been demonstrated. For the moment, these relationships can only be formulated in a very rough and global way, and many questions remain unanswered.

Especially the subtle influences of social expectations, for example the expectations of parents, teachers, friends, but also of mass media and public opinion, on the development of the adolescents' future orientation are so far hardly known.

4. Interaction Processes

Recent studies on the Pygmalion effect in the classroom (Rosenthal & Jacobson, 1968; LeVine & Wang, 1983) point out the impact of teachers' expectations on the self-concept and expectations of students. Results from our own studies on the relationship between teachers' expectations and the future orientation of pupils very clearly indicate strong interdependencies between both: Adolescents who are expected to be successful later in their life, hold a more optimistic future orientation and believe more in internal control of their future (Trommsdorff, 1983). Here, the question arises to what extent preexisting cognitive-motivational schemata determine which information is selected and how it is integrated into one's future orientation; and on the other hand, how one's future orientation determines one's decision making and behavior — which, in turn, may influence the way other people evaluate one's self, anticipate one's future, and then direct their interpersonal behavior accordingly.

These questions on the presumably complicated processes of interactions between one's future orientation and behavior, and the expectations and behavior of one's social environment, are especially interesting when studying the development of future orientation in adolescents.

As far as the first part of this interaction is concerned, we have to assume that the relationship between future orientation and behavior is mediated by other person variables such as self-concept, anxiety, problem solving abilities, etc., and by given situational variables which may activate certain hopes or fears. We have enough reason to expect complicated interrelations between these variables, which are not unidirectional in their effect. However, our present data do not yet allow for testing the sequence of such interactions.

In the following, I will give some examples to demonstrate the close relationship between future orientation, individual behavior, and social environment. Let me refer to a selected group of adolescents — juvenile delinquents.

Future Orientation and Behavior

A less extended and less complex future-time perspective of delinquents as compared to nondelinquents has often been interpreted as a precondition for delinquency, and an indicator of delinquents' inability to control their impulses and to delay gratifications (e.g., Barndt & Johnson, 1955; Stein, Sarbin & Kulik, 1968; Black & Gregson, 1973). However, the relationship between delinquency, delay of gratification, and extension of future time perspective is not so clear. These relationships were tested for male (Trommsdorff & Lamm, 1980) and for female delinquents (Trommsdorff, Haag, & List, 1979).

In the following, I will present our study on (drug-using and nonusing) female delinquents.

Method. In this study, our sample was composed of 55 female delinquents (15 were on probation, 30 were nonusing delinquents in prison, and 10 were imprisoned because of diverse drug problems); 30 female workers served as a control group. Due to the small sample size, the data should be interpreted with caution.

The subjects were rather homogeneous with respect to age (18 to 24 years) and socio-economic background. All subjects completed a questionnaire containing possible future life events that had been noted by other delinquents in a pilot study as relevant hopes and fears (e.g., to feel accepted by neighbours; to have friends; to have solved financial problems). For each item, subjects were asked to indicate the probability (expectation) and the desirability (evaluation) of the event's occurence, and the time when the event would occur (extension).

Results. Contrary to the often assumed difference in extension of future time perspective between delinquents and nondelinquents, no such differences occurred for positive events (hopes).

However, with respect to fears, female delinquents (drug-using and nonusing) had a significantly less extended future orientation as compared to nondelinquents. Furthermore, they judged the occurrence of feared events as being more probable.

This result is in contrast to the often assumed wishful thinking of delinquents (Landau, 1975; 1976). To summarize, our data demonstrate that delinquents have a rather pessimistic view of their future. That was also true for male delinquents (Trommsdorff & Lamm, 1980). Let us now have a look at drug using vs. nonusing female delinquents.

Delinquent Drug Users vs. Nondelinquent Females

Our results demonstrated an overall tendency of institutionalized delinquents (drug users *and* nonusers) to be more pessimistic than nondelinquents. This was shown for both components of future orientation, extension and probability estimations.

Substance users had a less extended future orientation for negative future events (fears); they also indicated higher probability estimations for the occurrence of feared events than nondelinquents ($t = 2.52$, $df = 28$, $p < .02$; $t = -2.74$, $df = 12.9$, $p < .02$) (see Table 1).

As for specific domains of life, delinquent users as compared to nondelinquents believed more strongly in the probability of occurrence of their fears in the economic and personal spheres.

Table 1. Future orientation of drug-using adolescents

	A Non-drug-using delinquents	B Non-drug-using nondelinquents	C Drug-using delinquents
Extension[1]			
Hopes			
Economic	9.51	8.41	5.77
Social	2.57	4.18	4.63
Self	4.82	4.85	3.86
Total	5.63	5.81	4.76
Fears			
Economic	5.57	9.85	3.80
Social	17.40	19.24	10.43
Self	8.98	16.52	6.23
Total	10.59	15.20	6.82
Probability Estimation[2]			
Hopes			
Economic	5.81	7.15	6.18
Social	7.83	8.00	7.13
Self	7.27	7.82	7.76
Total	6.97	7.66	7.02
Fears			
Economic	5.09	3.28	5.70
Social	4.12	4.34	5.77
Self	4.52	3.23	5.07
Total	4.57	3.62	5.51

$p < 0.05$ for A vs. C; $p < 0.05$ for B vs. C
[1] Number of years from now
[2] 0 = not at all probable ... 10 = very certain

Furthermore, delinquent drug users were more pessimistic than nondelinquents with respect to the belief that their self-centered fears will soon come true ($t = 2.36$, $df = 34$, $p < .03$) (see Table 1).

Delinquents: Drug Users vs. Nonusers

Extension. Looking at differences between *drug-using and nonusing delinquents* in more detail, we found that for only one domain of life, drug users were more optimistic than nonusers: They believed their hopes for economic well-being would be fulfilled in the near future ($t = 2.34$, $df = 24$, $p < .03$). However, especially with respect to social acceptance and integration, drug-using delinquents were more pessimistic than nonusing delinquents ($t = 2.19$, $df = 53$, $p < .03$).

Probability Estimation. Delinquent drug users believed more strongly than delinquent nonusers in the fulfillment of their fears concerning social integration ($t = 2.41$, $df = 54$, $p < .02$) (see Table 1).

To summarize, these results show that the future orientation of drug-using delinquents was generally more pessimistic than that of nonusers. This is indicated by their relatively less extended future orientation and high probability judgments with respect to fears.

Discussion. Studying the future orientation of drug-using and nonusing adolescents, one may hypothesize that the respective future orientation of these groups mirrors their past but also their probable future experiences. Experience of failure and lack of social acceptance may have affected the generalized attitude that self-ideal and social reality are too far apart, and self-fulfillment cannot be expected in the future. This generalized pessimism – the feeling of hopelessness and worthlessness – may have contributed to the decision to take drugs. On one hand, such a decision may help to deal with one's fears; on the other hand, however, fears concerning the distant future increase. Furthermore, such a decision for socially disapproved behavior supports negative responses from the social environment.

Here, we may observe a vicious circle between future orientation (as cognitive-motivational predisposition for such decision) and environmental conditions; the latter are influenced by these individual decisions in such a way that they reinforce the negative anticipations and fears of the adolescents and consequently contribute to their alienation. Thus, an imbalanced, pessimistic future orientation gains self-fulfilling qualities.

Development of Future Orientation and Behavioral Correlates: A Representative Study

So far we have discussed some conditions for the development of future orientation and pointed out the relation between future orientation and behavior, and the interrelations between both and the social environment.

The studies I have reported above had been designed to analyze some aspects of future orientation, and to test some specific conditions for its development and behavioral relevance. However, the scope of all of these studies is rather limited; they are all based on relatively small samples and focus only on some selected variables. Therefore, we have to question the generalizability of our results and the ecological validity of the data.

In search for more information about the empirical foundation of our hypotheses and post-hoc interpretations on the development and behavioral relevance of future orientation, we may turn to look at a recently published representative study on attitudes, life styles, and future orientation of German adolescents – the Shell study (Jugendwerk der Deutschen Shell, 1982).

Though this study must be criticized because of its methodological shortcomings (Hübner-Funk, Lösch, Rathgeber, & Schefold, 1982/83), and though future orientation has been conceptualized differently here, we may nevertheless refer to this study and some specific data which are of interest for our question. Here, we have the chance to get data on future orientation gathered in a broader context and in connection with other data on the social background and behavioral intentions of adolescents.

The general finding of the Shell study is that 58% of German adolescents are predominantly pessimistic about their future. Now, let us have a closer look at the concept of future orientation used, and at some correlated data.

The Shell Study: Some Results

In the Shell study (1982), several scales measuring future time perspective are used, all of them focussing on environmental, not on private aspects, of the future.

Belief in Control of the Future. One of these scales is especially interesting. It measures a *person's belief in his/her personal control of social environmental change* (p. 346 ff). The results show that adolescents low as compared to high in this belief:

1. differ with respect to *other aspects of their future orientation:* they tend to
− have less extended expectations about their future;
− be less interested in becoming adult soon;
− be more pessimistic about political, social, environmental, and economic aspects of their future;
2. differ with respect to their *social background and roles:* they tend to
− belong to lower social status groups and are females;
3. differ with respect to their behavioral preferences, tending to:
− be less active in sports clubs;
− feel closer to punkers;
− support "alternative" groups and green political parties more frequently.

Optimism/Pessimism. Another question (unfortunately consisting of one item only) focusses on *general optimism/pessimism.*

With respect to their *social roles,* the following differences are noted: The more pessimistic groups tend to:
− consist of girls, older pupils, and students;
− stem from the middle class;
− have experienced little parental acceptance but much conflict with parents.

Another scale measuring optimism/pessimism includes 12 items describing possible future economic, social, and environmental developments.

The results are quite similar to the findings cited above: More pessimistic adolescents have tried earlier in their development to become independent, however, they now prefer to postpone adult responsibilities and "independence"; they feel closer to peers than to parents, and they support protest movements.

Concerning other aspects of their future orientation, they have fewer goals and hopes for the future, and they believe themselves to be less in personal control of their future.

Conclusion

When summarizing the results from the empirical studies reported so far, we may come to the following hypotheses on the development and behavioral relevance of future orientation:

1. The more social settings require the testing of one's competence and allow for the awareness of one's abilities and options, the more subjective relevance is attached to this domain, and the more *differentiated* one's future orientation is structured with respect to this domain.

We have observed this relationship in the development of future orientation: Working adolescents structured the occupational domain more precisely as compared to nonworking adolescents. We have also observed a more differentiated structure of the family domain in girls' as compared to boys' future orientation.

To state this hypothesis in a more generalized way: The structure of specific areas of one's future orientation depends on the development of social motives and related goals.

2. The more social settings require and reinforce personal responsibility and independence, the more one's future orientation focuses on the *belief in personal control.*

According to the Shell study, lower-class adolescents are less convinced of personal control of environmental and social changes, possibly because of perceived difficulties in gaining influential positions later in their life. However, what the question of controlability of one's personal future is concerned, adolescents with lower status may well develop such belief if they are given the chance to take some responsibility for their actions, as we have seen in our study on working adolescents (Trommsdorff et al., 1978 b).

The data from the Shell study and our own studies are in accordance with respect to the sex-specific difference in this aspect of future orientation: Females believe less than males in personal control of their private and public future. Possibly, female adolescents experience less opportunities for testing their abilities and taking responsibility for activities that they would like to engage in. They trust less in their own abilities, as has been shown in other studies (Feldman-Summers & Kiesler, 1974).

3. Here we hit a related aspect of future orientation: the positive or negative evaluation of the future. The less social settings allow for the experience of success and social acceptance, the more pessimistic one's future orientation is colored.

According to the data from the Shell study, girls are more pessimistic than boys. This is in line with our findings that girls experience more internal conflicts when structuring their future; they anticipate more difficulties and uncertainties in attaining their goals (Trommsdorff et al., 1980). Other studies on life satisfaction and well-being of female as compared to male adolescents support this notion that girls have greater difficulties in defining their self-identity (Burke & Weir, 1978).

Referring again to our hypothesis, we should also expect a rather negative and pessimistic future orientation for those adolescents whose social environment has not offered enough opportunities to test their abilities, to experience success and acceptance even in case of failure.

As a matter of fact, data from the Shell study and our own studies are in line with this hypothesis. According to Trommsdorff et al. (1978a), those adolescents who have experienced little parental acceptance and who report conflicting interactions with their parents, have a more pessimistic future orientation than those adolescents who feel accepted. The pessimistic group in the Shell study rather prefers interactions with peers than with their parents; here they may receive social support and warmth which they are missing in their family.

How can we explain the more pessimistic future orientation of middle- as compared to lower-class adolescents? The less educated adolescents had to enter the adult role much earlier, they had to take over adult responsibilities and had experienced controlability of their situation. In contrast, the more highly educated middle class adolescents are living in a rather artificial world; real life has only been mediated by symbolic cognitive processes in school or mass media, but rarely by the experience of real consequences of decision making and behavior. As long as adolescents are not required to take personal responsibility for their behavior, they may not learn to structure means-ends relationships to cope with frustrating situations, restructure goals and make realistic judgments about their own competence, the responsiveness of the environment, and the interaction between both in the future. They will fail in one crucial developmental task: to develop a positive self-concept, a related positive future orientation, and realistic life planning.

4. Let us finally discuss the hypothesis dealing with the relationship between future orientation and behavior. The more future orientation is pessimistic and structured in terms of low personal control and negative action outcomes, the less adolescents are likely to accept and conform to common social norms; the more they tend to choose "alternative" life styles even if these are linked to negative sanctions. The data from the Shell study (e.g., preference for punkers; alternative groups; protest movements) and our own data on male and female delinquents are generally in line with this hypothesis.

When anticipating primarily negative outcomes, it seems less worthwhile to undertake investments, to control oneself, to tolerate frustrations, or to pursue far-reaching goals. Since it does not matter anyhow what one does, one might as well look for self-fulfillment in the very near future and choose activities which are socially disapproved and which have negative consequences for one's distant future.

Conflicts with parents and negative sanctions from the adult world will only reinforce the adolescents' existing cognitive schemata about the self and the environment and strengthen the tendency to reject or postpone adult roles and responsibilities. Thereby, one will further avoid realistically testing one's abilities and options and reinforce environmental responses of rejection.

Thus, in the process of adolescent development, an imbalanced pessimistic future orientation may stabilize and gain self-fulfilling qualities.

Outlook

Further systematic studies on the development and behavioral consequences of future orientation should clarify the function of future orientation for the development of adolescents. According to our present knowledge on the behavioral aspects of future orientation, one may assume that future orientation functions as a means to cope with developmental tasks by structuring and evaluating one's future. Especially in modern industrialized societies where changes in the social and economic system progress rapidly and affect a person's course of life, it seems necessary to develop a realistic, differentiated, well-structured, extended, and positive future orientation which allows for anticipating future developments and alternatives in order to prepare for taking over new roles, adapting to new situations, and solving new problems.

However, in our society, lack of responsibility and participation in the adult world will make it extremely difficult for adolescents to develop a well-balanced and realistic future orientation. Social learning is mostly mediated by symbolic and cognitive processes in school and by mass media, but rarely by concrete experiences and real consequences of decision making in other areas of life. This makes it difficult to learn the structuring of means-ends relations, to cope with given situations, solve problems, endure frustrations, restructure one's goals, and to make judgments about one's own competence, environment, and future. When adolescents finally enter the adult world without having had a chance to adequately prepare for taking these roles and responsibilities, disappointment and frustrations may result – an effect which is frequently reported for students after their first year of work (Burger & Seidenspinner, 1979).

Further factors may contribute to these difficulties. One is related to the pluralistic value system of our society. Adolescents are offered many alternative goals to strive for; clear value priorities are not available, and they have to find out for themselves which way of life is best for them. It may well be that such variety of goals and life styles creates insecurity for adolescents in search of self-identity and criteria for self-evaluation.

Furthermore, it is difficult for adolescents in our society to face the actual uncertainty of whether they will ever be able to achieve a social status and a standard of living which is comparable to that of their parents. In times of social change when the previously observed social and economic progress has come to an end and stagnation or retrocession takes on, the insecurities which adolescents have to face are increasing. Under these circumstances, who is surprised if a pessimistic future orientation and related experience of alienation stabilizes?

It is probably most difficult for adolescents in our society to find the right balance between extreme pessimism and unrealistic optimism as long as they are given only limited opportunities to empirically test their competence and the actual possibilities of their environment. However, this is only one side of the coin: it is not only the society which deprives our adolescents of participation in the adult world. Such deprivation also results from their future orientation. A pessimistic future orientation can block the motivation for any such activities and thus serves as reinforcing factor in a vicious circle of constructing one's future according to one's future orientation.

One may even ask whether a certain degree of unrealistic optimism and "illusion of control" is necessary to start acting on one's environment according to one's goals. Such optimism may allow one to face the manyfold problems lying ahead, it may serve as an excuse in case of failures, it may allow one to tolerate frustrations which come up in the process of dealing with these problems and it may encourage to continue even in case of failure. For example, the study of Wilpert (1980) on Turkish adolescents in the FRG (West Germany) shows that this deprived minority group is characterized by an enormous level of aspiration and extreme optimism in pursuing seemingly unrealistic goals.

Here, we have to ask whether the development of such illusions and unrealistic optimism depends on *more* than our before mentioned conditions. It may be difficult to find these specific economic, ecological, and cultural conditions in our own society. Therefore, one may think of broadening our knowledge about the function of future orientation for development-as-action by cross-cultural studies, possibly including such cultures where adolescent development is embedded in a specifically future-oriented value system.

References

Atkinson, J. W. (1964) *An introduction to motivation.* Princeton, N. J.: Van Nostrand
Barndt, R. J. & Johnson, D. M. (1955) Time orientation in delinquents. *Journal of Abnormal and Social Psychology, 51*, 343–345

Black, W. A. M. & Gregson, R. A. M. (1973) Time perspective, purpose in life, extraversion and neuroticism in New Zealand prisoners. *British Journal of Social and Clinical Psychology, 12*, 50–60

Bouffard, L. (1981) La perspective future chez les Africaines. Unpublished manuscript, Collège de Sherbrooke, Québec

Brock, T. & Del Giudice, C. (1963) Stealing and temporal orientation. *Journal of Abnormal and Social Psychology, 1*, 91–94

Burger, A. & Seidenspinner, G. (1979) *Berufliche Ausbildung als Sozialisationsprozeß*. Munich: Juventa

Burke, R. & Weir, T. (1978) Sex differences in adolescent life stress, social support, and well-being. *Journal of Psychology, 98*, 277–288

Feldman-Summers, S. & Kiesler, S. B. (1974) Those who are number two try harder: The effect of sex on attributions of causality. *Journal of Personality and Social Psychology, 30*, 846–855

Gjesme, T. (1981) Is there any future in achievement motivation? *Motivation and Emotion, 5*, 115–138

Heckhausen, H. (1980) *Motivation und soziales Handeln*. Berlin Heidelberg New York: Springer

Hübner-Funk, S., Lösch, H., Rathgeber, R., & Schefold, W. (1982/83) Die Shell-Studie '81: ein Bild von Jugend. Zwei aktuelle Themen: Jugend und Zukunft. *Literatur-Rundschau der Neuen Praxis*

Jugendwerk der Deutschen Shell (Ed.) (1982) *Jugend '81. Lebensentwürfe – Alltagskulturen – Zukunftsbilder*. Opladen: Leske & Budrich

Klineberg, St. L. (1967) Changes in outlook on the future between childhood and adolescence. *Journal of Personality and Social Psychology, 7*, 185–193

Lamm, H., Schmidt, R. W., & Trommsdorff, G. (1976) Sex and social class as determinants of future orientation (time perspective) in adolescents. *Journal of Personality and Social Psychology, 34*, 317–326

Landau, S. F. (1975) Future time perspective of delinquents and non-delinquents: The effect of institutionalization. *Criminal Justice and Behavior, 2*, 22–36

Landau, S. F. (1976) Delinquency, institutionalization, and time orientation. *Journal of Consulting and Clinical Psychology, 44*, 745–759

LeShan, L. L. (1952) Time orientation and social class. *Journal of Abnormal and Social Psychology, 47*, 589–592

LeVine, J. & Wang, M. (1983) *Teacher and student perceptions: Implications for learning*. Hillsdale, N. J.: Erlbaum

Lewin, K. (1948) Time perspective and morale. In: K. Lewin (Ed.), *Resolving social conflicts* (pp. 103–124). New York: Harper

Lewin, K. (1965) Group decision and social change. In: H. Proshansky & B. Seidenberg (Eds.), *Basic studies in social psychology* (pp. 423–437). London: Holt/Rinehart/ Winston

Mischel, W. (1974) Processes in delay of gratification. In: L. Berkowitz (Ed.), *Advances in experimental social psychology. Vol. 7*. New York: Academic Press

Piaget, J. (1946) Le développement de la notion de temps chez l'enfant. Paris: P. U. F.

Piaget, J. (1966) Time perception in children. In: J. P. Frazer (Ed.), *The voices of time* (pp. 202–216). New York: G. Braziller

Rosenthal, R. & Jacobson, L. (1968) *Pygmalion in the classroom*. New York: Holt, Rinehart & Winston

Rotter, J. B. (1966) Generalized expectancies for internal versus external control of reinforcement. *Psychological Monograph, 80* (No. 609)

Shannon, L. (1975) Development of time perspective in three cultural groups: A cultural difference or an expectancy interpretation. *Developmental Psychology, 11*, 114–115

Shannon, L. (1976) Age change in time perception in native Americans, Mexican Americans, and Anglo Americans. *Journal of Cross-Cultural Psychology, 7*, 117

Stapf, U. H., Herrmann, Th., Stapf, A., & Stäcker, K. (1972) *Psychologie des elterlichen Erziehungsstils*. Bern/Stuttgart: Huber

Stein, K. B., Sarbin, T. R., & Kulik, J. A. (1968) Future time perspectives: Its relation to the socialization process and the delinquent role. *Journal of Consulting and Clinical Psychology, 32,* 257−264

Trommsdorff, G. (1983) Future orientation and socialization. *International Journal of Psychology, 18,* 381−406

Trommsdorff, G., Burger, C., Füchsle, T., & Lamm, H. (1978a) *Erziehung für die Zukunft*. Düsseldorf: Schwann

Trommsdorff, G., Burger, C., & Füchsle, T. (1980) Geschlechtsdifferenzen in der Zukunftsorientierung. *Zeitschrift für Soziologie, 9,* 366−377

Trommsdorff, G., Burger, C., & Füchsle, T. (1982) Social and psychological aspects of future orientation. In: M. Irle (Ed.), *Sociopsychological aspects of decision-making* (chapter 6). Berlin: De Gruyter

Trommsdorff, G., Haag, C., & List, R. (1979) Zukunftsorientierung, Belohnungsaufschub und Risikobereitschaft bei weiblichen jugendlichen Delinquenten. *Kölner Zeitschrift für Soziologie und Sozialpsychologie, 3,* 732−745

Trommsdorff, G. & Lamm, H. (1975) An analysis of future orientation and some of its social determinants. In: J. T. Fraser & N. Lawrence (Eds.), *The study of time* (pp. 342−361). Berlin Heidelberg New York: Springer

Trommsdorff, G. & Lamm, H. (1980) Future orientation of institutionalized delinquents and nondelinquents. *European Journal of Social Psychology, 10,* 247−278

Trommsdorff, G., Lamm, H., & Schmidt, R.-W. (1978b) A longitudinal study of adolescents' future orientation (time perspective). *Journal of Youth and Adolescence, 8,* 131−147

Vroom, V. H. (1964) *Work and motivation*. New York: Wiley

Wilpert, C. (1980) *Die Zukunft der zweiten Generation − Erwartungen und Verhaltensmöglichkeiten ausländischer Kinder*. Frankfurt a. M.: Campus.

VIII. Prosocial Motives from 12 to 18: A Comparison of Adolescents from Berlin (West) and Warsaw [1]

R. K. SILBEREISEN*, K. BOEHNKE*, & J. REYKOWSKI**

Introduction

Research on age-related change in prosocial behavior from the preadolescent through adolescent years is usually limited to the question of whether
the frequency of this behavior increases or decreases as children grow older.
Frequency, however, is not consistently related to age. Data from existing research do not support the view that there is any simple unidirectional trend.
Increases, no changes, and decreases have been found — depending on the
behavior under scrutiny, the method of investigation, and the age group (cf.
Radke-Yarrow, Zahn-Waxler & Chapman, 1983). Consequently, there is a
growing belief that developmental profiles should be based on more qualitative dimensions; that studying change in the motivational base of prosocial
behavior may resolve inconsistencies in earlier results (cf. Reykowski,
1982 a; Rushton, 1976). Yet few empirical studies have dealt with the issue
of prosocial motivation directly; one of the few is the subject of the following
report.

The chapter is organized into three main parts: (a) A theoretical classification of prosocial motives is outlined and discussed and earlier approaches
are reviewed. (b) A series of three studies on age-related differences in prosocial motives of German and Polish adolescents is then reported. The cross-
sectional and longitudinal data were gathered using the Prosocial Motivation Questionnaire (PSMQ), an instrument developed on the basis of the
theoretical classification. (c) Conclusions are drawn on the development of
prosocial motivation.

[1] All studies were conducted in collaboration with a research group at the Polish Academy
of Science (principal investigator: J. Reykowski). This research was supported in part by
German Research Council Grant Si 296/1-1 through 4 (principal investigators: R. K.
Silbereisen and K. Eyferth) and in part by a grant awarded to J. Reykowski by the Polish
Academy of Science. The paper was prepared during a sabbatical leave made possible
by German Research Council Grant Si 296/2-1 to R. K. Silbereisen. The authors thank
Nancy Eisenberg for helpful comments on an earlier version of this chapter.

* Technical University of Berlin, Department of Psychology, Dovestrasse 1 – 5,
D-1000 Berlin 10, West Germany
** Polish Academy of Sciences, Department of Psychology, Pl. Małachowskiego 1,
PL-00-063 Warszawa

Development as Action in Context
Ed. by R. K. Silbereisen et al.
© Springer-Verlag Berlin Heidelberg 1986

Classification of Prosocial Motives

The point of departure (cf. Reykowski, 1982a, 1982b) is the assumption that prosocial behavior is goal-oriented toward a state of affairs that produces benefits for someone else. As with goal-oriented behaviors in general, the performance of a prosocial act can be understood as a function both of the value of the goal and of the expectation that the goal can be achieved under given circumstances (cf. Atkinson & Birch, 1978). Leaving the expectation issue aside, attribution of value to a specific prosocial goal seems to constitute the "core" of prosocial behavior (Staub, 1978).

The process of value attribution is based on evaluative standards that are conceived here as cognitive schemata charged with valence. We assume that there are three distinct sources of those standards: organismic processes, societal influences, and conceptual functioning; and each of them can attribute value to prosocial goals. The functional characteristics of prosocial acts will differ according to the type of standards controlling them. Depending on the interplay between situational factors and personal characteristics, any given prosocial behavior may be governed by a variety of evaluative standards.

Standards of Organismic Origin

Interaction between organism and environment instigates affective states which become cognitively encoded. We call them *hedonistic standards*, because the objects or events that match them evoke, respectively, pleasure or pain. There are various possible sources of affective states (physical stimulation of sensory organs, motor activity, bodily states, changes in level of activation, etc.) and various forms of cognitive encoding (visual patterns, words, cognitive categories, and dimensions). When hedonistic standards are operating, the performance of prosocial behavior is controlled by some promise of pleasure or protection from pain involved in the situation.

Standards of Societal Origin

Societal influences can be sources of evaluative standards, since society provides schemata with evaluative content. This may occur via conditioning (Miller & Dollard, 1972; Mowrer, 1960), modeling (Bandura, 1971), power execution (Hoffman, 1970), and possibly other means. The standards that develop as a product of societal influences operate on the principle of conformity to demands of external authority or peer group. We call them *conformity standards*. The targets evaluated acquire positive (or negative) value to the extent that they match the opinions or examples provided by other people. While in many novel situations, or in early stages of development, opinions and models can have direct control over behavior, in the more advanced stages regulation is based on internalized standards requiring no evaluative input from others. When conformity standards are operating, the performance of prosocial behavior depends on the presence of explicit or implicit demands by an authority or reference group.

Standards of Conceptual Origin

Conceptual standards develop because cognitive processing can be an intrinsic source of affect (Hebb, 1949; Hunt, 1965; Zajonc, 1968, 1980). For an analysis of social behavior, it is of special importance to note that such an affect can be evoked by cognitive representations of social objects (individual persons, groups, symbolic systems, etc.). Every major change in an object (e.g., in appearance, in physical or psychological state, in location) can produce an affective state if it is incongruent with a subject's expectations concerning the given object. The well-established expectations (or beliefs) concerning social objects possess the characteristics of evaluative standards: information about events acquires positivity or negativity depending on the degree of correspondence with those expectations.

There are different kinds of objects represented in a cognitive system, and hence different kinds of standards are possible. *Standards of self-interest* (ipsocentric standards) are related to the representation of the self. Prosocial motivation is aroused whenever a person perceives that his or her interests can be protected or enhanced by prosocial activity. It may also be aroused when the interests of an object regarded as useful for the self are at stake. *Other-oriented standards* (allocentric standards) are generated by representations of other people. This type of prosocial motivation is aroused by another person's need. *Task-oriented standards* are embedded in those cognitive structures that represent the accomplishment of tasks (individually or socially defined). Prosocial motivation is aroused by requirements inherent in accomplishing the task, irrespective of self-interest or other's interest. *Sociocentric standards* concern social groups and systems. The well-being and needs of these social objects regulate one's prosocial behavior. *Axiological standards* are related to higher-order cognitive organizations consisting of a set of principles organized around abstract concepts (e.g., "democracy").

Prosocial behavior regulated by self-interest, conformity, and hedonistic standards may be called *extrinsic*, since it is only incidentally related to the well-being of the person in need. Behavior regulated by other-oriented, task-oriented, sociocentric, and axiological standards may be called *intrinsic*, since the motivation is aimed at benefit to another person or state of affairs.

Comparison with Other Models

The proposed classification scheme shows some resemblance to earlier models of other researchers. Yet it is more explicit in theoretical foundation and more highly differentiated, for example, than Staub's (1978) distinction of other-oriented and self-oriented prosocial motivation or that of Karylowski (1982), who distinguished prosocial behavior motivated by a desire to bring about positive changes in one's self-esteem (endocentric) and prosocial behavior motivated by a desire to improve someone else's situation (exocentric). Hoffman (1970) suggested that moral behavior can be regulated by three orientations: what he called external moral orientation resembles self-interest standards; in both, anticipating consequences for oneself is the core element. His conventional rigid orientation implies a strong adherence to social norms and is thus similar to conformity standards. Finally, his flexible humanistic orientation resembles other-oriented standards, as both denote an interest in the well-being of someone else. Eisenberg (1982) differentiated five stages of what she called reasoning regarding prosocial behavior. Compared with Hoffman, she broadened the scope by differentiating five levels of prosocial orientation, viz., hedonistic/self-focused orientation, non sympathetic needs-of-others orientation, others' approval and stereotyped images of good and bad, empathic orientation, and the strongly internalized stage where prosocial behavior is based on "internalized values, norms, or responsibilities, the desire to maintain individual and societal contractual obligations, the belief in the dignity, rights and the equality of all individuals" (p. 234).

There are also some important differences from earlier models: Eisenberg's hedonistic orientation, for example, subsumes what we have differentiated into hedonistic and self-oriented standards (reflecting separate processes of value attribution).

Eisenberg and her colleagues (cf. Eisenberg, 1982) assume age-related changes in an individual's dominant prosocial motive. An increase in other-oriented and a parallel decrease in self-oriented patterns of motivation is expected. But research on prosocial motives, like that on development of prosocial behavior in general, has concentrated on young children (cf. Radke-Yarrow et al., 1983). The following series of studies was conducted to further elucidate age and culture — specifically, to investigate and compare age-related differences in the prosocial motivation of German and Polish adolescents of different educational strata.

Study I[2]

The aim of the first study was to describe grade- and education-related relative importance and structural organization of evaluative standards in prosocial behavior. Data were gathered in schools in Berlin (West) from sixth-, ninth-, tenth-, and twelfth-graders. The sample includes students from sev-

---

[2] Data were gathered by A. Claar and S. Nagel; their work was additionally funded by a grant from the Technical University of Berlin.

eral school types. These school types were chosen to represent different educational levels distinguished by the range of possible curricula and leaving certificates.

Hypotheses

Gathering data on motives is a formidable task, given the intangible and highly private nature of the construct. In contrast to rather indirect, projective procedures applied in research on achievement motivation (cf. Atkinson & Birch, 1978), developmental studies on prosocial motivation used fairly direct methods. Two principal approaches characterize earlier research: (a) Children are asked in open-ended interviews about cognitions concerning the motivational base either in hypothetical prosocial situations, or right after their own prosocial behavior in natural settings. This approach was used by Eisenberg in her studies (1982) and elicits what she calls "prosocial reasoning." (b) Children are asked to select or rate preferences from a given list of motivational alternatives. Representative of this approach is a study by O'Connor, Cuevas & Dollinger (1981). Research on moral judgment (cf. Staub, 1978) has demonstrated that these two approaches produce somewhat different results. The second approach tends to exaggerate developmental levels; the actual complexity of moral judgment is overestimated if subjects are allowed to express their preferences among preformulated statements, instead of having to formulate their own arguments. It may also be difficult to formulate a list of alternatives broadly enough to avoid unduly restricting the respondent.

The *Prosocial Motivation Questionnaire* (PSMQ) was developed according to the second approach. Respondents are asked to rate motivational alternatives for their own behavior in hypothetical prosocial situations. The items depict five of the seven evaluative standards: hedonistic, conformity, self-interest, task-oriented, and other-oriented. Helping and nonhelping situations were used.

Mean Profiles. The categories used in relevant studies vary in designation and definition. To allow comparability in the formulation of hypotheses, approximate equivalent evaluative standards are included in parentheses following the categories discussed.

O'Connor et al.'s (1981) response format is highly similar to that of the PSMQ. Comparing grades 3, 5, and 7, they found a consistent decrease with increasing grade in preference for egocentric, relationship, and reciprocity (self-interest); and for authority (conformity) and empathy (other-oriented). The only exception was conceptual/normative reasons (axiological). These increased with grade; they were the overwhelmingly preferred category in all grades. Battistich, Watson & Solomon (1983) used an open-ended interview format. Here, pragmatic considerations (task-oriented) and benefit to the helped person (other-oriented) are most frequently mentioned for grades K, 2, 4, and 6, but showed no change. The other categories: self-concern and joint benefit (self-interest), role obligation (?), and helping as a value (axio-logical) showed a slight increase. Eisenberg's data (cf. 1982) concerning grades 2, 4, 6, 9, 11, and 12 showed a clear decrease in hedonistic reasoning (self-interest) and approval/interpersonal (conformity) with increasing grade, and a clear increase in most other empathic and internalized catego-ries (other-oriented, axiological).

Bearing in mind the differences in procedure used and the age-groups studied, the hypothesis emerges that hedonistic, conformity, and self-interest standards are rated lower and show a decreasing trend, whereas other- and task-oriented standards are rated higher and show an increasing trend with increasing grade.

Hypotheses about differences between school types are based on speci-ficities in student recruitment and school climate. The strong relationship between educational level and socioeconomic background is well known. For example, a higher proportion of vocational school students than high school (Gymnasium) students is of working-class background.

Thus, class-related differences in value structures (cf. Kohn & Schooler, 1973) may produce differences in conformity, with vocational school students scoring higher than age-matched high school students. As to school climate, high schools have one significant peculiarity: interaction among students is more competitive than in other school types. Crockenberg, Bryant & Wilce (1976) found that negative effects on prosocial behavior result from competitive school socialization. Thus, lower other-oriented standards might be expected in high schools. These predictions are tentative; neither social background nor school climate was actually measured.

Structural Organization. More than one hypothesis seems plausible. Given the resemblance of three of the standards to Hoffman's (1970) classification, self-interest, conformity, and other-oriented standards can be expected to form separate factors. One may speculate about a link between those three and the remaining two standards. The task-oriented standard is presumably linked with the other-oriented standard because both represent intrinsic, conceptually generated standards. Hedonistic standards may be associated with self-interest because of the shared extrinsic quality. On the other hand, one could simply assume a two-dimensional scheme of extrinsic and in-trinsic standards — not positing conformity as a separate factor.

Concerning grade-related differences in organization, no hypotheses were formulated.

Helping versus Non-Helping
The preceding assumptions are considered valid for helping situations. Eisenberg-Berg (1979) differentiated between helping and non-helping. Her subjects rarely used any sort of reasoning other than hedonistic when re-fraining from help. Other data are not available. Thus the study is explora-tory on non-helping motivation.

Method

Subjects. A sample of 357 students (302 complete data sets: 165 girls, 137 boys) was drawn from schools[3] in Berlin (West). It consisted of 74 sixth-graders from elementary schools (*Grundschule*), 92 ninth-graders and 77 tenth-graders from comprehensive schools (*Gesamtschule*) and senior high schools (*Gymnasium*), and 59 twelfth-graders from vocational schools (*Berufsschule*) and senior high schools. Thus, the major school types at these grades are represented. Students came from up to four different classes in the same grade; in some cases two classes were sampled from different schools of the same type.

Prosocial Motivation Questionnaire. To measure an individual's tendency to use the various evaluative standards in the context of prosocial behavior, the Prosocial Motivation Questionnaire (PSMQ) was developed. This proceeded in several stages, including extensive pretesting. In its final form, the PSMQ consists of 24 statements. Each statement contains the description of a situation that provides an opportunity to help. These descriptions have to be somewhat ambiguous, in order to allow interpretations equally relevant for all standards. In 12 of the situations, the addressee ("you" in the stories) helped; in the other 12, he or she refrained from helping; thus a decision mode, helping or non-helping, is already formulated in the statement. For each statement, five reaction categories are offered: the reason given for the addressee's behavior corresponds to the functional characteristic of a standard.

An example from the 120 items (12 situations × 2 modes × 5 reaction categories) is: (*Situation*) "You eat lunch with your mother. Afterwards she has to go and do some urgent errands." (*Mode*) "You tidy up the kitchen for her." (*Reaction*) "What could have been the reasons for you to do so?" (a) It is good physical exercise for you (hedonism); (b) Others would have done it as well (conformity); (c) You sometimes get extra pocket money for extra work (self-interest); (d) If you don't clean up the kitchen right away, it's much more work to do it later (task-orientation); and (e) You knew it would make your mother happy (other-interest).

Subjects had to rate every category on a verbally anchored five-point rating scale offering the German colloquial equivalent of "I would probably think that way": not at all (later coded as 1); probably not (2); perhaps (3); quite probably (4); certainly (5). Thus, each rating is a self-attribution of a motive representing one of the five evaluative standards. This procedure provides more information than the simpler multiple-choice format used by O'Connor et al. (1981).

---

[3] Grade 6 was chosen because it precedes a transition between school types in Berlin; grade 9 precedes this transition in Warsaw. Grade 10 was chosen because it can be a school-leaving year in Berlin; grade 12 can be a school-leaving year in both cities.

In the parallel non-helping situation, the addressee leaves the dishes on the table after having lunch with his or her parents; the five response choices were: (a) You don't like to touch dirty dishes (hedonism); (b) You want to be like the others, and nobody else from your class would stay home for something like that (conformity); (c) You wanted to get to the swimming pool as fast as you could (self-interest); (d) You were in a hurry and surely would have broken something (task-orientation); (e) Your parents would not be happy if you stayed indoors instead of going out into the sun (other-interest).

The 12 statements of age-typical prosocial situations were formulated after several informal interviews with adolescents. The following examples show how the addressee's age and the occasion for helping (parallel formulations concerning non-helping not repeated) varied. (School-related assistance to younger peers): "You're at home doing your homework. Your younger sister comes in and asks you to test her on her vocabulary. Someone else then comes into the room. You say okay, and start reading out your sister's vocabulary list to her." (Assistance to older disabled persons): "You're on your way to the shopping center. You see a man in a wheelchair having trouble getting up the steps. Somebody else is coming along. You help the handicapped man." (Assistance in improving/protecting the environment): "There is danger of forest fires. Flammable debris is lying around in a clearing. You pitch in and help others who are cleaning up."[4]

Psychometric Quality. The PSMQ data were aggregated to form five helping and five non-helping scales: hedonism as a helping standard (HH), conformity as a helping standard (CH), self-interest as a helping standard (SH), task-orientation as a helping standard (TH), and other-orientation as a helping standard (OH); in the same manner, hedonism, conformity, self-interest, task orientation, and other orientation as non-helping standards (HN, CN, SN, TN, and ON).

The psychometric quality of the 12 items per scale was checked in a procedure combining factor analysis and item analysis. Items were deleted which did not have substantial loadings on the general factor of their particular scale (a > .40), and if the corrected item-total correlation was low (r_{it} < .15). If this procedure resulted in a scale shorter than nine items, the best of the deleted items was reincluded. The procedure produced one 9-item scale (SH), eight 10- or 11-item scales, and one 12-item scale (CH)[5].

Calculation of internal consistencies showed alpha coefficients ranging from .60 to .86 for the revised scales, with median .78.

---

[4] The PSMQ was pretested in a preliminary study (Boehnke & Silbereisen, 1984) and then optimized in discussions with the Polish research group. Some items were then changed to obtain an instrument of comparable ecological validity for both Warsaw and Berlin.

[5] Item selection also took Polish data (reported in Study II) into account. An item was deleted if it did not fulfill these requirements in both cities.

Results

Mean Profiles. To examine for differences concerning grade and educational level, multivariate and univariate analyses of variance were computed with sex as the first factor. Because grade and school type are necessarily confounded, the second factor is a combination of grade and school type with seven levels: elementary school, grade 6; comprehensive school, grade 9; senior high school, grade 9; comprehensive school, grade 10; senior high school, grade 10; vocational school, grade 12, and senior high school, grade 12. The multivariate analysis of variance was run separately for helping and non-helping standards. The interaction of the two factors sex and grade by school type was not significant in either multivariate or univariate analyses.

Main Effect Sex. The multivariate F (Pillais F) was significant for helping $[F_{(5,310)} = 10.62, p < .001]$, and for non-helping $[F_{(5,303)} = 5.88, p < .001]$. Furthermore, the univariate analyses were significant for six evaluative standards. Boys scored higher on self-interest in helping (SH: $F = 14.9, p = .001$) and on three non-helping scales (HN: $F = 4.6$, $p = .003$; CN: $F = 5.0$, $p = .026$; SN: $F = 5.0$, $p = .030$). Girls scored higher on task- and other-oriented helping standards (TH: $F = 8.5$, $p = .004$; OH: $F = 10.6$, $p = .001$). In sum, girls are more prone to endorse intrinsic motives for helping and boys, extrinsic non-helping. In other words, boys seem to show a less "social" attitude to some extent, conforming to the stereotype.

Main Effect Grade by School Type. The multivariate F was significant for helping $[F_{(30,1570)} = 4.12$, $p < .001]$ and non-helping $[F_{(30,1535)} = 4.95$, $p < .001]$. The univariate analyses were significant on all helping scales (HH: $F = 9.7, p = .001$; CH: $F = 11.5, p = .001$; SH: $F = 5.0, p = .001$; TH: $F = 2.8$, $p = .012$; OH: $F = 4.3, p = .001$) as well as on three of the non-helping scales (CN: $F = 10.3, p = .001$; TN: $F = 4.0, p = .001$; AN: $F = 10.3, p = .001$; i.e., no significant differences were found for HN and SN. Means of the seven grade by school type levels are depicted in Table 1 (next page)).

Single Comparisons. The rather complex pattern of grade and/or school type differences was analyzed using a series of systematic Scheffé tests ($p < .05$, cf. subscripts in Table 1).

First, senior high school grades 9, 10, and 12 were compared with grade 6 and among themselves. There were six significant declines from grade 6 to either grade 9 or 12: hedonistic and self-interest helping, task- and other-oriented non-helping, and conformity for both helping and non-helping. The only difference among senior high school was between grades 12 and 9 on other-oriented non-helping, rated significantly lower by the older subjects. No significant increase was observed.

Grades 9, 10, and 12 of comprehensive school (vocational school seen as its grade 12 equivalent) were then compared with grade 6 and among them-

Table 1. Means of the Berlin (West) cross-section[a]

Grade	6	9		10		12	
Type of school	Elementary school	Comprehensive school	Senior high school (Gymnasium)	Comprehensive school	Senior high school (Gymnasium)	Vocational school	Senior high school (Gymnasium)
Standard							
HH[b]	2.68	2.78	2.20[dg]	2.30[de]	2.15[d]	2.44	2.05[dg]
HN[c]	2.22	2.25	2.17	2.22	2.19	1.90	2.18
CH[b]	3.10	3.16	2.56[dg]	2.82	2.50[dg]	2.59[df]	2.18[dg]
CN[bc]	2.19	2.01	1.69[d]	2.05	1.65[d]	1.60[de]	1.44[d]
SH[bc]	2.40	2.37	2.09	2.11	2.01[d]	1.90[d]	1.83[d]
SN[c]	2.07	2.09	2.15	2.30	2.19	1.96	2.11
TH[bc]	3.83	4.01	3.68	3.68	3.70	4.07[e]	3.53[g]
TN[b]	2.47	2.52	2.29	2.44	2.29	2.28	1.92[d]
OH[c]	4.09	4.12	3.84	3.73[e]	3.76	4.06	3.77
ON[b]	2.34	2.54	1.94[dg]	2.24	1.84[dg]	1.94[d]	1.52[dfg]

[a] $p < .05$ for all tests
[b] Significant grade by school type effect
[c] Significant sex effect
[d] Significant single comparison (sc) with elementary school
[e] Significant sc with preceding grade from same school type
[f] Significant sc with grade 9 of same school type (vocational school substituted as 12th-grade equivalent of comprehensive school, which has no 12th grade)
[g] Significant sc of different school types at one grade

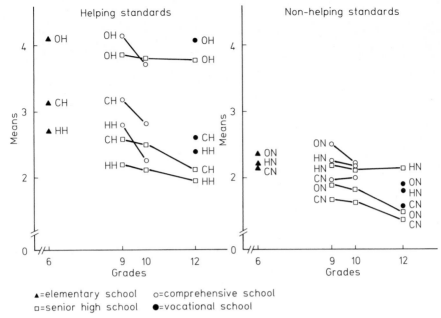

Fig. 1. Mean profiles [Berlin (West)] by grade for hedonistic, conformist, and other-oriented standards of evaluation

selves. There were four significant declines from grade 6 to grade 12: self-interest helping, other-oriented non-helping, and conformity for both helping and non-helping. Hedonistic helping also decreased from grade 6 to grade 10. In comprehensive school pupils, hedonistic and other-oriented helping declined from grades 9 to 10, conformity helping from 9 to 12, and conformity non-helping and task-oriented helping from 10 to 12. Again, no significant increase was observed.

Finally, differences between comprehensive and senior high school were tested among grades. Senior high school students of grades 9, 10, and 12 rated conformity helping and other-oriented non-helping significantly lower than their age-mates from comprehensive school. In hedonistic and task-oriented helping, subjects from grade 12 scored lower.

The results of both the overall tests and the single comparisons revealed two broad patterns of change: extrinsic helping and intrinsic non-helping decline; intrinsic helping and extrinsic non-helping do not change. Although scores in grade 9 pupils in senior high school were lower than those in grade 6, generally no further decline was observed through subsequent grades. For comprehensive school there was more change among grades, but no difference from grades 6 to 9. Thus, the two educational levels show patterns similar in course but different in time of onset of change; and conformity and other-oriented non-helping seem to be especially sensitive to differences in educational level and grade. Figure 1 (above) shows examples of the different trends with means found in the data. Hedonistic, conformistic, and other-oriented motives are depicted for both helping and non-helping.

Structural Organization. The structure of the evaluative standards was studied with confirmatory factor analyses. The LISREL procedure (cf. Jöreskog & Sörbom, 1981) was used. The optimal solution was approximated in a stepwise procedure guided by the hypotheses as well as information provided by LISREL.

Grade-Specific Solutions. First, two null models were tested: (a) All ten scales were assumed to be completely unrelated. The resulting goodness-of-fit indices (GFI) were extremely low (grade 6: .32; grade 9: .29; grade 10: .35; grade 12: .45), so this model was rejected.[6] (b) The five evaluative standards were postulated to form five orthogonal factors, each one combining helping and parallel non-helping decision modes. Thus, instead of scales, standards are assumed to be unrelated. Goodness-of-fit was not improved (grade 6: .38; grade 9: .33; grade 10: .39; grade 12: .50). Some parameters of the models revealed that orthogonality of the factors, and the assumption of a common structure of helping and non-helping, should be abandoned.

Two substantive models were then tested: (c) A non-orthogonal model was postulated with separate factors for helping and non-helping. This model matched the extrinsic-versus-intrinsic motivation scheme taken as one of the hypotheses; i.e., hedonism, conformity, and self-interest were assumed to be one factor, and task- and other-orientation to be the other. There were four factors in all: two for helping and two for non-helping. This model fitted the structure much better (grade 6: .80; grade 9: .63; grade 10: .68; grade 12: .72). Parameters of this model revealed that assuming correlated errors between the parallel helping and non-helping scales could improve goodness of fit further. This assumption seems feasible considering the feature of the PSMQ whereby helping and non-helping scales share a common situation. (d) Deviations between data and model structure were then analyzed to improve goodness of fit further. Here, differences between grades appeared. For grades 6 and 12, the LISREL program's built-in modification indices lead to the conclusion that conformity constitutes a separate factor within the helping as well as the non-helping standards. The resulting six-factor model, which resembles Reykowski's (1982b) propositions to some degree (hedonism plus self-interest, conformity, task- plus other-orientation, separately for helping and non-helping) showed a further improvement in goodness of fit. Following the same data-induced strategy of optimization, a different model had to be postulated for grades 9 and 10. For helping, each one of the former extrinsic evaluative standards constitutes a separate factor. The intrinsic factor remains unchanged. For non-helping, hedo-

---

[6] Models are deemed satisfactory if GFI > .80.

nism and self-interest are combined (as for grades 6 and 12). But conformity in non-helping is no longer a separate factor; it is linked to intrinsic non-helping. This six-factor structure shows improved goodness of fit (grade 9: .82; grade 10: .85).

General Solution. Given the two grade-specific solutions, the question occurs as to how distinct the models actually are. Therefore, in a multisample analysis, additional confirmatory factor analyses were run assuming either the one or the other model for *all* grades. Unfortunately, a clear decision cannot be made; the overall chi-square coefficients show a more or less identical validity; perhaps the extrinsic-conformity-intrinsic model (originally grades 6/12) has the edge for adequacy (grades 6/12: chi-square = 132.3, $df = 72$; grades 9/10: chi-square = 161.6, $df = 84$). Thus, instead of different grade-specific models, this model will be used from now on to describe the entire data. However, this involves a risk of overlooking grade specificities.

Table 2 depicts factor loadings and validity information for this general model, using the entire data set.

Table 2. Factor loadings for the Berlin (West) and Warsaw cross sections

Factors	Extrinsic helping		Conformist helping		Intrinsic helping		Extrinsic non-helping		Conformist non-helping		Intrinsic non-helping	
	B[a]	W[a]	B	W	B	W	B	W	B	W	B	W
Standard												
HH	.82	.83										
HN							.89	.99				
CH			1.00	1.00								
CN									1.00	1.00		
SH	.85	.92										
SN							.86	.74				
TH					.82	.75						
TN											.83	.82
OH					.87	.87						
ON											.92	.85

Berlin (West)	chi-square = 84.78, $df = 22$
	GFI = .86
	RMSR[b] = .04
Warsaw	chi-square = 65.27; $df = 22$
	GFI = .82
	RMSR = .05

[a] B = Berlin (West); W = Warsaw
[b] RMSR = root mean square residual

Discussion

As the confirmatory factor analyses showed, helping and non-helping do not form a common structure, although a similar three-dimensional pattern emerged in both cases, viz. extrinsic, conformist, and intrinsic motives. This scheme, however, resembles Reykowski's (1982b) proposition. Grade-specific structures were highly similar in the present sample; no serious indications of discontinuity in the development of prosocial motivation were observed.

The difference between helping and non-helping situations is still more clearly revealed by the results of analyses of variance and single comparisons. Whereas in helping situations extrinsic motives decreased and intrinsic motives remained unchanged, the opposite was true of non-helping: intrinsic motives decreased and extrinsic ones were stable. Conformity, however, decreased in both situations.

It may at first appear curious that in contrast to other studies, none of the helping motives increased. There are two possible explanations: (a) Using preference-type data, O'Connor et al. (1981) found a general decrease except for conceptual/normative reasons. These increased and were also the most popular. But no evaluative standard resembling that category is represented in the PSMQ. Thus, the present results may apply to the study's particular selection of standards and response format. (b) There is a slight but significant decline in overall grade means ($F = 8.74$, $p < .001$; 2.79, 2.65, 2.58, 2.49 for grade 6, 9, 10, and 12 means). Recalling the difference in results obtained by preference ratings vs open-ended interviews, the tendency of adolescents at higher grades and/or educational levels to give lower ratings may proceed from cognitive differentiation. They may take a broader range of alternatives into consideration and thus be more reserved in judgment. In an attempt to correct for that tendency, all ratings were adjusted gradewise to standard deviation units, separately for helping and non-helping. All analyses of variance for mean profiles were then rerun using these standardized data. The results did indeed show an increase for intrinsic helping and a decrease for extrinsic and conformity helping. Compared with the original data, decrease was not as rapid, and unchanged profiles gave way to a slight increase. This pattern more closely resembles that described by Eisenberg (1982). Because the rationale for standardizing the data is problematic, however, we will continue to report on analyses of raw data.

One important difference is that in level between school types as exemplified by conformity in helping and other-orientation in non-helping situations. Both are lower with senior high school than comprehensive school students, raising the question as to whether the effect is due to school-specific socialization or selective placement of students in schools. Unfortunately, the design does not allow us to determine an answer. At grade 6, placement into different school types has not yet occurred; at grade 9, the students have attended their second school for 3 years. Thus the variance among scores by school type might depict variance in standards of evaluation that existed prior to school changes. On the other hand, there are also indications of differential socialization; viz. differences in "slope" (cf. Fig. 1): for comprehensive schools the decline is sharper, but occurs later. There are also some instances of apparent increase between grade 10 of comprehensive school and vocational school grade 12. These represent genuine increases, however, only if one assumes that all comprehensive school students later attend vocational school (true for approx. 80%). When all these facts are taken together, there is evidence for both selective placement and differential socialization of evaluative standards by school type. The cross-cultural comparison accomplished with study II will shed more light on this issue: In the Warsaw sample, for example, it is possible to compare grades 6 and 9 within the same school track.

Generally speaking, however, all interpretation is premature: The data are still cross-sectional; and what has been called decline is actually difference. Thus, longitudinal data are mandatory.

Study II

The aim of this jointly planned study was to investigate the generalizability of the results obtained. To this end the data gathered in Berlin (West) were compared with equivalent data recorded for adolescents from Warsaw. The questions posed and the methods used were identical with those of study I, as were the purposes: (a) To analyze differences in mean profiles among grades, among types of school, and between sexes; and (b) to assess the structural organization of the standards of evaluation.

Method

Subjects. Due to differences between Warsaw and Berlin (West) in the school systems, it was not possible to match both grade and age. A sample of 125 students (124 complete data sets: 77 girls, 47 boys) was drawn from schools in Warsaw. It consisted of 18 fifth-graders and 22 eighth-graders from primary school (*szkola podstawowa*), 29 first-graders from senior high school (*liceum*), business high school (*liceum ekonomiczne*) and vocational school (*szkola zawodowa*), and 55 fourth-graders from these three school types plus technical school (*technikum*).[7] The selected groups are equivalent to the German sample in age, not grade. To simplify presentation, we will

---

[7] Grade designations differ in Warsaw and Berlin. Grade 6 in Berlin equals grade 5 in Warsaw; grade 9 in Berlin equals grade 8 in Warsaw. Tenth grade is called grade 1 again in Warsaw secondary schools, and twelfth grade, grade 4. The classes included for the oldest age group (referred to as grade 12 throughout) are comprised of students from grades 3 (vocational school) and 4 (*liceum*, business high school, and technical school) in Warsaw. This change from the design of Study I made it possible to include final school years for all types of secondary schools in Warsaw. But it should be remembered that in Warsaw the interval between grade 10 (1) and 12 (4) is 3 (not 2) years.

use the nomenclature of Study I throughout. Thus, the groups will be referred to as grades 6, 9, 10, and 12. The reader must bear in mind, however, that the picture is somewhat distorted by this.

This sample is only one-third of the original size; the remaining two-thirds were excluded from the following analysis because the instructions subjects were given for PSMQ were not equivalent to those given to subjects in Study I.

Prosocial Motivation Questionnaire. A Polish version of the PSMQ was prepared. Most items are literal translations of the corresponding German formulation. A few items, however, had to be revised to assure meaning equivalency: "Volkswagen van" became a well-known Polish brand of van; an Italian boy to whom help is refused, and a Turkish boy who is helped both became "a stuttering boy" in Polish.

An attempt was made to assess differences in the ecological validity of the PSMQ between Berlin and Warsaw. Upon finishing the questionnaire, participants in Studies I and II were asked to rate the everyday reality of the statements. Each subject rated helping and non-helping situations (one each in Berlin; two each in Warsaw), answering the question, "How often do situations like this one occur in your everyday life: very seldom (later coded as 1), seldom (2), sometimes (3), often (4), very often (5)?" The statements to be rated by subjects were chosen randomly from the entire set. They were tested in a balanced way: one-twelfth (Berlin) or one-sixth (Warsaw) of the sample rated a given couplet of situations; e.g., one-twelfth rated situations 2 and 14, another twelfth 8 and 16, etc.

In general, the Polish subjects rated the statements less ecologically valid: Their mean rating for helping situations is 3.23 (range 2.51 – 3.81); the mean rating in Berlin is 3.79 (range 3.23 – 4.32). The mean rating for non-helping is 2.78 (range 1.90 – 3.12) in Warsaw and 3.35 (range 2.54 – 3.79) in Berlin.

The PSMQ was used with three different instructions. They were Polish colloquial equivalents of (a) "What could have been the reasons for you to do so?" (the sole PSMQ instruction used in Berlin); (b) "My teachers would expect me to give this reason;" (c) "My close friend would give this reason." Data on (b) and (c) are not reported here.

Psychometric Quality. The PSMQ data were aggregated as in Study I. Thus, five helping and five non-helping scales resulted: HH, CH, SH, TH, OH; and HN, CN, SN, TN, ON. Alpha coefficients of internal consistency ranged from .59 to .84, with median .75.

Results

Mean Profiles. As with the Berlin cross section, multivariate and univariate two-way analyses of variance were calculated with sex and grade by school type as factors. Owing to differences between the school systems of Berlin and Warsaw, however, the grade-by-school-type factor has nine levels: primary school, grade 6; primary school, grade 9; senior high school, grade 1; business high school grade 10; vocational school, grade 10; senior high school, grade 12; business high school, grade 12; vocational school, grade 12; and technical school, grade 12. The interaction of the two factors sex and grade by school type were not significant on either multivariate or univariate analyses.

Main Effect Sex. The multivariate F (Pillais F) was significant for helping $[F_{(5.105)} = 2.84, p = .019]$ and for non-helping $[F_{(5.104)} = 2.46, p = .038]$. The univariate analyses were significant for five motives: Boys scored higher than girls on hedonism and conformity in both helping and non-helping (HH: $F = 5.3, p = .023$; HN: $F = 8.4, p = .005$; CH: $F = 10.2, p = .002$; CN: $F = 9.9, p = .002$) and on self-interest helping (SH: $F = 12.1, p = .001$).

Main Effect Grade by School Type. The multivariate F was significant for helping $[F_{(40,545)} = 1.95, p = .001]$ and non-helping $(F_{(40,540)} = 1.55, p = .019)$. With the exception of task-orientation, the univariate analyses were significant for all helping scales (HH: $F = 4.5, p = .001$; CH: $F = 4.4, p = .001$; SH: $F = 7.2, p = .001$; OH: $F = 2.2, p = .034$), for intrinsic non-helping (TN: $F = 2.2, p = .034$; ON: $F = 2.5, p = .017$), and for conformity non-helping (CN: $F = 4.0, p = .001$).

The means of the nine grade-by-school-type levels are reported in Table 3 (next page).

Single comparisons. As in Study I, Scheffé tests $(p < .05$, cf. subscripts in Table 3) were used to analyze the pattern of grade and/or school type differences.

First, grades 6 and 9 were compared. The comparison is particularly valuable because Polish cohorts are not split into different school system tracks until after grade 9. Self-interest in helping situations declined significantly. Intrinsic helping did not change. In general, the scales tended to decline, although not significantly.

Grades 10 and 12 were then compared within school types. No single comparison within senior high or business school types revealed a significant difference, though scores tended to decrease from grade 10 to 12. The opposite was true of vocational and technical school: for both, grade 12 scores were noticeably (but not significantly) higher than grade 10 scores.

Finally, grades 10 and 12 were compared among school types. For grade 10, business school scores were significantly higher than those of vocational school. Other differences were not significant; but vocational school scores were higher than those of senior high for most scales, with business school scores in between. For grade 12, three comparisons between senior high school and vocational school showed significant differences: vocational school hedonistic, self-interest, and conformity helping scores were higher.

Table 3. Means of the Warsaw cross section[a]

Grade	6	9		10			12		
Type of school	Primary school	Primary school	Sr.h.s. (*liceum*)	Business h.s.	Vocational school	S.h.s. (*liceum*)	Business h.s.	Vocational school	Technical school
Standard									
HH[bc]	2.78	2.31	2.35	2.57	2.62	2.04[de]	2.29	2.82	2.70
HN[c]	2.27	1.98	2.02	2.02	2.41	2.02	1.89	2.04	2.47
CH[bc]	3.21	2.75	2.54	3.01	3.07	2.35[de]	2.72	3.54	3.02
CN[bc]	2.40	1.90	1.86	2.02	2.27	1.74[d]	1.76	2.29	2.34
SH[bc]	2.64	1.96[d]	1.96[d]	1.90	2.42	1.75[defg]	1.86	2.69	2.41
SN	2.57	2.34	2.38	2.47	2.62	2.51	2.22	2.71	2.78
TH	3.71	3.72	3.78	3.99	3.61	3.66	3.91	4.11	3.76
TN[b]	2.76	2.26	2.44	2.60	2.68	2.53	2.49	2.77	2.79
OH[b]	3.84	3.81	3.86	4.04[e]	3.40	3.63	3.97	4.13	3.76
ON[b]	2.57	2.02	2.24	2.25	2.38	1.97	1.92	2.46	2.29

[a] $p < .05$ for all tests
[b] Significant grade-by-school-type effect
[c] Significant sex effect
[d] Significant single comparison (sc) with grade 6
[e] Significant sc with vocational school at the same grade
[f] Significant sc with business high school at the same grade
[g] Significant sc with technical school

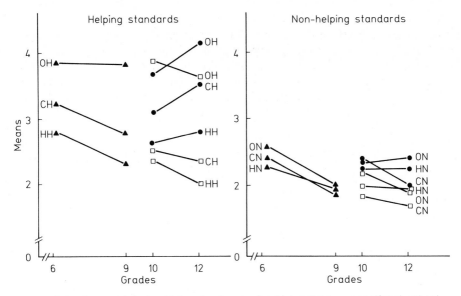

▲=elementary and junior high school ▫=senior high school ●=vocational school

Fig. 2. Mean profiles (Warsaw) by grade for hedonistic, conformist, and other-oriented standards of evaluation

Taking overall tests and single comparisons together, a more or less pronounced decline occurs between grades 6 and 9 for all scales except intrinsic helping, which remained unchanged. This same decline occurs between grades 10 and 12 of senior high and business school. Vocational school students' scores, however, were altogether different: 12th-graders scored higher than 10th-graders; and the increase was greatest for conformity, task-, and other- orientation in helping situations.

Figure 2 shows examples of different trends in mean found in the Warsaw data. Hedonistic, conformistic, and otheroriented motives are depicted for both helping and nonhelping. Only senior high school and vocational school are included for grades 10 and 12.

Mean Profiles (Warsaw-Berlin Comparison)

To gain information about gross differences between the data from Warsaw and those from Berlin (West), a three-way analysis of variance with sex, grade, and city as factors was calculated for the ten scales on the entire cross-sectional sample from both cities. The main effect city is significant for CH ($F = 6.1$, $p = .014$), CN ($F = 17.3$, $p = .001$), SN ($F = 33.9$, $p = .001$), TN ($F = 16.0$, $p = .001$), and ON ($F = 9.0$, $p = .003$). The students from Warsaw have higher scores on all these motives. Neither the main sex and grade effects nor the grade by sex effects are reported either because they have been reported above or because they are inconclusive since schools tracks have been combined that are not comparable.

Significant differences were found for all types of interactions in which city is involved. Sex by city was significant for HH ($F = 5.7$, $p = .017$) and TN ($F = 4.2$, $p = .041$). Grade by city was significant for SH ($F = 4.2$, $p = .037$), TN ($F = 4.9$, $p = .002$), and ON ($F = 3.2$, $p = .024$). The triple interaction was significant for HH ($F = 3.0$, $p = .030$), SH ($F = 4.5$, $p = .004$), and ON ($F = 2.9$, $p = .032$).

In sum, differences between Warsaw and Berlin (West) were observed for helping motivated by conformity and most non-helping motives. In both cases, adolescents from Warsaw scored higher.

Structural Organization. The structure of the evaluative standards could not be tested separately per grade in Study II because, gradewise, sample sizes are too small to meet the minimum sample size requirement of the LISREL procedure (cf. Bentler & Bonett, 1980). Thus the models tested per grade in Study I were tested for the whole cross section in Study II. The goodness of fit for the two null models (10 unrelated scales or 5 unrelated standards) was inadequate (GFI = .35 and GFI = .38). The four-factor model, assuming intrinsic and extrinsic factors for both helping and non-helping, has a GFI of .65. The model which assumes extrinsic, conformistic, and intrinsic factors for both helping and non-helping has a GFI of .82. Thus, one can accept this model for the Warsaw cross section as well as for the Berlin sample.

Table 2 showed the factor loadings together with validity information for the six-factor model for Warsaw. The factors are less homogeneous in Warsaw than they are in Berlin. The largest differences in loadings within one factor were found for extrinsic non-helping and for intrinsic helping.

To test the hypothesis of structural equivalence of the Warsaw and the Berlin cross sections, a multisample LISREL analysis was calculated including the two data sets. Overall goodness of fit is not quite satisfactory; chi-square is 152.53, $df = 44$; but proportions of unexplained variance are very low [Warsaw RMSR (root mean square residual) = .046; Berlin RMSR = .040].[8] Thus one may conclude that the three by two factor model (with extrinsic, conformistic, and intrinsic standards for both helping and non-helping) is still an acceptable model for both Warsaw and Berlin.

Discussion
The predominant impression is that results were fairly similar in the Polish and the German samples. Yet the disparate sample sizes for Warsaw and Berlin (West) must be borne in mind when mean profiles are compared. Thus, to be significant, critical Scheffé test differences have to be twice as high for Warsaw data as for Berlin data.

---

[8] Proportions of unexplained variance are deemed satisfactorily low if RMSR < .10.

Three generalizations may be drawn from the mean profiles of the two samples: (a) Intrinsic helping does not change, but the other scales decline more or less markedly with increasing grade. (b) Senior high school and vocational school mark the scores' extremes, with senior high students at the low extreme and vocational students at the high extreme. (c) Vocational school stands out as distinctly different from the other school types. From grade 10 to grade 12, conformity and other-oriented helping increases – an opposite trend to that evident in senior high school data. When the longitudinal data are available it will be possible to test whether the disparity in prosocial motivation at these extremes of educational level does indeed widen, as suggested, over the span of school life.

The main differences in mean profiles between the two samples are to be found in overall score levels. Warsaw students generally scored higher in non-helping situations; there were no gross differences for helping situations. This might be seen as a reflection of differences in the ecological validity of the PSMQ; but because validity was rated lower in Warsaw it can be eliminated as an explanation: validity-induced differences would have affected helping and non-helping trends similarly. Thus, it may be said that Warsaw adolescents, in general, showed higher acceptance of excuses offered in non-helping items.

The fact that differentiation into different school types occurs following grade 6 in Berlin but following grade 9 in Warsaw inspires further speculation on the issue of selection versus socialization. If selective placement were solely responsible for the differences in school specific profiles, the interval between time of differentiation into tracks and time of measurement would be irrelevant. This interval is about 3 years in Berlin and 1 year in Warsaw. In support of the socialization hypothesis: differences between comprehensive and senior high school were found to be significant in ninth-graders from Berlin, but not in tenth-graders from Warsaw (cf. Figs. 1 and 2).

Again the caution: all data are cross-sectional so far.

Study III

The aim of Study III was to determine whether some of the differences found between grades and among school types can be confirmed in a longitudinal study.

Method

Subjects. In Berlin, one comprehensive school ninth-grade class and one senior-high ninth-grade class were studied again 10 months after the cross sections. Of the 45 students from these two classes, it was possible to contact 41 for retesting (attrition rate 8.9%): 20 girls and 21 boys. Reexamination of 17 sixth-grade primary school students took place in Warsaw (attrition rate 5.6%): 10 girls and 7 boys. Also, 16 tenth-graders from three different school types were reexamined in Warsaw (attrition rate 27.2%): 13 girls and 3 boys. For pragmatic reasons, only those students who had not changed their school type during the interval between measurements were reexamined (grade 9 for Berlin and grades 6 and 10 for Warsaw).

A comparison of equally spaced age groups is possible with the Berlin ninth-grade cross section and the followup. For Warsaw, this is not the case; thus, in comparing differences within the cross section with changes that appear in the followup, the unequal time lag must be kept in mind. For the younger longitudinal subsample in Warsaw, the time lags are 3 years in the cross section and (about) 1 year in the followup. For the older subsample, the time lags are 2 or 3 years[7] in the cross section and 1 year in the followup.

The form of PSMQ used for the followup was identical with that used in the earlier studies.

Results

Univariate three-way analyses of variance were run separately for each scale, with sex, school type (senior high school and comprehensive school in Berlin; senior high school, business high school and vocational school in Warsaw), and time of measurement as factors for grade 9 in Berlin and grade 10 in Warsaw. For grade 6 in Warsaw only sex and time of measurement were included, because all students came from the same type of school.

To avoid redundancy in presentation, only the main effect of time of measurement and its interaction with school type is reported. The three-way design was chosen to provide appropriate error terms for significance testing.

Differences for the time-of-measurement factor are reported in Table 4 (next page), which presents mean differences for all scales between adjacent (cross-section and followup) age groups for Warsaw and Berlin. Superscripts indicate significant single comparisons for the cross section and significant time-of-measurement effects ($p < .05$) for the followup.

Table 4 shows that for the Berlin sample, all ten signs of mean differences from the cross-sectional study are confirmed by the direction of change in the longitudinal study. Scores for hedonistic, conformist, and selfish motives for non-helping (only the latter significantly; $F = 5.94$; $p = .020$) increase from grade 9 to grade 10. Agreement with all other standards declines, significantly for four of the five helping scales (HH: $F = 11.43$, $p = .002$; CH: $F = 5.73$, $p = .022$; SH: $F = 10.02$, $p = .003$; OH: $F = 19.39$, $p = .001$). In Warsaw, the picture is somewhat less impressive, but it must be borne in mind that here the time lags between adjacent age groups in the cross-sectional and longitudinal parts of the study differ: 3 years as against 1 year.[7] Seven differences from the cross section show the same direction as the change in the longitudinal study of the younger group, whereby only the decrease in the conformistic helping motive is significant

Table 4. Differences in means in adjacent grades in cross sections and longitudinal samples

	Warsaw		Berlin		Warsaw	
	Cross-section (6–9)	Longitudinal sample (6–7)	Cross-section (9–10)	Longitudinal sample (9–10)	Cross-section (10–12)	Longitudinal sample (10–11)
Standard						
HH	− .47	− .01	− .21	− .32[a]	− .18	− .20[a]
HN	− .29	+ .11	+ .01	+ .11	− .05	− .14
CN	− .46	− .24[b]	− .14	− .23[a]	− .15	− .09
CN	− .50	− .14	+ .03	+ .07	− .09	− .28
SH	− .68[b]	− .13	− .14	− .27[a]	− .04	− .14
SN	− .23	− .11	+ .11	+ .21[a]	+ .04	− .06
TH	+ .01	+ .30	− .12	− .10	− .02	+ .22[a]
TN	− .50	− .07	− .02	− .01	− .03	− .02
OH	− .03	+ .26	− .20	− .32	+ .01	+ .09
ON	− .55	− .05	− .14	− .08	− .20	− .26[a]

[a] Significant time-of-measurement effect ($p < .05$)
[b] Significant single comparison ($p < .05$)

($F = 5.88, p = .028$). Seven of the ten cross-sectional differences also appear in the longitudinal study for the older group; declines in hedonistic motive for helping ($F = 5.45, p = .038$) and other-oriented motive for non-helping ($F = 7.62, p = .017$) are significant.

School type by time of measurement interaction is significant only for other-oriented non-helping ($F = 5.05, p = .031$) in Berlin, with senior high school students declining much more sharply than comprehensive school students. In Warsaw, no interaction of school type with time of measurement was significant. Triple interactions were not significant in either city.

The longitudinal extension in Warsaw and Berlin (West) generally showed no differences between cross-sectional and equivalent longitudinal data. Thus, the cross-sectional differences may be interpreted as indicating intraindividual change.

Conclusions

All data are self-reported and hence susceptible to particular kinds of bias; some subjects, for example, may tend to preserve congruence of reported reasoning with opinions of the self they wish to maintain. Helping versus non-helping, furthermore, is a socially evaluated matter. And even the relatively anonymous ticking off of questionnaire items as a group activity in the classroom remains a social, communicative situation. These general reservations, however, apply to most studies on prosocial reasoning.

Prosocial Motivation Questionnaire

The PSMQ showed favorable psychometric characteristics. The reasons or motives in a revised questionnaire, however, should encompass the full range of standards as conceptualized in the theoretical outline. In its present version, two of the proposed conceptual standards, viz. sociocentric and axiological standards, are excluded. Given the high popularity of similarly conceptualized motives in O'Connor et al.'s (1981) study, the declining trend in the Berlin sample overall means may be partly attributable to the restricted range of motivational alternatives the PSMQ offers. The decline may also signify a greater reluctance of older adolescents to accept preformulated reasons; presumably, they appreciate the complexity of regulation of prosocial behavior better. The overall decline in means did not, however, appear in Warsaw − a fact for which there is no explanation.

Students in Warsaw generally rated the ecological validity of both helping and non-helping hypothetical situations lower than their age mates in Berlin (West) did − although situations were adapted to Polish everyday life. It is not possible to determine whether the lower ecological validity is due to the specific situational circumstances formulated in the items or whether it expresses a lower everyday validity of helping issues in general. Polish adolescents' higher agreement with non-helping motives, i.e., reasons for refusing to help, support the latter interpretation to some extent.

Structural Organization of Prosocial Motives

Confirmatory factor (LISREL) analyses clearly demonstrated that one of the proposed models fitted the data when helping and non-helping were taken separately. Thus, there are two separate three-dimensional motive structures expressing the functional characteristics of extrinsic, intrinsic, and conformity standards of evaluation. Although Reykowski's (1982a, 1982b) approach appears to be confirmed by the triple classification, his earlier analysis allowed the assumption of identical motivational structures for both helping and non-helping, because of the common standards. As it turns out, however, there is a clear categorical difference between reasons for helping and for non-helping. The only comparable evidence stems from Eisenberg (cf. 1982); in open-ended interviews, she found predominantly hedonistic justifications for not helping. In her study, however, the choice between helping and non-helping was determined by the subjects, and not by the researcher as in the present study. No other comparable study is known.

If we suppose that the model obtained (cf. Table 2) reflects more than the organization of concepts used to interpret prosocial behavior in a socially appropriate manner, some comment on the developmental formation of extrinsic and intrinsic clusters is necessary. Although hedonistic and self-interest standards are seen as functionally different, they collapsed into one

Table 5. Correlation of motive factors, Berlin and Warsaw combined

	Extrinsic helping (EH)	Conformist helping (CH)	Intrinsic helping (IH)	Extrinsic non-helping (EN)	Conformist non-helping (CN)	Intrinsic non-helping (IN)
EH	1.00					
CH	.72	1.00				
IH	.30	.43	1.00			
EN	.56	.22	− .31	1.00		
CN	.72	.57	− .06	.68	1.00	
IN	.70	.44	.00	.80	.77	1.00

factor. One may hypothesize that organismic and self-originated standards merge during the course of development; both become integrated within the self-structure. The self-structure develops as a specific cognitive organization discriminating between stimuli originating within the person and those originating without. Hence, the signals produced by changes in states of organism are very probably processed in the self-structure. The result may be an incorporation of organismic standards into self. Also, the lack of discrimination between other- and task-oriented standards may indicate that different forms of representation of external goals are not well separated, at least not at this stage of development.

The organizational scheme of prosocial motives is highly differentiated. This does not mean, however, that the dimensions were independent; the LISREL models explicitly allowed correlated factors, and these correlations were in fact substantive. They are depicted in Table 5 (for a model not reported in detail), which combines all the Berlin and Warsaw data into one set.

Table 5 shows that factor scores for extrinsic and conformist helping closely parallel those for intrinsic and conformist non-helping. The last two are themselves highly correlated. In contrast, intrinsic helping appears to be "exclusive," i.e., scores are more or less independent of all other motives. Thus, we may tentatively postulate two higher-order factors: (a) "hypothetical egoism" combining purely selfish reasons for helping with selfish or even cynical justification of non-helping ("It is in his/her best interests . . ."); and (b) "true altruism," in which task-oriented and empathic reasons are combined.

Gender Differences
Conforming to the widely held sterotype, boys showed a somewhat less "social" attitude than did girls. It is well known (cf. Radke-Yarrow et al., 1983) that self-reports on prosocial behavior tend to repeat gender stereotypes.

Developmental Profiles and Educational Level

Generally, the ratings for intrinsic helping motives were more or less identically high, whereas extrinsic motives decreased with increasing grade. The opposite was true of non-helping: intrinsic excuses decreased, and extrinsic ones were unchanged. Conformity decreased in both situations. Whatever comparable data earlier studies provide accord with this basic pattern. Intrinsic helping motives rank highest and remain so during adolescence in the present study as in those of O'Connor et al. (1981), Battistich et al. (1983), and Eisenberg-Berg (1979). The lack of increase in our profiles as compared with Eisenberg-Berg's is understandable: Her increasing scores are probably valid only for intrinsic arguments formulated by the subjects themselves. O'Connor et al. (1981), who gathered preference-type data that resemble the PSMQ response format, found a decrease in extrinsic and conformity reasons, as we did. On closer inspection, most of the increasing trends reported by Eisenberg (cf. 1982) could not apply to adolescents. The major changes appeared earlier in development.

The results of the present study do call for a qualification of the evidence collected in earlier investigations. As intended, a systematic comparison of educational levels in two countries with different bases for assigning birth cohorts school tracks produced a differential perspective on developmental patterns. In both countries a gap is evident between the traditional higher and lower educational strata. On the whole, senior high school students scored lower than vocational school students. A facile interpretation would be that senior high school students are capable on average of higher cognitive differentiation, and that this higher cognitive differentiation produces more reserved judgments. Arguing strongly against this interpretation, however, are the increasing trends in both Berlin (West) and Warsaw in higher grades of vocational school. An interpretation in terms of differential socialization according to differences in the life circumstances seems more feasible.

Yet another possibility must be mentioned, viz. that differences in score level between school tracks reflect differential placement according to preexisting differences; that the school system differentially places students according to variables correlated to prosocial motivation. The fact that differentiation into tracks in the two school systems occurs at different stages of the school career was used in 1-year follow-ups to test precisely this point. Data appear to show that differential socialization and selective placement both influence the scores. Further support is lent by the patterns of grade differences, which turn out to be similar to each other in course but school type specific in time of onset of change.

In sum, we have an opposition of the traditionally highest and lowest educational levels, confirming the hypotheses. Class-related differences in value structures (cf. Kohn & Schooler, 1973; Kohn, 1981) and school-type-specific interpersonal climate (cf. Crockenberg et al., 1976) may perhaps explain the opposition. Direct measurements of those variables are needed. At present, it remains speculative whether, for example, the increase in vocational school students' prosocial conformity motivation indicates a higher pressure for obedience which, in turn, may be required for successful job performance at particular levels within industrial and bureaucratic organizations (cf. Alwin, 1984).

Cross-Cultural Differences

In an earlier investigation, Eisenberg, Boehnke, Schuhler & Silbereisen (1985) compared American (USA) and West German children and found only minor differences. The present study did not actually measure cultural variables. It was a first attempt to learn to what extent single-culture German or Polish results can be generalized. All differences observed appeared small compared with educational level effects. Yet there are indications of some differences: Polish adolescents score higher in helping because of conformity and they also show higher acceptance of reasons for not helping, irrespective of the evaluative standard. Interestingly enough, Alwin (1984) found that among several other populations, parents of Polish descent ranked "obedience" highest (although the high value placed on it has declined over the past 2 decades).

Outlook

These results require further confirmation in independent, especially longitudinal samples. The present study, with its developmental-descriptive paradigm, allowed only an indirect assessment of parental values, socioecological data, and differential socialization versus selective placement; these need to be measured explicitly. Aspects omitted thus far (e.g., consequences for actual prosocial behavior) also need to be investigated.

Nor is this wishful thinking. Data collection on these questions has been in progress since 1982 in Berlin (West) and since 1985 in Warsaw as part of a 7-year longitudinal study involving a normal population of several thousand adolescents in the two cities.

References

Alwin, D. F. (1984) Trends in parental socialization values: Detroit, 1958 to 1983. *American Journal of Sociology, 90*, 359–382

Atkinson, J. W. & Birch, D. (1978) *Introduction to motivation.* New York: Van Nostrand

Bandura, A. (1971) *Psychological modelling.* Chicago: Aldine

Battistich, V., Watson, M., & Solomon, D. (1983) Children's cognitions about helping relationships. Paper presented at the annual meeting of the American Psychological Association, Anaheim, CA, August, 1983

Bentler, P. M. & Bonnett, D. G. (1980) Significance tests and goodness of fit in the analysis of covariance structures. *Psychological Bulletin, 88*, 588–606

Boehnke, K. & Silbereisen, R. K. (1984) Zur Entwicklung von Werthaltungen bei Jugendlichen. *Forschungsberichte aus dem Institut für Psychologie der Technischen Universität Berlin* (84–7)

Crockenberg, S. B., Bryant, B. K. & Wilce, L. S. (1976) The effects of cooperatively and competitively structured learning environments on inter- and intra-personal behavior. *Child Development, 47,* 386 – 396

Eisenberg, N. (1982) The development of reasoning regarding prosocial behavior. In: N. Eisenberg (Ed.), *The development of prosocial behavior* (pp. 219–249). New York: Academic

Eisenberg, N., Boehnke, K., Schuhler, P. & Silbereisen, R. K. (1985) The development of prosocial behavior. *Journal of Cross-cultural Psychology, 16,* 69 – 82

Eisenberg, N. (1979) The development of children's prosocial moral judgment. *Developmental Psychology, 15,* 129 – 137

Hebb, D. O. (1949) *The organization of behavior.* New York: Wiley

Hoffman, M. L. (1970) Moral development. In: P. Mussen (Ed.), *Handbook of child psychology.* New York: Wiley

Hunt, J. McV. (1965) Intrinsic motivation and its role in psychological development. In: D. Levine (Ed.), *Nebraska symposium on motivation.* Lincoln: University of Nebraska Press

Jöreskog, K. G. & Sörbom, D. (1981) *Lisrel V user's guide.* Chicago: International Educational Services

Karylowski, J. (1982) Two types of altruistic behavior: Doing good to feel good or to make the other feel good. In: V. Derlega & J. Grzelak (Eds.), *Cooperation and helping behavior* (pp. 397–413). New York: Academic

Kohn, M. L. (1981) Personality, occupation, and social stratification: a frame of reference. In: D. J. Treiman & R. V. Robinson (Eds.), *Research in social stratification and mobility,* vol. 1 (pp. 267–297). New York: JAI

Kohn, M. L. & Schooler, C. (1973) Occupational experience and psychological functioning: An assessment of reciprocal effects. *American Sociological Review, 38,* 97 – 118

Miller, N. E. & Dollard, J. (1972) *Social learning and imitation.* New Haven: Yale University Press

Mowrer, V. H. (1960) Learning theory and the symbolic processes. New York: Wiley

O'Connor, M., Cuevas, J., & Dollinger, St. (1981) Understanding motivations behind prosocial acts: A developmental analysis. *Journal of Genetic Psychology, 139,* 267 – 276

Radke-Yarrow, M., Zahn-Waxler, C., & Chapman, M. (1983) Children's prosocial dispositions and behavior. In: P. Mussen (Ed.), *Child psychology,* vol. IV (vol. ed., E. M. Hetherington) (pp. 469 – 545) New York: Wiley

Reykowski, J. (1982a) Motivation of prosocial behavior. In: V. Derlega & J. Grzelak (Eds.), *Cooperation and helping behavior* (pp. 357 – 376). New York: Academic

Reykowski, J. (1982b) Development of prosocial motivation: A dialectic process. In: N. Eisenberg (Ed.), *The development of prosocial behavior* (pp. 377–394). New York: Academic

Rushton, J. (1976) Socialization and the altruistic behavior of children. *Psychological Bulletin, 83,* 898–913

Staub, E. (1978) *Positive social behavior and morality. Social and prosocial influences, vol. 1.* New York: Academic

Zajonc, R. B. (1968) Cognitive theories in social psychology. In: G. Lindzey & E. Aronson (Eds.), *The handbook of social psychology* (pp. 320–411). New York: Addison-Wesley

Zajonc, R. B. (1980) Feeling and thinking: preferences need no inferences. *American Psychologist, 35,* 151–175

C. Development and Problem Behavior

IX. Resourceful and Vulnerable Children: Family Influence in Hard Times[1]

G. H. ELDER, Jr.*, A. CASPI, & T. VAN NGUYEN

Introduction

Periods of drastic economic decline generally represent times of jeopardy for the welfare of children. In the Great Depression, observations pointed to a lost generation of young people. How would the large number of children growing up in families on public aid be able to withstand and possibly rise above their misfortune? Homeless, abused, and hungry children brought similar questions to mind. For all of the concern it is remarkable that we have so little evidence of uniform impairment among 'children of the Great Depression' (Elder, 1979). Even in the worst of times, some children manage to come through without undue strain or damage. But how is this achieved? What factors determine why only some children are adversely influenced by hard times? These questions are the orienting theme of our examination of factors that differentiate resourceful from vulnerable children in deprived families of the 1930s. In diverse economic situations, research on coping resources (Kasl, 1979; Kobasa, 1979) has brought greater appreciation for the resilience of individuals and their families. Within the field of developmental psychology, there is growing recognition of the need to identify and examine the adaptive and resilient individual and familial attributes that may condition the relationship of stress to children's impairment (Garmezy, Masten, & Tellegen, 1984).

This chapter examines selected personal and social resources (e.g., child's age and physical attractiveness, mother's support) that had important implications for the resilient or vulnerable status of children in two Depression cohorts (Elder, 1974; 1981): an adolescent cohort based on the Growth Study of children who were born in 1920−21 and grew up in the city of Oakland, California; and a cohort of preschool children who were born shortly before

---

[1] This study is based on a program of research on social change in the family and life course. Support from the National Institute of Mental Health (Grant MH-34172) and from the National Science Foundation (Grant SES82-08350) is gratefully acknowledged (Glen H. Elder, Jr., principal investigator). We are indebted to the Institute of Human Development, University of California, Berkeley, for permission to use archival data from the Oakland Growth and Berkeley Guidance Studies. We are grateful to Urie Bronfenbrenner for helpful discussion of this chapter.

* University of North Carolina, Chapel Hill, NC 27514, USA

Development as Action in Context
Ed. by R. K. Silbereisen et al.
© Springer-Verlag Berlin Heidelberg 1986

the Great Depression (1928 – 29) in the city of Berkeley, California. They are members of the Berkeley Guidance Study (Macfarlane, 1938).

Each cohort experienced a distinctive sequence of economic conditions and stresses. The 167 members of the Oakland cohort were children during the relatively prosperous 1920s and entered the adolescent years as the economy collapsed. They left high school just prior to war mobilization and the beginning of World War II. The 214 members of the Berkeley cohort experienced the Great Depression through the family during their early years of childhood. In many cases, hard times and family insecurity did not end until their adolescence in the Second World War. Each cohort's experience across the Depression years was recorded year by year through observations and interviews. As of 1929, three-fifths of the Oakland and Berkeley families were positioned in the middle class.

The resilience or vulnerability of children during a stressful time, such as the Great Depression brings two issues to mind: 1. the process by which economic hardship entails substantial health and developmental risks for children; and 2. factors that minimize or accentuate such risks. We begin this chapter by specifying causal paths linking family hardship to children's lives. Deprivational effects are traced through family adaptations, especially changes in father's behavior, in response to a changing environment. Next, two organizing propositions structure our analysis of conditional variations. Here we refer to variations in the causal process by which Depression hardship adversely influenced the welfare and development of children.

The first proposition centers on the personal resources of children in both cohorts, Oakland and Berkeley. We review evidence from our research on the role of children in modifying their own social environment, particularly the behavior of fathers under economic stress. Specifically, we consider the implications of children's age and sex, physical attractiveness, and temperamental characteristics (ill-tempered, irritable) before the economic crisis in shaping their family experiences and treatment by fathers.

The second proposition draws upon the resources of the Berkeley archive for an empirical test of the role of mothers in protecting children from economic stress and paternal maltreatment. The expansion of analytic models from a dyadic unit (i.e., father–child) to a family system (i.e., mother–father–child) requires knowledge of how interactions between two people influence and are influenced by a third person (e.g., Clarke-Stewart, 1978). The response of each person to the other is conditioned by their joint relationship to a third person. Thus, changes within any individual or relationship may affect all other persons and relationships. Bronfenbrenner (1979) has coined the term *second order effect* as a generic concept for these influences. Similar schemes for understanding the array of psychological influences that occur in social units larger than the dyad have been proposed by Parke, Power, and Gottman (1979) and Lewis and Feiring (1982).

The presentation of our results corresponds with progressively more complex elements in a model of the process by which families and children adapt to hard times (Moen, Kain, & Elder, 1983): 1. Social and economic macro change is linked to children's lives through alterations in family relationships; 2. family relations take place in a reciprocal social system which involves mutual accommodation and adjustment between parent and child; and 3. parent–child relations are embedded in a network of family relationships. Thus, change in any one set of relationships inevitably influences others. We view stress in families as an interacting process. This requires identifying both the objective and subjective meanings of drastic change events; the salient attributes of families as a system of interactional personalities; and, finally, the resources individuals bring to change situations.

Harsh Fathers in Stressful Times

The father's behavior during the Great Depression emerges as the critical causal link between family deprivation and children's well-being. Children were most likely to suffer adverse consequences when fathers became more explosive, tense, and emotionally unstable. Four studies using the Berkeley sample have explored the key role of fathers in mediating the influence of macroeconomic change on family relations and children's lives.

The first study examined father behavior as a link between heavy income loss and marital discord. In a second study, we extended these findings to an analysis of the arbitrary and punitive behavior of fathers during the early 1930s. A third project identified circumstances under which men were most and least likely to become explosive and unstable in stressful circumstances, and a fourth analysis traced the interplay of unstable men and unstable families across four generations. Families that suffered heavy income losses become more discordant in the marital relationship, owing largely to rising financial disputes and the more irritable, tense, and volatile state of men (Liker & Elder, 1983). The latter change represented a primary determinant of the abusive parenting behavior of men (Elder, Liker, & Cross, 1984). The more irritable men became under economic pressure, the more they tended to behave punitively and arbitrarily toward their offspring. Finally, economic stress generally accentuated the explosive behavior of men, but it did so primarily when they ranked initially high on this characteristic (Elder, Liker, & Jaworski, 1984). Hard times made explosive men more explosive.

From an intergenerational perspective, irritable, explosive husbands and fathers emerged as a primary source of family instability. In turn, family turmoil and instability increased the prospects of an irritable, unstable pattern of behavior in the lives of children (Elder, Caspi, & Downey, 1985). Within a single generation of the Berkeley study, unstable family relationships made no significant difference in the unstable behavior of men. Their causal role is intergenerational, from family of origin to the behavioral style of children and then to the latter's family behavior in adulthood. The thread of continuity extends across four generations, although its strength varies greatly according to specific conditions.

In all of the Depression research to date, we find that mothers did not become more unstable under economic stress and income loss did not directly increase their punitive or arbitrary behavior. A good many women were relatively unstable before the economic crisis and, just as for fathers, these qualities increased the likelihood of child disturbance. However, only men's behavior linked economic stress to the experience of children in the Great Depression. One possible explanation for this sex difference centers on the more personal nature of income and job loss among men than among wives and mothers. Family misfortune was often regarded as a consequence of men's losses. Women were deprived of family support when their husbands lost jobs and income, but men lost a core dimension of their social significance. Indeed, the overall pattern of men's reactions to sudden economic loss conforms to a theory of force in regaining control over life circumstances (Goode, 1971). Loss of control over one's life situation prompted efforts to regain control. Force is one means to this end.

Economic hardship was often a change agent of family life, and the father's behavior emerged as a critical link between Depression hardship and the family experience of the children. But children's characteristics also played an important role in determining their experiences in hard-pressed families. Project research has identified some attributes and behavior of children that moderated the adverse influence of economic hardship and father maltreatment on their own development and well-being.

Children as Agents of Their Family Experience

The interplay of family stressors and parent behavior is partly a function of the attributes and behavior of children. Increasingly, studies are showing the influence of children on the behavior of parents (Lerner & Spanier, 1978). In this section we review evidence of children as potential agents of their own family experience in the Great Depression, especially as collaborators in their treatment by deprived fathers. Using the Oakland and Berkeley cohorts, our studies identify four factors that bear upon the resourceful or vulnerable status of children and on their insulation from, or increased exposure to, parental maltreatment in hardpressed families: age, sex, physical attractiveness, and temperamental characteristics.

Age and Sex Variations

Drastic change affects people of different ages in different ways. This variability is reflected, in part, by the options and coping resources people of different ages bring to the adaptation process. The Oakland adolescents in *Children of the Great Depression* (Elder, 1974) encountered hard times when they were beyond the years of family dependency and they entered adult-

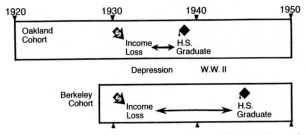

Fig. 1. Interaction of depression hardship and life stage. A comparison of the Berkeley and Oakland cohorts

hood after the economy had begun to revive. By contrast, children in the Berkeley cohort, seven to eight years younger than their Oakland counterparts, were less than two years old when the economy collapsed and they remained exclusively within the family through the worst years of the decade. Figure 1 presents the key contrasts in this comparison of the two cohorts.

Cohort differences between the Oakland and Berkeley samples appear in this age contrast, and in the variable sequence of hard times and prosperity from early childhood to the adult years. Comparison of the Oakland Growth and the Berkeley Guidance samples offered a rare opportunity to examine age and sex variations in vulnerability to economic hardship. Both studies were launched within the same research institute and they relied upon similar measures of social, psychological, and family behavior. The two cohorts also shared the same ecological setting within the eastern region of the San Francisco Bay area.

Children's age and sex during the Depression crisis had implications for their roles and vulnerability within the family. In the Oakland families, adolescent boys and girls in deprived circumstances were often called upon to assume major responsibilities within and outside the household. Girls took on greater household responsibilities when their mothers worked and a good many held paid jobs, as did boys from similar circumstances. Family change of this sort enhanced the social independence of boys. But for girls greater family involvement also meant greater exposure to family discord, tension, and abuse. From theory and research, we expected the effect of Depression hardship to be even more severe in the lives of young children (Berkeley cohort), when compared to adolescents of the Oakland cohort (Elder, 1979). Moreover, this difference should be especially pronounced among young boys in view of their known vulnerability to family stress, marital tension and the abusive behavior of fathers (Rutter, 1979).

In order to assess the effect of children's age in their family experience, we used similar measurements from the Oakland and Berkeley cohorts to construct and estimate a simple causal model. The effects of family deprivation (1929–33) and social class (1929) were estimated on scales of adolescent and adult (age 40) functioning. For both cohorts, income change was measured by comparing 1929 family income and the figure for 1933 (or the worst year). Taking into account the sharp decline in cost of living within the San Francisco Bay area (about 25% in 1933) and the correlation between income and asset loss, all families that lost at least 35 percent of their income were classified as economically deprived. Smaller losses placed families in the nondeprived category. The two-factor Hollingshead index of family standing before the Depression (in 1929) was used in both cohorts. One factor is father's education and the other is his occupational status. California Q-sort (Block, 1971) items were available on both cohorts for the adolescent and adult years. From correlational analyses, we constructed identical sets of measures of psychosocial functioning for the two cohorts in both time periods (see Elder, 1979). The scales tapped feelings of self-inadequacy, goal orientation, passive-submissive behavior, and social competence. Some illustrative results from the analysis of self-inadequacy are summarized in Fig. 2.

In adolescence and at mid-life (age 40), the effects of family deprivation were negative primarily among the Berkeley males. The sons of deprived parents were more likely to be judged relatively low on self-adequacy, goal orientation, and social competence in adolescence, when compared with their nondeprived counterparts. By comparison, no such disadvantage was observed among the Oakland males in adolescence. Indeed, the costs of family deprivation for young boys in the Berkeley cohort were matched in some respects by the developmental gains of older boys in the Oakland cohort. In the latter group, boys from deprived homes were judged even more resilient and resourceful than the nondeprived, while in the Berkeley cohort deprived boys were consistently at a disadvantage.

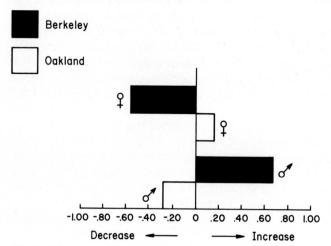

Fig. 2. Effects of family deprivation on ratings of self-inadequacy. Metric regression coefficients (adjusted for effects of class origin, 1929)

Among females, the short-term effects of family deprivation were generally positive in the Berkeley (preschool) cohort and moderately negative in the Oakland (adolescent) cohort. The same pattern emerged in adulthood although it was not as pronounced. At least on psychological well-being, the Berkeley girls from deprived families had more in common with the Oakland boys than with males of similar age. In combination, these results suggest that risk factors vary in type and relative influence along the life course and between the sexes. Consistent with previous research (Rutter & Madge, 1976), family stress seems more pathogenic for boys than girls in early childhood, though not in early adolescence. During the latter period girls appear to be at greater risk than boys (cf. Werner & Smith, 1982). Acute social pressures and developmental change in early adolescence may have contributed to the psychological risk observed among adolescent girls. Other longitudinal studies (e.g., Simmons, Blyth, Van Cleave, & Bush, 1979) are beginning to identify early adolescence as a time of distinctive vulnerability for girls.

The Conditional Effects of Physical Attractiveness

Hard times caught the Oakland girls in transition to the social world of adolescence with its pressures for popularity and dating. The psychic costs of this pressure were especially acute for girls who lacked appropriate dress and material resources for social dating. Earlier analyses (Elder, 1974: Chapter 6) found that the Oakland girls, but not boys, were judged "less well-groomed" during early adolescence if they came from deprived families in the '30s, whether middle or working class. Some implications of this handicap appear during junior high school. On self-reports, girls from deprived families in both social classes scored higher than the nondeprived on social unhappiness and on feelings of being excluded from student activities. Mothers also perceived differences of this sort. Mothers from deprived families ranked their daughters higher on hurt feelings, worries, and self-consciousness than mothers from nondeprived families.

Some of this emotional distress may have stemmed from parental maltreatment within the family, especially from the father. Adolescent girls were less powerful from a physical standpoint than boys of similar age, and consequently they may have been more vulnerable to abusive behavior by the father. This logic applies even more readily to the least attractive girls in the Oakland cohort. In this section we review some evidence on the physical characteristics of girls that may have prompted their maltreatment by fathers in hard times.

Physical maturation often influences the way in which one is seen by others and the expectations that are held by these others (Clausen, 1975). Physically attractive children are more often the recipients of positive attributions from others. Adults also tend to assign less blame to physically attractive children, regardless of the facts (Dion, 1972). Moreover, attractive children generally think well of themselves (Sorell & Nowak, 1981). They rank high on self-confidence and assertiveness, qualities that are not characteristic of the victimized. Overall, we assumed that the least attractive members of the Oakland cohort would be at greater risk than attractive children, and that this risk was greatest among adolescent girls. Research suggests that evaluations along social dimensions are affected not only by the attractiveness level, but also by sex, with more differences appearing between attractive and unattractive females than between similarly grouped males (e.g., Bar-Tal & Saxe, 1976). Hence, we expected attractiveness to operate as a powerful conditional factor among adolescent girls in the Great Depression.

Project research (Elder, Van Nguyen, & Caspi, 1985) tends to confirm this reasoning with newly developed measures of rejecting, exploitive, and supportive behavior of fathers. All measures were constructed from parenting data in 1931–1934. The rejecting parent, indexed by four ratings, is described as "negatively responsive to child," "neglecting," "rejecting," and "not dependable." The exploitive parent, indexed by two ratings, is "overdemanding," and "exploitive." Parental supportiveness is indexed by a single rating. Using a general index of physical attractiveness derived from observational ratings in junior high school, we classified girls as "unattractive" if they had scores below the median. All other girls were placed in the "attractive" category. For each group, we estimated the effects of economic hardship on father's behavior, with adjustments for social class before the onset of Depression hardship. The results are summarized in Fig. 3.

Girls' attractiveness made a substantial difference in the parenting outcomes of economic deprivation among Oakland fathers but not among mothers. Economic hardship increased father's rejecting behavior only when daughters ranked low on physical attractiveness. In addition, if girls were unattractive, family hardship accentuated father's exploitive behavior and diminished his supportiveness. Of additional interest is the direction of observed relationships in the contrasting adolescent subgroups. In two of the models the signs of the coefficients are reversed. Attractive girls were not simply insulated from the psychic costs of economic hardship. In some cases, hard times actually increased the supportive and benign qualities of their fathers. Comparable analyses for attractive and unattractive adolescent boys revealed no significant effects or variations of economic hardship on father's behavior toward sons. The conditional effect of physical attractiveness is restricted to adolescent girls.

The strength of this conditional outcome is especially noteworthy when we consider data limitations, in particular our reliance on reports by wives, children, and staff workers for information regarding the behavior of fathers. The Oakland fathers were never interviewed, whereas their wives were interviewed on three occasions, 1932, 1934, and 1936. Whatever the full implications of this data source, they are likely to work against the attractiveness effect. According to a variety of studies of neglect and abuse in the

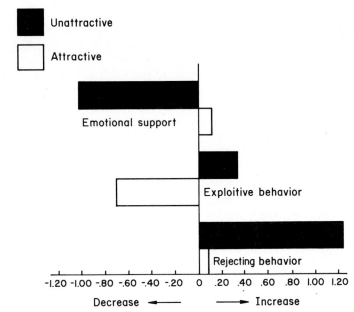

Fig. 3. Deprivation effects on father's behavior toward daughter by her physical attractiveness. Metric regression coefficiencts (adjusted for effects of class origin, 1929)

family (Kadushin & Martin, 1981), the evidence suggests that wives and mothers are apt to underreport the paternal abuse of children. If so, the link between income loss and paternal maltreatment among relatively unattractive daughters would represent an underestimate of the actual causal relation.

Problem Child and Problem Father

Another view of the socially unattractive child is provided by behavior which has negative implications for parents. Examples include temper outbursts and quarrelsome behavior. From research completed on the Berkeley cohort (Elder et al., 1984), it is clear that young boys and girls (about 18 months old) who were observed as problematic in behavior (e.g., inclined toward tantrums, irritability, negativism) before the Depression experienced a greater risk of arbitrary and punitive treatment by father during the worst years when compared to less problematic children. The Institute staff encountered some difficulty in achieving an accurate reading on behavior at 18 months, even with the detailed reports of mother. For this reason, a problem child index was constructed as the best alternative under the circumstances. The index represents the percentage of all assessments on the child (some 35 items) that indicate some form of a behavior problem. Not surprisingly, items that had the most variance and hence dominated the index were typically overt, disruptive behaviors such as temper tantrums.

Problem boys and girls in 1930 were not distinguished by fathers with hostile feelings at that time, but three years later in the Depression they were more likely to encounter extreme and arbitrary (inconsistent) discipline by father than nonproblematic children (r's = 0.28, 0.21). Extreme behavior refers to an exaggerated disciplinary style, such as severe punishment and indifference. Arbitrary behavior refers to inconsistent disciplinary practices. Even with adjustments for the initial irritability of the fathers (1930), these correlations remain the same. In order to specify these relationships more precisely in the Depression years, we estimated the effect of a child's initial problem behavior on the father's behavior under two conditions: among fathers who were hostile toward the child before the economic crisis (in 1930) and among those who ranked below average on this scale. We expected to find the strongest effect of problem children on the arbitrary behavior of fathers in the hostile group.

Contrary to expectations, relatively hostile fathers were not locked into a cumulative exchange of problem behavior with children. This dependency was more common among initially warm or friendly fathers. The status of the problem child in 1930 was only predictive of the father's arbitrariness when the father had a positive relationship to the child in question ($\beta = 0.34$, vs. -0.08). Upon reflection, the findings suggest that father hostility minimized a contingent relationship between father and child. That is, hostile fathers were apt to behave arbitrarily toward children *regardless* of how their children behaved. By comparison, affectionate fathers were more likely to behave arbitrarily in *response* to the problem conduct of their children. Such conduct served to elicit similar behavior from the father.

Our studies of parent–child behavior in hard times began with the premise that influence flows from parent to child and from child to parent. The results we have summarized support this premise. The effect of hard times on children in the 1930s depended on whether fathers became more arbitrary and punitive, but this process also varied according to the stimulus characteristics of the child. Factors such as the child's age, sex, physical attractiveness and temperament conditioned father–child dynamics and the effects of economic hardship. But what about mothers? They are absent from this causal sequence. The following section adds mothers to the picture of hardpressed families during the 1930s.

Unstable Fathers, Problem Children, and Economic Stress: The Moderating Influence of the Mother

The Berkeley children entered the Depression crisis with different relationships to their mothers. Some were the recipients of maternal warmth and affection, while others lacked such nurturance. The implications of this pre-

Depression variation are suggested by the dependency of young preschool children on their family environment and especially on the mother. Maternal responsiveness to child cues affects both immediate and long-term adaptations by children (Schaffer, 1977), and, in times of stress, the emotional support and assurance of mother can protect children from conflicts and overwhelming demands (Caplan, 1976). Using data from the Berkeley archive, we now examine the effects of family hardship and punitive fathers on the behavior of children whose mothers differ sharply on expressed affection. Following this analysis, we consider the effects of children on fathers and of fathers on children under different conditions of maternal affection.

Maternal Affection and Family Stress

Our general model defines children's temper outbursts (1933−35) as the outcome of a process whereby father instability and Depression income loss increased the likelihood of arbitrary behavior by father. The more arbitrary the discipline of father, the greater the likelihood of temper outbursts by his children. According to project research, unstable fathers and heavy income loss were especially conducive to children's temper outbursts, and this influence was largely mediated by father's arbitrary behavior (Elder et al., 1984). The important question at this point is the extent to which the affectional support of mother moderated the influence of income loss and father instability on child behavior.

Before turning to the analysis itself, we will describe the key measures. A more detailed account can be found in Elder et al. (1984). Behavior ratings on the parents in 1930 are based on judgments by an interviewer (with the mother and father) and a home observer. An example is the index of father's instability, a measure based on the average of three behavior ratings: irritable, nervous instability, and tense-worrisome (average $r = 0.51$). The arbitrary discipline of father for 1933−35 represents an average of annual ratings on a five-point scale. Data were obtained from interviews with mothers only. Arbitrary refers at the extreme to inconsistent discipline that expresses the mood of the parent such that the "child never knows what to expect." The child temper tantrum index includes two ratings: severity and frequency of tantrums. Severe tantrums take the form of "biting, kicking, striking, throwing things and screaming." Tantrum frequency ranged from one per month to several times a day. The temper index was created by obtaining the product of severity and frequency of tantrums for 1933−35. This measure captures a key identifying characteristic of children classified as aggressive (Achenbach, 1978). Moreover, severe and frequent tantrums have been shown to be highly contingent on the disciplinary strategies of parents (Patterson, 1982).

To investigate the moderating influence of maternal sentiment, we stratified the Berkeley sample by a pre-Depression measure (1930) of mother's

A. Mother affectionate, 1930 (N=49)

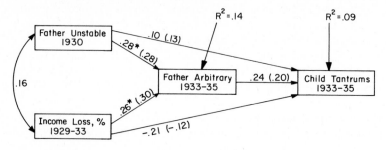

B. Mother undemonstrative, 1930 (N=44)

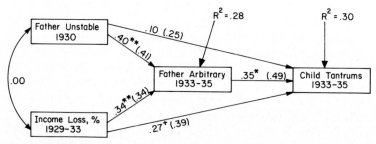

Fig. 4. Linking family hardship to children's lives by maternal demonstrativeness, 1930. Regression coefficients in standard form. Zero-order correlations in parentheses
$^+ p < 0.10;$ * $p < 0.05;$ ** $p < 0.01$

Table 1. Effects of income loss and father's instability on children's temper tantrums by mother's demonstrativeness, 1930[a]

Effects	Family Contexts of Berkeley Children	
	Mother affectionate N = 44	Mother undemonstrative N = 49
Income loss %		
Direct effect	−0.21	0.27
Indirect effect via arbitrary father	0.06	0.12
Total effect	−0.15	0.39
Father unstable		
Direct effect	0.10	0.10
Indirect effect via arbitrary father	0.07	0.14
Total effect	0.17	0.24

[a] Direct effects are represented by standardized regression (path) coefficients; indirect effects represent the product of two path coefficients; total effects represent the sum of all direct and indirect path coefficients

demonstration of affection toward the child. For purposes of analysis, we classified mothers as 'undemonstrative' if they had scores below the median and as 'affectionate' if they had scores above the median. The rating of mother's demonstrativeness is *not* significantly correlated with the antecedent variables in this model.[2]

Mother's attitude toward the study child was found to have implications for father's behavior toward the child under conditions of severe income loss. The results in Fig. 4 suggest that we gain valuable information about the determinants of arbitrary parenting by treating the contrasting family subgroups separately. In particular, a family context defined by an initially undemonstrative mother is most likely to lead to the outward expression of the father's anger through physical and verbal force, especially when prompted by economic misfortune. Moreover, income loss is positively related to the temper outbursts of children only in families with an undemonstrative mother.

When measured prior to the Depression as a sentiment ranging from expressive of affection to undemonstrative, this orientation tells us a good deal about the influence of economic hardship on child disturbance and on the nature of father's action under stress. The overall pattern in Panel B of Fig. 4 (undemonstrative) suggests a lack of fatherly regulation in the household, or the absence of effective normative constraints in hard times. All paths leading to child disturbance are accentuated in this group and the total variance explained is three times that of the corresponding model with affectionate mothers (Panel A of Fig. 4). The aversive dynamics of family stress were relatively limited when mothers were affectionate toward the study child. Family units with strong affective mother–child bonds restrained the arbitrary treatment of children by Depression fathers, and children with warm, affectionate mothers were under some protection from economic hardship. A summary of the direct, indirect, and total effects of income loss and father's instability on child temper tantrums is provided in Table 1. Drastic income loss increased the risk of children's problem behavior, but only in families characterized by a weak mother–child bond.

Mother's initial attitude toward the study child differentiates contrasting family trajectories under the economic pressures of the 1930s. One leads toward the maltreatment of children and their subsequent problem behavior; the other involves a more benign course in which the child is sheltered from the adverse influence of Depression hardship and the punitive hand of fathers. The contrasting dynamics of the two groups highlight the

---

[2] Subgroup analyses may introduce artifactual results if, as a result of selection procedures, the distributional characteristics (e.g., ranges and variances) of other nonselection variables in those subgroups are also affected. Selection by maternal demonstrativeness (1930) does not significantly alter these distributional characteristics of the antecedent and mediating variables included in the reported models.

explanatory usefulness of comparing family processes under different conditions. The mother's relationship to the study child before the onset of hard times emerges as an important contextual determinant of how that child fared in Depression families. Warm affective ties to the child diminished the risk of impairment through economic pressures and the father's arbitrary behavior. Hard times were most likely to turn into bad times when children lacked the affectional and emotional support of their mothers.

Maternal Affection and Father–Child Influences

From previous results we know that children modified the nature of fathers' responses in hard times. Bearing in mind the likelihood of reciprocal influences, the analysis moves now to consider how the mother's relationship to the child modified father–child interactions. Does this process vary by the mother's initial attitude toward the child, whether negative or positive?

Different approaches are available for estimating the reciprocal influence of fathers and children in the 1930s. If we view the timing of influences as a lagged process, the influence model shown in Fig. 5 is most appropriate. This model assumes a recursive process and was estimated using two ordinary least squares regression analyses. The first equation links the problem behavior of father and child in 1930 to the arbitrariness of father in 1933–35. The second equation relates the same independent variables to child tantrums in 1933–35.[3]

This is not a two-wave, two-variable model since we do not have repeated measures over time, yet it is encouraging to note that the 1930 father and child measures substantially affect their corresponding measures in 1933–35.[4] Unstable fathers at Time 1 were likely to be arbitrary in the De-

---

[3] Other, alternative approaches to the estimation of reciprocal influences are available. One approach views the influence process in terms of a simultaneous two-wave stream; at any given point, child influences parent and parent influences child. Estimation of this simultaneous model requires demanding assumptions. For example, to estimate effects in the two-way process between father's arbitrary behavior and child temper outbursts in 1933–35, we must use earlier measures of father and child (1930) as instruments for later behavior. This approach assumes the cross-time effect of the father/child instrument on child/father behavior at Time 2 is indirect, and the unmediated effects are weak. However, attempts to estimate this model revealed both mediated and unmediated effects, rendering any interpretation difficult.
A second approach brings time and sequence to the reciprocal process: for example, parent behavior elicits child behavior which in turn elicits parent behavior. Patterson's research (1982) uses conditional probabilities to represent such interdependencies between parent and child actions. But find-grained measurements over time are required for this type of analysis, a requirement that is not met by the relatively crude temporal categories and global measurements of the Berkeley archive.

[4] Given archival limitations, we were not able to use similar father and child measures in both time periods. Instability was used for fathers since this index represents the most

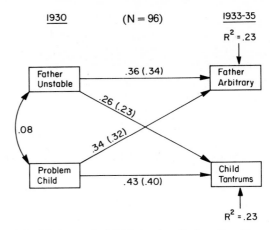

Fig. 5. A two-wave, cross-lagged model of father and child behavior. Each path with a straight arrow is described by a standardized regression coefficient and a zero-order correlation coefficient within parentheses. All regression coefficients are statistically significant at the 0.05 level

pression ($\beta = 0.36$) and problem children were prone to temper tantrums over this time period ($\beta = 0.43$). The evidence also supports the assumption of reciprocal influences between father and child. However, it is impractical to draw inferences about the relative strength of father and child effects. These coefficients are sensitive to the sample variance of the particular indicators examined and either the 1930 father or child measures may include greater error variances which would dilute the cross-time effect.

The important question at this point is the extent to which the affectional support of the mother conditioned these influences. The cross-lagged model was reestimated separately for the contrasting family subgroups (affectionate vs. undemonstrative). These results are presented in Fig. 6. The first equation, linking the problem behavior of the father and child in 1930 to the father's arbitrariness in 1933–35, shows no appreciable difference between the groups. For example, children classified as 'problematic' were likely to elicit the father's arbitrary behavior regardless of maternal sentiments. This significant effect, even in the face of potentially buffering or moderating influences, attests to the strength of children's capacity to influence parents.

Turning to the second equation, we note the accentuation of father and child problem behavior when mothers were undemonstrative. We use the concept of *accentuation* to describe an increase in emphasis of an already

---

relevant measure in 1930. For a pre-Depression measure of problem behavior on the Berkeley children, we used the general problem behavior index that was constructed at age 18 months, or about 1930. The problem child index represents the percentage of all assessments on the child (35 items) that indicate some form of behavior problem.

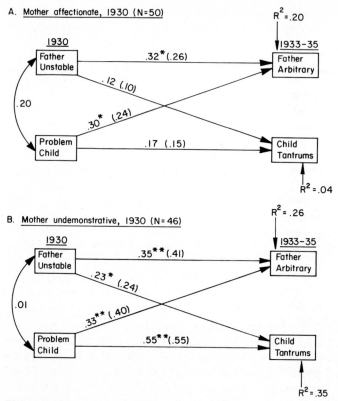

Fig. 6. Two-wave, cross-lagged model of father and child behavior by maternal demonstrativeness, 1930. Regression coefficients in standard form. Zero-order correlations in parentheses. * $p < 0.05$; ** $p < 0.01$

prominent characteristic due to its reinforcement by selected contexts and settings (e.g., Feldman & Weiler, 1976). As expected, the initial problem status of father and child is magnified in the context of undemonstrative mothers. Only in families with undemonstrative mothers were problem children likely to persist in their out-of-control, aggressive behavior ($\beta = 0.55$ vs. 0.17). The father's problem status shows a similar, though nonsignificant trend. In the 'affection' context, initial problem behaviors (both father's and child's) are less pronounced and their variation has little bearing upon the subsequent temper tantrums of children.

The findings summarized in this section underscore the critical nature of the ecological niche occupied by children and their families as well as highlighting major limitations of global descriptive research on socioeconomic factors in the lives of children and adults. All too often research proceeds no further than the demonstration of a simple association between two variables (e.g., socioeconomic stress or change with indicators of child behavior) which are assumed to be ordered in a causal sequence. Project research suggests that this bivariate relationship is more accurately specified by intervening mechanisms, such as alterations in family relationships and the predictability or coherence of a home environment. Moreover, the influence of environmental stressors must be considered in terms of the family context in which they operate (e.g., Bronfenbrenner & Crouter, 1983), and personal relationships within the family should be considered in terms of a network of interactions (e.g., Hinde, 1979). These features are central to the ecological study of human development.

Conclusion

Drastic change and life stress do not have uniform effects on all children. Whether a given child is adversely affected by income loss depends on other variables that moderate the impact of that change. A critical question for research on stressful life events concerns the nature of those variables that determine which individuals are likely to be adversely affected by drastic change and which are likely to be spared its attendant hardships (Johnson & Sarason, 1979). What is different about the children who rise above disadvantage? What are the protective or ameliorating circumstances? Conversely, we may ask, what factors accentuate the adverse influence of stressful times on children's lives?

To understand the impact of economic hardship on the personality and behavior of children requires knowledge of adaptations chosen and played out by parents. The effects of hard times are not necessarily exercised directly. They may be produced indirectly through their disorganizing effect on family relations. Fathers represent the critical link between Depression hardship and children's experience. But the punitive and arbitrary behavior of fathers in the 1930s was expressed only when potentiating factors surpassed compensatory ones. Thus, economic loss increased the instability of fathers who were initially unstable, and thereby increased the developmental risk of young children. The risk was much less for children of initially resourceful fathers who were relatively calm under stress.

Turning to the child, project research identifies several factors that protected children from harsh parenting in Depression families. The physical attractiveness of adolescent girls proved to be a valuable asset, and this resource conditioned father's behavior toward them in hard times. Whether through impression management or implicit attribution processes, children often shaped the way they were treated, and especially their father's behavior. Moreover, under certain conditions, children's overt behavior (e.g., ill-tempered, irritable) accelerated family tensions and the risk of their maltreatment by hard-pressed fathers. Consistent with a social interactional perspective (Patterson & Reid, unpublished manuscript), our findings suggest that characteristics and reactions of victimized children often strengthened and maintained the aversive behaviors of fathers.

To explicate the nature of family dynamics in hard times requires a synthetic framework that links family members. To this end, the dyadic model orienting much of our research proved to be deficient. An exclusive focus on father–child dynamics obscures variability within particular family contexts and ignores the interplay among different family systems. In the Depression era, mothers were not as directly affected by income loss as fathers, but they played a major role in their children's development. To understand the differing, but mutually consequential, roles of father and mother in the 1930s, it is necessary to order them in relation to the sequential phases of economic crisis and family adaptation.

Fathers are prominent in our analysis of Depression families because economic misfortune was typically the first-hand experience of men. Their response to this loss intensified the social consequences of income loss. By contrast, mothers in Depression families stand out as coping and recovery figures. Following the trauma of economic crisis and the impairment of husbands and fathers, the story of family survival often centered on the role of women in the household economy and in the labor force (Elder, 1974), and, as the present findings additionally suggest, in the lives of children. Patterns of family relations (i.e., mother–child) prior to the deprivation event emerge as particularly critical determinants of subsequent family relations (i.e., father–child) and child outcomes. The influence of economic hardship, as well as father's behavior, vary by the family context in which the child resides, and stresses in family life were often countered by the mother's nurturant relationship to the child. These findings are consistent with results from studies of families with a parent diagnosed as having a psychiatric disorder. Rutter (1979) notes that conduct disorders of children in such discordant homes were much less evident if children had a good relationship with at least one parent. Effective coping with difficult times thus represents a product of interacting persons; it is not merely individual behavior in isolation from the actions and attitudes of others.

. External events, such as the Great Depression, can affect children, as well as their parents, in different ways. Drastic changes are not synonymous with stressful changes and hard times do not necessarily foreshadow bad times. The causal sequence bridging Depression hardship and children's welfare is conditioned by a host of individual and contextual factors. These factors are underscored by recognizing children as agents of their own family experience and the multiple relationships which define patterns of family adaptation in hard times.

References

Achenbach, T. M. (1978) The child behavior profile. I: Boys aged 6 through 11. *Journal of Consulting and Clinical Psychology, 46,* 478 – 488

Bar-Tal, D. & Saxe, L. (1976) Perceptions of similarly attractive couples and individuals. *Journal of Personality and Social Psychology, 33,* 772 – 781

Block, J. (1971) *Lives through time.* Berkeley, CA: Bancroft

Bronfenbrenner, U. (1979) *The ecology of human development.* Cambridge, Mass: Harvard University Press

Bronfenbrenner, U. & Crouter, A. C. (1983) The evolution of environmental models in developmental research. In W. Kessen (Ed.), *Handbook of child psychology, Vol. I. History, theory, and methods.* New York: Wiley

Caplan, G. (1976) The family as support system. In G. Caplan & M. Killilea (Eds.), *Support systems and mutual help: Multidisciplinary explorations.* New York: Grune and Stratton

Clarke-Stewart, K. A. (1978) And daddy makes three: The father's impact on mother and young child. *Child Development, 49,* 466 – 478

Clausen, J. A. (1975) The social meaning of differential physical and sexual maturation. In S. E. Dragstin & G. H. Elder, Jr. (Eds.), *Adolescence in the life cycle: Psychological change and social context.* New York: Halsted

Dion, K. (1972) Physical attractiveness and evaluations of children's transgressions. *Journal of Personality and Social Psychology, 24,* 207 – 213

Elder, G. H., Jr. (1974) *Children of the Great Depression.* Chicago: University of Chicago Press

Elder, G. H., Jr. (1979) Historical change in life patterns and personality. In P. B. Baltes & O. G. Brim, Jr. (Eds.), *Life span development and behavior, Vol. 2.* New York: Academic

Elder, G. H., Jr. (1981) Social history in life experience. In D. H. Eichorn, J. A. Clausen, N. Haan, M. P. Honzik, & P. H. Mussen (Eds.), *Present and past in middle life.* New York: Academic

Elder, G. H., Jr., Caspi, A., & Downey, G. (1985) Problem behavior and family relationships: A multi-generational analysis. In A. Sorensen, F. Weinert, & L. Sherrod (Eds.), *Human development and the life course. Multidisciplinary perspectives.* Hillsdale, NJ: Erlbaum

Elder, G. H., Jr., Liker, J. K., & Cross, C. E. (1984) Parent–child behavior in the Great Depression: Life course and intergenerational influences. In P. B. Baltes & O. G. Brim, Jr. (Eds.), *Life span development and behavior, Vol. 6.* New York: Academic

Elder, G. H., Jr., Liker, J. K., & Jaworski, B. J. (1984) Hard times in lives: Historical influences from the 1930s to old age in postwar America. In K. McCluskey & H. W. Reese (Eds.), *Life span developmental psychology: Cohort and historical effects.* New York: Academic

Elder, G. H., Jr., Van Nguyen, T., & Caspi, A. (1985) Linking family hardship to children's lives. *Child Development, 56,* 361 – 375

Feldman, K. A. & Weiler, J. (1976) Changes in initial differences among major-field groups: An exploration of the "accentuation effect." In W. H. Sewell, R. M. Hauser, & D. L. Featherman (Eds.), *Schooling and achievement in American society.* New York: Academic

Garmezy, N., Masten, A. S., & Tellegen, A. (1984) The study of stress and competence in children: A building block for developmental psychopathology. *Child Development, 55,* 97 – 111

Goode, W. J. (1971) Force and violence in the family. *Journal of Marriage and the Family, 33,* 624 – 636

Hinde, R. A. (1979) *Towards understanding relationships.* London: Academic

Johnson, J. H. & Sarason, I. G. (1979) Moderator variables in life stress research. In I. G. Sarason & C. D. Spielberg (Eds.), *Stress and anxiety, Vol. 6.* Washington: Hemisphere

Kadushin, A. & Martin, J. A. (1981) *Child abuse: An interactional event.* New York: Columbia University Press

Kasl, S. V. (1979) Changes in mental health status associated with job loss and retirement. In J. E. Barrett (Ed.), *Stress and mental disorder.* New York: Raven

Kobasa, S. C. (1979) Stressful life events, personality, and health: An inquiry into hardiness. *Journal of Personality and Social Psychology, 37,* 1–11

Lerner, R. M. & Spanier, G. B. (Eds.) (1978) *Child influences on marital and family interactions.* New York: Academic

Lewis, M. & Feiring, C. (1982) Direct and indirect interactions in social relations. In L. Lipsitt (Ed.), *Advances in infancy research. Vol, 1.* Norwood, NJ: Ablex

Liker, J. K. & Elder, G. H., Jr. (1983) Economic hardship and marital relations in the 1930s. *American Sociological Review, 48,* 343–359

Macfarlane, J. W. (1938) Studies in child guidance. I: Methodology of data collection and organization.*Monographs of the society for research in child development, 3* (serial no. 6)

Moen, P., Kain, E. L., & Elder, G. H., Jr. (1983) Economic conditions and family life: Contemporary and historical perspectives. In R. Nelson & F. Skidmore (Eds.), *American families and the economy.* Washington, DC: National Academy

Parke, R. D., Power, T. G., & Gottman, J. (1979) Conceptualizing and quantifying influence patterns in the family triad. In M. E. Lamb, S. J. Suomi & G. R. Stephenson (Eds.), *Social interaction analysis: Methodological issues.* Madison: University of Wisconsin Press

Patterson, G. R. (1982) *Coercive family process: A social learning approach.* Eugene, OR: Castalia

Patterson, G. R. & Reid, J. B. (1985) Social interactional processes within the family: The study of moment by moment family transactions in which human social development is imbedded. *Journal of Applied Developmental Psychology, 5,* 237–262

Rutter, M. (1979) Maternal deprivation, 1972–1978: New findings, new concepts, new approaches. *Child Development, 50,* 283–305

Rutter, M. (1979) Protective factors in children's responses to stress and disadvantage. In M. W. Kent & J. E. Rolf (Eds.), *Primary prevention of psychopathology, Vol. 3. Social competence in children.* Hanover, NH: University Press of New England

Rutter, M. & Madge, N. (1976) *Cycles of disadvantage: A review of research.* London: Heinemann

Schaffer, R. (1977) *Mothering.* Cambridge, MA: Harvard University Press

Simmons, R. G., Blyth, D. A., Van Cleave, E. F., & Bush, D. M. (1979) Entry into adolescence: The impact of school structure, puberty and early dating on self-esteem. *American Sociological Review, 44,* 948–967

Sorell, G. T. & Nowak, C. A. (1981) The role of physical attractiveness as a contributor to individual development. In R. M. Lerner & N. A. Busch-Rossnagel (Eds.), *Individuals as producers of their own development.* New York: Academic

Werner, E. E. & Smith, R. S. (1982) *Vulnerable but invincible: A study of resilient children.* New York: McGraw Hill

X. Adolescents' Changing Values in a Changing Society

K. R. Allerbeck* & W. J. Hoag

Introduction

German youth has been a subject of interest as well as concern among political observers and social scientists alike for some time. One of the reasons for this is the assumption, occasionally borne out by facts, that the youth is a forerunner of future developments. Unfortunately, there is a paucity of good data that can be considered representative of German youth. Although there is an abundance of one-shot surveys of German youth conducted by pollsters, their reports do not present much more than the marginal distributions of the answers to the single questions. Thus, their contribution to knowledge about youth is minimal. Other serious methodological problems, like the distortions caused by the use of quota samples for surveys of youth are present. The main problem however, a point to which we will return shortly, is the lack of comparability between different studies.

We will present here some initial results from a comparative study of German youth.[1] The data base consists of interviews with 16- to 18-year-olds conducted in 1962 and 1983, using relatively large national samples drawn at random from the official registration records of the inhabitants (Einwohnermeldeamtsregister). We will focus on only a few of the substantive topics. Since our concern is also the methodology of studying change empirically, we will present variables that illustrate particular methodological problems in studying change.

* Johann-Wolfgang-Goethe-University, Department of Social Sciences, Senckenberganlage 15, D-6000 Frankfurt/Main

[1] The 1983 survey data were collected by means of the project: "Integrationsbereitschaft der Jugend im sozialen Wandel", funded by the Volkswagen Foundation for the period of Oct. 1, 1981 through Sept. 30, 1984. The fieldwork was conducted by Infratest, Munich. Interviews with youth, born during the years 1964–1967, took place in the spring of 1983. For any 1962/1983 comparisons only the data of those respondents who were 16–18 years old at the time of the interview were used. The 1962 study was funded by the WDR (West German Radio). The fieldwork was conducted by DIVO, Frankfurt. Interviews with youth 16–24 years old took place during the fall of 1962. For 1962/1983 comparisons, only the data of the 16- to 18-year-olds were used. The data from the 1962 survey are available at the German National Survey Data Archive in Cologne (Zentralarchiv für empirische Sozialforschung).

Development as Action in Context
Ed. by R. K. Silbereisen et al.
© Springer-Verlag Berlin Heidelberg 1986

Assertions with respect to change require comparable measurements taken at several points in time. Just how many measurements and at how many points in time is a matter for debate. What is certain, however, is that more than one measurement point is necessary. Although it may appear obvious, the requirement of at least two time points may not be relaxed if statements about change are to have any empirical basis.

Often ignored, but perhaps equally obvious methodologically, is the requirement that the measurements be comparable. Only if the method of measurement remains unchanged is it possible to measure change in the object being observed. Clearly it is not sufficient to compare literary documents from the past with the results of a survey conducted at the present. Any differences reported are not admissible as evidence of change. Differences may be attributed to the fact that literary documents and surveys capture different aspects of reality.

Equally inadmissible as evidence of change are differences between observations made by an observer at the present and his recollection of observations made in the past. This is not only due to the distortion of memory and the tendency to glorify the past, but also to the change in the observation perspective as a result of aging. It is well known, for example, that the world seen through the eyes of a student is different from that seen through the eyes of the teacher. Statements made with respect to change are often merely the result of a change in the perspective of the observer. Widely propagated statements concerning new forms of socialization, for example, may be partly explained by the fact that the propagators of these statements have changed from being the objects of socialization to becoming the agents of socialization.[2]

Recently it has become common practice to subdivide representative national surveys according to age and to interpret differences among these age groups as a form of value change. Such conclusions are admissible only if differences among the age groups are generational and not life-cycle related.

If we are to take seriously the obvious need for measurements at several points in time, then many widely spread theoretical belief systems about change, in general, and changes in values, in particular, would not be adequately supported because of the paucity of adequate data. Methodological considerations with respect to the study of change appear to have only negative consequences. How is it possible, then, to obtain a data base of the kind which would support empirical statements about change (or continuity)?

---

[2] The existence of a *neuer Sozialisationstyp* (new socialization type, frequently shortened to NST), has been postulated with psychoanalytic concepts by Thomas Ziehe (1975). Although empirical evidence is for the most part lacking, this concept has obtained considerable acclaim in Germany. An extensive recent critique of the concept and its foundation is provided by Martin Baethge et al. (1983)

This question was researched by O. D. Duncan (1969) in a short but pro-lific memorandum in which he explored the alternatives and recommended the replication of baseline studies for the measurement of change or con-tinuity. A reference to Duncan at this point is sufficient; we do not intend to discuss his arguments, but rather to use his conclusion as our starting point. We have employed Duncan's preferred strategy in a study of West German youth. Our findings, some of which we will present here, suggest that Duncan's strategy should be supplemented and adjusted. The gener-al conditions for measuring social change will be presented at the conclu-sion.

In our study, we are using representative surveys to compare different generations of youth. At the same time it is intended that our 1983 survey serve as a baseline study for future comparisons. Our goal is to contribute empirically anchored statements about change or continuity. With such a chosen strategy the selection of the baseline study is obviously of crucial im-portance. The baseline study we have chosen for our study was conducted in 1962. This unpublished youth study was conceptualized by L. von Friede-burg and E. Becker and fulfilled the most important criterion: that of using a random sample. In youth studies quota samples dominate, thus making any time comparisons extremely risky. It is primarily due to this criterion that this study was selected.

For any replication of importance is which questions were or were not asked in the baseline study. What a replication study can contribute with re-spect to statements about change is in great part dependent on the researcher who conceptualized the baseline study being replicated. Achievement of comparability requires that the measurement instrument not be changed. This precludes any well intended "improvements". All experience in survey research shows that even small changes in question wording or answer alternatives can result in substantial variation in the distribution of answers. (We are certainly aware, for example, that the following may take place: change in meaning of identically formulated questions, placement effect of questions in a questionnaire, differences in the composition of interviewer staffs and also perhaps differences in the willingness on the part of those se-lected to be interviewed.) To argue, however, that while exact replication is not possible due to the impossibility of controlling all sources of variation, is no excuse for deliberately tolerating the inclusion of even more incompara-bility. Such tolerance of incomparability is unfortunately prevalent with re-spect to comparisons over time. We do not intend, however, to explore these technical aspects in greater detail.

Of greater concern is the question of the importance of a two-decade-old replicated study for the present. Is there not the danger, due to progress in the social science community as well as in society in general, that the ques-tions asked are no longer relevant today? Looking back, it may also be the case that the questions were not even relevant at the time they were orig-inally asked. Did the researchers in 1962 anticipate the present interest in the change in values and the present variations of the issue *crisis?* To ask such questions logically requires that the study conducted in the past be constructed according to the wishes and needs of the present. The impossibility of the realization of such a wish leaves open any speculation about change.

In order to describe the most basic change in the composition of German youth between 1962 and 1983 we hardly needed a survey. We know that there has been an increase not only in the length of schooling, but also in the percentage of youth attending schools leading to higher degrees. Our data, as shown by Table 1, support this.

In 1962 only a minority (19.8%) of German youth were attending school, 38.8% were apprentices and 39.7% were employed. In 1983, however, the majority (59%) were attending school, whereas the minority were either apprentices (32%) or were in the "other" category (8%).

In sociology there has been a debate as to whether there is a separate subculture of youth (note Coleman, 1961; PSAC: youth 1974; Tenbruck, 1962). We do not have direct evidence concerning this, since survey data, by nature, have little direct bearing on this question. Atomistic in character, the sample survey dips occasionally into a social process, collects data from an individual and continues on to the next individual, as if these individuals did not exist within the context of a social structure. Thus, the survey, since it usually deals with one point in time, is not the proper method to settle this theoretical controversy. The appropriate data appear not to exist. We do, however, have survey data that point to some major changes with respect to youth's identification with youth.

There are two items in the 1962 study, which were replicated in 1983, that can be considered relevant in this context. The first question concerns membership in informal groups. The question text and marginal responses are presented in Table 2.

The second question is an item from the Frankfurt A-scale. This scale, which was patterned after the California F-scale by Adorno et al. (1948), was included in the 1962 study (von Freyhold, 1971). The text of the item is: "Most young people today have it too good: it is about time that they learn strict discipline again." Respondents could agree or disagree on a scale ranging from −3 to +3. Table 3 presents the means for 1962 and 1983 as well as the percent of agreement for both time points.

It is evident that young people in 1962 did not identify much with "youth". Since a large majority in 1983 reject this statement, it appears that young people today, however, identify much more with "youth". Even more revealing is an analysis by age: Even though 16- to 18-year-olds might not appear much of a range, there is a trend in the 1962 data. This trend can be seen in Table 4. If this measure can be taken as an indicator of an identification with youth, it is clear that in 1962 the 16-year-olds were more willing to identify with youth, whereas the 18-year-olds were not. The change between 1962 and 1983 is almost dramatic here. The agreement trend has almost dis-

Table 1. Status of german youth 1962/1983

	1962	1983
Attending school	19.8	59.0
Apprentices	38.8	32.4
Employed	39.7	4.6
Unemployed	0.0	2.7
Other	1.7	1.2
%	100.0	100.0
N	872	1528

Table 2. Membership in semipermanent informal groups of young people. Frequently young people are together with friends or other young people so often that they form a permanent group or true *Gemeinschaft* (clique), but not an association or organization. Do you or did you ever belong to such a group?

	1962	1983
Yes, belong	16.2	56.9
Yes, belonged before	3.0	9.3
No, never belonged	80.8	33.4
%	100.0	100.0
N	872	1528

Table 3. Young people have it too good 1962/1983. Most young people today have it too good; it is about time that they learn strict discipline again

	1962	1983
% Agreement	50.2	24.5
Mean response (Scale −3, +3)	0.01	−1.32

Table 4. Young people have it too good by age, 1962/1983

	Mean Response		% Agreement	
	1962	1983	1962	1983
16 year-olds	−0.2	−1.23	46.1	24.5
17 year-olds	0.1	−1.24	49.4	25.9
18 year-olds	0.8	−1.5	53.1	22.5

appeared in 1983 and younger and older respondents alike tend to disagree with the statement.

These indicators, taken together, clearly show that *youth* has greatly increased as a reference group for young people in Germany. Thus, there now appears to be more of a basis for a separate youth culture. This change is particularly interesting in that it has hardly been consciously noticed by anyone before. For our next topic the reverse seems to be true.

There has been a great deal of discussion about value changes and we have some data to contribute to this discussion. It should be noted that these are not, and cannot be, the proper data. Such concepts as *postmaterialism* gained wide acclaim only since the early seventies[3]. Thus there are no baseline measurements from the sixties or earlier. Talking about change without baseline data closely approaches speculation and presenting data broken down by age leaves one with the problem of interpreting the effects as aging or generational. In any event, a substantial portion of this debate has centered on the decline of work values and the dwindling of the work ethic. We do have, however, some data on these points.

The 1962 study included the question: "Everyone has his own opinion as to what work means for his life. Can you tell me which one of these opinions about work comes closest to that of your own?" The four alternatives are presented in Table 5.

It is apparent that there has been a decline, although only a slight one, in the importance of work in one's own life. The table of marginals, however, might be masking more important changes. It was evident from the analysis of the 1962 data that the answers to this question depended on the sex of the respondent, as indicated by Goodman and Kruskal's Gamma of -0.36. In 1983 the answers are less dependent on sex, demonstrated by a Gamma of -0.19. This can be interpreted as follows: for male youth the importance of work has declined, for female youth, increased. The overall trend points towards a decline in the importance of work. The gender gap, although it has narrowed, has not as yet disappeared.

Value changes are mostly observed in the political realm. Since 1978 a new party exists in Germany which draws its support predominantly from young voters. Clearly, this is a new development and there are no baseline data available for comparison. As in the 1962 study, a party preference question was included in the questionnaire. Although the respondents were not as yet eligible to vote, most had, however, a preference.

A comparison of the marginals for the two time points is distorted by the addition of the new party (the Greens). Of greater interest is a comparison

---

[3] The conception and widespread application of the term *postmaterialism* is owed to Ronald Inglehart (1977). This concept has attracted the attention of a number of German social scientists interested in *Wertewandel* (value change). All German data used to investigate postmaterialism share a common fault: they are cross-sectional, from one point in time only, thus making any longitudinal inference rather risky

Table 5. Importance of work 1962/1983. Everyone has his own opinion as to what work means for his life. Can you tell me which one of these opinions about work comes closest to that of your own?

	1962	1983
One could lead a happy life even without work	6.1	8.3
Some work is part of a happy life	38.2	48.6
Without work, a happy life is hardly possible	42.1	37.8
Only by working does one become truly happy	13.1	4.0
%	100.0	100.0
N	872	1531

Table 6. Party preference 1962/1983. Note: Missing data (Don't know, refusals) are not included in the above table

	1962	1983
Like no party	23.9	15.6
Social Democrats (SPD)	25.0	33.2
Christian Democrats (CDU/CSU)	45.3	36.5
Free Democrats (FDP)	4.9	2.0
Greens	–	12.0
Deutsche Partei (DP)	0.4	–
GDP–BHE	0.2	–
German Peace Union (DFU)	0.2	–
Other Parties	0.1	0.8
%	100.0	100.0
N	833	1154

of a higher order. As in 1962, perceived party preference of respondent's father was also asked. Thus for both time points, we can cross-tabulate party preference of the child with party preference of the father. These tables can then be compared.

Although a more refined analytical treatment is required, such as log-linear modelling for example, it is nevertheless apparent that the transmission of party identification in 1983 is as effective as it was in 1962. The only exception is that of the new party, which seems to represent a genuine generational effect. Preference for this party does not demonstrate any sign of rebellion against parental beliefs. This becomes even clearer if one breaks down parental orientation. Voting for the Social Democratic Party has several meanings, depending on whether one is a member of the working or middle class. For the former it is milieu voting and for the latter progressive

Table 7. Party preference of 16–18 year-olds in 1962 by party preference of father

Youth	Father				
	SPD	CDU-CSU	Other party	None	Percent
SPD	65.6	4.9	9.8	5.9	26.8
CDU-CSU	17.2	82.7	17.1	32.4	50.1
Other party	1.8	3.1	65.9	5.9	8.4
None	15.3	9.3	7.3	55.9	14.7
Percent	100.0	100.0	100.0	100.0	100.0
N	163	225	41	34	463

Table 8. Party preference of 16–18 year-olds in 1983 by party preference of father

Youth	Father				
	SPD	CDU-CSU	Other party	None	Percent
SPD	68.3	9.0	29.6	0.0	33.1
CDU-CSU	7.9	66.3	7.4	15.0	39.9
Other party	14.5	12.8	44.4	30.0	14.9
None	9.4	11.9	18.5	55.0	12.1
Percent	100.0	100.0	100.0	100.0	100.0
N	331	454	27	20	832

voting. We found that those children of SPD-fathers having completed more than the required schooling were twice as likely than children of SPD-fathers having completed only the required schooling to prefer the Greens.

Another topic that has occasionally been of concern is the existence of neo-nazism and antisemitism among German youth. Some observers claim that these have been on the increase. We have two items, in addition to the A-scale, to investigate this. The following questions from the 1962 study, for example, were replicated in the 1983 study: "Today when you think of the period of the Third Reich, would you say, all things considered, that it had more bad or good points?" and "Are you of the opinion, that the Jews themselves were partly responsible for what happened to them during the Third Reich or are you not of this opinion?".

The results of our analysis of these questions do not lend support to statements proclaiming a rise of neo-Nazi support among the youth. In fact, the proportion of those answering "more good points" or "as many good as bad points" to the Third Reich question has decreased. In like manner, there is a decrease in the porportion of those maintaining that the Jews were at least partially to blame for what happened to them.

Of perhaps greater significance is the change in the proportion of respondents willing to give an opinion to such questions. With respect to the Third Reich question, 7% of the 1983 respondents answered with "don't know", compared to almost 27% giving this response in 1962. Controlling the proportion of "don't know" response to these questions by sex resulted in the finding that the greatest reduction over time of "don't know" responses occurred among the female youth.

Looking at the distribution of responses for those having an opinion, however, revealed that no sex differences existed, neither in 1962, nor in 1983. One could draw several conclusions from these findings: First, female youth over time have become more willing to express their opinions. This conclusion is borne out by responses to the question as to whether Jews were at least partially responsible for what happened to them. Only 66% of the female youth as compared to 79% of the male youth voiced an opinion in 1962. In 1983, however, 93% of both groups gave an opinion.

A second conclusion which could be made, at least with respect of these questions, is that there is no "female" or "male" opinion. Increase in the size of the opinion pool has not resulted in a change in the distribution of opinion.

It can be argued that the attitudes of youth today toward national socialism and Jews are no longer relevant and that, for them, the period of the Third Reich is only a point in history. As a result, the tolerance of, or willingness to accept other groups cannot be measured by such questions. Of importance today are the attitudes of the Germans with respect to the guest workers. In 1962 the guest workers were not an issue and therefore no questions about guest workers were included in the 1962 questionnaire. In our 1983 study, however, a battery of questions concerning contact with, and attitudes toward, guest workers was included.

The measurement of change with respect to the nature of prejudice or tolerance of other groups cannot be accomplished by exact replication, when, as in this case, the groups as well as the characteristics of the groups have changed. We are presently exploring the extent to which functional equivalents for measurements of tolerance of groups can be employed in the study of change. That is, we are investigating the extent to which attitudes toward Jews can in any way be equated with attitudes toward guest workers. Our findings, at this point in time, are too premature to present here.

In the 1962 study the theme *family*, both present and future, was given considerable attention. Here, we will present only some of the results of replication in this area, mainly those questions pertaining to having a child without being married and future concepts of partnership.

The following question elicited almost complete agreement among the respondents in 1962: "Is it important or not so important for a woman to be married when she has a baby?".

Table 9. Mother–child 1962/1983. Is it important or not so important that a woman be married when she has a child?

	1962	
	Male	Female
Not at all important	0.8	1.1
Not so important	3.6	3.7
Depends	5.4	5.8
Important	39.4	32.8
Very important	50.8	56.6
%	100.0	100.0
N	388	378

	1983	
	Male	Female
Not at all important	3.7	7.6
Not so important	25.8	41.0
Depends	7.0	11.4
Important	50.6	32.7
Very important	12.9	7.3
%	100.0	100.0
N	731	700

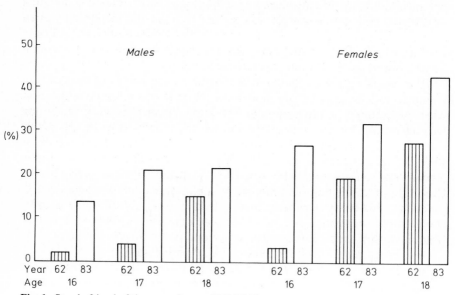

Fig. 1. Steady friend of the opposite sex 1962/1983

In 1962 circa 90% of the respondents, male as well as female youth, considered it to be "very important" or "important" that a woman be married. This almost total agreement voided the possibility of sex differences. In 1983, however, there is much less agreement on this issue. In addition, a sex difference has emerged. Whereas the majority of the male respondents (63.5%) consider it to be "important" or "very important" only (40.0%) of their female counterparts are of this opinion. Female youth today are more likely to give the answer: "not so important". They stress the importance of taking circumstances into account: what is best for the mother as well as for the child.

Strength of religious identification, which correlated with the responses given in 1962, continued to do so in 1983. Those strongly identifying with a religion are more likely to give the response: "very important" or "important". The difference as a result of religious identification in 1962 (Catholics more likely than Protestants to answer "very important" or "important") is also evident among the respondents in 1983.

Change was also apparent with respect to strength of relationship with the opposite sex. Our data support a widely held belief that youth today experience things at an earlier age. In the 1962 and 1983 surveys the respondents were presented with a list and requested to give the letter of the statement that applied to them. The statements were: "I have a fiancee". "I have a steady boy/girl friend", "I have a boy/girl friend". "I have no boy/girl friend".

The graph of steady-friend comparisons indicates that the sex difference present in 1962 is also existent in 1983. Girls continue to have a steady friend at an earlier age than boys. Youth in 1983, girls as well as boys and in all age groups, have more steady friends than the youth in 1962. Whereas a drastic increase occurred among the males between 17 and 18 years in 1962, a smaller increase in 1983 occurs between the ages of 16 and 17. Among the females, an increase also takes place earlier in the 1983 study: between 15 and 16 rather than between 16 and 17 as it did in 1962.

Although the desire for steady relationships has increased among the youth, the desire for future permanent steady attachments, of husbands and wives, has decreased.

Table 10 shows that sex differences evident in 1962 have decreased. Both male and female respondents in 1983 are less likely than the respondents in 1962 to answer "yes" to the question: "Would you eventually like to get married?". A relatively large increase in the percent answering "no" or "don't know" has taken place, especially among the female youth. The result is that among youth in 1983 there is no longer a large difference between girls and boys with respect to their wish to marry.

Our replication of future marriage plans and perspective family size questions in the 1962 study was restricted to the marriage wish question. The possibility of having a child without being married (demonstrated by the responses to the mother-child question discussed above) was not widely en-

Table 10. Marriage wish 1962/1983. Would you eventually like to get married?

	1962	
	Male	Female
Yes	79.2	91.3
No	3.1	1.5
Don't know	17.8	7.2
%	100.0	100.0
N	456	404
	1983	
	Male	Female
Yes	69.2	76.6
No	11.6	9.1
Don't know	19.2	14.3
%	100.0	100.0
N	818	705

tertained in 1962. As a result, a filter was placed into the 1962 questionnaire. Only those respondents not answering "no" to the wish to marry question were asked if they wanted to have children. In like manner, only married respondents were asked if they had children. A "don't know" category was not included among the answers alternatives for the question: "Would you like to have children?".

We were of the opinion that to pursue exact replication in this area would be too costly. It would result in a loss of important information with respect to partnership and desire for children among today's youth. We therefore attempted to allow for the existence of alternatives other than the classic pattern: first marriage, then sex, then children.

To mention just one result: over 80% of the 1983 respondents want to live together before marriage. We can only hope that our question battery in this area is sufficiently broad and flexible to allow for future replication.

We have presented data showing little change in areas where a lot of change was expected and data showing a lot of change where none was expected. In addition, we probably presented some data showing what everybody already knows.

We are convinced that one has to be faithful to the letter in the replication of those questions to be used in any investigation of change. We know that this is not completely attainable, but this goal should be kept in mind.

The primary source of any remaining differences is the variation in institute practices. The 1962 interviews were conducted by DIVO interviewers, the 1983 interviews by Infratest interviewers. What the instructions were in 1962 for reading out response alternatives, for example, we do not know. On the other hand, difficult as it may be, the rule of strict replication, including replicating errors, must be adhered to. Improvements are strictly forbidden, as they destroy the antire process. Only in this way can we measure change.

There have been frequent arguments as to the feasibility of the replication process, due to changes in language usage. Such critics maintain that questions asked at one point in time may have totally different meanings if asked at a later point due to change in language usage and word meanings. Our experience does not bear this out. Instead, it points to a different source of incomparability. This can best be demonstrated by the question as to whether it is important for a woman to be married if she has a child. In 1983 a frequent response to the open ended question: "Why is it important or not important", was that it is possible to live together without being married. In 1962 such a response was, of course, unthinkable. Thus, the question means different things in 1962 and 1983, despite the fact that every individual word has the same meaning at both points in time. In 1962 the implicit choice was living alone with child or living together married. In 1983, the choice is not necessarily that of living or not living together with the father, but primarily that of living together with father with or without a marriage certificate.

A serious problem of the replication strategy, however, is that it greatly underplays the amount of change that has taken place. As a matter of fact, not all the questions of a baseline study will be replicated. Some questions will be considered obsolete, others merely amusing. Such questions cannot be asked if the integrity of a study is to be maintained. Take, as an example, the following question from the 1962 study: "In many cases it is expected that unmarried young people not have sexual relations. Should young people be permitted to have sexual relations before marriage or not? What is your opinion?" To this question, the majority (58%) maintained that sexual relations should not be permitted. The text includes a stated assumption that is plainly invalid today. Hardly anybody, outside of hard-core religious circles, expects this anymore. Thus, we had to drop this question because there has been a tremendous change in sexual morals. But by dropping the question, we can no longer document nor quantify this change.

By omitting questions that appear obsolete, the replication strategy systematically distorts the picture of social change by exclusively focusing on gradual changes and totally omitting changes in kind or of a larger order of magnitude. We have addressed this problem in our study in the following manner. With respect to this topical realm we have included the opposite end of an underlying continuum: "Many young people live together before marrying. Others marry when they want to set up a common household. What do you think will be likely, will you live together with a partner before marriage or live together only after marriage?" For obvious reasons this question has no direct counterpart in 1962. Living together was so rare among young people that it would have been impossible to ask such a question. Although this question is not at all identical to the question about sexual relationships, we insist that the two questions can be compared, not in a quantitative but in a qualitative manner in order to document the changing consensus in an area.

We have presented only a few initial results from our rather complex study. The complete analysis will require considerable time since the data base also includes parent interviews and a mail panel supplement. The result of this analysis will be presented in due course. At this time, however, we are able to summarize our experience in the realm of survey replication. We believe that survey replications have important consequences for both the study of value changes and human development, and in conclusion we would like to stress the following three points:

1. Youth is perhaps the greatest challenge for the replication strategy. Social change occurs faster and questions become obsolete with greater speed than for other populations. A legitimate concern, therefore, is whether replication over a time span of decades is at all possible within this group. We have demonstrated that replication within a time span of over 20 years is indeed feasible. It can yield results that are both highly plausible (after the fact) and not available with other methods. To insure, however, that the data from several time points can be compared it is necessary to devote considerable attention to the fine details of data collection.

2. Replication, as a method, can only be utilized in studying particular types of social change. Only opinions with respect to events, issues, objects, etc. still relevant at the time point at which a replication study takes place can be utilized in an investigation of change. At the time of replication, those opinions which have become obsolete or have just appeared cannot, on the other hand, be used in an investigation of change. Omitting these changes by exclusively focusing on what can be measured by means of identical questions at both time points would produce a distorted view of social change. Thus the replication process must be updated periodically, not only by means of new questions but also by means of new techniques (electronic recording and analysis of answers to open ended questions, for example).

3. Those concerned with adolescent development, for example, are occasionally in danger of postulating a permanent sequence of developmental stages considered to be characteristic for a given society. Theorists of value changes are more likely to commit the opposite fallacy: they tend to provide explanations for a change they assume to have taken place, without first having proved the existence of this change. Survey replication can partially correct this error or bias by pointing out and documenting changes in those sequences considered to be permanent. The data we provided show some of these changes and we are certain that there may be others that could be subjected to analysis in this manner.

References

Adorno, T. W., Frenkel-Brunswik, E., Levinson, D. J., & Nevitt Sanford, R. (1948) *The authoritarian personality*. New York: Harper and Row

Baethge, M., Schomburg, H., & Voskamp, U. (1983) *Jugend und Krise – Krise aktueller Jugendforschung*. Frankfurt: Campus

Coleman, J. S. (1961) *The adolescent society*. New York: Free Press

Duncan, O. D. (1969) *Towards social reporting: next steps.* New York: Russel Sage

Freyhold, M. von (1971) *Autoritarismus und politische Apathie. Analyse einer Skala zur Ermittlung autoritätsgebundener Verhaltensweisen*. Frankfurt: Europäische Verlagsanstalt

Inglehart, R. (1977) *The silent revolution. Changing values and political styles among western publics*. Princeton: Princeton University Press

Tenbruck, F. H. (1962) Jugend und Gesellschaft. Soziologische Perspektiven. Freiburg: Rombach

Youth – Transition to adulthood (1974). Report of the panel on youth of the President's Science Advisory Comittee. Chicago: University of Chicago Press

Ziehe, T. (1975) Pubertät und Narzißmus. Frankfurt: Syndikat

XI. Processes of Peer Influences in Adolescence[1]

D. B. KANDEL*

Introduction

Adolescence is traditionally considered to be the period in life when peer influences are most intense. Because adolescents are still members of parental family units and occupy the social roles of children toward whom parents have since their births exerted important socialization functions, a basic issue in adolescent socialization is the extent to which adolescent development proceeds in response to peer or to parental influences (Brofenbrenner, 1970; Hartup, 1979; Kandel & Lesser, 1972). A pervasive notion is that there is a "generation gap", with adolescents assumed to function completely independent and in opposition to the world of adults. Social commentators such as the late Margaret Mead (1970) or the noted sociologist James S. Coleman (1970, 1973) stress the emergence of strong adolescent subcultures and the increased separation between parents and their adolescent children. The emergence of these distinct subcultures has been attributed to structural changes in social organization: the fact that adolescents spend most of their lives segregated in schools with peers of their own age; the lengthening of schooling; and the reduced responsibilities for participation in the labor force. Insulation from parents and other adults is assumed to result in the elimination of parental ability to influence their adolescent children.

It is this very thesis that I would like to challenge today, a thesis that I believe to be too simple-minded. The understanding of the role of friendships in adolescence that I present here derives from the research on adolescent development that my colleagues and I have carried out over the last decade. Selected findings from that research are reviewed to provide an overview of what has been learned about the nature and the role of friendships in adolescence. By bringing together the results of different analyses, a comprehensive perspective on peer influences in adolescence emerges.

[1] Preparation of this paper was partially supported by research grants DA 0064 and DA 01097 and Research Scientist Award DA 00081 from the National Institute on Drug Abuse. The assistance of Mark Davies and Victoria Raveis is gratefully acknowledged.

* Columbia University, College of Physicians and Surgeons, Department of Psychiatry, 722 West 168th Street, New York, NY 10032, USA

Development as Action in Context
Ed. by R. K. Silbereisen et al.
© Springer-Verlag Berlin Heidelberg 1986

I will address the following aspects of friendships and peer influences in adolescence:

1. similarity among adolescents who make friends with each other;
2. the process of friendship formation and dissolution in adolescence;
3. the nature of the influence of friends compared to the influence of parents;
4. the mechanisms underlying interpersonal influences.

On the Nature of Friendship Studies

Before presenting the results, I need to point out the conceptual and methodological contributions of this research to the study of adolescent friendships. We have examined real-life adolescent friendships, and we have examined them not in isolation but within the context of parental relationships. Thus, in their methodology, these studies differ in important respects from most other studies of friendships. Friendship studies have been carried out almost exclusively among young children, adolescents, and college students. Simplifying to some extent, it appears that specific methodologies typify studies at different stages in the life span. Studies of young children rely for the most part on behavioral observations in the classroom or in the playground, as exemplified by the work of Furman and Childs (1981), or of Berndt (1981). Adolescent studies rely for the most part on the subjects' reports of the characteristics of their friends (Blyth, 1982); the nature of the influence process is inferred from the effect of the perceptions of friends' characteristics on the adolescents' own behaviors or attitudes (e.g., Huba, Wingard & Bentler, 1980) or from the youths' responses to hypothetical situations involving potential conflicts between parents and peers (e.g., Berndt, 1979; Brittain, 1963; Bronfenbrenner, 1970; Youniss, 1980). Studies of young adults rely for the most part on laboratory experimental investigations of interpersonal attraction based on paper and pencil tests administered to college students (e.g., Byrne, 1971). Three notable exceptions with regards to adult friendships include surveys of the general population in which respondents were asked to describe in detail the nature of their social network, including their best friends, carried out in Detroit and in Germany by Laumann (Laumann, 1973; Verbrugge, 1977, 1979) and in California by Fischer (1982). Studies of real-life friendships in which independent data are obtained from one or more friends are rare; longitudinal studies of friendships are even rarer. Newcomb's classic 1961 study of the *Acquaintance Process* still stands as a model of such longitudinal investigations. Other important and more recent research on real-life friendships among children and adolescents includes the work by Hallinan on friendship formation among elementary school children (Hallinan, 1979; Hallinan & Tuma, 1978); the studies of friendships among high school students by Epstein (1978) and Coleman (Coleman, 1961; Taylor & Coleman, 1979; Waldorf

& Coleman, 1971), the further analyses of the Coleman data by Cohen (1977), as well as the work of Duck and his collaborators in England (Duck & Craig, 1978; Duck & Allison, 1978).

Our own studies are based on large scale relational samples of adolescent—best friend dyads and adolescent—best friend—parent triads. Because we obtained independent assessments of each interacting member in the dyads or triads, we could investigate such issues as actual similarity in friendship pairs, the intergenerational transmission of values, or interpersonal influence without having to rely exclusively on the respondents' reports of the other persons' attributes. This strategy has very strong methodological advantages. Indeed, we have demonstrated that the perceptions of another's characteristics, which are generally indexed as sources of interpersonal influences, are partially determined by the perceiver's own attributes which these perceptions are assumed to explain (Davies & Kandel, 1981) or by the perceiver's social roles (Jessop, 1982). In addition, because we followed a sample of friendship pairs over time we could analyze the processes of friendship formation and dissolution, as I will describe in greater detail shortly. Such relational longitudinal samples are relatively rare, but include several of the studies cited earlier (Newcomb, 1961; Curry & Kenny, 1974; Duck & Craig, 1978; Epstein, 1978; Hallinan, 1979; Taylor & Coleman, 1979; Waldorf & Coleman, 1971; Cohen, 1977).

Two major studies were carried out: one in 1965 with Gerald Lesser (Kandel & Lesser, 1972); and a second study carried out in 1971 and 1972. To the extent that similar issues were addressed in both studies, the results of the second one replicate the results of the first. Most of the present data derive from the second study, to be discussed below. Although the data were collected more than ten years ago, most of the analyses pertaining to friendships have been published only relatively recently.

Methods

A large scale longitudinal survey was carried out on a representative sample of the adolescent population attending public secondary schools in New York State in 1971−72, drawn from 18 public high schools throughout the state. Students were given self-administered questionnaires in their classrooms twice in the course of a school year, in Fall 1971 and Spring 1972, at a 5 to 6 month interval. The self-administered structured questionnaire included closed multiple-choice or Likert-type questions. In five of these schools, adolescents were asked to nominate their best friend in school and everyone in the school was questioned in order to simultaneously collect a questionnaire from a focal respondent and from his/her best friend in school. In addition, a questionnaire was mailed to every parent of every student in the 18 schools, alternating mothers and fathers, in order to obtain independent data from one parent for each adolescent. Sixty-six percent of the parents returned their questionnaires.

Fig. 1. Relational samples available for analysis

	N	Per cent of eligible sample	Number in eligible sample
Student–parent dyads	4,033	49.1	8,206
Student–best school friend dyads	1,879	38.3	4,911
Triads: Matched student–best school friend– parent	1,112	22.6	4,911
Panel of friendship pairs followed at 5–6 months interval	959	51.0	1,879

The following samples are available for analysis (see Figure 1):
– 4,033 adolescent–parent dyads
– 1,879 adolescent–best school friend dyads, and
– 1,112 triads of adolescent–best school friend–parent.

In addition, 959 identified friendship dyads could be traced over the 5- to 6-month interval.

Details of the methodology have been reported in several publications (Kandel, Single & Kessler, 1976; Kandel, 1978b, 1983). In the majority of cases, the friendships were of long duration: 73% of the adolescents had known their friend three or more years, only 11% one year or less. Forty-one percent of the choices were reciprocated.

It is important to note that the restriction of the best friend nomination to a best friend in school still allows us to generalize to best friends in general, since in 79% of the cases adolescents reported that their best school friend was also their best friend overall, in and out of school. Furthermore, the very limited relevant data available in the literature suggest that data on a single best friend provide acceptable estimates of the influence of a group of close friends. For example, the zero-order correlation between adolescents' and best friends' educational aspirations has been reported at 0.45 when based on five friends (Otto & Haller, 1979) compared with 0.37 for a single friend (Duncan, Haller & Portes, 1968), these estimates based on the same data set. The similarity in these correlations suggest that social networks are characterized by a substantial amount of homophily.

Similarity in Friendship Pairs

The first theme to be addressed about friendship in adolescence pertains to the characteristics shared in common by friends, since similarity may indirectly throw light on the determinants of interpersonal attraction and interpersonal influence. Who becomes friends with whom? As noted above, most of our knowledge about friendships and interpersonal attraction beyond childhood derives from laboratory studies. These have suggested that similarity in values and attitudes provides the most important basis for interpersonal attraction. However, these results may be determined by the research paradigm that underlies these inquiries, in which individuals are asked to express their degree of liking for a stranger or a fictitious person on the basis of values and attitudes attributed to that person by the experimenter. By restricting information about another person to certain characteristics specifically selected by the experimenter and by requiring subjects to attend to these elements, laboratory studies may artificially distort the relevance of certain factors in interpersonal attraction (Murstein, 1971).

Indeed, results from our research on real life adolescent friendship pairs indicate that the most frequent attributes shared in common by friends are not values and attitudes but sociodemographic characteristics such as age and sex (Kandel, Lesser, Roberts, & Weiss, 1968; Kandel & Lesser, 1972; Kandel, 1978a). Shared demographic attributes are also most important among adults (Verbrugge, 1977; Fischer, 1982). Behaviors, especially the use of illicit drugs, are next in importance. Similarity is lowest on psychological factors and attitudes (Figures 2a & 2b).

The extraordinary role of illicit drugs in adolescent friendships is illustrated further by the next slide (Figure 3) that shows the proportion of focal adolescents who report having ever used marijuana as a function of the degree of self-reported lifetime marijuana experience of the nominated best school friend. When the best friend reports never having used marijuana, only 15% of the focal adolescents report having used marijuana; when the best friend has used marijuana 60 times or over, 79% of the choosers also used marijuana.

Interestingly, the important role of the peer group in the use of illicit drugs is also observed at a later stage in the life span. We reinterviewed a subsample of these adolescents nine years later at the average age of 24.7 years. Perceived extent of marijuana use in one's social networks was the strongest predictor of current marijuana involvement in young adulthood (Kandel, 1984). Social networks for single people included their friends and for those married or living with a partner, the social network included the spouse or partner as well as friends.

However, in noting the seemingly unimportant role of similarity on personality or attitudinal attributes in these adolescent friendships, one must keep two points in mind. First, the assessments that were carried out were limited with respect to the variety and extensiveness of the scales included to measure personality and attitudinal constructs. Second, as stressed by Duck (Duck, 1973; Duck & Craig, 1978), different aspects of personality may be important at different stages in the course of a relationship, with personality attributes more important in the early stages, values being important some time later, and personal constructs, that is psychological meanings assigned to objective phenomena, in the most advanced stage of friendship. (The time intervals defined empirically by Duck in a test of his hypothesis were one,

Fig. 2a. Similarity on selected characteristics within adolescents friendship dyads. (Kandel, 1978a)

Characteristic	All pairs (N = 1,879)	Boys (N = 733)	Girls (N = 1,106)
Sociodemographic			
Grade in school	0.837	0.814	0.853
Sex	0.810	–	–
Ethnicity	0.655	0.604	0.679
Age	0.638	0.623	0.648
Religion	0.370	0.379	0.359
Program in school	0.281	0.310	0.252
Father's education	0.132	0.118	0.139
Use of drugs ever			
Smoking	0.338	0.308	0.350
Drinking hard liquor	0.251	0.230	0.265
Drinking beer or wine	0.228	0.233	0.216
Marijuana	0.459	0.439	0.471
Psychedelics	0.407	0.485	0.360
School activities			
Educational aspirations	0.309	0.280	0.305
Self-reported grade average	0.288	0.296	0.282
Classes cut per week	0.285	0.280	0.284
Time spent on homework	0.229	0.208	0.215
Days absent from school	0.161	0.099	0.197

Similarity measured by weighted kappas
Coefficients significant at 0.001 except where designated otherwise
 * $P < 0.05$
** $P < 0.01$

three, and eight months.) Failure to make the necessary distinctions in the stage of the friendship, as is true of the analyses reported here, could lead to certain null findings. However, analyses where the dyads were classified according to the number of years the members had known each other did not lead to different conclusions. Similarity on such constructs as depressive symptomatology, normlessness, social isolation or self-esteem was low and did not vary systematically as a function of the duration of the friendship, with the exception of depressive mood. There was a slight suggestion that similarity increased with length of association, from 0.040 among friends who had known each other one year or less, to 0.140 among those who had known each other two years, 0.191 among those friends with each other for three to four years but 0.159 among those who knew their friends for five or more years.

Fig. 2b. Similarity on selected characteristics within adolescents friendship dyads. (Kandel, 1978a)

Characteristic	All pairs (N = 1,879)	Boys (N = 733)	Girls (N = 1,106)
Other activities			
Index of peer activity	0.274	0.279	0.271
Attending religious services	0.238	0.208	0.250
Participation in political activities	0.238	0.313	0.182
Listening to records	0.192	0.216	0.174
Index of minor delinquency	0.217	0.123	0.270
Time spent watching TV	0.131	0.112	0.130
Relationships with parents			
Closeness to father	0.074	0.076**	0.057*
Closeness to mother	0.073	0.078**	0.069**
Parent-peer orientation	0.147	0.099	0.123
Intrapersonal			
Political orientation	0.160	0.147	0.165
Depressive mood	0.135	0.100**	0.117
Self-esteem	0.103	0.066, ns	0.118
Normlessness	0.053**	0.032, ns	0.066**
Drug-related Attitudes			
Marijuana use a few times harmful	0.242	0.147	0.305
Marijuana should be legalized	0.234	0.229	0.237

Similarity measured by weighted kappas
Coefficients significant at 0.001 except where designated otherwise
 * $P < 0.05$
** $P < 0.01$

Process of Friendship Formation

To the extent that similarity among friends exists on certain attributes, how is it obtained? Similarity among individuals at one point in time could result from one or both of two processes: selection (or assortative pairing) and socialization. Under selection, similarity between friends would preexist the friendship and would be a causative factor in the association. An alternate explanation for similarity in friendship pairs is socialization, in which similarity develops over time as the result of interpersonal association and its resulting interpersonal influence. An unusual set of relational longitudinal data on stable and unstable friendship pairs and their associated members-to-be, newly chosen members, and relinquished members allowed us to address this issue (Kandel, 1978b).

A sample of 959 friendship pairs drawn from the same schools in the fall and spring of the same academic year was identified. In a number of these pairs (N = 290), the person named as best friend changed over time. Because

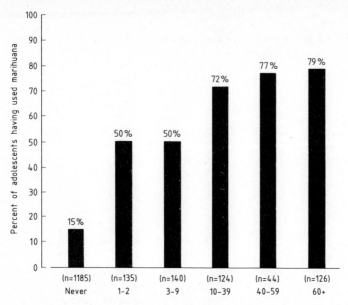

Fig. 3. Adolescent marihuana use correlated with self-reported marihuana use of best schoolfriend. Dyads comprise students and best schoolfriends in five schools. In Fall 1971. (Kandel, 1973)

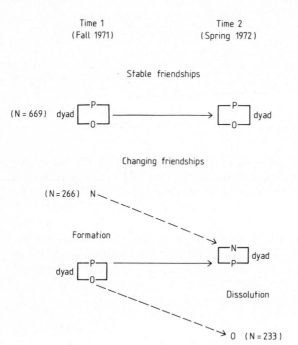

Fig. 4. Available longitudinal data on friendship dyads. P = adolescent; O = old friend; N = new friend

the friendship choices were restricted to school friends, and because everyone in the school was sampled, a serendipitous feature of the data soon became obvious to us. For a number of these changing unstable pairs, information was available not only about the two members of the dyad at each point in time, but also about a third person: Information at Time 1 about the friend-to-be, and information at Time 2 about the former friend (Figure 4). The relatively short time interval between the measurement points allowed close monitoring between potential changes in individual attributes and changes in friendship patterns. These data provide an unusual opportunity to assess similarity among adolescents before they become friends, while they are friends, and after they cease being friends. Inferences could be made about the role of similarity in the formation and dissolution of friendships.

We found that both processes, selection and socialization, are important. Adolescents who share certain characteristics are more likely to become friends and those who associate with each other become more similar over time. We investigated similarity on four attributes that can change over time: marijuana use, educational aspirations, participation in minor delinquency, and political attitudes. Overall levels of similarity in friendship dyads decrease from the first to the last of these four attributes.

Some very interesting patterns emerge (see Figure 5). Levels of similarity vary systematically with the stage of the friendship: whether it is in the process of formation, in a stable phase, or has recently dissolved. Similarity in existing friendships measured at Time 1 shows differences in levels according to the subsequent fate of the friendship, a fate that was not yet known at the time of the initial measurement. These patterns are most striking for marijuana use. When the pairs are classified according to their subsequent history, those that would dissolve between the fall and the spring of the school year are characterized by lower similarity *prior to the dissolution* (see row 1) than those that remained stable (row 4). Newly formed pairs are more similar than pairs of friends-to-be (row 3 versus row 2). Among the stable pairs, similarity further increases over time, as can be noted by comparing row 5 with row 4. The highest similarity is observed among stable reciprocated pairs (row 7); stable unreciprocated pairs have much lower similarity. Interestingly enough, at Time 1, *similarity is higher among friends-to-be* (row 2) *than among existing friendships that are going to dissolve over the next several months* (row 1). *As regards marijuana use, similarity is lowest in the unstable friendships, both prior to the dissolution* (row 1) *and especially afterwards* (row 6). Similar patterns are obtained among the other three characteristics: educational aspirations, political attitudes, and participation in minor forms of delinquency, although the differences are most striking with respect to marijuana and least striking with respect to levels of educational aspirations. Similarity is lowest prior to the dissolution of the friendship and after its dissolution; it is highest during the active phase of the friendship itself.

Fig. 5. Homophily* on behaviors and attitudes among friendship dyads at various stages of formation and dissolution. (Kandel, 1978 b)

Type of friendship dyad**		Time when homophily assessed+	Frequency current marijuana	Educational aspirations	Political orientation	Minor delinquency
1. Unstable: changed friend at T2	A_1F_1	Time 1	0.239	0.327	0.145	0.158
2. Friends-to-be at T2	A_1N_1	Time 1	0.327	0.348	0.107	0.248
3. New friends	A_2F_2	Time 2	0.405	0.406	0.106	0.296
4. Stable pairs	A_1F_1	Time 1	0.451	0.349	0.201	0.255
5. Stable pairs	A_2F_2	Time 2	0.505	0.382	0.248	0.286
6. Former friends (Friends at T1)	A_2O_2	Time 2	0.220	0.380	0.185	0.167
7. Stable pairs: Reciprocated	A_1F_1	Time 1	0.580	0.369	0.263	0.307
8. Stable pairs: Unreciprocated	A_1F_1	Time 1	0.302	0.327	0.127	0.203

* As measured by Kendall's T_B

** A = Adolescent chooser; F = friend chosen; N = friend-to-be; O = former friend

+ Time 1 = fall; Time 2 = spring

It is clear that the sharing of certain characteristics contributes to interpersonal attraction and is strengthened further as the result of association. Statistical analyses (Kandel, 1978b) indicate that selection and socialization are about equal in importance in contributing to resulting levels of intrafriendship similarity or agreement observed at one point in time.

On the Relative Influence of Parents and Peers

Given that adolescents share similarity in various behavioral and attitudinal domains with their friends and that similarity increases further as the result of association, what is the overall role of peer influence in the adolescent's life? How strong is that influence relative to the influence of other potential sources of socialization, especially parents?

My thesis is that both parents and peers are influential, but that each have their realms of influence. The proper question to ask is not: To what extent are adolescents under the general influence of their friends as compared to their parents? But: What are the areas of influence for friends and what are the areas of influence for parents? Indeed, in certain areas, peers are most influential; in other areas, parents are the influential force. For issues and concerns of immediate relevancy to the adolescent's life, such as drug involvement, peers play a crucial role. For issues relevant to basic values, such as religiosity, and to the adolescent's future, such as educational aspirations, parents are much more important than peers.

These processes are illustrated strikingly when one considers interpersonal influences in two different realms, marijuana use and educational aspirations, for the same group of adolescents in the sample of matched adolescent–best school friend–parent triads.

Two alternative explanations of adolescent's involvement in illicit drugs have been posited. According to one interpretation, adolescent involvement in illicit drugs results exclusively from peer influences; that is, participation in a drug subculture and association with other drug using peers. According to an alternative interpretation, even a behavior such as marijuana use, which is typical of the youth culture and deviant according to adult standards, could represent continuity between the generations and constitute a juvenile manifestation of behaviors engaged in by adults. Adolescent drug users may come from families in which the parents themselves use a variety of drugs, either socially accepted drugs, such as alcohol, or medically prescribed psychoactive drugs, such as tranquilizers or stimulants.

In order to test these two alternative hypotheses, the drug behavior of focal adolescents was examined as a function simultaneously of the parents' self-reported use of alcohol (or medically prescribed psychoactive drugs) and of the best school friend's use of marijuana (Kandel, 1973, 1974; Kandel & Andrews, in press; Kandel, Kessler & Margulies, 1978a, b; Kandel, Margulies & Davies, 1978). Figure 6 shows lifetime prevalence rates of ado-

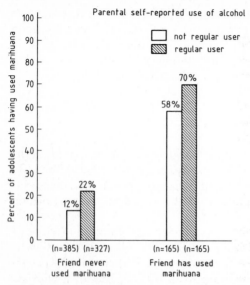

Fig. 6. Adolescent marihuana use correlated with self-reported marihuana use of best schoolfriend and self-reported alcohol use of parents. Regular user uses alcohol at least once a week

lescent marijuana use as a function of the best friend's marijuana experience and parental drinking.

While parents and best friends both have an independent effect on adolescent's marijuana use, the effect of peers is much larger than the effect of parents. This is best seen in those triads in which the adolescent is exposed to conflicting role models because parent's and friend's behaviors diverge, one using drugs and the other not. When faced with such conflict, adolescents are much more responsive to peers than to parents. In this particular sample, 58% of adolescents used marijuana when their best friends also used marijuana although their parents did not drink alcohol (distilled spirits) regularly. By contrast, only 22% of adolescents used marijuana when their parents drank regularly but their best friends had not used marijuana. Parental influence can, however, work synergistically with and potentiate peer influence. The highest rates of adolescent marijuana use (70% in this sample) occurred when both parent and peer reinforced each other's influence on the adolescent; the lowest rate (12%) when neither used drugs. Given particular patterns of peers' use of drugs, parental behavior becomes important in moderating peer influences. Children of nondrug using parents are somewhat *less* likely to be using drugs than their peers, whereas children of drug using parents are *more* likely to do so. The same trends appear when the parental behavior is indexed by parental use of medically prescribed drugs, or when the adolescent's behavior is the drinking of hard liquor. When adolescent's drinking of hard liquor is examined as a function both of drinking

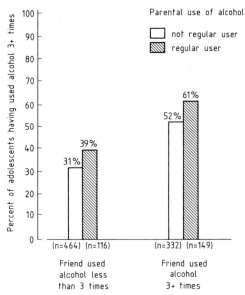

Fig. 7. Adolescent alcohol use correlated with self-reported alcohol use of best school-friend and self-reported alcohol use of parents. Regular parental user uses alcohol at least once a week

by parents and by the best school friend, results similar to those with respect to marijuana are observed, although the differences among the groups are not as striking (see Figure 7). The preeminent influence of peers as compared to that of parents is still very evident.

Estimates of influence based on a causal path model indicate that the total modeling effect of peer marijuana use on adolescent marijuana use is ten times as high as the effect of parental alcohol use among girls (0.52 versus 0.05) and almost seven times higher among boys (0.47 versus 0.07) (see Figure 8).

Completely opposite patterns of influence appear in connection with the formation of educational aspirations in *these same triads of respondents.* Levels of educational aspirations were examined as a function of the parent's aspirations for their children and the best friend's aspirations for themselves (Davies & Kandel, 1981). The effect of parents on adolescent's aspirations is much stronger than the effect of the best friend, a conclusion also reached in our earlier study (Kandel & Lesser, 1969). The differential impact of parents and peers on adolescents' college aspirations is displayed graphically on the next figure (Figure 9). The contrast with drug behavior is striking. Coefficients estimated in a causal path model indicate that the effect of parents is several times as strong as the effect of the best friend: seven times as strong in the case of boys and one and a half times as strong in the case of girls (Figure 10).

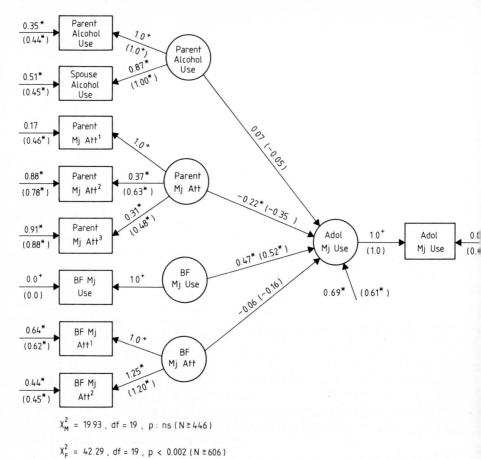

Fig. 8. Model of interpersonal influences of parents and peers on adolescent marijuana use. Based on self-reports by parents and peers. Standardized coefficients for males (N=446) and for females (N=606) in parentheses.
Mj Att 1 = Believes casual marijuana use is harmful; *Mj Att 2* = Believes regular marijuana use is harmful; *Mj Att 3* = Parent is not tolerant of child's marijuana use.
* greater than twice standard error; + fixed parameter

Furthermore, there is also some inferential evidence that parental influence may have a longer lasting impact than the influence of peers made at a particular point in time. Suggestive differences appear in the predictive power of parental and peer influences in explaining initiation to marijuana use in longitudinal investigations that make these predictions over differing time intervals. When the interval and time lag is short, as the five to six month interval of our own study, peer influence is much stronger than parental influence (Kandel, et. al, 1978 a, b). Over a longer three year interval,

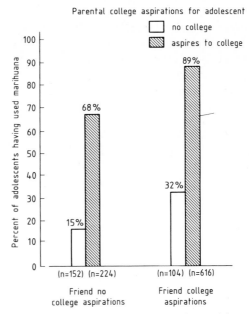

Fig. 9. Adolescent college aspirations correlated with self-reported aspirations of best schoolfriend and self-reported parental aspirations for the adolescent

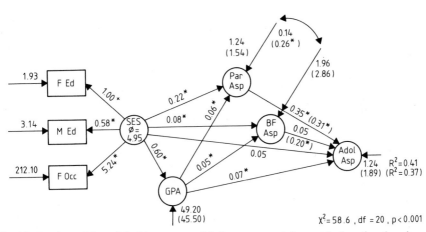

Fig. 10. Psychosocial model of interpersonal influences on adolescents' educational aspirations. Parental influence measured by the parent's self-report of aspirations for their child (N = 762). Standardized coefficients for males and females (in parentheses) are presented. Single coefficient is presented for parameters constrained to be equal across sex. Variables: F Ed = Father's education; M Ed = Mother's education; F Occ = Father's occupation; SES = Socioeconomic status; GPA = Grade point average; BF Asp = Friend's educational aspiration; Par Asp = Self-reported parental aspiration; Adol Asp = Adolescent's educational aspiration. + Fixed parameter; * greater than twice standard error (Davies and Kandel, 1981)

by contrast, other investigators found that peer factors did not have any effects (Brook, Lukoff & Whiteman, 1980). Similarly, Lucas, Grupp & Schmitt (1975) found that perceived marijuana use by college students' reference group in the freshman year weakly predicted marijuana initiation two years but not four years later. Because peer attachments may change relatively rapidly over the course of adolescence, the results suggest an important hypothesis about the nature of peer influence to be tested in future work. Namely, that peer influences are immediate and relatively transitory in comparison to parental influences.

Differentiation of Adolescent Subcultures

Not only must peer versus parental influences be conceptualized in terms of specific issues, but peer influences and peer groups themselves must be differentiated according to their prevailing orientation. Not all peer groups promote an antiadult ideology. There exist striking differences in the behaviors and values of adolescents in different adolescent subgroups (Kandel, 1978 c). In our sample of adolescents, two contrasting subgroups were identified among all the adolescents who interacted actively with their peers. An index of degree of peer interaction was constructed based on five items that measured the frequency of getting together with friends outside of school, dating, attending parties, hanging around with groups of kids, and driving around with friends. Adolescents scoring in the upper third of the distribution were defined as high in peer involvement. We then classified these high interacting youths according to the extent of perceived marijuana use among their friends. Adolescents answering that "most" or "all" of their friends had used marijuana (10.3% of the sample) were considered to move in circles with high levels of exposure to marijuana use; they were contrasted to those reporting that "none" of their friends were users (6.7% of the sample). Both groups of adolescents were actively involved with their peers, as reflected, for example, in the fact that 59% and 65% respectively, reported seeing their best friend daily out of school. These two groups are characterized by very different values, orientations and behaviors (Figure 11). Compared to members of nonmarijuana using groups, those who belong to marijuana using groups are more likely to be using other drugs, to be less close to their parents but closer to their friends, to perform less well in school, to be less religious, to be more depressed, and to hold more liberal political attitudes.

That different peer groups and cliques are different in their behaviors and attitudes appears an obvious and trite finding. Obviously, peer groups are going to be different to the extent that their individual members share different attributes. Yet, in discussions of peer influences in adolescence, these variations and differentiations are most often disregarded and the discussions are oriented as if all peer groups were consistently antagonistic

Fig. 11. Variations in adolescent subcultures. (Kandel, 1978 c)

Adolescent characteristics	High peer involvement	
	No friend uses marijuana %	Most friends use marijuana %
Drug use:		
Ever used hard liquor	65	93
Ever used marijuana	5	89
Ever used other illicit drugs	9	76
Parental relationships:		
High closeness to mother (index)	64	40
High closeness to father (index)	55	33
Respect parents' opinions more than friends	50	30
High on index of peer orientation	32	56
Would continue to see friends even if parents objected	62	90
Academic performance:		
Absent from school 2 days or less since past year	27	11
Overall grade average: A + B	51	41
Aspires to college	34	38
Spends 1–1/2 hours or more on homework every day	32	15
Intrapersonal characteristics:		
Attends religious services 1–2 times a month	40	19
Political beliefs: is liberal, radical	29	62
High on depression index	26	45

toward adults. As documented by the data we have presented, the crucial factor in the adolescent's feelings toward adults is not involvement in peer groups per se but involvement in certain groups, for example a group in which the members use marijuana. A high degree of interaction with peers can coexist without necessary rejection of parents.

Processes of Interpersonal Influence

The last issue I would like to address pertains to processes of interpersonal influence. To the extent that adolescents influence each other, how does this influence come about? Social learning theory provides a useful framework for addressing the question (Akers, Krohn, Lanza-Kaduce & Radosevich, 1979; Maccoby, 1968; Bandura & Walters, 1963). Interpersonal influence can arise out of two processes: (1) imitation, in which one person models the behavior or values of another; and (2) social reinforcement, in which one per-

Fig. 12. Modeling versus defining: Parental and peer effects on ongoing adolescent drug behavior. Standardized path coefficients obtained in Lisrel models

	Alcohol		Marijuana	
	Boys	Girls	Boys	Girls
Parental				
Attitude	0.06	−0.02	−0.22*	−0.35*
Alcohol use	0.30*	0.12*	0.07	0.05
Best friend				
Attitude	−0.02	0.02	−0.06	−0.16
Drug use	0.23*	0.36*	0.47*	0.52*

son adopts the values of another which in turn affects his or her behavior. These two principles of social learning correspond to the functions of significant others as role models, on the one hand, and as definers, on the other (Woelfel & Haller, 1971).

A test of these two hypotheses was carried out with respect to ongoing use of alcohol and marijuana. We examined the effects of the significant others' self-reported use and attitudes about each drug on the focal adolescent's own use of that same drug. The test for peers could be carried out with more precision than for parents, since the drug behaviors and drug related attitudes were the same as those of the focal respondent, either alcohol or marijuana. Modeling of parental drug behavior was indexed by the consumption of hard liquor (distilled spirits) since very few parents had used marijuana. We found modeling of peers' drug use to be consistently a stronger factor than social reinforcement (Figure 12). The influence of parents, by contrast, appears to derive from their role as definers of norms and standards with respect to marijuana, and as role models to be imitated with respect to drinking of alcohol.[2] The only other investigators to have addressed this issue, on the basis of perceived characteristics of parents and peers in a small sample of adolescents (N = 149), concluded that peers were influentials as role models and parents as the definers of standards (Biddle, Bank & Marlin, 1980).[3]

---

[2] These results, however, may be partly determined by the format of the questions, since identical drugs were asked about to measure modeling of peers by the adolescents but not modeling of parents.

[3] Analyses reported elsewhere suggest also that the relative impact of parents and peers as role models and as definers for drug involvement varies not only depending upon the particular drug, but also for initiation as compared to ongoing use. Parents have stronger influence as role models in the initiation phase of involvement in a particular drug as compared to later phases, while the reverse is true for peers (Kandel & Andrews, in press).

Boys and Girls

Adolescent friendships and peer influences have been discussed without any differentiation being made regarding the adolescent's sex. Yet, there are both similarities and differences in adolescent friendships between boys and girls. The trends that we have observed will be briefly summarized. General processes underlying the formation and dissolution of friendships are very similar for both sexes, as are the factors underlying interpersonal attraction. Differences appear, however, in the relative influence of parents and peers. Girls, in general, appear to be more generally receptive than boys to interpersonal influences, whether those of parents or of their friends, and within this trend, to be more influenced by their peers than by their parents. We found this to be true both as regards involvement in drug use (Margulies, Kessler & Kandel, 1977) and the formation of educational aspirations (Davies & Kandel, 1981). The greater susceptibility of girls than boys to interpersonal influences is consonant with results reported by others and the observation that girls tend to form a greater number and more intimate ties than boys (Blyth, Hill & Thiel, 1982; Eder & Hallinan, 1978; Epstein, 1978; Hansell, 1981; Hartup, 1983; Kon, 1981; Maccoby & Jacklin, 1974).

Conclusion

The findings reviewed here provide only a modest beginning understanding of the role of friendships in adolescent development.

Longitudinal sociometric data provide insights into processes underlying the formation and dissolution of friendships and the nature of peer influence that are not available from cross-sectional data. Adolescents coordinate their choice of friends and their behaviors and attitudes, in particular the use of marijuana, so as to maximize congruency within the friendship dyad. If there is a state of unbalance, such that the friend's attitude or behavior is incongruent with the adolescent's, the adolescent will either break off the friendship and seek another friend or will keep the friend and modify his or her own behavior and attitude.

Prior similarity (or homophily) on a variety of behaviors and attitudes is a determinant of interpersonal attraction as documented by the finding that friendships in the process of formation are more similar than friendships that will dissolve. Similarity increases further as the result of sustained association. Thus, similarity between friends at one point in time results from two complementary processes, selection and socialization, whereby adolescents who share certain prior attributes tend to associate with each other and subsequently tend to influence each other as the result of continued association. While the importance of selection and socialization varies for different areas of adolescents' lives, the respective importance of each process within each area is approximately equal.

The finding that selection and socialization are approximately equal in importance has important implications for much of the published literature on the degree of interpersonal influence attributed to peers. Indeed, much of this influence is inferred from observed similarity at one point in time between friends, either on the basis of independent self-reports but most often on the basis of perceived attributes of the friend. For example, in investigations of educational aspirations or of involvement in illicit drugs, interpersonal influence is inferred on the basis of (observed or perceived) current similarity in aspirations or marijuana use among friends. The results presented here lead to the conclusion that these estimates are inflated, since they fail to take into account the role of prior similarity in friendship formation.

The data also document clearly that both parents and peers can have strong influences on adolescents, the degree of influence depending upon the arena of interest. The results of our investigations, and those of others, support unequivocally the conclusion that peer influences predominate on current lifestyles, while parental influences are especially strong with respect to basic values and future life goals and aspirations (e.g., Brittain, 1963; Jennings & Niemi, 1974; Troll & Bengston, 1979). Furthermore, parents and peers are not necessarily antagonistic to each other. As reported elsewhere, there can be continuity of values across the generations and parents and their adolescent children can maintain close relationships with one another (Kandel et al., 1968; Kandel & Lesser, 1972). A high proportion of adolescents, at least half the sample, report feeling extremely or very close to their mothers (62%) and their fathers (51%). Exclusive theories of interpersonal attachment in adolescence that stress attachment either to peers or to parents are too simplistic. Our task is to specify the domains of life and the conditions under which one type of influence predominates over the other.

Furthermore, to the extent that interpersonal influences of peers operate, they are more the result of modeling than of social reinforcement, while parental influence derives in part from the role of parents in setting standards and promulgating values for behaviors.

These insights provide a very modest understanding of the process of peer influences and of the role and nature of friendships in adolescence. The limitations of this understanding are many. No attention has been paid to individual factors, such as stage of cognitive or personality development, that may influence the type of developing interpersonal interactions (Epstein, 1978; Youniss, 1980). Hansell (1981), for example, has documented that level of ego development is related to the nature of dyadic and clique interactions among adolescent girls, with those at the middle levels most likely to be involved in reciprocated dyadic relationships. Although balance (Heider, 1958) and social exchange (Emerson, 1976; Homans, 1961) theories provide the most popular explanatory frameworks for conceptualizing interpersonal relations, our understanding of the rewards and costs that underlie adolescents' choice of friends is primitive. Yet, progress can only be made if more sophisticated accounting schemes that specify the kinds of needs, interests and power that individuals have in and toward each other and how these elements affect dynamically the nature of interpersonal exchanges are developed and tested (Taylor & Coleman, 1979; Coleman, 1983). Furthermore, dyadic involvements represent but a limited aspect of peer influences. The adolescents' relationships to their larger and more complex peer networks must also be examined. Thus, children in elementary and junior high school have been reported by one investigator (Hallinan, 1979) to name five persons when asked to nominate their best friends in school without restrictions as to number of nominations. Future research on adolescent friendship ought to stress longitudinal field surveys based on large relational samples and careful monitoring of developmental changes in adolescent behaviors and values.

Many additional issues relevant to our understanding of adolescent friendships are unresolved. I would like to speculate about two issues in particular. One question is why do peer groups come to have the prominence that they have in adolescence? The answer, I would suggest, is found in structural societal factors, on the one hand, and in biological factors, on the other. The importance of peers in adolescence may represent the conjunction of two conditions. One condition is the segregation of young people in schools, which are social structures that are completely age stratified and age homogenous (Coleman, 1973). This setting provides the restricted age range of like-aged persons from whom young people can choose their friends, and leads to the absence of ties with other persons of different ages in society (Coleman, 1973). As stressed by Feld (1981, 1982), people select their friends from the different foci around which their activities are organized, foci being "social, psychological, legal or physical objects", such as families, schools, or work settings (Feld, 1981: 1016). These foci create structural constraints on the types of interpersonal choices that individuals can make. Because such settings are commonly homogenous with respect to age, association with age-similar individuals is likely to result over and beyond any specific overt preference for friendship with same-age individuals. Furthermore, internal organizational features of these foci may create additional differential opportunities for association with specific types of persons, as is true of track placement or classroom organization within schools (Karweit, Hansell & Ricks, 1979). As stressed by James Coleman (1973), these structural characteristics and social conditions come to affect the way young people behave: their increasing reliance and psychic attachment to one another and their increasing drive for autonomy from adults.

The second condition that favors the emergence of reliance on peer groups is the experience of the same biological event within a relatively narrow age range, namely puberty (Petersen & Spiga, 1982). Interpolating from Festinger's (1954) theory of social comparison and Schachter's work on affiliation and anxiety (Schachter, 1959), Petersen has suggested that the occurrence of extensive physiological changes coupled with uncertainty about how to handle these changes intensifies adolescents' need for affiliation. Schachter's experimental studies suggest that anxiety would intensify the need of adolescents to associate with other young people who experience the same biological changes. Furthermore, adolescents would also prefer to associate with other adolescents in order to determine appropriate standards. "Uncertainty about the capacity to adapt causes the adolescent to look to peers not only for ways to adapt but also for comparisons against which to measure his or her actions." (Petersen & Spiga, 1982: 519)

A second issue concerns the functions played by variations in the relative salience of peers and parents in different arenas of life. The differentiated attachment to peers and to parents across issues that is observed in adolescence may represent an important structural mechanism with positive functional properties for social systems. Differentiated attachment creates solidarity within and across generations and in this way insures generational continuity and stable evolution of social life across different cohorts.

The last several years have witnessed an explosion of theoretical and methodological discussions of interpersonal dyadic relationships (e.g., Burgess & Huston, 1979; Duck & Gilmour, 1981 a, b, c) and more recently of social networks (e.g., Burt & Minor, 1983; Mardsen & Lin, 1982). The study of adolescent friendships should be integrated within this broader intellectual tradition. Ideally, our understanding of friendships in adolescence will be enhanced by models that incorporate structural, biological, and personality factors within a developmental framework.

Acknowledgements. The assistance of Mark Davies and Victoria Raveis is gratefully acknowledged.

References

Akers, R. L., Krohn, M. D., Lanza-Kaduce, L., & Radosevich, M. (1979) Social learning and deviant behavior: A specific test of a general theory. *American Sociological Review, 44,* 635–655

Bandura, A. & Walters, R. H. (1963) *Social learning and personality development.* New York: Holt

Berndt, T. J. (1979) Developmental changes in conformity to peers and parents. *Developmental Psychology, 15,* 608–616

Berndt, T. J. (1981) Prosocial behavior between friends and the development of social interaction patterns. Paper presented at the Biannual Meeting of the Society for Child Development, Boston, April

Biddle, B. J., Bank, B. J., & Marlin, M. M. (1980) Parental and peer influence on adolescents. *Social Forces, 58,* 1057–1079

Blyth, D. A. (1982) Mapping the social world of adolescents: Issues, techniques and problems. In F. C. Serafica (Ed.), *Social-cognitive development in context.* New York: Guilford

Blyth, D. A., Hill, J. P., & Thiel, K. S. (1982) Early adolescents' significant others: Grade and gender differences in perceived relationships with familial and non-familial adults and young people. *Journal of Youth and Adolescence, 11,* 425–449

Brittain, C. V. (1963) Adolescent choices and parent—peer cross-pressures. *American Sociological Review, 28,* 385—391

Bronfenbrenner, U. (1970) Reaction to social pressure from adults versus peers among Soviet day school and boarding school pupils in the perspective of an American sample. *Journal of Personality and Social Psychology, 15,* 179—189

Brook, J. S., Lukoff, I. F., & Whiteman, M. (1980) Initiation into adolescent marihuana use. *Journal of Genetic Psychology, 137,* 133—142

Burgess, R. L. & Huston, T. L. (Eds.) (1979) *Social exchange in developing relationships.* New York: Academic

Burt, R. S., Minor, M. J., et al. (1983) *Applied network analysis, A methodological introduction.* Beverly Hills: Sage

Byrne, D. (1971) *The attraction paradigm.* New York: Academic

Cohen, J. M. (1977) Sources of peer group homogeneity. *Sociology of Education, 50,* 227—241

Coleman, J. S. (1961) *The adolescent society.* New York: Free Press

Coleman, J. S. (1970) Interpretations of adolescent culture. In J. Zubin and A. M. Freedman (Eds.), *The Psychopathology of adolescence.* (pp. 20—29). New York: Grune and Stratton

Coleman, J. S. (1973) *Youth: Transition to adulthood.* A report of the panel on youth of the President's Science Advisory Committee. Washington, D.C.: U.S. Government Printing Office

Coleman, J. S. (1983) Purposive action embedded in social networks. Paper presented at Conference on Social Networks, San Diego, California

Curry, J. & Kenny, D. A. (1974) The effects of perceived and actual similarity in values and personality in the process of interpersonal attraction. *Quantity and Quality, 8,* 27—44

Davies, M. & Kandel, D. B. (1981) Parental and peer influences on adolescents' educational plans: Some further evidence. *American Journal of Sociology, 87,* 363—387

Duck, S. W. (1973) *Personal relationships and personal constructs.* New York: Wiley

Duck, S. & Allison, D. (1978) I liked you but I can't live with you: a study of lapsed friendships. *Social Behavior and Personality, 6,* 43—47

Duck, S. W. & Craig, G. (1978) Personality similarity and the development of friendship: A longitudinal study. *British Journal of Social and Clinical Psychology, 17,* 237—242

Duck, S. W. & Gilmour, R. (Eds.) (1981 a) *Personal relationships: Vol. 1. Studying personal relationships.* New York: Academic

Duck, S. W. & Gilmour, R. (Eds.) (1981 b) *Personal relationships: Vol. 2. Developing personal relationships.* New York: Academic

Duck, S. W. & Gilmour, R. (Eds.) (1981 c) *Personal relationships: Vol. 3. Personal relationships in disorder.* New York: Academic

Duncan, O. D., Haller, A. O., & Portes, A. (1968) Peer influences on aspirations: A re-interpretation. *American Journal of Sociology, 74,* 119—137

Eder, D. & Hallinan, M. T. (1978) Sex differences in children's friendships. *American Sociological Review, 43,* 237—250

Emerson, R. M. (1976) Social exchange theory. In A. Inkeles, J. Coleman and N. Smelser (eds.), *Annual review of sociology:* Vol. 2. Palo Alto, California: Annual Reviews

Epstein, J. L. (1978) *Friends in school: Patterns of selection and influence in secondary schools.* (Report No. 266, November). Baltimore, MD: Johns Hopkins University Center for Social Organization of Schools

Feld, S. L. (1981) The focused organization of social ties. *American Journal of Sociology, 86,* 1015—1035

Feld, S. L. (1982) Social structural determinants of similarity among associates. *American Sociological Review, 47,* 797—801

Festinger, L. A. (1954) A theory of social comparison processes. *Human Relations, 7,* 117—140

Fischer, C. S. (1982) *To dwell among friends: Personal networks in town and city.* Chicago: University of Chicago Press

Furman, W. & Childs, M. K. (1981) A temporal perspective on children's friendship. Paper presented at the bi-annual meeting of the Society for Child Development, Boston, April

Hallinan, M. T. (1979) Structural effects on children's friendships and cliques. *Social Psychology Quarterly, 42,* 43–54

Hallinan, M. T. & Tuma, N. B. (1978) Classroom effects on change in children's friendships. *Sociology of Education, 51,* 270–282

Hansell, S. (1981) Ego development and peer friendship networks. *Sociology of Education, 54,* 51–63

Hartup, W. W. (1979) The social worlds of childhood. *American Psychologist, 34,* 944–950

Hartup, W. W. (1983) The peer system. In Mussen, P. H. and Hetherington, E. M. (eds.), *Carmichael's manual of child psychology* (4th ed.) (Vol. 4, pp. 1–282). New York: Wiley

Heider, F. (1958) *The psychology of interpersonal relations.* New York: Wiley

Homans, G. (1961) *Social behavior: Its elementary forms.* New York: Harcourt Brace & World

Huba, G. J., Wingard, J. A., & Bentler, P. M. (1980) Longitudinal analysis of the role of peer support, adult models, and peer subcultures in beginning adolescent substance use: An application of setwise canonical correlation methods. *Multivariate Behavioral Research, 15,* 259–280

Jennings, M. K. & Niemi, R. G. (1974) *The political character of adolescence: The influence of families & schools.* Princeton: Princeton University Press

Jessop, D. J. (1982) Topic variation in levels of agreement between parents and adolescents. *Public Opinion Quarterly, 46,* 538–559

Kandel, D. B. (1973) Adolescent marihuana use: Role of parents and peers. *Science, 181,* 1067–1070

Kandel, D. B. (1974) Inter- and intra-generational influences on adolescent marihuana use. In V. Bengston and R. Laufer (Eds.), Special issue on generations and social change. *Journal of Social Issues, 50,* 107–135

Kandel, D. B. (1978a) Similarity in real-life adolescent friendship pairs. *Journal of Personality and Social Psychology, 36,* 306–312

Kandel, D. B. (1978b) Homophily, selection, and socialization in adolescent friendships. *American Journal of Sociology, 84,* 427–436

Kandel, D. B. (1978c) On variations in adolescent subcultures. *Youth and Society, 9,* 373–384

Kandel, D. B. (1984) Marijuana users in young adulthood. *Archives of General Psychiatry 41:* 200–209

Kandel, D. B. & Andrews, K. (in press) Processes of adolescent socialization by parents and by peers. *International Journal of the Addictions, 22*

Kandel, D., Kessler, R., & Margulies, R. (1978a) Adolescent initiation into stages of drug use: A developmental analysis. In D. Kandel (Ed.), *Longitudinal research on drug use: Empirical findings and methodological issues* (pp. 73–100). Washington, D.C.: Hemisphere- Wiley

Kandel, D., Kessler, R., & Margulies, R. (1978b) Antecedents of adolescent initiation into stages of drug use: A developmental analysis. *Journal of Youth and Adolescence, 7,* 13–40

Kandel, D. B. & Lesser, G. S. (1969) Parental and peer influence on educational plans of adolescents. *American Sociological Review, 34,* 212–223

Kandel, D. B. & Lesser, G. S. (1972) *Youth in two worlds.* San Francisco: Jossey-Bass

Kandel, D. B., Lesser, G. S., Roberts, G. C., & Weiss, R. (1968) *Adolescents in two societies: Peers, school, and family in the United States and Denmark.* Final report submitted to the Office of Education, U.S. Dept. of Health, Education and Welfare

Kandel, D. B., Margulies, R. S., & Davies, M. (1978) Analytical strategies for studying transitions into developmental stages. *Sociology of Education, 51,* 162–176

Kandel, D. B., Single, E., & Kessler, R. (1976) The epidemiology of drug use among New York State High School students: Distribution, trends and change in rates of use. *American Journal of Public Health, 66,* 43–53

Karweit, N. L., Hansell, S., & Ricks, M. A. (1979) The conditions for peer associations in Schools (Report No. 282). Baltimore, MD: Johns Hopkins University Center for Social Organization of Schools

Kon, I. (1981) Adolescent friendship: Some unanswered questions for future research. In Duck, S. and Gilmour, R. (Eds.), *Personal relationships: Vol. 2. Developing personal relationships.* New York: Academic

Laumann, E. D. (1973) *Bonds of pluralism. The form and substance of urban social networks.* New York: Wiley

Lucas, W. L., Grupp, S. E., & Schmitt, R. L. (1975) Predicting who will turn on: A four-year follow-up. *International Journal of the Addictions, 10,* 305–326

Maccoby, E. E. (1968) The development of moral values and behavior in childhood. In J. S. Clausen (Ed.), *Socialization and society.* Boston: Little, Brown

Maccoby, E. & Jacklin, C. (1974) *The psychology of sex differences.* Stanford: Stanford University Press

Mardsen, P. V. & Lin, N. (Eds.) (1982) *Social structure and network analysis.* Beverly Hills: Sage

Margulies, R., Kessler, R. C., & Kandel, D. (1977) A longitudinal study of onset of drinking among high school students. *Quarterly Journal of Studies on Alcohol, 38,* 897–912

Mead, M. (1970) *Culture and commitment.* New York: Natural History Press–Doubleday

Murstein, B. (Ed.) (1971) *Theories of attraction and love.* Berlin Heidelberg New York: Springer

Newcomb, T. (1961) *The acquaintance process.* New York: Holt, Rinehart and Winston

Otto, L. B. & Haller, A. O. (1979) Evidence for a social psychological view of the status attainment process: Four studies compared. *Social Forces, 57,* 887–914

Petersen, A. C. & Spiga, R. (1982) Adolescence and stress. In Goldberger, L. and Breznitz, S. (Eds.), *Handbook of stress: theoretical and clinical aspects.* Chapter 31. New York: Free Press

Schachter, S. (1959) *The psychology of affiliation.* Stanford: Stanford University Press

Taylor, D. G. & Coleman, J. S. (1979) Equilibrating processes in social networks: A model for conceptualization and analysis. In Holland, P. W. and Leinhardt, S. (Eds.), *Perspectives on social network research.* New York: Academic

Troll, L. & Bengston, V. (1979) Generations in the family. In Burr, W. R., Hill, R., Nye, F. I., & Reiss, I. L. (Eds.), *Contemporary theories about the family* (Vol. 1, pp. 127–161). New York: Free Press

Verbrugge, L. M. (1977) The structure of adult friendship choices. *Social Forces, 56,* 576–597

Verbrugge, L. M. (1979) Multiplexity in adult friendships. *Social Forces, 57,* 1266–1309

Waldorf, F. & Coleman, J. (1971) Analysis and simulation of reference group processes. In J. M. Dutton and W. H. Starbuck (Eds.) *Computer simulation of human behavior.* New York: Wiley

Woelfel, J. & Haller, A. O. (1971) Significant others, the self-reflexive act and the attitude formation process. *American Sociological Review, 36,* 74–87

Youniss, J. (1980) *Parents and peers in social development.* Chicago: University of Chicago Press

XII. The Coping Function of Adolescent Alcohol and Drug Use[1]

E.W. Labouvie *

Introduction

It is widely accepted by both the lay public and scientific experts (e.g., Freed, 1978; Lettieri, 1978; Pandina, 1982) that individuals often rely on alcohol and/or drugs to manage and control the subjective experience of their internal affective states. These states are assumed to include both moods and emotions. Presumably, moods are more general and diffuse, representing central tendencies in affect and motivation with some degree of continuity and stability over time and situations. In comparison, emotions are more specific, more discontinuous, and less stable (Ketai, 1975; Lazarus, Kanner, & Folkman, 1980). Furthermore, it is generally believed that the self-regulation of subjectively experienced, affective states represents an important aspect of an individual's attempts to cope with, and adapt to, the environment (Breger, 1974).

In contrast to this commonly held view, however, more detailed and specific theories of alcohol and drug use differ considerably with regard to their conceptualization of the underlying coping processes (Hochhauser, 1981; Lettieri, 1978; Lettieri, Sayers, & Wallenstein Pearson, 1980). One reason for this lack of consensus is simply the fact that some theories do not include the concept of coping at all or only implicitly (e.g., Lettieri, 1978). For instance, none of the four theories deemed most promising by Kandel (1980) for an understanding of adolescent drinking and drug use makes explicit reference to either the concept of affective self-regulation or the concept of coping. Furthermore, among the theories that do incorporate these concepts, viewpoints differ with regard to (a) the relative role of negatively and positively toned emotions, and (b) the relevant sources of stress assumed to precipitate the experience of negative emotions (Lettieri et al., 1980). In other words, it is not clear under what circumstances and to what extent the substance use of individuals in general and of adolescents in particular is motivated by a need to reduce tension and relieve negative emotions or by a desire to ex-

[1] Writing of this paper was supported by grant no. AA 05823-01 from the National Institute on Alcohol Abuse and Alcoholism and grant no. DA 03395-01 from the National Institute on Drug Abuse.
* Rutgers-The State University of New Jersey, Health and Human Development Project, P.O. Box 788, Piscataway, NJ 08854, USA

Development as Action in Context
Ed. by R. K. Silbereisen et al.
© Springer-Verlag Berlin Heidelberg 1986

perience positive emotions, or a combination of both (Braucht, Brakarsh, Follingstad, & Berry, 1973; Freed, 1978; Lettieri et al., 1980; Pohorecky, 1981). Similarly, the presumed sources of stress and of negative emotions vary considerably ranging from the self, to the proximal social and physical environment, to society at large and the more abstract notion of existential meaning (Lettieri, 1978; Lettieri et al., 1980).

In view of this state of affairs it would seem desirable and useful for theory and research in the area of substance use to formulate a theoretical framework which can provide an explicit integration of the concepts of emotional self-regulation, stress, and coping. In addition, it would seem important that such a framework give consideration to the role of both positive and negative emotions and emphasizes a view of the individual as an actively self-monitoring and self-regulating organism (Gaines, 1981; Lisansky Gomberg, 1982).

The purpose of this chapter is to discuss Lazarus' cognitive-phenomenological theory of stress and coping as a promising candidate for such a theoretical framework (Folkman & Lazarus, 1980; Lazarus, 1966; Lazarus & DeLongis, 1983; Lazarus & Launier, 1978; Lazarus et al., 1980). Instead of providing a detailed account of the theory and its key concepts, however, attention will be primarily focused on those aspects of the theory that may require some modification, extension, or clarification in order to address the issues raised above.

Due to space limitations the present discussion will have to ignore a number of issues that have been important in the study of substance use. More specifically, no attempt will be made to tackle definitional problems of concepts such as drug abuse, drug dependence, and drug addiction. Nor will there be any explicit consideration of different types of drugs or of different phases of drug use such as initiation, continuation, cessation, and relapse. It should, however, be quite obvious that a more comprehensive discussion of the proposed theoretical framework and its usefulness will have to take these issues into account.

The Theoretical Framework

The cognitive-phenomenological theory of stress and coping as elaborated by Lazarus and his colleagues (e.g., Folkman & Lazarus, 1980; Lazarus & DeLongis, 1983; Lazarus et al., 1980) is based on a process-oriented view of individuals' transactions with their environment. Cognitive appraisal and coping are the two key processes assumed to mediate between environmental events/conditions and emotional responses with cognitive reappraisal providing continuous feedback. Thus, appraisal, coping, and emotions are all in flux and subject to change throughout a particular coping episode. Empirically, this view is reflected in attempts to assess individuals' coping efforts in response to specific problems and hassles (e.g., Folkman &

Lazarus, 1980), presumably making the question of stability a purely empirical one. In line with arguments presented in connection with the situationism-personologism controversy (Mischel, 1977, 1979) it should be pointed out, however, that the issue of temporal stability is, at least in part, preempted by the definition of one's concepts (Epstein, 1979, 1980). Assuming that those definitions are reflected in the measures used (Labouvie, 1982), the question of stability and change is obviously a conceptual, as well as an empirical one. This conclusion has particular relevance for the present discussion which originates from a more developmentally oriented perspective. That is, given a focus on both short- and long-term continuity and discontinuity in human behavior, it would seem more profitable and empirically less cumbersome to conceptualize coping as a middle level concept (Labouvie, 1982; Mischel, 1979). Without going to the other extreme of a trait-like approach we, therefore, propose a definition of coping in terms of intraindividual hierarchies of action tendencies with those high in the hierarchy being executed more frequently and over a wider range of situations than those ranking low in the hierarchy. Although aspects of stability and continuity are, at least partially, attributed to intraindividual factors, this notion of coping does not preclude the possibility that combinations of coping actions and their sequential patterning may be relatively specific across different situations.

The proposed definition of coping in terms of hierarchically organized repertoires of action tendencies seems also useful when considering two other issues. First, in line with the assumption that coping processes mediate between environmental events and emotional responses, the present definition implies that one important goal, although not always the only one, of any attempted coping action involves the monitoring and regulation of one's subjectively experienced emotions and moods. In that sense, so-called emotion-focused coping actions (Lazarus et al., 1980) are more direct while situation- or problem-focused coping actions are more indirect in trying to achieve emotional self-regulation through the management of person—environment relationships. It should be noted that this notion of coping actions is not meant to imply that emotional self-regulation is necessarily an end in itself. It is more likely that emotional self-regulation often serves to facilitate behavioral/motoric and cognitive self-regulation. For instance, an athlete may try to regulate his emotional state in order to achieve maximum performance in a sports event. What remains unclear, however, is the question of the target values and optimization principles used by individuals to guide such self-regulation. Most psychological theorizing has been limited to a consideration of simple maximization or minimization principles with little regard for more complex heuristics that may actually be used (e.g., Labouvie, 1984; Labouvie & Pandina, 1983; Oerter, 1982).

The second issue relates to the fact that emotional self-regulation involves both positive and negative emotions. In other words, it is not limited to the management of emotions such as fear, anxiety, guilt, anger, and rage which are typically experienced in response to hassles and problems that happen to the individual. Instead, emotional self-regulation also involves positive emotions such as sensual pleasure, love, security, excitement, and joy which are often brought about and experienced through the individual's active seeking and shaping of opportunities and goals. Despite its explicit emphasis on individual-environment transactions, the cognitive-phenomenological theory of stress and coping tends to project a mechanistic view. That is, it portrays individuals as primarily responding *reactively* to the occurrence of events and situations that are imposed by the environment largely without any intent on the part of the individuals involved. In turn, little attention is given to the fact that individuals may, and do, *actively* seek out, select, and produce desired situations and opportunities for the experience of emotional uplifts. A more balanced consideration of the role of both positive and negative emotions and introduction of the concept of anticipatory coping in recent elaborations of the theory (e.g., Lazarus et al., 1980) do not fully overcome the mechanistic bias of the theoretical framework. Therefore, we propose to extend the notion of anticipatory coping into an explicit distinction between reactive and active coping actions as outlined below.

Reactive Coping Actions

As already pointed out above, coping actions are generally thought to be initiated and carried out reactively in response to demands, hassles, and problems as they are dealt out to individuals by their environments. Although the occurrence of such events is often expected, it is, for the most part, unwanted except for the case of challenging situations. But even then the individual is not seen as having been actively involved in producing that situation. Obviously, since the presence of most events that are considered in the coping literature (e.g., hassles, threats, losses) is assumed to be unintended and unwanted, it is not surprising that the study of coping has almost exclusively focused on the experience of negative emotions and their relief (Lazarus et al., 1980) in line with an emphasis on tension/stress reduction models.

Active Coping Actions

According to an organismic view, human behavior is often better understood if one assumes that individuals are actively engaged in the construction of their own experiences (e.g., Lerner, 1983; Reese & Overton, 1970). Accordingly, individuals actively seek out and bring about the occurrence of desired events and situations including the experience of challenges and emotional uplifts (Kanner, Coyne, Schaefer, & Lazarus, 1981). Similar to reactive coping, active coping actions may be primarily situation-focused in trying to obtain a desired circumstance that is associated with the experience of a positive emotion, or more directly emotion-focused in trying to achieve a certain positive emotional state, or they may involve a combination of both. Conceptually, the notion of active coping is broader than, but shares similarities with, Lazarus' concept of anticipatory coping (Lazarus et al., 1980) and Zuckerman's concept of sensation seeking (Zuckerman, Buchsbaum, & Murphy, 1980).

Considering the role of active coping in human development, several aspects need to be emphasized. First, similar to the suggested role of anticipatory coping, active coping is assumed to counterbalance and buffer the impact of negative emotions that are experienced in anticipation of, during, or after specific hassles and problems. In that sense, it serves to sustain and restore reactive coping efforts of the individual (Lazarus et al., 1980). At the same time, however, it is also seen to have a more general function. In particular, it is assumed that individuals, on the basis of actual and vicarious experiences of their daily living, develop the belief or expectation that (a) a life without unwanted hassles and problems is highly unlikely, and (b) a successful mastery of today's and yesterday's hassles does not guarantee or promise a hassle-free tomorrow. On the background of that belief, active coping serves to sustain and promote, even in the face of unsuccessful reactive coping efforts, a positive mood including (a) a sense of hope, and (b) a sense of personal control (Fiske Lowenthal, 1977). In line with the work of Bower (e.g., Bower, Gilligan, & Monteiro, 1981), we assume that maintenance of a positive mood in general and of hope and a sense of personal control in particular is important in monitoring and regulating one's cognitive appraisal of unwanted, unintended, or unexpected events and circumstances. That is, individuals maintaining a positive mood are more inclined to interpret such events as minor hassles or even challenges rather than as major hassles and threats. This view obviously stresses the fact that the cognitive appraisal of events does not take place initially in an emotional vacuum and affirms the position that emotional monitoring serves to regulate cognitions and their content to the same extent that cognitive monitoring serves to regulate emotions (Beck, 1971; Lazarus et al., 1980). Finally, to the extent that successful active coping fosters feelings of hope and of personal control and efficacy (Bandura, 1977, 1982), it plays an essential role in the development and maintenance of personal commitments (Fiske Lowenthal, 1977; Lazarus & DeLongis, 1983). It is generally agreed that adolescence represents an important period for the formulation and initial crystallization of such commitments (Conger, 1977; Feather, 1980; Marcia, 1980).

Drinking and Drug Use as Active and Reactive Coping

Based on available empirical evidence (e.g., Cahalan, 1982; Cahalan, Cisin, & Crossley, 1969; Kandel, 1980) it is reasonable to assume that a good deal of substance use, at least in the low to moderate range of intensity and especially the use of alcohol, takes place in the context of desired and emotionally uplifting circumstances such as social gatherings of friends or celebrations. In the most straightforward sense, this implies that the use of alcohol and/or drugs is simply a part of some of the situations that individuals find desirable and emotionally uplifting. On the basis of such associations, however, individuals may develop the belief that (a) substance use helps to enhance the quality of such situations and uplifts (Christiansen, Goldman, & Inn, 1982), and/or (b) substance use is a necessary element to make a particular situation a desirable and emotionally uplifting one. For instance, an individual may come to believe that a social gathering of friends or a party is not enjoyable unless it is accompanied by the consumption of alcohol or the smoking of marijuana. Furthermore, such associations may also lead to the expectation that the use of alcohol and drugs is sufficient in itself to bring about the experience of emotional uplifts and sensual pleasures even in otherwise neutral or even undesirable contexts. Obviously, to the extent that these beliefs and expectations are reinforced through direct or vicarious experiences and to the extent that availability of, access to, and experience of desired circumstances and emotional uplifts without the presence of alcohol or drugs are limited, individuals will tend to incorporate substance use into their hierarchy of active coping actions.

Many cultures provide prescriptions for the use of alcohol or drugs in conjunction with desirable and emotionally uplifting occasions (e.g., religious ceremonies, social celebrations) (Heath, 1982). Therefore, it is reasonable to expect that substance use in connection with active coping efforts is more normative than, and emerging developmentally prior to, use in connection with reactive coping efforts. Most theories interested in the more extreme range of use intensity, however, tend to focus on the latter.

In view of the fact that medication and self-medication have become culturally accepted and widely used ways of relieving negative physical and psychological states (Lennard, Epstein, Bernstein, & Ranson 1971; Mellinger, 1978; Mellinger, Balter, Parry, Manheimer, & Cisin, 1974), it is not at all surprising if those strategies are extended to include the use of 'nonmedical' substances such as alcohol and illicit drugs. In addition, if individuals have come to believe that alcohol and drug use can enhance a desired situation, they may readily accept the logic that "if substance use can make a good thing even better, it will certainly help to make a bad thing more tolerable".

In the most direct sense then, alcohol and drug use are seen to provide an emotion-focused reactive coping action expected to yield a relatively reliable and immediate relief of negative emotions. Furthermore, the action itself requires little physical and cognitive effort and very few skills on the part of the individual. As a consequence, substance use may be relied upon to facilitate the application of other reactive coping actions, especially those problem-focused actions that are intrapsychic and involve a cognitive reappraisal of the problem situation. Thus, alcohol and drug use may become a pivotal aspect of reactive coping to the extent that an individual believes that (a) emotion-focused coping actions have to precede problem-focused coping in order for the latter to be more effective, and (b) the use of alcohol or drugs represents the only or the fastest and most effective action to relieve negative emotions ("First I need a drink; then I'll be able to start thinking about the problem").

From the preceding discussion it becomes quite clear that alcohol and drug use may serve a dual coping function. Its attractiveness as both a re-active and an active coping action is further strengthened by the fact that the successful attainment of desired events and of emotional uplifts is frequently preceded by the experience of negative emotions such as feelings of insecur-ity and fear of failure or rejection. In such cases, alcohol and drugs may be used with the expectation of simultaneously relieving negative emotions and enhancing positive ones. At the present time, available evidence does not help to clarify whether and to what extent use patterns are related to both active and reactive coping efforts, nor is it clear how individuals combine and differentiate both functions in their own use. Nevertheless, the present discussion does suggest that it is probably not very useful to consider the two functions separately and independently of each other when studying their role in individuals' alcohol and drug use.

The Period of Adolescence

Adolescent Drinking and Drug Use

According to a recent review by Kandel (1980), substance use typically be-gins in late childhood and early adolescence when the use of legal drugs (al-cohol and cigarettes) is most frequently initiated in the context of the family. During adolescence the use of legal drugs tends to intensify and is often ac-companied by a sequentially patterned exposure to marijuana and 'harder' illicit drugs (Labouvie & Pandina, 1983). Presumably the peak of legal drug use in early adulthood is followed by a plateau that extends at least into the fifties while a similar peak in illegal drug use during the same age period gives way to a rapid decline that parallels the assumption of adult social roles – employment, marriage, and parenthood.

The empirical evidence on which these age trends are based, comes for the most part from cross-sectional observations. In addition, the bulk of the available longitudinal evidence is restricted to a relatively narrow range of birth cohorts and a particular historical time period. Consequently, in-ferences about ontogenetic patterns of substance use are based on data that may lack both internal and external validity. For instance, it is not at all clear whether individuals born in the 1960s and early 1970s will exhibit a sharp decline in illegal drug use (especially the use of marijuana) as they be-gin to enter into adult roles.

Given man's increasing use of chemical substances (with and without knowledge of its potential side-effects) to manage and control aspects of his environment, given the widespread use of medical drugs (with and without expert supervision) to manage and regulate physical and psychological well-being, and given the widespread use of tobacco, alcohol, and psychoactive drugs in a variety of cultures and societies, it seems hardly useful to put special emphasis on labels such as 'problem behavior', 'risk-taking behavior', or 'health-threatening behavior' (e.g., Jessor & Jessor, 1977; Jessor, 1982) when referring to adolescent substance use as described above. According to Breger (1974), the core conflicts of human life — independence and dependency, pleasure and renunciation, aggression and its control — are not resolved at any stage or period of human development but have to be faced all through life. Consequently, problem behaviors, risk-taking behaviors, and health-trheatening behaviors as an expression of individuals' attempt to deal with these conflicts are not the hallmark of any particular developmental period. In the same sense, we do not believe that the potential employment of substance use as an active or reactive coping action is in any way unique to the period of adolescence.

The Psychological Experience of Adolescence

Even though the potential coping function of substance use is not assumed to be uniquely linked to adolescent development, it is, nevertheless, important to consider its role in relation to the particular intra- and extrapersonal circumstances which characterize that period of the human life span. Theoretically, adolescent development has most often been viewed from two general perspectives: (a) as a period of transition from childhood to adulthood involving significant biological, cognitive, and social changes (e.g., Havighurst, 1972; Olbrich, 1983), and (b) as a time for the exploration and development of a personal identity (e.g., Erikson, 1974; Oerter, 1982). Obviously, it is beyond the scope of this chapter to provide a detailed discussion of each perspective. Instead, we will briefly outline how the two viewpoints may be related to the theoretical framework proposed above. In particular, we will consider the notion of transition in terms of a shift in the sources of both stress and emotional uplifts, and emphasize the role of emotional self-monitoring and self-regulation as a salient aspect of adolescent identity formation.

As is well known, adolescence represents a period of significant biological changes and heightened sexual awareness and responsiveness. At the same time, cognitive changes bring about the capacity to introspect, to reflect about one's thoughts and emotions, and to think about possibilities and ideals. Socially, the adolescent is expected to make appropriate adjustments in his relationships to parents, adults, and peers. The psychological experience of this multitude of changes is multifaceted.

First of all, actual and anticipated change does not only bring about feelings of curiosity, excitement, and achievement. To the extent that routinized actions and familiar behavioral programs have to be given up, it will also elicit intense feelings of insecurity and anxiety (Olbrich, 1983). Second, the combination of biological, sexual, and cognitive changes is likely to increase adolescents' self-awareness and to focus their attention on issues of self-monitoring and self-regulation. Finally, an intensified cognitive exploration of present and future realities in comparison to possibilities and ideals may not only lead to a hopefully only temporary lack of valued goals and commitments, but may also produce cognitive content that is itself unpleasant and a source of stress. Consequently, a cognitively based approach to problem-solving may be curtailed in favor of a more emotion-focused one.

In the context of such experiences it is not at all surprising if the emotional uplifts sought by adolescents take on a narcissistic and hedonic quality (Kanner et al., 1981) with a focus on present emotional well-being. Substance use becomes a viable means for the exploration of emotional experiences and for emotional self-regulation. Adding to its attractiveness are the expectation of reliable and immediate effects, the belief that emotional experiences are under one's own control, and the fact that its 'successful' performance does not require much cognitive effort.

Conclusion

According to the position taken here, substance use has the potential of being employed as an active and/or reactive coping action in connection with emotional self-regulation as an end in itself or as a facilitator of cognitive and motoric self-regulation. Since adolescence is a period of heightened self-awareness and self-monitoring and of increased responsiveness to emotional experiences, it is reasonable to expect that adolescents will explore the regulative utility of various drugs, especially if they are readily available. In exploring this utility, it is quite possible that different drugs are employed differentially for active or reactive coping purposes. In other words, individuals may learn to use some drugs for the purpose of enhancing emotional uplifts, others in order to relieve negative emotions.

Obviously, substance use as active or reactive coping action does not have to represent problem use or abuse. In fact, it could be argued that such use has some adaptational utility, within certain limits, especially if it does facilitate the use of other coping actions. On the other hand, as suggested by various theories of drug addiction, such use can easily evolve into problem use and dependence if it becomes an indispensable element in an individual's repertoire of coping actions and if its expected effects and/or their subjective experience are susceptible to tolerance.

References

Bandura, A. (1977) Self-efficacy: Toward a unifying theory of behavioral change. *Psychological Review, 84,* 191—215

Bandura, A. (1982) Self-efficacy mechanism in human agency. *American Psychologist, 37,* 122—147

Beck, A. T. (1971) Cognition, affect and psychopathology. *Archives of General Psychiatry, 24,* 495—500

Bower, G. H., Gilligan, S. G., & Monteiro, K. P. (1981) Selectivity of learning caused by affective states. *Journal of Experimental Psychology: General, 110,* 451—472

Braucht, G. N., Brakarsh, D., Follingstad, D., & Berry, K. L. (1973) Deviant drug use in adolescence: A review of psychosocial correlates. *Psychological Bulletin, 79,* 92—106

Breger, L. (1974) *From instinct to identity. The development of personality.* Englewood Cliffs, NJ: Prentice-Hall

Cahalan, D. (1982) Epidemiology: Alcohol use in American society. In E. Lisansky Gomberg, H. Raskin White, & J. A. Carpenter (Eds.), *Alcohol, science and society revisited.* Ann Arbor: University of Michigan Press

Cahalan, D., Cisin, I. H., & Crossley, H. M. (1969) American drinking practices; a national study of drinking behavior and attitudes (Monograph No. 6). New Brunswick, NJ: Rutgers Center of Alcohol Studies

Christiansen, B. A., Goldman, M. S., & Inn, A. (1982) Development of alcohol-related expectancies in adolescents: Separating pharmalogical from social-learning influences. *Journal of Consulting and Clinical Psychology, 50,* 336—344

Conger, J. J. (1977) *Adolescence and youth. Psychological development in a changing world* (2nd ed.). New York: Harper & Row

Epstein, S. (1979) The stability of behavior: I. On predicting most of the people much of the time. *Journal of Personality and Social Psychology, 37,* 1097—1126

Epstein, S. (1980) The stability of behavior: II. Implications for psychological research. *American Psychologist, 35,* 790—806

Erikson, E. H. (1974) *Dimensions of a new identity.* New York: Norton

Feather, N. T. (1980) Values in adolescence. In J. Adelson (Ed.), *Handbook of adolescent psychology.* New York: John Wiley

Fiske Lowenthal, M. (1977) Toward a sociological theory of change in adulthood and old age. In J. E. Birren & K. W. Schaie (Eds.), *Handbook of the psychology of aging.* New York: Van Nostrand Reinhold

Folkman, S. & Lazarus, R. S. (1980) An analysis of coping in a middle-aged community sample. *Journal of Health and Social Behavior, 21,* 219—239

Freed, E. X. (1978) Alcohol and mood: An updated review. *The International Journal of the Addictions, 13,* 173—200

Gaines, L. S. (1981) Cognition and the environment: Implications for a self-awareness theory of drinking. In T. C. Harford & L. S. Gaines (Eds.), *Social drinking contexts* (Research Monograph No. 7). Rockville, Maryland: National Institute on Alcohol Abuse and Alcoholism

Havighurst, R. J. (1972) *Developmental tasks and education* (3rd ed.). New York: Davis McKay

Heath, D. B. (1982) In other cultures, they also drink. In E. Lisansky Gomberg, H. Raskin White, & J. A. Carpenter (Eds.), *Alcohol, science and society revisited.* Ann Arbor, MI: University of Michigan Press

Hochhauser, M. (1981) Learned helplessness and substance abuse in the elderly. *Journal of Psychoactive Drugs, 13,* 17—24

Jessor, R. (1982) Critical issues in research on adolescent health promotion. In T. Coates, A. Petersen, & C. Perry (Eds.), *Promoting adolescent health: A dialog on research and practice.* New York: Academic

Jessor, R. & Jessor, S. L. (1977) *Problem behavior and psychosocial development: A longitudinal study of youth.* New York: Academic

Kandel, D. B. (1980) Drug and drinking behavior among youth. *Annual Review of Sociology, 6,* 235–285

Kanner, A. D., Coyne, J. C., Schaefer, C., & Lazarus, R. S. (1981) Comparison of two modes of stress measurement: Daily hassles and uplifts versus major life events. *Journal of Behavioral Medicine, 4,* 1–39

Ketai, R. (1975) Affect, mood, emotion, and feeling: Semantic considerations. *American Journal of Psychiatry, 132,* 1215–1217

Labouvie, E. W. (1982) Issues in life-span development. In B. B. Wolman (Ed.), *Handbook of developmental psychology.* Englewood Cliffs, NJ: Prentice-Hall

Labouvie, E. W. (1984) Sequential strategies as quasiexperimental designs: Possibilities and limitations in explanatory analysis. In J. R. Nesselroade & A. von Eye (Eds.), *Individual development and social change: Explanatory analysis.* New York: Academic

Labouvie, E. W. & Pandina, R. J. (1983) Jugend und Drogengebrauch. In R. K. Silbereisen & L. Montada (Eds.), *Entwicklungspsychologie. Ein Handbuch in Schlüsselbegriffen.* Munich: Urban & Schwarzenberg

Lazarus, R. S. (1966) *Psychological stress and the coping process.* New York: McGraw-Hill

Lazarus, R. S. & DeLongis, A. (1983) Psychological stress and coping in aging. *American Psychologist, 38,* 245–254

Lazarus, R. S., Kanner, A. D., & Folkman, S. (1980) Emotions: A cognitive-phenomenological analysis. In R. Plutchik & H. Kellermann (Eds.), *Emotion. Theory, research, and experience.* Vol. 1. New York: Academic

Lazarus, R. S. & Launier, R. (1978) Stress-related transactions between person and environment. In L. A. Pervin & M. Lewis (Eds.), *Perspectives in interactional psychology.* New York: Plenum

Lennard, H. L., Epstein, L. J., Bernstein, A., & Ranson, D. E. (1971) *Mystification and drug misuse.* San Francisco: Jossey-Bass

Lerner, R. M. (Ed.) (1983) *Developmental psychology. Historical and philosophical perspectives.* Hillsdale, NJ: Erlbaum

Lettieri, D. J. (1978) Theories of drug abuse. In D. J. Lettieri (Ed.), *Drugs and suicide. When other coping strategies fail.* Beverly Hills: Sage

Lettieri, D. J., Sayers, M., & Wallenstein Pearson, H. (1980) *Theories on drug abuse. Selected contemporary perspectives.* Rockville, Maryland: National Institute on Drug Abuse

Lisansky Gomberg, E. (1982) Alcoholism: Psychological and psychosocial aspects. In E. Lisansky Gomberg, H. Raskin White, & J. A. Carpenter (Eds.), *Alcohol, science and society revisited.* Ann Arbor, MI: University of Michigan Press

Marcia, J. E. (1980) Identity in adolescence. In J. Adelson (Ed.), *Handbook of adolescent psychology.* New York: Wiley

Mellinger, G. D. (1978) Use of licit drugs and other coping alternatives: Some personal observations on the hazards of living. In D. J. Lettieri (Ed.), *Drugs and suicide. When other coping strategies fail.* Beverly Hills: Sage

Mellinger, G. D., Balter, M. B., Parry, H. J., Manheimer, D. I., & Cisin, I. H. (1974) An overview of psychotherapeutic drug use in the United States. In E. Josephson (Ed.), *Epidemiology of drug use.* Washington: V. H. Winston

Mischel, W. (1977) On the future of personality measurement. *American Psychologist, 32,* 246–254

Mischel, W. (1979) On the interface of cognition and personality: Beyond the person-situation debate. *American Psychologist, 34,* 740–754

Oerter, R. (1982) Jugendalter. In R. Oerter & L. Montada, *Entwicklungspsychologie.* Munich: Urban & Schwarzenberg

Olbrich, E. (1983) Übergänge im Jugendalter. In R. K. Silbereisen & L. Montada (Eds.), *Entwicklungspsychologie. Ein Handbuch in Schlüsselbegriffen.* Munich: Urban & Schwarzenberg

Pandina, R. J. (1982) Effects of alcohol on psychological processes. In E. Lisansky Gomberg, H. Raskin White, & J. A. Carpenter (Eds.), *Alcohol, science and society revisited.* Ann Arbor, MI: University of Michigan Press

Pohorecky, L. A. (1981) The interaction of alcohol and stress: A review. *Neuroscience & Biobehavioral Reviews, 5,* 209 – 229

Reese, H. W. & Overton, W. F. (1970) Models of development and theories of development. In L. R. Goulet & P. B. Baltes (Eds.), *Life-span developmental psychology. Research and theory.* New York: Academic

Zuckerman, M., Buchsbaum, M. S., & Murphy, D. L. (1980) Sensation seeking and its biological correlates. *Psychological Bulletin, 88,* 187 – 214

XIII. Adolescent Problem Drinking: Psychosocial Aspects and Developmental Outcomes[1]

R. Jessor*

Introduction

The multiple functions that the use of drugs can serve for adolescents is by now well established (Jessor, 1984). Drug use by adolescents can be a way of affirming independence from parents, signalling commonality with the peer group, expressing opposition to the norms and values of the larger society, coping with stress and with apprehensions about personal inadequacy and social role failure, and establishing a sense of personal identity. In addition, drug use can serve an important *developmental* function; it can constitute a claim on transition from a less mature to a more mature status and represent, symbolically, the passage out of adolescence and entrance into the stage of youth or young adulthood. Since all of these functions are central to the adaptations of adolescent life, it is not surprising that the use of drugs has become a salient issue for young people.

In this paper, my aim is to elaborate a psychosocial framework for the understanding of youthful drug use, and to present some of the developmental findings that have emerged from our ongoing longitudinal research (Jessor & Jessor, 1984). While the present focus will be on alcohol use rather than the illicit drugs, the general framework has been shown to apply to the latter as well, and the findings for other drugs are consonant with those for alcohol use.

A Brief Overview of Problem-Behavior Theory

The conceptual framework we have developed over the past quarter of a century was originally formulated for research on drinking behavior in a tri-

[1] The research reported in this paper was carried out in longterm collaboration with Dr. Lee Jessor and, more recently, with Dr. John Donovan; it could not have been accomplished without them. I am grateful to Drs. John Donovan and Frances Costa for the special analyses of the data. Support for the research has been provided by Grant No. AA-03745 from the National Institute on Alcohol Abuse and Alcoholism (NIAAA). The material in this paper was also presented at the ceremony designating NIAAA a Collaborating Center of the World Health Organization, Washington, D.C., November 2, 1983.

* University of Colorado, Institute of Behavioral Science, Campus, Box 483, Boulder, CO 80309, USA

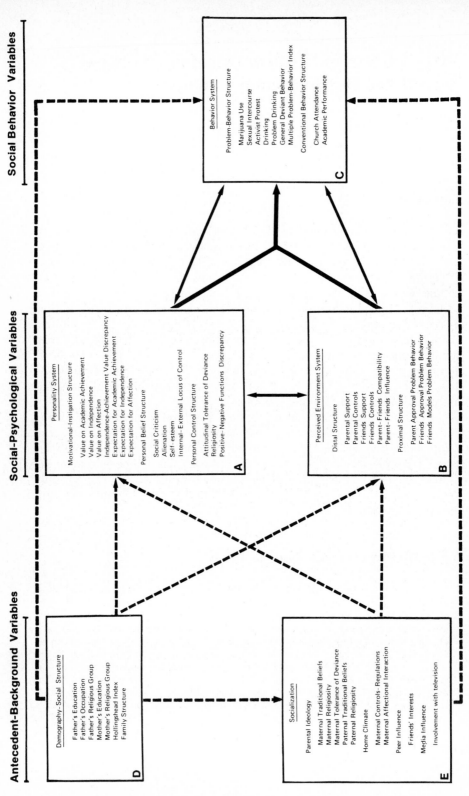

Fig. 1. The conceptual structure of Problem-Behavior Theory (Jessor & Jessor, 1977)

Antecedent-Background Variables

Social-Psychological Variables

Social Behavior Variables

Demography-Social Structure

Father's Education
Father's Occupation
Father's Religious Group
Mother's Education
Mother's Religious Group
Hollingshead Index
Family Structure

D

Socialization

Parental Ideology

Maternal Traditional Beliefs
Maternal Religiosity
Maternal Tolerance of Deviance
Paternal Traditional Beliefs
Paternal Religiosity

Home Climate

Maternal Controls-Regulations
Maternal Affectional Interaction

Peer Influence

Friends' Interests

Media Influence

Involvement with television

E

Personality System

Motivational-Instigation Structure

Value on Academic Achievement
Value on Independence
Value on Affection
Independence-Achievement Value Discrepancy
Expectation for Academic Achievement
Expectation for Independence
Expectation for Affection

Personal Belief Structure

Social Criticism
Alienation
Self-esteem
Internal-External Locus of Control

Personal Control Structure

Attitudinal Tolerance of Deviance
Religiosity
Positive-Negative Functions Discrepancy

A

Perceived Environment System

Distal Structure

Parental Support
Parental Controls
Friends Support
Friends Controls
Parent-Friends Compatibility
Parent-Friends Influence

Proximal Structure

Parent Approval Problem Behavior
Friends Approval Problem Behavior
Friends Models Problem Behavior

B

Behavior System

Problem-Behavior Structure

Marijuana Use
Sexual Intercourse
Activist Protest
Drinking
Problem Drinking
General Deviant Behavior
Multiple Problem-Behavior Index

Conventional Behavior Structure

Church Attendance
Academic Performance

C

ethnic community (Jessor, Graves, Hanson, & Jessor, 1968). Later modified for studies of a variety of adolescent problem behaviors, including delinquency, drug use, and precocious sexuality, it is currently referred to as Problem-Behavior Theory (Jessor & Jessor, 1977). Three major sources of psychosocial variation are incorporated into Problem-Behavior Theory. They are shown, in Figure 1, as the Personality System, the Perceived Environment System, and the Behavior System in boxes A, B, and C, respectively. The theoretical variables within each system are all considered to be the outcome of social learning and social experience, and each has directional implications for the likelihood of occurrence of problem behavior in youth. (Problem behavior, parenthetically, is defined as behavior that departs from the norms of the larger society and that tends to elicit some kind of social control response, whether mild criticism or social rejection or even incarceration.) Each theoretical variable specifies, therefore, a *proneness* toward engaging in normative transgression; the greater the proneness within each system, the more likely the occurrence of problem behavior.

Since the rationale for the variables in the theory has been described in detail elsewhere (Jessor & Jessor, 1977), it is useful here just to summarize the key features of problem behavior proneness within the three theoretical systems. Proneness toward problem behavior in the Personality System is represented by lower value on academic achievement, higher value on independence, higher value on independence relative to academic achievement, greater social criticism, greater alienation, more external control, greater tolerance of deviance, and less religiosity. In the Perceived Environment System, problem behavior proneness implies less parent and friends' support and controls, lower compatibility between the expectations of parents and those of friends, lower perceived influence of parents, relative to friends, greater friends' approval and lower parental disapproval of problem behavior, and more models for problem behavior among friends. In the Behavior System, problem behavior proneness refers to higher actual involvement in various problem behaviors (other than the one being predicted, of course) and lesser involvement in conventional behaviors. Taken together, the three systems yield an overall characterization of psychosocial proneness toward engaging in problem behavior, a theoretical pattern or profile specifying the greater or lesser likelihood of its occurrence.

The relevance of such a conceptual framework to adolescent alcohol use and abuse ought already to be obvious. Given both the legal and the social norms prevalent in American society, drinking per se is widely considered a transgression when adolescents are below a certain age. In addition, the excessive use of alcohol by adolescents, for example, to the point of drunkenness, or its inappropriate use, for example, before driving, are viewed with disapproval by society and generally elicit some sort of negative social sanction. Adolescent alcohol abuse can therefore be subsumed under the rubric of problem behavior, and that makes our formulation of problem behavior proneness apposite as a potential account of variation in problem drinking.

The variables in Problem-Behavior Theory should, in other words, constitute a set of *psychosocial risk factors* for adolescent problem drinking. That very possibility is what our research has, in fact, enabled us to explore.

The Design of the Research

The larger project from which the data on problem drinking will be drawn is a longitudinal study that began in 1969 and is still in progress. It has been carried out in two phases and has involved six waves of data collected on each participant over the years between 1969 and 1981. The first phase began in 1969 with samples of 7*th*, 8*th*, and 9*th* grade boys and girls drawn from three junior high schools in a small Rocky Mountain city. They filled out questionnaires annually for four successive years through 1972, at which time they had reached the 10*th*, 11*th*, and 12*th* grades. Thus, all the participants had by then made the transition from junior high school to senior high school. From 1972 until 1979 there was no further contact with any of the participants; after that seven-year hiatus, all of the former participants were located and asked to resume participation in the second phase of the study, now called the "Young Adult Follow-Up Study." The fifth data wave was then collected in 1979, and the sixth one was carried out in 1981. By then, the former junior high school cohorts were 25, 26, and 27 years of age. The cohort-sequential longitudinal design for the High School Sample is shown in Figure 2.

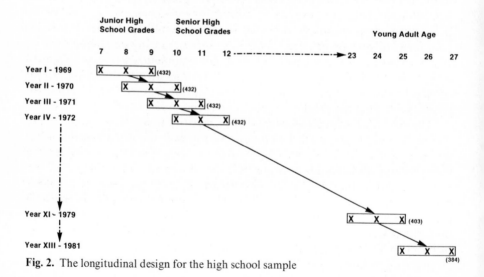

Fig. 2. The longitudinal design for the high school sample

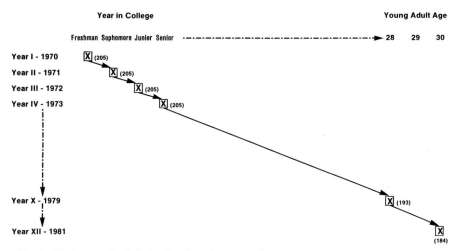

Fig. 3. The longitudinal design for the college sample

Most of the data to be presented in this paper will refer to the cohorts in this High School Sample; they are mostly middle class in socioeconomic status and Anglo in ethnicity. It should be noted, however, that an entirely independent longitudinal study was carried along in tandem with this one, also taking place in two phases. The first phase of the latter study began in 1970 with a sample of freshmen, both male and female, in the College of Arts and Science at the local university in the same city; they were tested annually for four successive years through 1973. After a six-year hiatus, the College Sample youth were located and invited to resume participation in the Young Adult Follow-Up Study, and they then also filled out questionnaires in 1979 and 1981. By 1981, they had reached the age of 30. The simple longitudinal design for the cohorts in the College Sample, a largely upper middle class, Anglo group, is shown in Figure 3.

As can be seen in both Figures 2 and 3, retention between Phase One and Phase Two for both the High School and College Samples was unusually high, thereby safeguarding the longitudinal integrity of the cohorts. For the High School Sample, fully 94 percent of the 1972 core participants resumed the study in 1979, and 96 percent of those continued with the study in 1981. For the College Sample, 95 percent of the 1973 core participants resumed the study in 1979, and 96 percent of those also continued in 1981. These retention rates testify to the commitment of the participants to the research and suggest that the quality of the data would be enhanced.

Data were collected in each of the six waves by a theoretically derived questionnaire that exceeded 60 pages in length and mapped all of the variables shown in the conceptual framework in Figure 1. Most of the variables were measured by psychometrically-developed, construct-validated, multiple-item scales. Many of the measures were retained unchanged across both phases of the longitudinal study; others had to be adapted to accommodate the obvious developmental changes taking place; and still other measures were added in the Young Adult Follow-Up Study to cover some entirely new domains such as marriage, family, child rearing, and work.

Further details about sampling, measurement, and design can be found elsewhere (Jessor & Jessor, 1977; Jessor & Jessor, 1984; Donovan, Jessor, & Jessor, 1983).

The Prevalence of Adolescent Problem Drinking

Although the definition of problem drinking is inherently arbitrary, there are two kinds of criteria about which, especially for young people, there is reasonable consensus as to their relevance. One criterion is frequent drinking to the point of drunkenness or intoxication, and the other is drinking that results in negative social consequences and that compromises role obligations and interpersonal relationships. We have relied on both criteria, jointly, in our studies, their correlation ($r = 0.48$) in the High School Sample in 1972 being significant, as expected, but not indicating a great deal of overlap. To be classified as a problem drinker, an adolescent had to report having been drunk six or more times in the past year, *or* having experienced negative consequences due to drinking at two or more times in the past year in each of three or more life areas out of the following six: trouble with teachers, difficulties with friends, trouble with parents, criticism from dates, trouble with the police, and driving while under the influence of alcohol. Exploration of two alternative operational definitions with data from a national sample of adolescents is reported in Donovan and Jessor (1978), and the psychosocial findings tend to remain relatively invariant. Relying on this joint frequency of drunkenness and/or frequency of negative consequences criterion yields the results shown in Table 1.

It is apparent in the table that there is significant prevalence of problem drinking among these adolescents. Aged 16, 17, and 18 in 1972, and in grades 10, 11, and 12, the High School Sample shows that one out of four of the young men and one out of six of the young women qualify as problem drinkers. These are not inconsequential rates, especially when one considers that they are contributed to primarily by the drunkenness component of the joint criterion and that this is an age group with access to motor vehicles. Indeed, the actual frequency of drunkenness reported by the problem drinkers is much higher than the cutpoint of six might suggest. For the young men classified as problem drinkers, the mean frequency of drunkenness in the

Table 1. Percent in each drinker status. High school sample: Year IV (1972)

Drinker status	Males (N = 188)	Females (N = 244)
Abstainer	21	21
Former drinker	4	7
Minimal drinker	2	2
Nonproblem drinker	46	55
Problem drinker	28	16
Total	100%	100%

Note: *Abstainers* have not had a drink more than 2 or 3 times in their lives; *former drinkers* have not had a drink in the past 6 months; and *minimal drinkers* have a very low level of alcohol intake per occasion – less than a can of beer, a glass of wine, or a drink of spirits

past year was 23.9, about twice a month; for the young women problem drinkers, the mean frequency of drunkenness was 17.8. By sharp contrast, the mean frequency of drunkenness in the past year among the *non*problem drinkers was 1.7 for the males and 1.8 for the females.

It is clear from these figures that adolescent problem drinkers are engaging in a behavior – drunkenness – that can place them seriously at risk, and with a frequency that raises public health concern. While this statement applies equally to both males and females, there is an important gender difference in the *prevalence* of problem drinking. As Table 1 indicates, the problem drinking rate among males (28 percent) is nearly twice the rate among females (16 percent).

Despite the arbitrariness of any classification system, the criteria used have yielded a reasonable distribution of problem and nonproblem drinkers. Not only do those classified as problem and nonproblem drinkers differ substantially in frequency of drunkenness, as just described, but the former also report 2 to 3 times the daily alcohol intake as the latter. These behavioral differences contribute support for the validity of the problem drinker classification. That accomplished, we are in a position to pursue the more fundamental issues of accounting for variation in problem drinking and for its continuity/discontinuity over time.

Problem Drinking and the Syndrome of Problem Behavior

Before taking up those issues, however, it is important to locate problem drinking more explicitly within the conceptual framework of Problem-Behavior Theory shown in Figure 1. If it is indeed part of the Behavior System, then it should have systematic relationships with other behaviors assigned to

Table 2. Relationship of drinker status to other problem behaviors. High school sample: Year IV (1972)

Drinker status	% Who are marijuana users		% Who are nonvirgins		% Who are high in deviance		% Who are high in church attendance	
	Males	Females	Males	Females	Males	Females	Males	Females
Abstainers	0	2	5	4	15	2	64	52
Nonproblem drinkers	31	42	23	39	40	34	23	33
Problem drinkers	79	80	52	73	73	43	27	18

that same conceptual domain. To permit exploration of that question, the association of drinker status with involvement in other problem behaviors was examined, and the data are shown in Table 2.

The Abstainer group (those who have not had a drink more than two or three times in their lives) has been included in Table 2 to provide a benchmark for the contrast between the Nonproblem Drinkers and the Problem Drinkers. It is immediately apparent from Table 2 that being a problem drinker is associated with high rates of involvement in other adolescent problem behaviors such as marijuana use, sexual intercourse experience, and protodelinquency. It is also apparent that the rates of involvement for problem drinkers are approximately *twice as high* as those for nonproblem drinkers, a difference of major epidemiological significance. Thus, 80 percent of the female problem drinkers have used marijuana as against only 42 percent of the nonproblem drinker women; and 73 percent of them had had sexual experience as against only 39 percent of the female nonproblem drinkers.

The compellingness of these positive associations between problem drinking and other adolescent problem behaviors is further accentuated by two other observations that can be made about Table 2. One of these is the *negative* association that is obtained between problem drinking and a conforming or conventional behavior, in this instance, frequency of church attendance in the past year. For involvement in this behavior, the rate for *non*problem drinker women is nearly twice as high as it is for the problem drinker women, a complete reversal of direction, as theoretically expected. Although that particular finding doesn't hold for the males, the overall reversal of direction is apparent for them as well, once reference is made to the abstainers' rate.

The second noteworthy observation remaining about Table 2 is the very low absolute rates of the abstainer group; almost none of the abstainers has had experience with or involvement in other problem behaviors (the males are a slight exception in relation to high deviance). What this suggests is that the decision to begin to drink is a critical one − remaining an abstainer may function as an insulating status against engaging in any problem behavior, whereas beginning to drink – even as a nonproblem drinker – represents a watershed crossed in regard to involvement in other problem behaviors. Inclusion of the abstainer data in Table 2 also makes clearer that intensity of involvement with alcohol (from no involvement up to problem drinking) varies directly with involvement in those other problem behaviors.

While these data have focused on variation in drinker status and in rates of involvement in other behaviors, the basic issue of the covariation of problem drinking with other behaviors can also be explored in another way, employing now continuous rather than discrete measures (except for sexual experience for which no continuous measure is available). In Table 3, Pearson intercorrelations among the various behaviors are presented, and much the same conclusions emerge. For both males and females, there are significant correlations among the various problem behaviors, and the two component measures of problem drinking (frequency of drunkenness and negative consequences of drinking) correlate with the other measures of problem behavior. It is of interest to mention that similar analyses of national sample data collected in 1978 are consonant with these findings, yielding somewhat higher correlations of the problem drinking measures with the other problem behavior measures, and linking them significantly with another problem behavior, involvement with cigarette smoking, as well (cf. Table 3.1 in Jessor, Donovan, & Widmer, 1980).

The covariation among problem behaviors indicated by the data in Tables 2 and 3 does not reveal whether the behaviors tend to be engaged in together, that is, on the same occasion or at the same time. We inquired about this in the Young Adult Follow-Up Study, in both 1979 and 1981. More than 80 percent of the men and about 60 percent of the women report using both alcohol and marijuana on the same occasion "at least some of the time." A

Table 3. Intercorrelations among problem behavior measures. High school sample: Year IV (1972)

Problem behavior measures	Times drunk past year	Negative consequences of drinking	Marijuana involvement	Deviant behavior	Church attendance
Times drunk/past year	1.00	0.41	0.23	0.19	-0.10^{ns}
Neg. consequences of drinking/past year	0.52	1.00	0.20	0.34	-0.05^{ns}
Involvement with marijuana	0.41	0.30	1.00	0.52	-0.30
General deviant behavior	0.36	0.29	0.49	1.00	-0.14
Church attendance/ past year	-0.01^{ns}	-0.11^{ns}	-0.12^{ns}	-0.14	1.00

Note: Females above the diagonal, males below

considerable amount of simultaneous engagement in different problem behaviors would thus appear to be taking place.

In sum, the evidence suggests that problem drinking is not an isolated behavior reflecting something unique about the effects of alcohol. Rather, it would seem more appropriate to consider adolescent problem drinking as part of a *syndrome* of problem behavior, a larger pattern of covarying behaviors all of which in one way or another depart from the expectations of conventional society about acceptable adolescent comportment. The significance of such a conclusion is far from trivial. On the one hand, it confirms the theoretical stance of Problem-Behavior Theory concerning problem behavior as a system of interrelated actions that can serve similar psychological functions. On the other hand, it suggests that since alcohol-related problems are embedded in a lifestyle, a coherent pattern of engagement in other problem behaviors, attempts at intervention and prevention that ignore that fact are likely to be less successful.

Accounting for Variation in Adolescent Problem Drinking

It is possible now to turn to one of the enduring concerns of our research efforts, namely, to explore the reach of a psychosocial approach to explaining variation in problem drinking. Having established the measures of problem drinking among the adolescent cohorts in our longitudinal study, we are able to examine how well the concepts in Problem-Behavior Theory can account for variation on those measures. Rather than deal with each individual variable in the theory, it will be more expeditious to examine simultaneously the multiple variables that constitute the key systems in the theory. For this purpose, multiple regression analyses were run employing the major variables in the Personality System, in the Perceived Environment System, in the two systems taken together (to capture the emphasis of Kurt Lewin's field theoretical approach to explanation), and finally, in an Overall Set that also includes the Behavior System variables. These different sets of theoretical measures

Table 4. Multiple correlations (Rs) of adolescent (1972) theoretical measures with adolescent (1972) problem drinking. High school sample

Adolescent (1972) Theoretical measures	Times drunk past year		Problem drinker status	
	Males	Females	Males	Females
Personality system	0.36	0.29	0.48	0.49
Perceived environment system	0.46	0.35	0.61	0.59
Field pattern	0.58	0.40	0.72	0.70
Overall set	0.60	0.43	0.79	0.76

were regressed against two measures of problem drinking, one a continuous measure, namely, frequency of drunkenness in the past year, and one a dichotomous measure, namely, problem-versus-nonproblem drinker status. The results of these multiple regression analyses are presented in Table 4.

The usefulness of Problem-Behavior Theory is evident in the findings in Table 4. Each of the explanatory systems is significantly correlated with both measures of problem drinking, although the multiple correlations are considerably higher with the problem drinker status criterion measure than they are with the times-drunk measure. The Perceived Environment System measures account for a somewhat higher percentage of the variance than do the Personality System measures, probably reflecting the fact that the components of the former are more proximal to problem drinking behavior whereas the components of the latter are more distal.[2] When the two systems are taken together as in the Field Pattern, there is a significant increment in variance explained for both sexes, and the Overall Set yields yet another increment. The multiple correlations of the Overall Set with problem drinker status ($Rs = 0.79$ and 0.76) account for about 60 percent of the variance for both males and females; that represents a substantial contribution to a psychosocial explanation of adolescent problem drinking.

What that psychosocial explanation implicates is the pattern of *proneness* toward problem drinking that underlies the multiple correlations for each system. Proneness toward problem drinking in the Personality System, as reflected by the individual measures typically entering the regression equations, includes:

— lower value on academic recognition
— higher value on independence
— independence valued more highly relative to academic recognition
— lower expectation for academic recognition
— greater attitudinal tolerance of deviance
— lesser religiosity.
   Proneness in the Perceived Environment System includes:
— lower compatibility between parental and friends' expectations
— greater perceived influence from friends than parents
— greater friends approval for problem behavior
— greater friends models for problem behavior.
   Proneness in the Behavior System includes:
— greater involvement in proto-delinquent behavior
— greater involvement with marijuana use
— less attendance at church.

---

[2] The proximal-distal distinction refers to the degree to which a predictor variable directly and explicitly implicates the criterion variable. Thus, "peer models for drunkenness" is more proximal to adolescent problem drinking whereas "peer expectations for academic achievement" would be more distal from it (cf. Jessor & Jessor, 1977)

Table 5. Multiple correlation (Rs) of theoretical measures with problem drinking. Independent national samples: 1974 and 1978

Theoretical measures	Times drunk/past year				Problem drinker status			
	Males		Females		Males		Females	
	1974	1978	1974	1978	1974	1978	1974	1978
Personality system	0.43	0.44	0.45	0.47	0.37	0.39	0.37	0.41
Perceived environment system	0.47	0.42	0.49	0.42	0.40	0.35	0.39	0.36
Field theoretical pattern	0.55	0.54	0.56	0.54	0.47	0.46	0.46	0.47
Overall set	0.65	0.69	0.67	0.71	0.56	0.60	0.55	0.62

Note: Male Ns: 1974 (2006); 1978 (1666)
Female Ns: 1974 (1989); 1978 (1848)
Grades 10–12, drinkers only

This profile of psychosocial proneness to problem drinking follows from the conceptual structure of Problem-Behavior Theory, and these data provide strong support for the theory. The basic underlying dimension that would seem to capture best the various components in the profile is a dimension of *psychosocial unconventionality*, implying a generalized skepticism about societal values, a rejection of its norms, and a readiness for nonconformity. The pattern is similar to, even isomorphic with, that emerging from comparable analyses of other problem behaviors, such as marijuana use, delinquency, or sexual precocity.

That these results are not merely parochial and confined to the idiosyncratic nature of the local sample of high school youth employed, or to the particular 1972 year of data examined, can be seen in Table 5. The key measures, albeit abbreviated, of Problem-Behavior Theory were incorporated into two different national sample surveys carried out by the Research Triangle Institute in 1974 and 1978 (Rachal *et al.*, 1975; Rachal *et al.*, 1980; Jessor, Donovan, & Widmer, 1980). Analyses of frequency of drunkenness and problem drinker status in both of these large sample surveys, for both sexes, yield further support for the psychosocial explanatory account provided by Problem-Behavior Theory. The two independent, cross-sectional, national samples replicate to a large extent the findings from the small local samples we have been following over time. In this case, frequency of drunkenness is better explained than problem drinker status, with better than 40 percent of the variance accounted for, and the Personality System is here no less predictive than the Perceived Environment System, but on the whole the relevance of Problem-Behavior Theory is again apparent. Further, these data, collected during a turbulent decade two and six years later than those for the High School Sample, suggest some degree of invariance of the psychosocial account over at least this portion of historical time (see also Jessor, Chase & Donovan, 1980; Donovan & Jessor, 1983).

Continuity of Problem Drinking: Adolescence to Young Adulthood

Up to this point, we have been looking at problem drinking in adolescence, its prevalence and its psychosocial correlates. Our focus has been cross-sectional, concerned with a particular point in time and with providing an account of variation between persons in problem drinking at that time. The employment of a longitudinal design in our research, however, makes possible a concern with very different questions, ones that have large social importance. First, it becomes possible to inquire about the natural history of problem drinking beyond adolescence, that is, about the course of development that problem drinking takes from adolescence into young adulthood. Is there continuity and to what extent? Once a problem drinker, always a problem drinker? Second, longitudinal design permits us to examine whether the course of development of problem drinking is merely adventitious or whether, instead, it is actually systematic and predictable from antecedent measures in adolescence. Is it possible to predict young adult problem drinking from psychosocial characteristics measured in adolescence? Can we identify early – that is, in adolescence – those youth who are likely to have alcohol-related problems as young adults?

To examine continuity of problem drinking between adolescence and young adulthood, it was necessary to classify the High School Sample participants on their drinker status in the two later waves of data as well, those collected in young adulthood, both in 1979, when they were 23, 24 and 25, and again in 1981, when they were 25, 26, and 27 years of age. The same joint criterion as had been used with their adolescent data was again employed, relying on the same cutting points for frequency of drunkenness and for negative consequences, but now over the preceding 6 months as the time interval rather than the preceding year. This change in time interval was made to take account of the generally higher level of alcohol use in this later life stage. In these analyses, our operational specification designated as a young adult problem drinker anyone who met the joint criterion for problem drinking in *either* 1979 *or* 1981, or in both years. Nonproblem drinkers in young adulthood, it follows, had to be so classified consistently, that is, in *both* 1979 *and* 1981. The data on the continuity of drinker status between adolescence and young adulthood are presented for both sexes in Table 6.

It is interesting to observe in Table 6 that there is considerable discontinuity or instability in drinker status between adolescence and young adulthood. Among the males who were problem drinkers in adolescence, fully half of them are no longer classified as problem drinkers as young adults; for females, the discontinuity is even more striking – three quarters of the adolescent problem drinker women are no longer problem drinkers as young adults. Another kind of discontinuity in drinker status can be seen when the adolescent *non*problem drinkers are followed into young adulthood: among the males, 40 percent have *onset* problem drinking by young adulthood, and among the females, 20 percent have done the same. As for the adolescent ab-

Table 6. Continuity of drinker status in adolescence and young adulthood. High school sample

Adolescent (1972) Drinker status		Young adulthood (1979/81) Drinker status		
		% Abstainer	% Not problem drinker	% Problem drinker
Males	Abstainer (N = 31)	16	81	3
	Not problem drinker (N = 86)	0	60	40
	Problem drinker (N = 45)	0	49	51
Females	Abstainer (N = 49)	8	86	6
	Not problem drinker (N = 138)	0	80	20
	Problem drinker (N = 35)	0	74	26

stainers, nearly all of them have become drinkers by young adulthood, almost all classified as nonproblem drinkers.

Although merely descriptive, such "natural history" data are uniquely valuable since little is known about this particular portion of the life trajectory, and such information can only be gotten by following lives through time. What these descriptive, developmental data reveal is that having been a problem drinker as an adolescent is, *in itself*, not very predictive about the likelihood of problem drinking later on as a young adult. The chances of a male adolescent problem drinker being a problem drinker as a young adult are about 50:50; for females, the probability is clearly greater that they will be nonproblem drinkers rather than problem drinkers. The outcome of adolescent problem drinking, therefore, even for males, is no more likely to be inexorable chronicity than it is to be "maturing out," and, for females, the latter outcome is, in fact, much more likely to be the case.

Clearly, risk for young adult problem drinking is greater for men than it is for women in this sample: a larger proportion of male adolescent problem drinkers remain problem drinkers in young adulthood than is true for comparable females (51 percent versus 26 percent); at the same time, a larger proportion of male adolescent nonproblem drinkers onset problem drinking by young adulthood than is true for comparable females (40 percent versus 20 percent). Whether these important gender differences reflect differential cultural expectations and controls, gender-linked variation in role obligations, or women's apprehensions in relation to possible childbearing is not something we are able to determine from our information.

In addition to examining the degree to which drinker status in adolescence predicts drinker status in young adulthood, it is possible for us to address a related but different question: does adolescent drinker status predict *other* kinds of outcomes in young adulthood? Stated otherwise, is adolescent problem drinking *consequential* for later life status, for subsequent life events, for achievement, or for other life outcomes? Does it portend a legacy for the future? The most general answer to this question turns out, with some qualifications, to be negative. Nearly 300 different measures obtained in young adulthood were analyzed in relation to the three adolescent drinker statuses: abstainer, nonproblem drinker, or problem drinker. Only a tiny handful of the measures yielded systematic differences, and some of these reflect, at least partially, the current drinker status in young adulthood rather than the earlier drinker status as an adolescent.

A few of the findings are nevertheless of interest to mention. Among the young adult males, the percent *ever arrested* is 48, 20, and 0 for those classified as problem drinkers, nonproblem drinkers and abstainers in adolescence, respectively; for females, the respective percentages are 23, 9, and 2. These differences hold, for both sexes, even when young adult drinker status is controlled. Among males, the percent who *smoke half a pack or more of cigarettes per day* is, in the same group order, 38, 24, and 0; among females, the percentages are 46, 23 and 6. Among males, the percent with a *history of divorce* is 11, 6, and 7; among females it is 23, 18, and 2. Finally, among males, the percent *graduating college or beyond* is 49, 50, and 61; among females, it is 35, 41, and 71. Although such findings do suggest that there may be some systematic outcomes in later life related to degree of involvement with alcohol in adolescence, their sparseness among 300 different measures is noteworthy, and it is not possible to rule out chance as being responsible.

Overall, it seems clear and worth emphasizing that adolescent drinker status *per se* does not predict very much about either drinker status or a large variety of other attributes and outcomes later in young adulthood. This conclusion would seem to be just another reflection of the degree of discontinuity of drinker status between adolescence and young adulthood that was noted earlier in Table 6. Such findings are of major importance because they suggest that post-adolescent development and attainment are not necessarily mortgaged by adolescent problem drinking. They should also alert us to the possibility that premature labeling and social processing of adolescents as problem drinkers might very well set up expectations for chronicity that unnecessarily restrict the developmental options that our data suggest are, indeed, there.

Predicting Young Adult Problem Drinking

Although adolescent drinker status, per se, has been shown not to be predictive of young adult problem drinking, the question still remains whether young adult problem drinking may be predictable from other kinds of adolescent characteristics, perhaps the very ones that are mapped by the concepts of Problem-Behavior Theory. It is to that question that we turn in this section.

Table 7. Multiple correlations (*R*s) of adolescent theoretical measures with young adult problem drinking (*Among* 1972 problem drinkers). High school sample

Adolescent (1972) Theoretical measures	Young adult (1979/81) Problem drinker status	
	Males (N = 45)	Females (N = 35)
Personality system	0.60	0.29
Perceived environment system	0.51	0.49
Field pattern	0.71	0.49
Overall set	0.74	0.56

Analyses Among Adolescent Problem Drinkers

In order to answer this question with our longitudinal data, we have phrased it as follows: Among adolescent problem drinkers, are the theoretical measures obtained in adolescence predictive of continuation/discontinuation by young adulthood? In other words, do the Problem-Behavior Theory measures serve to identify early, that is, in adolescence, those whose problem drinking will be chronic and those who will "mature out" of problem drinking by young adulthood?

The analyses again employed multiple regression. Drinker status in young adulthood (the dichotomy of problem drinker versus nonproblem drinker) was regressed on the measures of the multivariate systems of Problem-Behavior Theory collected in adolescence. Drinker status in adolescence was controlled, of course, since these analyses were run *within* the adolescent problem drinker group. The relevant results are presented in Table 7 for both males and females.

Among adolescent problem drinkers, the pattern of psychosocial proneness to problem behavior that obtains in adolescence significantly predicts continuation/discontinuation of problem drinking by young adulthood, that is, seven and/or nine years later. The Overall Set of adolescent measures accounts for a substantial portion of the young adult criterion variance, 55 percent for the men ($R = 0.74$), and 31 percent for the women ($R = 0.56$). Although the variance accounted for among the males is nearly twice that among the females, both multiple correlations are significant beyond the 0.001 level. This interesting difference between the genders is largely due to the greater predictiveness of the adolescent Personality System measures for the males ($R = 0.60$) than for the females ($R = 0.29$); in fact, for the former, it is a more important source of variance than the Perceived Environment System ($R = 0.51$) and, in interaction with the latter, yields a substantial increment in multiple R for the Field Pattern ($R = 0.71$).

Analyses Among Adolescent Nonproblem Drinkers

The predictability of continuity/discontinuity of drinker status between adolescence and young adulthood can be addressed within the adolescent nonproblem drinkers as well. Retaining our concern for predicting problem drinking in young adulthood from measures obtained in adolescence, the research question is phrased as follows: Among adolescent nonproblem drinkers, are the theoretical measures obtained in adolescence predictive of the onset of problem drinking by young adulthood? Data relevant to this inquiry are shown in Table 8.

Again the findings indicate significant multiple correlations between the theoretical system measures in adolescence and the problem drinker vs. nonproblem drinker criterion in young adulthood. However, the amount of criterion variance accounted for is considerably less, for both sexes, than it was in the preceding analysis for the adolescent problem drinkers. As in those analyses, there is a gender difference here with predictability once more better for men than women.

Both sets of analyses confirm the theoretical expectation that the course of development of adolescent drinker status — and the likelihood of young adult problem drinking — are systematic rather than adventitious or circumstantial outcomes. Both analyses have shown the relevance of Problem-Behavior Theory as a systematic account of the likelihood of continuing or initiating problem drinking in the post adolescent period. Although predictability is greater for adolescent problem drinkers than nonproblem drinkers, and for males than for females, it is nevertheless significant for both groups and both genders. The profile of adolescent theoretical attributes that is implicated in these longitudinal multiple correlations is similar to the profile that accounted for variation in problem drinking cross-sectionally in adolescence. The typical components of that profile of psychosocial proneness to problem behavior were listed in an earlier section of the paper. Such invariance between the cross-sectional and the longitudinal accounts has been noted before (Jessor & Jessor, 1977); it serves to strengthen con-

Table 8. Multiple correlations (Rs) of adolescent theoretical measures with young adult problem drinking (Among 1972 not problem drinkers). High school sample

Adolescent (1972) Theoretical measures	Young adult (1979/81) Problem drinker status	
	Males (N = 84)	Females (N = 137)
Personality system	0.36	0.23
Perceived environment system	0.33	0.24
Field pattern	0.43	0.33
Overall set	0.58	0.35

viction about the relevance of Problem-Behavior Theory as an explanation of the developmental course of adolescent problem drinking.

It should be cautioned that while the analyses reported in this section show statistically significant predictiveness, it is not of a magnitude that would permit prediction at an individual level. Nevertheless, the findings surely are germane to considerations of early identification and the design of prevention/intervention efforts. They underscore the necessity to go beyond the phenotypic level of overt behavior, that is, whether an adolescent is a problem drinker or not, and to address the underlying, or "causal," or genotypic level, that is, the degree of psychosocial proneness to problem behavior that characterizes that adolescent. The targeting of adolescents at risk — either for chronicity or for onset of problem drinking — will inevitably require knowledge of their profile of psychosocial risk factors.

Continuity of Problem Drinking Within Young Adulthood

The discontinuity of problem drinking that has been discussed thus far emerged from a consideration of data collected at two rather different life stages, adolescence and young adulthood. Since adolescence is a time of rapid change and the interval between the adolescent data and the young adult data was rather long — from 1972 to 1979/81, discontinuity and instability might well have been expected. It seems important, then, to consider whether discontinuity of problem drinking is apparent over a shorter time interval and one that takes place within the same life stage.

Continuity/Discontinuity of Young Adult Problem Drinking

Because the young adult phase of our larger longitudinal study is itself longitudinal in design, it is possible to address that issue. Within young adulthood, two waves of data were collected, one in 1979 when the High School Sample cohorts were ages 23, 24, and 25, and the other in 1981 when they were 25, 26, and 27. This two-year time interval, 1979–1981, occurs near the middle of the third decade of life for our participants, well within the life stage of young adulthood.

In the preceding analyses, the young adult problem drinker criterion measure was based upon data from *both* 1979 and 1981; problem drinking in *either* year qualified a participant as a young adult problem drinker. The reasons for employing such a "liberal" criterion were our anticipation of some degree of instability in drinking pattern but, more importantly, a desire to deal with any indication of problem drinking as part of young adult life rather than requiring that it be a consistent characteristic. Such an approach obviously yields a higher prevalence of young adult problem drinking and thus decreases the likelihood of discontinuity of problem drinking for adolescent problem drinkers. Despite such a definition, one that would tend to maximize continuity, considerable discontinuity is what we have seen. In the present analyses, we separate the 1979 and 1981 drinker status classifications and then examine the degree of continuity that is obtained between them across that two-year interval within young adulthood. The relevant findings can be seen in Table 9; drinker status shown as "Not Problem Drinkers" includes abstainers, minimal drinkers, and former drinkers, as well as nonproblem drinkers.

Even across a relatively short interval of time and within the same stage of life, there is substantial discontinuity of problem drinking. Among the men who were classified as problem drinkers in 1979, more than a quarter of them no longer meet the very same criterion only two years later in 1981. Among the women, the data are much more striking; of those classified as problem drinkers in 1979, over half are no longer problem drinkers in 1981. Unlike the pattern of discontinuity between adolescence and young adulthood that was seen earlier in Table 6, discontinuity that involved *both* directions of change — from problem drinker to nonproblem drinker, and from nonproblem drinker to problem drinker — the discontinuity within young adulthood seems primarily to involve the *discontinuation of problem drinking*. As can be seen in Table 9, only 7 percent of the 1979 nonproblem drinker men and only 4 percent of the 1979 nonproblem drinker women are classified as problem drinkers in 1981; thus, there is little onset (or resumption) of problem drinking during this interval. The comparable figures from Table 6 for the percentage shifting from nonproblem to problem drinking were 40 percent for men and 20 percent for women. Overall, there is a decline in the actual prevalence of problem drinking between 1979 and 1981 of 4.3 percent for the men and 4.8 percent for the women.

Table 9. The continuity of problem drinking *within* young adulthood: 1979 to 1981. High school sample

1979 Problem drinker status		1981 Problem drinker status	
		% Not problem drinkers	% Problem drinkers
Males	Not problem drinkers (N=110)	93	7
	Problem drinkers (N=49)	29	71
Females	Not problem drinkers (N=189)	96	4
	Problem drinkers (N=32)	53	47

Note: Four people were missing drinking data in 1981 and have been omitted from this table

The data in Table 9, therefore, have special interest. They reemphasize the discontinuity of problem drinking that we had seen earlier, and now make clear that it is still substantial even for short time intervals. Second, they reaffirm the earlier observation of greater discontinuity among women than men and show that that difference also is obtained within young adulthood. But, perhaps most intriguing, they suggest that young adulthood – at least this portion of it – might be characterized as a time of maturing out of problem drinking, that is, as a time in which there are significant rates of discontinuation of problem drinking (especially for women) and very low rates of initiating or resuming it. If this were to prove to be the case, it would be a finding of major importance.

Psychosocial Change in Young Adulthood

In trying to consider the latter possibility further – namely, that this stage of the life trajectory, the late twenties, may be a time of maturing out of problem drinking – it is important to recall that various studies have implicated an earlier age range as being the really high risk period for problem drinking and other problem behaviors. Thus, beyond the high risk 18 – 24 age period, some decline in prevalence might well be expected on the basis of those studies, and that may be what is reflected in the data from our somewhat older 25, 26, and 27 year-olds.

Unfortunately, such considerations do not provide an *explanation* for the decline, that is, for why it should occur. Our longitudinal psychosocial data, however, do make available certain findings that may contribute toward an answer. With six waves of data on each participant, it has been possible for us to plot the trajectories of development and change on many of the psychosocial variables from 1969 through 1981. Two developmental generalizations seem best to summarize those graphs or "growth curves." First, the course of psychosocial development in adolescence for the cohorts in this study seems to be in a direction of increasing problem behavior proneness; this is the conclusion we drew in our book on the earlier phase of the longitudinal study (Jessor & Jessor, 1977). Second, the course of psychosocial development in young adulthood seems to be in the opposite direction, one of decreasing problem behavior proneness; that is, there is now in young adulthood a clear developmental increase in conventionality and in psychosocial proneness toward conformity (Jessor, 1983). An almost paradigmatic illustration of both of these generalizations can be seen in Figure 4.

The measure charted in Figure 4 is a key Personality System variable, Attitudinal Intolerance of Deviance, that has excellent psychometric properties, established construct validity, and a stability coefficient of 0.41 for males and 0.47 for females between 1972 and 1979 (corrected for attenuation). Between 1969 and 1972 in Figure 4, there is a consistent developmental decline in intolerance of deviance. That means theoretically, of

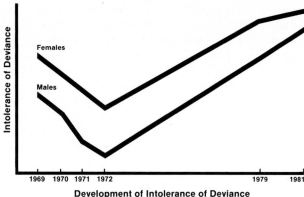

Development of Intolerance of Deviance
High School Sample: Males N=162; Females N=222

Fig. 4. Change over time in intolerance of deviance: high school sample

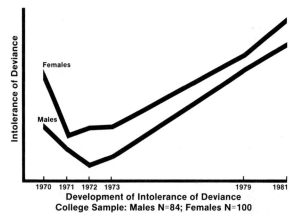

Development of Intolerance of Deviance
College Sample: Males N=84; Females N=100

Fig. 5. Change over time in intolerance of deviance: College sample

course, a consistent increase in problem behavior proneness. Although women are more intolerant of deviance than men throughout, the slope of their curve in those adolescent years is similar to that of the men. What is striking about these curves is their *reversal of direction* after adolescence, that is, between 1972 and 1979. Not only is there now a consistent *increase* in intolerance of deviance across this latter time interval, but by 1979 it reaches, for both sexes, a level higher in intolerance than that of 1969 when they were all in junior high school. The added data point for 1981 makes clear that we are observing a stable developmental trend rather than an artifact dependent upon having only a single measurement in young adulthood. Thus, the High School Sample data in Figure 4 strongly suggest that these cohorts are increasing in psychosocial conventionality as they reach their late twenties. Further corroboration of that direction of developmental change on this same measure can be seen in Figure 5.

Data from the College Sample, the parallel longitudinal study that was carried along in tandem with the High School Sample, have been used in Figure 5. Once again, the same major trends can be seen as were noted in Figure 4: a decline in intolerance of deviance in the initial years of the prior phase of the study beginning in 1970, and then a reversal by 1979 that is sustained in 1981 at which time the college sample had reached the age of 30. Thus, the two major developmental generalizations are supported by four separate, replicated curves. Although only a single measure, Intolerance of Deviance, has been presented here, similar findings have emerged on several other theoretical measures as well (see Jessor, 1983). Development, at least in the mid- and later twenties, appears to be in the direction of greater personality, perceived environment, and behavioral conventionality. That direction may well follow from the assumption of new life roles in work and family and the occupancy of new social contexts other than that of school, both factors constituting conventionalizing influences.

Obviously, these findings are constrained by the particular cohorts involved and by the time in history when the data were collected. It is not possible, therefore, to infer that the increasing conventionality observed in our sample in young adulthood is an invariant developmental characteristic of that life stage rather than being simply a reflection of the increasing conventionality of the larger society and the historical shift away from the radicalism of the early Seventies. In this regard, however, it is most intriguing to note that, for the College Sample cohorts in Figure 5, there is already an indication of a beginning reversal of direction in their curves *within* the first phase of the study, that is, in the early Seventies and *prior to* the historical shift just mentioned. The reversal can be seen to occur by 1972 for the females and by 1973 for the males, when they were, in fact, just beyond adolescence and at the beginning of their development as young adults at the ages of 21 and 22.

The intent in presenting the data in these two figures has been to invoke a possible psychosocial explanation for the suggested trend in the High School Sample toward maturing out of problem drinking by 1981, when the participants had reached their later twenties. That explanation involves the observed decline in psychosocial proneness to problem behavior in later young adulthood. According to the logic of Problem-Behavior Theory, such a decline would result in a corresponding decline in involvement in problem behavior, including, of course, problem drinking, our present concern.

Conclusion

I have sought in this paper to provide an overview of the cumulative outcome of more than two decades of psychosocial inquiry about adolescent problem drinking. Throughout this period, our research − both cross-sectional and longitudinal − has been guided by a general psychosocial perspective and by a more specific conceptual framework, namely, Problem-Behavior Theory. In the latter framework, variation in adolescent problem drinking is accounted for by three explanatory systems: personality, environment, and behavior. What the research has shown is that each of these explanatory systems is significantly associated with problem drinking, and, together, they can account for a substantial portion of its variation.

But the research, especially the longitudinal study following up adolescents into young adulthood, has contributed more than just support for a particular theory. It has corroborated that problem drinking in adolescence is a serious public health issue, with one out of four young men and one out of six young women in our sample of normal high school youth meeting our criteria for problem drinking. It has also demonstrated that problem drinking, rather than being an isolated behavior, is associated with and embedded in a larger pattern or syndrome of adolescent problem behavior.

Following lives through time has enabled us also to observe the course of development and change of problem drinking as adolescents move into the third decade of life and become young adults. What has emerged from the research is a strong sense of the discontinuity or instability of problem drinking over time. Although the gap in our data *between* adolescence and young adulthood, that is, between 1972 and 1979, precludes our describing what the drinking pattern has been during that interval, it is apparent that there is considerable turnover in drinker status between those two times of measurement. About 50 percent of the males who were problem drinkers as adolescents are no longer problem drinkers as young adults; for females the discontinuity is even greater, and the comparable figure is about 75 percent. Discontinuity is observed, also, over the much shorter 1979–1981 interval within young adulthood, with more than a quarter of the 1979 male problem drinkers and more than half of the 1979 female problem drinkers no longer problem drinkers in 1981.

These findings about discontinuity are important in helping to temper a perspective on adolescent problem drinking that would emphasize inexorable chronicity and an inescapable legacy for later life. Equally important, the findings make clear that the observed discontinuity over time is not simply random or adventitious, but systematic and predictable to a significant degree. The prediction of young adult continuity/discontinuity of problem drinking rests, however, not on the antecedent adolescent drinker status but on an assessment of antecedent psychosocial proneness to problem behavior in adolescence. These developmental findings provide further support for the usefulness of Problem-Behavior Theory.

The difficulties of deriving from explanatory research its logical implications for prevention/intervention cannot be overestimated. Nevertheless, at least two possible implications from our findings should be emphasized: the importance of interventions that deal with multiple problem behaviors simultaneously; and the advisability of seeking change in all three psychosocial systems – personality, the environment, and behavior.

The research described in this paper has led us, we think, at least a small distance in the direction of greater understanding of adolescent problem drinking. If that proves to be the case, it will have been a scientific journey well worth the traveling.

References

Donovan, J. E. & Jessor, R. (1978) Adolescent problem drinking: Psychosocial correlates in a national sample study. *Journal of Studies on Alcohol, 39,* 1506–1524

Donovan, J. E. & Jessor, R. (1983) Problem drinking and the dimension of involvement with drugs: A Guttman scalogram analysis of adolescent drug use. *American Journal of Public Health, 73,* 543–552

Donovan, J. E., Jessor, R., & Jessor, L. (1983) Problem drinking in adolescence and young adulthood: A follow-up study. *Journal of Studies on Alcohol, 44,* 109–137

Jessor, R. (1983) The stability of change: Psychosocial development from adolescence to young adulthood. In: Magnusson, D., and Allen, V., (Ed.) *Human development: An interactional perspective* (pp. 321–341). New York: Academic

Jessor, R. (1984) Adolescent development and behavioral health. In: Matarazzo, J. D., Weiss, S. M., Herd, J. A., Miller, N. E, and Weiss, S. M. (Eds.) *Behavioral health: A handbook of health enhancement and disease prevention.* New York: Wiley

Jessor, R., Chase, J. A., & Donovan, J. E. (1980) Psychosocial correlates of marijuana use and problem drinking in a national sample of adolescents. *American Journal of Public Health, 70,* 604–613

Jessor, R., Donovan, J. E., & Widmer, K. (1980) *Psychosocial factors in adolescent alcohol and drug use: The 1978 national sample study, and the 1974–78 panel study* (pp. 1–161) Boulder: Institute of Behavioral Science, University of Colorado

Jessor, R., Graves, T. D., Hanson, R. C., & Jessor, S. L. (1968) *Society, personality, and deviant behavior: A study of a tri-ethnic community.* New York: Holt, Rinehart, & Winston

Jessor, R. & Jessor, S. L. (1977) *Problem behavior and psychosocial development: A longitudinal study of youth.* New York: Academic

Jessor, R. & Jessor, S. L. (1984) Adolescence to young adulthood: A twelve-year prospective study of problem behavior and psychosocial development. In: Mednick, S., and Harway, M. (Eds.) *Longitudinal research in the United States.* New York: Praeger

Rachal, J. V., Williams, J. R., Brehm, M. L., Cavanaugh, B., Moore, R. P., & Eckerman, W. C. (1975) *A national study of adolescent drinking behavior, attitudes, and correlates* (NTIS Report No. PB-246-002, pp. 1–159). Springfield, VA: U.S. National Technical Information Service

Rachal, J. V., Guess, L. L., Hubbard, R. L., Maisto, S. A., Cavanaugh, E. R., Waddell, R., & Benrud, C. H. (1980) *Adolescent drinking behavior, Vol. I: The extent and nature of adolescent alcohol and drug use: The 1974 and 1978 national sample studies* (pp. 1–140). Research Triangle Park: Research Triangle Institute

XIV. Structural Modeling with Large Data Sets and Non-Normal Continuous Variables[1]

P. M. BENTLER *

Introduction

Although there are a number of different paradigms for the study of developmental trajectories of youth in various social contexts, the multivariate statistical approach that allows a test of structural hypotheses specified by the researcher represents a powerful approach to testing person/ situation theories (Bentler, 1980). This approach intrinsically involves data from a large number of subjects, assessed on multiple occasions and on a substantial number of variables. The availability of data from large numbers of subjects allows for the use of newly developed methods of structural modeling that are distribution-free, or that make relatively mild assumptions in comparison with currently popular methods that rely on assumptions of multivariate normality. In many cases, however, the data base available to the researcher outstrips the analytic capability of the statistical methods, at least in practice if not in theory. More specifically, as the number of variables increases, the number of parameters in structural equation models with latent variables can quickly grow to several hundred or more, making it difficult to use statistical estimation involving iterative nonlinear optimization methods. Not only does an iterative process take geometrically longer to converge to an appropriate solution, but the expense of obtaining such a solution also quickly gets out of hand. Some feasible estimators have recently been proposed to solve this problem. The nature of these recent developments, and their relevance to multivariate person/ ecology data, are reviewed.

Effects of Excessive Data

Researchers stemming from a manipulative hypothesis-testing tradition, especially a univariate experimental design tradition, can probably hardly conceive of a research context involving excessive data. In such situations,

[1] This report was prepared in part with the support of USPHS grants DA01070 and DA00017.

* University of California, Department of Psychology, 1282a Franz Hall, Los Angeles, CA 90024, USA.

Development as Action in Context
Ed. by R. K. Silbereisen et al.
© Springer-Verlag Berlin Heidelberg 1986

only a few dependent variables are examined, a highly limited number of manipulative variables are utilized, and few if any control variables are used. In contrast, research on naturalistic flows of development require massive numbers of dependent and independent variables as well as control variables because, typically, the research questions being asked are far broader than those considered in experimental psychology, the reliabilities of the variables are somewhat low, the nature of cause-effect relations are more poorly understood, and the absence of randomization requires a consideration of a variety of competing explanations whose possible impacts must be controlled statistically. Combining these general problems of quasi- or nonexperimental research with a longitudinal design, or a design involving person and ecology, has the effects of multiplying the number of variables that could or should be assessed in practice to an almost unmanagable amount. Thus, even if it were possible to consider a study of naturalistic development focussing only upon some twenty key variables, measuring these variables in the context of only five ecologies across five occasions, yields a total of 500 scores per individual. Such massive data bases require not only specialized skills in strategies for approaching the analytic task in the context of a developmental theory, but also requires a great deal of care in the selection of psychometric and statistical methods to be used. It will be obvious, for example, that if the sample of subjects consists of 100 individuals, in the design considered above there would be too many parameters to estimate per subject. Unless analytic methods that yield highly stable results with small subject pools are utilized, or carefully considered methods of data reduction are implemented, one can be in the dangerous situation of having more parameters to estimate from the data than there are subjects in the study.

There are hardly any dangers associated with having too many subjects in a study. It is known that estimates of parameters become more stable as the size of a subject sample increases, and that one can then evaluate differences between conditions and variables with greater confidence. Large subject pools make it possible to divide a sample judiciously into multiple groups, such as those based on sex, socioeconomic status, or age, and possibly to their combination, and to analyze data for within and between group consistency. Clean cross-validation studies are possible when the sample can be split: part of the data can be used to develop models and to make empirical modifications to yield statistically acceptable results, while the other part of the data can be used to provide clean tests as to the adequacy of such mixed theoretical-empirical models. In the absence of very large subject pools such analyses could not even be considered, because the effective sample size within any subgroup can become so small that the number of parameters to be estimated can exceed the size of the sample. This is an impossible situation; it is well known that even a simple mean based on independent observations for a single variable requires more than a few cases to yield relatively stable results. In order to have just five subjects per parameter, a 200 parameter structural model would require 1000 subjects. Furthermore, as will be noted below, recent developments in structural modeling, which also apply to more traditional methods such as multiple regression and correlation, can take advantage of large subject pools by enabling the use of methods that do not rely on strong statistical assumptions. These asymptotically distribution-free methods can allow the tests of hypotheses in data bases for which the only extant methods, based on maximum likelihood methods associated with multivariate normal distribution theory, are really not appropriate.

Just about the only potential problem of excessively large numbers of subjects in structural modeling is that statistical power of the goodness of fit test becomes so large as to enable the rejection of almost any realistic model. That is, while a model may well explain virtually all of the variation and covariation in the data, a nonzero amount of covariation is not explained and the statistical test can verify that this residual covariation is not strictly zero. In order to reduce such residual covariation, many researchers are tempted into utilizing empirically determined parameters, so-called "junk" parameters, just to make a model fit with an acceptable statistical probability level. These types of problems can be dealt with by utilizing a perspective on model fitting concerned more with relative model acceptability that with a magic 0.05 probability level, as espoused for example by Bentler & Bonett (1980) in their development of normed and nonnormed goodness of fit indices. For additional perspectives, see Huba & Bentler (1982a).

The main difficulty, then, of excessive data is that associated with the multiplying effect of number of variables and parameters relative to a fixed and insufficiently large sample size. All indications are that massive data sets, such as are appropriate to fully investigate the development of person or ecological development, are difficult to conceptualize in all their complexity, and harder still to analyze and report in a relatively straightforward manner. Inevitably, excessive data require the use of massive data reduction techniques such as factor analysis and a compromise of confirmatory theory-testing approaches to allow for exploratory analyses. A great deal of inventiveness is required to organize and sequence the data reduction and analysis in such a way as to minimize capitalization on chance and to maximize the extraction of meaning and stable findings from the data. Although there are various strategies for dealing with problems, one that seems to work well in the context of research problems as are addressed here is that of submodeling, as developed and applied by Huba in a longitudinal study of adolescent development and drug use started by the author many years ago (Huba & Bentler, 1982b; in preparation). In this approach meaningful aspects of the data are evaluated via models, and the models are replicated in a wide variety of ecologies, for example across time. This latter point is relevant to some advantages of excessive data that should be noted as well.

The availability of a large number of observations per individual allows the data reduction into variables that have higher reliability, greater generality, and greater validity – as noted, for example, by Epstein (1979). In addition to such effects as might be predicted from reliability theory, the ability to target in on constructs of broader meaning through multiple operationalizations across a variety of settings and contexts provides for greater meaningfulness of the resulting measures and greater hope for dealing with constructs and variables that have fundamental significance to the field – here, to adolescent development. In the context of structural modeling, the possible advantages are even greater. The ability to use indicators that range across the relevant domain of generalization also implies that latent variables that might be defined on such variables will have broader generality. Furthermore, such latent variables will be totally freed from the effects of random error, while the Epstein type of approach could only reach such limits with an arbitrarily large number of variables (which is, of course, not practical). In addition, in contexts such as longitudinal data one can utilize designs that allow the replication of effects in order to evaluate the stability of a phenomenon, for example, do attitudes affect future behavior more strongly than behavior affects future attitudes? (See Bentler & Speckart, 1981; Speckart & Bentler, 1982.) Of special interest in the current context is the question of whether hypothesized causal influences would show themselves similarly in a variety of ecologies.

In the remainder of this paper, some recent developments relevant to structural modeling with large data bases will be reviewed. First, factor analytic models that can be applied with very large numbers of variables will be discussed. Then, some recent developments that make possible structural modeling in large data sets by reducing the computational burden will be discussed. Some of these methods make substantially fewer assumptions than are associated with LISREL (Jöreskog & Sörbom, 1981) or related normal theory methods. Finally, a distribution-free estimator is discussed which yields correct statistical conclusions in situations where the normal theory chi-square can be primarily a test of multivariate normality rather than a test of a hypothesized structural model.

Factor Analytic Methods for Large Data Sets

One of the fundamental needs in the analysis of large data sets is to have methods of data reduction on the one hand, and methods for understanding the structure of data on the other. It is well known that factor analysis serves both of these functions. Exploratory factor analysis is particularly suited to these tasks in a context of raw empiricism, while confirmatory factor analysis tends to be more appropriate when testing structural hypotheses. Although exploratory factor analysis has received a bad reputation for its ability to be applied in essentially all research contexts with quantitative data, its apparent ability to make something out of nothing is vastly overrated. In fact, explicit data gathering designs and quality theories about potential constructs operating in a given situation are critical to the ability of the technique to yield results that do not necessarily require cross validation (though that is always desirable). Drawing appropriate conclusions about the number of factors and their meaning is certainly aided by adequate theory.

As noted above, longitudinal and person-ecology data sets can easily have several hundred variables to be analyzed. Current methods of factor analysis have great difficulty being implemented in such large data situations. Of course, principal components can probably be extracted from very large data sets, but these components do not allow confirmatory variants and are not really consistent with the factor model (although they are apparently sometimes empirically indistinguishable from them; see e.g., Lee & Comrey, 1979; Jackson & Chan, 1980). Recently, Hägglund (1982) and Bentler (1982a) introduced methods of factor analysis that involve little more than the solution of linear equations which can be done quickly and cheaply. These methods provide a foundation for factor analysis for large data sets, since they do not require iterative recalculation of parameter estimates. The Hägglund estimator, however, requires substantially more computations than the Bentler estimator, and it has been developed primarily for the exploratory model and not the confirmatory model. The Bentler estimator has been developed for both situations, and consequently it will be emphasized in the discussion below.

Without being too technical, the concepts underlying the Bentler non-iterative estimator can be easily described. All of the variables to be analyzed are divided into two sets. The first set is small, consisting of variables that are chosen to be good indicators of the underlying factors. Thus with 30 hypothesized factors, 30 variables would be chosen as marker variables and the remaining several hundred variables would be placed into another set. These marker variables are presumed to have unit loadings on their respective factors, as is typically executed in LISREL applications. As a consequence, these marker variables are rather simply decomposed as

$$\mathbf{x} = \xi + \varepsilon_x$$

with covariance matrix

$$\Sigma_{xx} = \Phi + \Psi_x \, .$$

Here, ξ is the vector of factors, and Φ is the covariance matrix of these factors, while ε_x is the residual vector with covariance matrix Ψ_x. The remaining variables, say, the $\mathbf{y}$ variables, are decomposed in the traditional way as

$$\mathbf{y} = \Lambda \xi + \varepsilon_y \, .$$

Associated with this decomposition is the covariance structure of the $(\mathbf{y}, \mathbf{x})$ and $(\mathbf{y}, \mathbf{y})$ sets

$$\Sigma_{yx} = \Lambda\Phi$$
$$\Sigma_{yy} = \Lambda\Phi\Lambda' + \Psi,$$

where Ψ is the covariance matrix of the ε_y. So far, this matrix decomposition looks pretty much like traditional decompositions. The trick of the method is to realize that since $\Sigma_{yx} = \Lambda\Phi$, one can rewrite Σ_{yy} as

$$\Sigma_{yy} = \Sigma_{yx}\Phi^{-1}\Sigma'_{yx} + \Psi$$

and then estimate Σ_{yx} via the sample covariance matrix S_{yx}. Then it follows that

$$\Sigma_{yy} \cong S_{yx}\Phi^{-1}S'_{yx} + \Psi.$$

The importance of this decomposition is the following: The covariance structure for Σ_{yy} is now a linear rather than nonlinear function of the remaining parameters Φ^{-1} and Ψ. Thus, one can use least squares or generalized least squares to estimate these parameters, and the solution method simply involves solving some linear equations (e.g., as in regression). Once the estimates $\hat{\Phi}^{-1}$ and $\hat{\Psi}$ are obtained, further linear equation solutions yield the estimates $\hat{\Lambda}$ and $\hat{\Psi}_x$. Thus, the complicated problem of nonlinear estimation has been reduced to the solution of linear equations, and the estimates can be obtained far more cheaply than principal components analysis which is a method typically chosen for its computational cheapness rather than its theoretical elegance.

The computational elegance of the method can be illustrated by considering slightly confirmatory versions of the above. Consider a situation with 220 variables and 20 factors. Then there are 20 $\mathbf{x}$ variables and 200 $\mathbf{y}$ variables. In the exploratory factor model Λ has $200 \times 20 = 4{,}000$ parameters, Φ has $(20 \times 21)/2 = 210$, Ψ has 200 parameters and Ψ_x has 20 parameters. Such a problem could certainly not be entertained by a LISREL type method, in which, as was noted above, 200 parameters is already stretching the limits of the method. If one considered a marginally confirmatory variant of such a model with say, 200 parameters taken as known zeros, this would leave 4,230 parameters to be estimated. Such a problem could not be entertained with maximum likelihood methods, but the most difficult part of the current computation involves solving a linear system involving a 200×200 symmetric matrix. This is not beyond current computational capability, even if the numerically nonoptimal method involving matrix inversion is used for this purpose. It should be noted, of course, that this hypothetical example ideally requires a very large number of subjects. Except in national surveys, it may actually be impossible to achieve any desired ratio of subjects/parameter in practice. However, preliminary indications are that the factor model is a very remarkable model yielding quite stable results in very adverse circumstances. Although it has not yet been studied, it would not be surprising to find quite acceptable results in a sample of 1,000 subjects in this situation of over 4,000 parameters (the ratio is just the reverse of what it ought to be), providing that the variables have been carefully structured to yield hypothesized factors in a systematic manner. (With "garbage in," "garbage out" may well be expected.)

The method may be illustrated in a small problem of nine psychological variables and three factors, taken from Bentler (1982a). The left part of Table 1 presents the noniterative factor solution, while the right side of the table shows the maximum likelihood solution. It will be obvious that the solutions are extremely similar. Note that the variables having 1.0 and 0.0 loadings only served as the x marker variables for the problem. As would be expected, when some variables serve as markers with unit loadings, the factors have been identified with the scale of the variables and thus the factors do not have unit variance (see factor covariance matrix). It is a simple matter to rescale the results to yield the traditional solution with unit variance factors.

Although the noniterative estimator is a consistent estimator of the parameters of the factor analytic model, it does not directly yield statistical tests of goodness of fit of the model to data. In large samples, such tests are not particularly meaningful in any case, as noted above, and consequently,

Table 1. Confirmatory factor solution for nine psychological variables

Variable	Noniterative Estimator ($W=I$)				Maximum likelihood			
	Factor Loading Matrix			Unique variance	Factor Loading Matrix			Unique variance
	I	II	III		I	II	III	
1	1.0[a]	0[a]	0[a]	0.52	1.0[a]	0[a]	0[a]	0.48
2	0.92	0[a]	−0.28	0.60	0.85	0[a]	−0.22	0.64
3	1.10	0[a]	−0.45	0.40	1.03	0[a]	−0.36	0.44
4	0[a]	1.0[a]	0[a]	0.28	0[a]	1.0[a]	0[a]	0.29
5	0.18	0.80	0.11	0.38	0.09	0.86	0.11	0.37
6	0.22	0.85	0[a]	0.32	0.19	0.88	0[a]	0.32
7	0[a]	0[a]	1.0[a]	0.35	0[a]	0[a]	1.0[a]	0.33
8	0.79	−0.37	0.88	0.24	0.76	−0.33	0.89	0.26
9	0.84	−0.24	0.58	0.46	0.92	−0.28	0.60	0.41
			Factor covariance matrix					
I	0.48				0.52			
II	0.34	0.72			0.34	0.71		
III	0.15	0.25	0.65		0.11	0.23	0.67	

[a] Parameter was fixed during estimation

normed fit indices may well be more informative than chi-square tests. In cases where statistical statements are desired, Bentler (1983a, b) and Bentler & Dijkstra (1985) have provided the relevant machinery. This machinery involves taking one iterative step towards a more optimal estimator such as the maximum likelihood estimator with normal variables, or the elliptical and distribution-free estimators discussed below. However, such a step will involve substantially heavier computations than noted above and hence will cut down substantially the effective problem size that can be analyzed comfortably.

Structural Methods for Large Data Sets

When relatively specific and complete structural models can be entertained for a data set, structural models involving indicators of latent variables and regressions among these latent variables can be entertained. Such models, sometimes known generically as LISREL models, due to the available computer program (Jöreskog & Sörbom, 1981), can be conceptualized in a variety of ways and also estimated in several ways. LISREL uses the Wiley-Keesling structural representation (Wiley, 1973), and the maximum likelihood method of estimation (Jöreskog, 1977). Recently, least squares methods (Browne, 1974) were also added as an option. A major alternative is the Bentler and Weeks (1979, 1980) conceptualization and statistical methods based on the above methods as well as generalized least squares approaches to elliptical and distribution free estimation (see e.g., Bentler, 1982b, 1985; Bentler & Weeks, 1982; Lee & Bentler, 1980). An introduction to the author's computer program EQS is provided in German by Bentler (in press), and in a developmental context by Doscher & Bentler (in press).

It has recently become apparent that the existing statistical machinery and computational implementations cannot handle the variety of data situations actually encountered. Even in cases where the distributional assumptions associated with existing methods can be met, that is, basically, multivariate normality of the measured and latent variables, their computations are sufficiently difficult and costly that they cannot be routinely employed in large problems. Some recent developments towards improving estimation and testing under nonstandard circumstances will be reviewed in three sections below. These new developments have been incorporated into EQS (Bentler, 1985). Excluded from the current review are new developments in the ability to deal with categorical data under assumptions of latent multivariate normal distributions (see e.g., Bartholomew, 1983; Muthén, 1983). Only the case of continuous variables is discussed below. Other critical issues, such as the use of covariance structure models with correlational (rather than covariance) data (cf. Bentler & Lee, 1983) or multiple population models (Lee & Tsui, 1982) is not addressed.

Multinormal Data

When a model has many parameters it becomes expensive to estimate via methods such as maximum likelihood (ML) that require the iterative optimization of a highly nonlinear function. This function is of the form

$$f = \log \det \mathbf{\Sigma} + \operatorname{tr} \mathbf{S\Sigma}^{-1} - \log \det \mathbf{S} - p,$$

where $\mathbf{\Sigma} = \mathbf{\Sigma}(\mathbf{\theta})$ is a function of a parameter vector $\mathbf{\theta}$, $\mathbf{S}$ is the sample covariance matrix, det refers to the determinant, and tr refers to the sum of diagonal elements in the subsequent matrix product. If the model $\mathbf{\Sigma}(\mathbf{\theta})$ (e.g., the LISREL or Bentler-Weeks specialized model) is true and the normality assumption is met, in large samples of size N, at the minimum $(N-1) \cdot f$ is distributed as chi-square with degrees of freedom corresponding to the difference between the number of nonduplicated elements in $\mathbf{S}$ and the number of free parameters in $\mathbf{\theta}$. This test can be used to evaluate proposed models, and a chi-square difference test is available to evaluate parameters that differentiate two nested models. Estimates of standard errors can be obtained via the associated inverse of the Fisher information matrix. See, for example, Bentler & Bonett (1980).

A breakthrough towards estimation of the factor model was mentioned above via the Hägglund (1982) and Bentler (1982a) noniterative approaches. These approaches do not minimize f. Jöreskog & Sörbom (1981) have extended Hägglund's method to allow the estimation of general linear structural models. The estimates that result from their procedure do not allow for tests of hypotheses or evaluation of model fit via chi-square goodness of fit tests.

A different approach was taken by Bentler (1983a). He suggested starting with any initial consistent estimate of parameters, such as might be obtained with least squares estimation, and then taking one iterative step towards the maximum likelihood estimator (i.e., performing one iteration of a so-called Gauss-Newton type of minimize f). Based on the theories of Ferguson (1958) and others, the resulting estimator is a best asymptotically normal estimator that has the large sample statistical properties of the maximum likelihood estimator and allows goodness of fit and other statistical tests. Thus, a great computational simplification has been achieved with no apparent loss of statistical efficiency.

In case of the noniterative factor analytic model estimator mentioned above, one iterative step is thus needed to make the resulting estimates statistically optimal in the sense of having minimal sampling variances and in allowing standard errors and goodness of fit tests. A step in such a direction for the data of Table 1 yields results that are virtually synonymous to those reported previously, and, hence, these results are not reported here.

The multivariate normality assumption, however, is a very problematic one. In a superb paper, Browne (1982) first pointed out how the standard errors and test statistics obtained from maximum likelihood methods such as LISREL based on minimizing f could be totally wrong when the variables have kurtoses that are nonzero. Thus, when the variables are more peaked and have heavier tails than would be expected on the basis of normality, the standard errors are underestimated and the chi-square goodness of fit test may be too large even when the model actually does represent the population. Thus, normal-theory based methods become tests of the normality assumption rather than model tests. Furthermore, it is possible for the fit tests to be wrong in the opposite direction, that is, the model may actually not be appropriate when a maximum likelihood test statistic presumes to conclude that it is. For these reasons, more general methods of estimation must be introduced. Two such methods involve elliptical distributions and distribution-free methods. In a final section of this paper, a small simulation study will illustrate the problems that can result from using the wrong statistical model with the right structural model.

An Elliptical Generalization

It has been recognized for some time that generalizations of multivariate normal distributions exist. An especially attractive generalization is the elliptical multivariate distribution which, in many ways, behaves like the normal distribution of which it is a generalization (see, e.g., Chmielewski, 1981; Kelker, 1970; Muirhead, 1982). In particular, elliptical distributions allow variables to have nonzero kurtoses, providing that this kurtosis is homogeneous across variables. Thus elliptical distributions may have heavier or lighter tails than the normal distribution. The ability to accept heavier tails is particularly valuable in data situations that appear to be normal-like but to have outliers. In recent years the relevance of elliptical distributions to a variety of multivariate situations have been studied. Browne (1982) noted their relevance to covariance structure models, and showed how in certain specialized circumstances an elliptical correction to normal based test statistics would provide more accurate results than standard LISREL-type maximum likelihood estimators.

Bentler (1983b) and Browne (1984) extended the initial results of Browne (1982). They developed the general theory for minimum modified chi-square estimation of data obtained from elliptical distributions, and showed how gradient, Hessian, chi-square statistic and standard errors would be affected by the incorrect assumption of normality. One such formula is presented in the next section. They also developed computational formulas for estimation that would yield quasi-maximum likelihood estimates for elliptical data. The computations required of such minimum modified chi-square (generalized least squares) or elliptical quasi-maximum likelihood estimates are approximately the same as those required by the comparable normal theory results. However, since the normal theory methods are a special case of the elliptical theory methods, the resulting procedures are more generally applicable and yield the correct specialization when needed, without special procedures having to be invoked.

Although it is comforting to have methods that are robust to violation of normality, the computational burden of these methods is still substantial in situations with such large data sets as are being considered here. Thus, the question arises as to how the elliptical estimator can be made more computationally acceptable. Browne (1984) emphasized that with a certain class of scale-invariant models, the normal theory maximum likelihood estimator remained appropriate, but that test statistics and standard errors needed alternative computations. Bentler (1983a) proposed that a more general approach involves the two-step improvement procedure outlined above. That is, initially obtain an estimate that is consistent, such as the ordinary least-squares estimate. Then, perform a single iterative step of the Gauss-Newton type improvement procedure based on elliptical theory. Such a step is very similar to that described in Bentler and Weeks (1980), except that the formulas must be modified slightly to accommodate the elliptical situation. Details are provided in Bentler (in press). After such a correction, the resulting estimates can be used with the appropriate formulas to yield correct standard errors, test statistics, etc.

Although it is certain that elliptical estimators would provide a general improvement over currently implemented normal theory methods, it should be noted that elliptical methods are not distribution-free either. It can be speculated that these methods come very close to distribution-free methods as the number of variables increases, because it can be supposed that the mean kurtosis (or multivariate kurtosis) of variables that are not homogeneous in kurtosis may well represent the general corrections for nonnormality needed in structural modeling. If such speculation is correct, then elliptical estimators could be used in circumstances when they are not theoretically appropriate. Some simulation studies need to be designed to evaluate this suggestion.

Distribution-free Methods

Browne (1982, 1984) recently proposed the utilization of a minimum modified chi-square estimator for covariance structures that is completely distribution free. Bentler (1983a) showed how Browne's procedure could be considered to represent a general quadratic form test statistic as described by Ferguson (1958) and others, using the covariance matrix of covariances described by Hsu (1949). In the general case, consider the quadratic form defined as

$$Q = (\mathbf{Z} - \mathbf{P})' \, \mathbf{W}^{-1} (\mathbf{Z} - \mathbf{P}) \, ,$$

where $\mathbf{Z}$ is a sample vector of means of identically distributed random variables, $\mathbf{P} = \mathbf{P}(\boldsymbol{\theta})$ is the vector of expectations of $\mathbf{Z}$ given $\boldsymbol{\theta}$, and $\mathbf{W}$ is the covariance matrix of $\mathbf{Z}$ given $\boldsymbol{\theta}$. Estimators that minimize Q are called minimum chi-square or minimum-distance estimators, having the property of being best asymptotically normal. Ferguson (1958) attributes to K. Pearson the modification of Q that replaces $\mathbf{W}$ with an estimator $\hat{\mathbf{W}}$, and he indicates that if $\hat{\mathbf{W}}^{-1}$ converges to $\mathbf{W}^{-1}$ in probability as $N \to \infty$, this minimum modified chi-square is also optimal. These and other properties of Q were developed by Browne (1974) in the context of covariance structure analysis via the form

$$g = (\mathbf{s} - \boldsymbol{\sigma})' \mathbf{W}^{-1} (\mathbf{s} - \boldsymbol{\sigma}) \, ,$$

where $\mathbf{s}$ and $\boldsymbol{\sigma}$ are the reduced vectors of $p(p+1)/2$ nonduplicated elements of $\mathbf{S}$ and $\boldsymbol{\Sigma}$, respectively. Clearly, $\mathbf{s}$ takes the role of $\mathbf{Z}$ in Q, being the mean of deviation cross-products, while $\boldsymbol{\sigma}(\boldsymbol{\theta})$ takes the role of $\mathbf{P}(\boldsymbol{\theta})$. Browne called the estimators that minimize g generalized least-squares estimators, and noted that, if the fourth-order cumulants of the multivariate observations are zero (this occurs, for example, when the variables are multinormally distributed), g can be written in the form

$$h = 2^{-1} n \operatorname{tr}[(\mathbf{S} - \boldsymbol{\Sigma}) \mathbf{W}^{-1}]^2 \, ,$$

where the weight matrix $\mathbf{W}$ has been reduced in size to order p, thus making computations much simpler. Here $\mathbf{W}$ can be estimated by any matrix that estimates $\boldsymbol{\Sigma}$ consistently. Browne showed that such generalized least squares estimators and test statistics derived from them have the same asymptotic properties as their maximum likelihood counterparts. Lee & Bentler (1980) showed how the statistical theory is modified when functional constraints are imposed on parameters. If $\mathbf{W} = \mathbf{I}$ in g or h, a least squares estimator is obtained. This estimator is not asymptotically (large-sample) efficient, though it is consistent.

Bentler (1983b) and Browne (1984), showed that when variables are elliptically distributed, g reduces to the form

$$j = (\varkappa + 1)^{-1} h - \alpha \, [\operatorname{tr}(\mathbf{S} - \boldsymbol{\Sigma}) \mathbf{W}^{-1}]^2 \, ,$$

where $\varkappa$ is a kurtosis parameter that is zero in normal samples and positive with heavier than normal tails, $\alpha = \varkappa n/[4(\varkappa + 1)^2 + 2p\varkappa(\varkappa + 1)]$, and the remaining terms are as in g. Note that if $\varkappa = 0$, $j = h$, the normal theory function results. With $\varkappa > 0$, the correction term in j is positive, indicating that h gives a test statistic that is too large when the data are not normal. Thus, researchers may well be rejecting statistically adequate models for data, based on the use of the wrong test statistic (i.e., normality based statistics when the data are not normal).

Although the statistical properties of Q and hence g have been known for some time, and although the general form of the covariance matrix $\mathbf{W}$ in g has also been known, it was not recognized until recently that the use of the general weight matrix in minimum modified chi-square estimation would lead to asymptotically distribution-free (ADF) estimates and test statistics. In a superb paper, Browne (1982) worked out most of the technical details, and demonstrated the effect of kurtosis on the test statistic and standard errors obtained from f and h. For example, he showed that the ML goodness of fit χ^2 cannot be trusted with nonnormal variables. In order to implement g in general, $\mathbf{W}$ can be estimated consistently via

$$\hat{w}_{ij,kl} = n^{-1}\left(v_{ijkl} - v_{ij}v_{kl}\right),$$

where

$$v_{ijkl} = N^{-1}\Sigma_r^N \left(x_{ri} - \bar{x}_i\right)\left(x_{rj} - \bar{x}_j\right)\left(x_{rk} - \bar{x}_k\right)\left(x_{rl} - \bar{x}_l\right)$$
$$v_{ij} = N^{-1}\Sigma_r^N \left(x_{ri} - \bar{x}_i\right)\left(x_{rj} - \bar{x}_j\right),$$

x_{ri} is the rth observation on the ith variable, and $\bar{x}_i$ is the sample mean. Any consistent estimate, for example, based on a model, can replace v_{ij} above. Bentler (1983b) shows how $\hat{\mathbf{W}}$ simplifies if the variables are multinormal or elliptical. Unfortunately, estimation based on minimizing g iteratively with a huge weight matrix such as $\hat{\mathbf{W}}$ is expensive; the costs can exceed LISREL by a tenfold amount. Consequently, there is need for simpler estimators.

A two-stage asymptotically distribution-free (2SADF) estimator was introduced by Bentler (1983a). It would have large sample statistical optimality no matter what the distribution of variables may be. First, a cheap consistent estimate $\hat{\boldsymbol{\theta}}$ is obtained, for example, by the noniterative methods, by minimizing g or h with $\mathbf{W} = \mathbf{I}$, or, more expensively, by minimizing f, or h with $\mathbf{W} = \mathbf{S}$. Second, an asymptotically efficient linearized improvement over $\hat{\boldsymbol{\theta}}$ is made. Bentler (1983a) noted that it can be implemented by taking one Gauss-Newton minimization iteration from the consistent estimate via g. Specifically, he proposed taking one step as follows in order to yield the optimal estimator

$$\bar{\boldsymbol{\theta}} = \hat{\boldsymbol{\theta}} + (\partial\hat{\boldsymbol{\Sigma}}\,\hat{\mathbf{W}}^{-1}\partial\hat{\boldsymbol{\Sigma}}')^{-1}\partial\hat{\boldsymbol{\Sigma}}\hat{\mathbf{W}}^{-1}(\mathbf{s} - \hat{\boldsymbol{\sigma}}),$$

where $\partial\hat{\boldsymbol{\Sigma}}$ is $\partial\boldsymbol{\Sigma}/\partial\boldsymbol{\theta}$, evaluated at $\hat{\boldsymbol{\theta}}$. The test statistic is given by g, evaluated at $\bar{\boldsymbol{\theta}}$, while $(\partial\hat{\boldsymbol{\Sigma}}\hat{\mathbf{W}}^{-1}\partial\hat{\boldsymbol{\Sigma}}')^{-1}$ estimates the variance-covariance matrix of the estimator. Both $\partial\hat{\boldsymbol{\Sigma}}$ and $\hat{\mathbf{W}}^{-1}$ can be updated to yield more efficient estimates of sampling variability, but a further iteration would not improve the parameter estimates or the test statistic, which are asymptotically equivalent to statistics that would be obtained with more expensive direct minimization of g. If the variables are multinormal or elliptical, $\bar{\boldsymbol{\theta}}$ can be obtained via Bentler's (1983b) simplification formulas. De Leeuw

(1983) was the first to propose the virtues of such a two-stage approach in the closely related area of correlation structure models. The general statistical theory is given by Bentler & Dijkstra (1985), who call the resulting two-stage estimators "linearized" estimators. Nothing is known about the small sample behavior of any of the ADF estimators, though Browne notes that bias may be smaller in correlation structures.

A difficulty with ADF estimators is that the size of the weight matrix needed for computations grows rapidly with number of variables. Thus with 20 variables, the weight matrix must be of order $(20)(21)/2 = 210$ by 210. With 100 measured variables, the weight matrix would be $(100)(101)/2$, that is, 5050 by 5050. The number of subjects should exceed the size of the weight matrix. Clearly ADF estimation cannot be used in very large problems. This limitation motivated the development of the elliptical case, described above, and further research is needed to evaluate its possibilities in situations where it is not strictly applicable. The weight matrix in the function j is only of the size of the number of variables.

A Small Simulation Study

Although most longitudinal data that researchers are likely to encounter will almost surely contain variables whose distributions are anything but multivariate normal, as noted above, structural models have until recently only been able to be estimated and tested on the assumption that the data were normally distributed. This practice has had the consequence of yielding conclusions about theories that may be incorrect: false models may be accepted, and correct models rejected, solely because the distributional assumption underlying the method (such as LISREL) is incorrect and not because of the validity or invalidity of the theory itself. It seems crucial to evaluate whether model evaluations can be seriously misled when such methods as maximum likelihood estimation based on multinormal theory are applied in inappropriate circumstances.

Bentler (1983a) reported a small simulation study of a data set that has some of the characteristics that would be encountered in longitudinal research. In particular, the model of Figure 1 was used as a basis for generating several data sets that either were or were not multinormally distributed.

As can be seen, the data consisted of nine variables that might be considered to have been obtained across three measurement occasions. The measured variables $V_1 - V_3$ represent data obtained at the initial time point, variables $V_4 - V_6$ represent data obtained at a second time point, and variables $V_7 - V_9$ represent variables measured at a third time point. It is assumed that at each time the variables are indicators of a single common factor (F_1, F_2, and F_3), but that the factor represents an autoregressive process in which scores on the factor at a later time point are dependent only upon the scores at a previous time point. In particular, F_3 is not

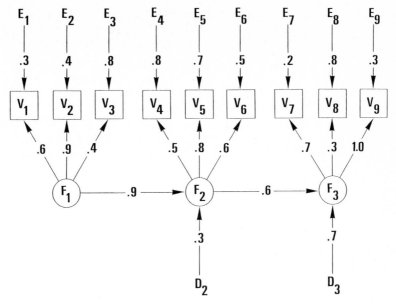

Fig. 1. Latent variable model for the nine measured variable $V_1 - V_9$. The three factors F_1, F_2, and F_3 are related by a simplex regression relation. The complete model contains nine measurement equations that relate manifest and latent variables, plus two construct equations that relate latent variables to each other. All twelve of the independent latent variables ($E_1 - E_9$, F_1, D_2, D_3) are mutually uncorrelated. The numbers represent parameter values used to generate the V_i from normal random variables obtained by a random number generator. The notation is consistent with the computer program EQS, so that $V_1 = 0.6*F_1 + 0.3*E_1$ is literally the form of model specification used in the program (stars represent free parameters)

regressed upon F_1, so that the influence of F_1 on F_3 is manifested only through the intermediary of F_2. The disturbances D_2 and D_3 represent the residuals for the latent regressions. As is typical in a factor analytic measurement model, each of the measured variables is also influenced by a residual error ($E_1 - E_9$).

Two sets of data were generated according to the model of Figure 1. Later, these two data sets were combined into a third data set, as described below. The two data sets were generated from a random number generator that could create normally distributed variables with a given mean and variance. In each case, twelve independent variables were created (E_1 to E_9, F_1, D_2, and D_3). These variables were taken as uncorrelated (there are no two-way arrows in the figure). In data set A, the variables were scaled to have means of zero and a variance of one, while in data set B the variables were scaled to have means of zero but a variance of nine. The measurement and construct equations with parameters as shown in Table 2 were then used to generate the remaining variables, the dependent variables in the

Table 2. Models generating simulated data associated with Figure 1

Measurement equations	Construct Equations
$V_1 = 0.6*F_1 + 0.3*E_1$	$F_2 = 0.9*F_1 + 0.3\ D_2$
$V_2 = 0.9*F_1 + 0.4*E_2$	$F_3 = 0.6*F_2 + 0.7\ D_3$
$V_3 = 0.4*F_2 + 0.8*E_3$	
$V_4 = 0.5*F_2 + 0.8*E_4$	
$V_5 = 0.8*F_2 + 0.7*E_5$	*Variances*
$V_6 = 0.6*F_2 + 0.5*E_6$	Data Set A (N=2500)
$V_7 = 0.7*F_3 + 0.2*E_7$	E_1 to $E_9 = 1.0$, $F_1 = 1.0$, $D_2 = 1.0$, $D_3 = 1.0$
$V_8 = 0.3*F_3 + 0.8*E_8$	Data Set B (N=250)
$V_9 = 1.0*F_3 + 0.3*E_9$	E_1 to $E_9 = 9.0$, $F_1 = 9.0$, $D_2 = 9.0$, $D_3 = 9.0$

system. Data sets *A* and *B* were also different in that the sample sizes were markedly different: 2,500, and 250, respectively. A summary of the data generation process is shown in Table 2.

Since data sets *A* and *B* represent data based on normally distributed variables, another data set had to be created that would not be normally distributed. This effect was achieved by simply combining data sets *A* and *B* into a third set *C*, consisting of 2,750 hypothetical subjects. When two normal distributions are combined in this manner, where the independent variables have markedly different variances, the resulting distribution has tails that are larger than would be expected for variables drawn from one normal distribution. It would thus be expected that data sets *C* should behave differently from data sets *A* and *B*, even though in all cases the structural model used was linear and of the form hypothesized. The key question is whether the statistical methods can determine the appropriateness of the model to the data.

Estimation of parameters of the model of Figure 1 and Table 2, in data set *A*, proceeded as follows. The equations had generated nine hypothetical measured variables $V_1 - V_9$, yielding a 2,500 by 9 data matrix. These data, and the resulting covariance matrix **S**, were used in attempt to recover the structure in the figure, that is, the "unknown" parameters, via three estimation methods: maximum likelihood (ML), Browne's (1982) asymptotically distribution-free method (ADF), and Bentler's (1983a) two-stage asymptotically distribution-free method (2SADF). The free parameters were taken as all the numbers in the figure except for the paths associated with D_2 and D_3, which when fixed served to identify the factors F_2 and F_3; the scale of F_1 was fixed by setting its variance to 1. Thus, there are $9(10)/2 = 45$ covariances and 20 free parameters, leaving 25 degrees of freedom. The test statistic results are shown in the first three rows of Table 3. Both ML and ADF methods recover the structure and agree that the data could have come from a population with the structure in Figure 1; 2SADF yields the same conclusion. Thus, all three methods work when the data are normally distributed.

Table 3. Results of an estimation study

Sample type	N	Estimation method	Chi-square	D.F.	Prob.
Normal A	2500	ML	24.79	25	0.47
Normal A	2500	ADF	24.82	25	0.47
Normal A	2500	2SADF	24.82	25	0.47
Normal B	250	ML	27.30	25	0.34
Normal B	250	ADF	34.24	25	0.10
Normal B	250	2SADF	34.45	25	0.10
A and B	2750	ML	60.38	25	<0.001
A and B	2750	ADF	22.82	25	0.59
A and B	2750	2SADF	22.84	25	0.59

The second sample, data set B, also was based on normally distributed variables, so that the estimation of parameters of the model and the chi-square goodness of fit test should verify that fact. As seen in the next three rows of Table 3, this is what is observed. All three methods allow the conclusion that the sample data could have been drawn from a population with the structure indicated in Figure 1. The probability levels exceed the usual 0.05 critical cut-off points for rejecting models.

When these two samples were combined into a third sample C, based on $N = 2,750$, the observed variables $V_1 - V_9$ have distributions with substantially longer tails than would be obtained with a normal sample: the individual kurtoses were in the range $3.5-6.0$, compared with $N = 2,500$ sample that had values in the range -0.18 to 0.06. The ML method incorrectly concludes that the data were not generated by the model of Figure 1. In contrast, both ADF and 2SADF methods yield the correct conclusion.

It is apparent that maximum likelihood estimation is fraught with dangers when the assumption of multivariate normality is not appropriate. As shown in the example, incorrect conclusions regarding the correctness of a model can easily be drawn. While the normality assumption should be rejected, and the model accepted, uncritical use of ML lead to the rejection of a correct model. The opposite can occur as well, where incorrect models are accepted.

Conclusions

Large data sets provide special challenges to the theorist as well as the methodologist. They bring in focus the underlying assumptions associated with methods and highlight the computational difficulties that might be associated with any attempt at structural modeling. The promises and problems associated with recent developments in structural modeling have been highlighted in this context.

Browne (1982, 1984) introduced distribution-free estimation into co-variance structure models. The two-stage, linearized estimator introduced by Bentler (1983a) primarily represents a computational simplification over the Browne approach. However, this computational savings can be substantial, since only one iteration is required with a very large weight matrix. As a consequence, the substantial expense associated with Browne's approach is avoided. Rather than being an order of magnitude more expensive than simpler estimators such as least-squares, as the Browne approach tends to be, the two-stage approach is only marginally more expensive than such methods as maximum-likelihood estimation favored by LISREL. The slight cost increase is, however, well worth expending since the conclusions reached thereby are likely to have greater statistical validity in the situations typically encountered in large sample longitudinal research. In addition, the two-stage estimator simplifies substantially with either elliptical or normal distributions (Bentler, 1983b; Bentler & Dijkstra, 1985). In such cases it is still more feasible than other, more computationally intensive approaches without any apparent loss of statistical information. It might be speculated that two-stage estimation may not be as successful in very small sample situations, but only further research can evaluate whether this suggestion is correct or not.

References

Bartholomew, D. J. (1983) Latent variable models for ordered categorical data. *Journal of Econometrics, 22*, 229–243

Bentler, P. M. (1980) Multivariate analysis with latent variables: Causal modeling. *Annual Review of Psychology, 31*, 419–456

Bentler, P. M. (1982a) Confirmatory factor analysis via noniterative estimation: A fast, inexpensive method. *Journal of Marketing Research, 19*, 417–424

Bentler, P. M. (1982b) Linear systems with multiple levels and types of latent variables. In K. G. Jöreskog & H. Wold (Eds.), *Systems under indirect observation: Causality, structure, prediction. Part I* (pp. 101–130). Amsterdam: North-Holland

Bentler, P. M. (1983a) Simultaneous equation systems as moment structure models: With an introduction to latent variable models. *Journal of Econometrics, 22*, 13–42

Bentler, P. M. (1985) *Theory and implementation of EQS, a structural equations program.* Los Angeles: BMDP Statistical Software

Bentler, P. M. (1983b) Some contributions to efficient statistics in structural models: Specification and estimation of moment structures. *Psychometrika, 48*, 493–517

Bentler, P. M. (in press) The EQS approach to structural equation models for normal and nonnormal continuous variables. In C. Möbus & W. Schneider (Eds.), *Kausalmodelle in den Sozialwissenschaften – zur Analyse von Längsschnitt und experimentellen Daten mit LISREL und verwandten Methoden.* Bern, Switzerland: Huber

Bentler, P. M. & Bonett, D. G. (1980) Significance tests and goodness of fit in the analysis of covariance structures. *Psychological Bulletin, 88*, 588–606

Bentler, P. M. & Dijkstra, T. (1985) Efficient estimation via linearization in structural models. In P. R. Krishnaiah (Ed.), *Multivariate analysis VI* (pp. 9–42). Amsterdam: North-Holland

Bentler, P. M. & Lee, S. Y. (1983) Covariance structures under polynomial constraints: Applications to correlation and alpha-type structural models. *Journal of Educational Statistics, 8,* 207–222, 315–317

Bentler, P. M. & Speckart, G. (1981) Attitudes "cause" behaviors: A structural equation analysis. *Journal of Personality and Social Psychology, 40,* 226–238

Bentler, P. M. & Weeks, D. G. (1979) Interrelations among models for the analysis of moment structures. *Multivariate Behavioral Research, 14,* 169–185

Bentler, P. M. & Weeks, D. G. (1980) Linear structural equations with latent variables. *Psychometrika, 45,* 289–308

Bentler, P. M. & Weeks, D. G. (1982) Multivariate analysis with latent variables. In P. R. Krishnaiah & L. Kanal (Eds.), *Handbook of Statistics, Vol. 2* (pp. 747–771). Amsterdam: North-Holland

Browne, M. W. (1974) Generalized least squares estimators in the analysis of covariance structure. *South African Statistical Journal, 8,* 1–24

Browne, M. W. (1982) Covariance structures. In D. M. Hawkins (Ed.), *Topics in applied multivariate analysis.* London: Cambridge University Press

Browne, M. W. (1984) Asymptotically distribution free methods for the analysis of covariance structures. *British Journal of Mathematical and Statistical Psychology, 37,* 62–83

Chmielewski, M. A. (1981) Elliptically symmetric distributions: A review and bibliography. *International Statistical Review, 49,* 67–74

de Leeuw, J. (1983) Models and methods for the analysis of correlation coefficients. *Journal of Econometrics, 22,* 113–137

Doscher, M. L. & Bentler, P. M. (in press) Structural equation modeling in cognitive development. In J. R. Bergan (Ed.), *Measuring cognitive development.* Westport, Conn.: Mediax

Epstein, S. (1979) The stability of behavior: I. On predicting most of the people much of the time. *Journal of Personality and Social Psychology, 37,* 1097–1126

Ferguson, T. S. (1958) A method of generating best asymptotically normal estimates with application to the estimation of bacterial densities. *Annals of Mathematical Statistics, 29,* 1046–1062

Hägglund, G. (1982) Factor analysis by instrumental variables methods. *Psychometrika, 47,* 209–222

Hsu, P. L. (1949) The limiting distribution of functions of sample means and applications to testing hypotheses. *Proceedings of the First Berkeley Symposium in Mathematical Statistics and Probability,* pp. 359–402

Huba, G. J. & Bentler, P. M. (1982a) On the usefulness of latent variable causal modeling in testing theories of naturally occurring events (including adolescent drug use): A rejoinder to Martin. *Journal of Personality and Social Psychology, 43,* 604–611

Huba, G. J. & Bentler, P. M. (1982b) A developmental theory of drug use: Derivation and assessment of a causal modeling approach. In P. B. Baltes & O. G. Brim, Jr. (Eds.), *Life-span development and behavior, Vol. 4* (pp. 147–203). New York: Academic

Huba, G. J. & Bentler, P. M. (in press) *Antecedents and consequences of adolescent drug use: A psychosocial study of development using a causal modeling approach.* New York: Plenum

Jackson, D. N. & Chan, D. W. (1980) Maximum likelihood estimation in common factor analysis: A cautionary note. *Psychological Bulletin, 88,* 502–508

Jöreskog, K. G. (1977) Structural equation models in the social sciences: Specification, estimation, and testing. In P. R. Krishnaiah (Ed.), *Applications of statistics.* Amsterdam: North-Holland

Jöreskog, K. G. & Sörbom, D. (1981) *LISREL V user's guide.* Chicago: International Educational Resources

Kelker, D. (1970) Distribution theory of spherical distribution and a location-scale parameter generalization. *Sankhya, A32,* 419–430

Lee, H. B. & Comrey, A. L. (1979) Distortions in a commonly used factor analytic procedure. *Multivariate Behavioral Research, 14,* 301 – 321

Lee, S. Y. & Bentler, P. M. (1980) Some asymptotic properties of constrained generalized least squares estimation in covariance structure models. *South African Statistical Journal, 14,* 121 – 136

Lee, S. Y. & Tsui, K. L. (1982) Covariance structure analysis in several populations. *Psychometrika, 47,* 297 – 308

Muirhead, R. J. (1982) *Aspects of multivariate statistical theory.* New York: Wiley

Muthén, B. (1983) Latent variable structural equation modeling with categorical data. *Journal of Econometrics, 22,* 43 – 65

Speckart, G. & Bentler, P. M. (1982) Application of attitude-behavior models to varied content domains. *Academic Psychology Bulletin, 4,* 453 – 466

Wiley, D. E. (1973) The identification problem for structural equation models with unmeasured variables. In A. S. Goldberger & O. D. Duncan (Eds.), *Structural equation models in the social science* (pp. 69 – 83). New York: Academic

D. Prospects

XV. Recent Advances in Research on the Ecology of Human Development

U. Bronfenbrenner*

Introduction

It is now more than a decade ago that, being somewhat younger, I presumed to challenge the then-prevailing conventions of my field by describing the developmental research of the day as "the study of the strange behavior of children in strange situations with strange adults for the briefest possible period of time" (Bronfenbrenner, 1974). Instead, I argued (as if it were simply a matter of choice), we should be studying development in its ecological context; that is, in the actual environments in which human beings lived their lives. I then proceeded to outline, in a series of publications, a conceptual framework for analyzing development in context, and to offer concrete examples of how various elements of the schema might be applied both to past studies and to studies yet to come. I also emphasized the scientific and practical benefits of a closer linkage, in both directions, between developmental research and public policy (Bronfenbrenner, 1975, 1977a, 1977b, 1979a, 1979b, 1981).

Now, 12 years later, one might think that I have good reason to rest content. Studies of children and adults in real-life settings, with real-life implications, are now commonplace in the research literature on human development, both in the United States and, as this volume testifies, in Europe as well. This scientific development is taking place, I believe, not so much because of my writings, but rather because the notions I have been promulgating are ideas whose time has come. Indeed, some of these ideas are not so new. Recently, in a chapter published in the new *Handbook of Child Psychology*, Nan Crouter and I were able to trace the evolution of ecological models in developmental research, beginning with investigations conducted in western Europe over 100 years ago (Bronfenbrenner & Crouter, 1983). In the same chapter, we also reported on discoveries made at the opposite pole of the time continuum. In the bibliography, we were able to cite over 40 research articles published since the previous comprehensive review, which had appeared only 4 years earlier (Bronfenbrenner, 1979a).

Clearly, if one regards such scientific developments as desirable, there are grounds for satisfaction. Yet, along with feelings of gratification, I must

* Cornell University, Department of Human Development and Family Studies, Martha Van Rensselaer Hall, Ithaca, NY 14853, USA

Development as Action in Context
Ed. by R. K. Silbereisen et al.
© Springer-Verlag Berlin Heidelberg 1986

confess to some discontent. My disquiet derives from two complementary concerns. The first pertains to one of the main roads that contemporary research has taken; the second, to some more promising pathways that are being neglected.

Alas, I may have to accept some responsibility for what I regard as the wayward course. It is an instance of what might be called "the failure of success." For some years, I harangued my colleagues for avoiding the study of development in real-life settings. No longer able to complain on that score, I have found a new bête noir. In place of too much research on development "out of context," we now have a surfeit of studies on "context without development." Some examples are cited below.

The principal aim of this chapter, however, is to report on more recent scientific advances, and to indicate their implications for present knowledge, for future research, and, where it seems appropriate, for practical application. In the scholarly world, it is customary to designate as "new findings" those that have been reported since the publication of the most recent comprehensive review. Strict adherence to this criterion would therefore argue for my excluding from the present essay any results or conclusions already reported in the recently published Handbook chapter mentioned above. However, since the Handbook may not be readily available to some readers of the present volume, especially those in Europe, I propose to use as the point of reference for defining new findings the somewhat earlier review contained in *The Ecology of Human Development* (Bronfenbrenner, 1979a).

The present chapter is organized in three major sections. The first gives a summary of the defining properties of ten explicit or implicit research paradigms that I had identified in two earlier publications (Bronfenbrenner, 1979a; Bronfenbrenner & Crouter, 1983). The second section contains concrete research examples of those paradigms that, in my judgment, are yielding the most fruitful scientific findings. Finally, in a brief third section, I attempt to specify combinations of paradigm elements that, in my judgement, offer the greatest promise for future scientific progress.

Current Paradigms for Research on Development in Context

The following paradigms are usefully distinguished:

Social Address Models

These exemplify one of the earliest strategies used for studying development in context (Schwabe & Bartholomai, 1870). The design is so simple and self-evident that it hardly seems to warrant the status of a paradigm, but it has certainly been applied as such is actual research. As documented by Bronfenbrenner & Crouter (1983) for about 6 decades − from the 1870s to the 1930s − it was one of only two models employed for studying the influence of real-life environments on human development. The design involves nothing more than comparison of the psychological characteristics of children or adults living in different social environments (e.g., class, nationality, family structure, etc.); hence the term, "social address" (Bronfenbrenner, 1979a).

The principal limitations of this model have been described by Bronfenbrenner & Crouter (1983) as follows:

> No explicit consideration is given ... to intervening structures or processes through which the environment might affect the course of development. One looks only at the "social address" − that is, the environmental label − with no attention to what the environment is like, what people are there, what they are doing, or how the activities taking place could affect the developing person (pp. 361−362).

Despite these limitations, the social address model is still in wide use today, and not without good reason. Because of its simplicity, and comparatively low cost, it is often the method of choice for assessing the potential scientific yield of a new, unexplored research area. For example, little is known as yet about the consequences for the development of children of a growing new family form in contemporary American society − the so-called "merged" or "reconstituted" family produced by remarriage. In this sphere, an appropriate first step is the application of a social address model comparing the psychological characteristics of children being raised in first-married vs remarried families, matched for relevant personal and social characteristics. Such a study was recently carried out by Koel (1984) and yielded provocative findings. For example, remarriage appears to bring psychological benefits for both spouses but to increase the psychological vulnerability of children, particularly those from the wife's previous marriage when her new spouse is childless.

Process Models

Such models go beyond simple "social address" designs by specifying the mechanisms through which particular aspects of the environment or of the person can influence the individual's development. On the environmental side, such mechanisms typically involve processes of social interaction, although more recently aspects of the physical environment have been implicated as well. A number of examples of both types are cited in Bronfenbrenner and Crouter (1983).

Bidirectional Models

Up until the mid-1960s environmental processes affecting development were thought of almost exclusively as unidirectional; that is, the environment was seen as affecting the development of the individual, with no recognition of the possibility of influences operating in the opposite direction. Although the concept of reciprocal effects was recognized earlier in the theoretical thinking and research of ethologists (e.g., Tinbergen, 1951), its application in studies of human development received its most powerful impetus in 1968 from Bell's (1968) influential paper on the "Reinterpretation of the Direction of Effects in Studies of Socialization."

Causal Path Models

Up until 10 years ago, studies of environmental influences on development were limited almost exclusively to the analysis of direct, single-step effects. To be sure, structural equations as a statistical tool for analyzing causal processes had been developed and applied in the field of genetics by Sewell Wright 50 years ago (1934). Their use in developmental investigations, however, as exemplified in several chapters of this volume, has been relatively recent.

Structural equation models, being purely abstract and mathematical in nature, of course do not in themselves constitute theoretical conceptions of development in context. They have nevertheless made a significant theoretical contribution by highlighting the importance of, and providing a method for analyzing, two types of phenomena that have turned out to be frequent and often critical features of developmental processes: bidirectional influences on the one hand, and direct vs indirect effects on the other.

An excellent example of the latter is given by Elder, Caspi, & van Nguyen (this volume). By applying structural analytic models, these investigators were able to show that the disruptive influence of economic hardship on children's development were not direct, but operated indirectly through the impact of economic stress on the behavior of fathers within the family.

As I shall suggest below, however, the impressive power of structural models for distinguishing reciprocal, direct, or indirect causal linkages may distract developmental researchers from recognizing important nonlinear processes that imply a paradigm of a different sort, requiring a different type of statistical design for its analysis. The "person-process-context" model, described below, exemplifies such a paradigm.

The next set of models differentiate the environment of the developing person in terms of three progressively more expanded regions of space and time.

Microsystem Models

These involve the analysis of processes taking place within a single immediate, face-to-face setting that becomes significant for the person's development (e.g., the home, the classroom, or the workplace). Until comparatively recently, microsystem designs were essentially limited to the investigation of relationships and interactions occurring within particular dyads, such as mother–child, brother–sister, teacher–pupil, or employer–employee. Expansion to a triadic, or more generally, to an $N + 2$ model introduces the possiblity of what Bronfenbrenner (1979 a) has referred to as a *second-order effect*, the influence of A upon the relation between B and C. An excellent example is found in the work of Seaver (1973), who demonstrated that a child's classroom performance varied systematically as a function of whether or not the teacher had taught the child's older sibling and, if so, how well that older sibling had performed academically. In other words, the teacher's experience with an older sibling affected his or her treatment of any younger brother or sister who subsequently entered that teacher's class.

Mesosystem Models

Whereas a microsystem is limited to processes taking place within a single immediate setting, mesosystem models take into account the joint effects of processes occurring within and between two or more settings, in each of which the developing person is an active participant. Because mesosystem paradigms are proving to be especially fruitful in illuminating how environmental forces affect the course of development, several investigations based on this model, along with their empirical findings, are summarized in the section: "Some Provocative Findings from Promising Paradigms."

Exosystem Models

These designs also encompass more than one setting; however, they go beyond the micro- or mesosystem level by including at least one setting that does *not* involve the developing person as an active participant, but in which events occur that affect what happens in the settings that do contain the developing person. The results of studies conducted in the last few years confirm the expectation that one of the most consequential exosystems in contemporary society is the parents' world of work as it influences the development of their children. Some recent research findings in this sphere are summarized below.

Chronosystem Models

A recent advance in contemporary research on development in context has projected the factor of time along a new dimension. Traditionally in the study of human development, the passage of time was treated as synonymous with chronological age. Beginning in the 1940s, however (Baldwin, 1947), and especially during the past decade, an increasing number of investigators have employed research designs in which time appears not merely as an attribute of the growing human being but also as a property of the surrounding environment (Baltes & Schaie, 1973). I have referred to designs of this kind as *chronosystems* (Bronfenbrenner, 1984). Two types have been usefully distinguished (Baltes, 1979): *Normative* (school entry, puberty, entering the labor force, marriage, retirement) and *non-normative* (a death or severe illness in the family, divorce, moving, winning the sweepstakes). Such transitions occur throughout the life-span, and often serve as a direct impetus for developmental change. For example, early on, Baldwin (1947) observed dramatic changes in the mother's behavior toward the first child before, during, and after her pregnancy with the second child.

The term *life transition* refers to the developmental impact of a single event during a person's life. Of even greater significance for the study of development in context are the often cumulative effects of particular sequences of transitions, which Elder (1974) has referred to as the *life course*.

Several examples of both types of chronosystem designs appear in the section: "Some Provocative Findings from Promising Paradigms."

Person-Process-Context Models

It is a commonplace principle and practice in behavioral science to view developmental outcomes as a joint function of properties of the person and of the environment. It is not so commonplace a principle or, especially, a practice to view developmental *processes* as joint functions of both sets of factors. On the contrary, in keeping with the scientific paradigms of physics, on which those of psychology are mainly based, developmental processes have typically been thought of, and correspondingly analyzed, as if they were invariant across both person and situation. Indeed, this assumption is sometimes even carried over to the analysis of developmental effects. Evidence of this is seen in the all-too-common practice, in studies of developmental processes and outcomes, of controlling for the possibly confounding effects of other variables, such as parental education, family size, or even sex of child, by means of a regression analysis. Such a procedure assumes that both processes and effects are invariant across these parameters. However, when investigators use research designs that treat the potentially confounding variables not simply as controls but as possible *moderating* factors, the more typical finding is that processes vary, not only in magnitude but sometimes even in direction, as a function of both the nature of the context and the characteristics of the person. For example, in a series of studies growing out of his doctoral dissertation, Tulkin (1977) found that the relation between maternal attitudes and behavior during infancy was consistently stronger among middle class than among working class families. Moreover, the same differential pattern appeared in the correlations of these factors with measures of the child's behavior and performance in school 5 years later.

As documented in the section: "Some Provocative Findings from Promising Paradigms," such *moderator effects* on developmental processes are quite common, particularly in relation to such personal characteristics as sex and age, or contextual variables of family structure, social class, or more recently, parental employment patterns. This fact takes on special significance for the interpretation of studies utilizing structural equation models, which are typically based on assumptions of homogeneity of regression and hence overlook the possibility that causal pathways may vary markedly for different subgroups within the total sample.

The use of a person-process-context model (Bronfenbrenner & Crouter, 1983) avoids such possible misinterpretations by taking into account variations in process as a function of characteristics of the person, the context, and any interaction between them. But that is not the principal benefit to be gained from the use of this paradigm. More important is the new knowledge that may be obtained about the often complex but nevertheless consistent interplay that takes place between organism and environment in determining the course of the individual's development.

Developmental Outcome Models

To speak of developmental outcome models as a special case in discussing research designs for analyzing development in context might well strike the reader as redundant if not down-right silly. Yet, it is a paradoxical fact that the proliferation of research on how the characteristics of persons and environments shape the course of development has not necessarily increased our understanding of the changes taking place in the psychological structure of the individual. This is so for two reasons:

First, the study of context and process is increasingly becoming an end in itself; for example, an investigation of the impact of social networks on family interaction may not examine any effects of such interaction on the development of particular family members. Such an inquiry of course represents an entirely appropriate and desirable scientific concern for developmental researchers, but, by itself, it does not provide any information about any resultant effects on the psyches of the individual participants.

A second limitation arises when the outcome measures used in studies of development in context are themselves bereft of psychological content. Examples include such dependent variables as whether or not the person graduates from school, gets married, achieves a particular occupational status, or dies at a given age. Indeed, in reviewing ecologically-oriented research on human development, I sometimes get the impression that the more sophisticated the design employed for the analysis of context and process, the more simplistic and psychologically impoverished are the measures being used to assess developmental outcomes.

And even when such measures possess significant psychological content, they are often one-sided. Thus one may have elaborate data on such attitudinal variables as self-esteem, locus of control, marital or job satisfaction, and general value preference, but no information about the actual behavior of the person in the several contexts under investigation. Conversely, one is provided with minute behavioral data based on the analysis of videotapes made in the home, school, or job setting, but the meaning of these contexts and behaviors to the participants is left to be inferred.

Most modern definitions of development encompass both the behavioral and the phenomenological aspects of human functioning. Hence, wherever possible, it is desirable to have both these facets represented in assessments of developmental outcomes.

Finally, as I have argued elsewhere (Bronfenbrenner, 1979a) development cannot be equated with mere behavioral change; to conclude that actual development has occurred, it is necessary to submit evidence that the observed patterns of behavior exhibit some degree of continuity across both space and time. All too often, the outcome measures used in studies that purport to investigate development in context are in fact situation specific.

Such examples define by default the requirements of a developmental outcomes model; namely, it should provide some information about the psychological state of the developing person in terms of both its behavioral and its phenomenological aspects. It should also present evidence that the observed psychological outcomes exhibit continuity across time and setting.

Having defined the major paradigms employed in research on development in context, we now turn to an examination of their choice scientific yield in recent harvests.

Some Provocative Findings from Promising Paradigms

Before discussing specific results, it is important to indicate a general conclusion emerging from research that has been conducted on the ecology of human development, especially during the past few years. The overall thrust of the findings is to underscore the pivotal role of the family in shaping the course of development over the life-span. This is not to imply, however, that the major forces influencing psychological growth are primarily those that operate *within* the family. Rather, the key factor lies in the *relation* between processes taking place within the family and those that occur in other contexts affecting human development. In operational terms, this means that the research paradigms that have proved most productive scientifically are those that involve linkages between the family and other settings across time. This fact, in turn, suggests a convenient framework for the presentation of substantive findings under the following six headings:

The Family and Parental Support Networks.
The Family and the Community.

The Family and the School.
The Family and the Peer Group.
The Family and the World of Work.
The Family and Environmental Change through the Life Course.

In the interest of brevity, I shall confine detailed discussion of particular studies to two or three examples in each domain.

The Family and Parental Support Networks

Unfortunately, up to the present time, researchers in this domain have limited their investigations almost exclusively to the mother–child dyads, particularly those in specially vulnerable situations such as teenage mothers, single-parent mothers, or families living in poverty. In general, this body of research revealed that support was more likely to come from kin than nonkin, with the father being the principal source of help, even in single-parent households; the mother's mother was next in line, followed by other relatives, and then friends, neighbors, and professionals (Belle, 1981; Brown, Bhrolchin, & Harris, 1975; Crockenberg, in press-a, in press-b; Tietjen & Bradley, 1982). Mothers who had access to stronger social networks during their pregnancy reported lower levels of stress, anxiety, and depression, a better marital adjustment, and a more positive attitude toward their pregnancy. Support from the husband was more effective than that from friends, neighbors, or relatives outside the home. Studies conducted in families with young infants revealed that low family support evoked maternal attitudes of hostility, indifference, and rejection of the child (Colletta, 1981), whereas mothers experiencing help and comfort, primarily from the immediate family and relatives, felt less stress and had more positive attitudes toward themselves and their babies (Aug & Bright, 1970; Colletta, 1983; Colletta & Gregg, 1981; Colletta & Lee, 1983; Mercer, Hackley, & Bostrom, in press). In the realm of maternal behavior, mothers receiving higher levels of social support responded more quickly when their infants cried (Crockenberg, in press-a, in press-b), and provided more adequate caretaking behavior (Epstein, 1980; Wandersman & Unger, 1983).

With respect to the children themselves, Furstenberg & Crawford (1978), working with a predominantly black sample of teenage mothers, found that children of mothers who continued to live with their families of origin experienced fewer behavior problems, showed less antisocial behavior, and scored higher on cognitive tests than did children of teenage mothers who lived alone without adult relatives.

Research by Crockenberg (1981) broke new ground in demonstrating the interaction of organism and environment in the effects of social support. Working with a middle-class sample, she found that support received by the mother when the infant was 3 months old was positively related to the strength of the infant's attachment to its mother, with the effect being most pronounced in families in which the infant exhibited an irritable temperament.

A broader picture emerges from Crockenberg's most recent study (1984), in which she compared English teenage mothers with a matched sample of their American counterparts. She found that "English mothers engaged in more smiling and eye contact, less frequent routine contact, and responded more quickly to their babies' crying than did American mothers". Control of possibly confounding variables through regression analysis pointed to the amount and type of social support as the factor accounting for the difference. Crockenberg elaborates as follows:

In the United States most mothers rely on private doctors to serve their own and their children's health needs . . . Public health nurses or social workers may be assigned to families in need of special assistance, but there is no comprehensive system designed to provide health-related and child care advice to parents.

In contrast, England incorporates community-based social support for parents in a comprehensive program of health care. This care begins before the child's birth and continues through his school years. . . . Midwives provide postnatal care for mothers and babies after they leave the hospital following delivery, and home health visitors see new mothers on a regular basis. . . . In England, mothers had only to be home and open their doors.

At the conclusion of her report, Crockenberg emphasizes that her findings contradict a view about health and social services widely held in the United States; namely, that "largescale efforts will be implemented with variable quality, and the modal performance will be, by qualitative standards, mediocre."

With respect to implications for future research, a major consideration is the fact that work in this area is plagued by a lack of precision in the operationalization of concepts and causal processes. First, agents and types of support need to be differentiated and related to the degree of environmental stress to which the family is subjected. Second, research designs must take into account the possibility that causal processes may actually be operating in the reverse direction, with supportive social networks being a creation rather than a condition of constructive family functioning. Finally, social network studies should be expanded to encompass the full, two-step causal sequence: first, from the network properties to family functioning (or vice versa); and second; from family functioning to the behavior and development of the child.

The Family and The Community

The outstanding studies in this domain have been those conducted by Rutter and his group, beginning with their classic comparison of rates of mental disorder in Inner London and the Isle of Wight (Rutter, Cox, Tupling, Berger and Youle 1975; Rutter and Quinton, 1977). To control for possible effects of migration, the investigators confined their samples exclusively to children of parents born and bred in the given areas. Their findings reveal that rates of psychiatric disorder were much more frequent in the metropolis. Nor could the observed effects be explained by any community differences with respect to ethnicity, social class, or demographic factors (Quinton, 1980; Rutter & Madge, 1976). Indeed, the same social class position appeared to have a different significance in urban vs rural environments, with low socioeconomic status being a much stronger predictor of mental illness in the city than in the country. In the light of this series of findings, Rutter (1981) concluded: "It seemed that there must be something about living in the city which predisposed to mental disorder" (p. 612).

What is this "something"? Rutter's own efforts to answer this question have yielded results of particular relevance for child development. For example, taking advantage of the longitudinal design of the London—Isle of Wight study, Rutter (1980) analyzed community differences as a joint function of age of onset and type of disorder.

The results were striking in showing that the biggest difference between London and the Isle of Wight applied to *chronic* disorders of *early* onset . . . The least difference was found with psychiatric conditions beginning in adolescence for the first time. Moreover, the difference applied mainly to disorders associated with serious family difficulties. In short, the problems most characteristic of city children were those beginning early, lasting a long time, and accompanied by many other problems in the family (Rutter, 1981, p. 613, his italics).

To clarify the causal pathway leading to such effects, Rutter and his group (Rutter et al., 1975, Rutter & Quinton 1977) developed an index of "family adversity," including such factors as marital discord and dissolution, mental disorder or criminality in the parents, large family size, and other conditions known to be associated with higher levels of psychiatric disturbance and social deviance. The results were revealing. With the degree of family adversity controlled, the difference between London and the Isle of Wight in rates of child psychiatric illness all but disappeared. The authors interpret this result as indicating that the main adverse effects of city life on children are indirect, resulting from the disruption of the families in which they live.

Similar evidence of indirect effects on the child via the family have also been found for juvenile delinquency. For example, using a longitudinal design that permitted control for prior characteristics both of the child and of the family, West (1982) was able to demonstrate that delinquency rates for boys declined after their families moved out of London. As Rutter notes in a personal communication (1984), what is lacking in studies of this kind (including his own) is an identification of the particular features of an area that produce the given effect, and the process through which the effect takes place. "It is all very well to note the stresses of inner-city life, but what is needed is to determine just what it is that makes inner-city life stressful for some families in some circumstances. Personally, I would see this as the most important needed direction for future research."

Finally, whereas the *indirect* effects of urban residence appear to be negative for *social and emotional development,* particularly in *young* children, there is evidence that the *direct* influence of the city environment may be beneficial for *intellectual development* among *older* children. The principal support for this conclusion comes from a two-stage investigation carried out in rural and urban areas of Switzerland. The first study (Meili & Steiner, 1965) was conducted with 11-year-old schoolchildren. The researchers found that performance in both intelligence and achievement tests increased as a direct function of the amount of industry and traffic present in the area. The relationship was still significant after controlling for social class, but the influence of the latter variable was more powerful than that of locality. In a follow-up study, 4 years later, Vatter (1981) undertook to investigate the nature of the more immediate influences accounting for this result. Drawing on earlier work by Klineberg (1935, 1938) and Wheeler (1942), Vatter hypothesized that the superior cognitive functioning observed in city children was a product of exposure to the richer and more differentiated cultural environment typifying the urban scene. To investigate his "stimulus hypothesis," Vatter obtained information from his subjects about their daily activities within the community, and about the nature of existing community facilities (e.g., availability and use of libraries, learning opportunities outside the home, etc.). In support of the author's hypothesis, there was a significant positive relation between indices of the community environment and mental test scores. Moreover, community factors appeared to exert a stronger influence than intrafamilial variables (median correlation coefficient r of .41 vs .26). Vatter acknowledges, however, that his design did not permit adequate control for migration effects, since his follow-up study did not include all the original cases, and it was impossible to identify and reanalyze Time 1 data for the Time 2 sample.

It is noteworthy that the great majority of systematic studies of community influences on families and children have been conducted in Europe. In addition to the British and Swiss studies reviewed above, a seminal line of investigation in France takes its impetus from the classic two-volume work by Chombart de Lauwe (1959–1960), *Famille et Habitation,* and focuses primarily on neighborhood and housing as physical environments. In German-speaking Europe, a research tradition stimulated by Muchow & Muchow's (1935) classic study of the life-space of city children has led to investigations that are more diversified. For example, a recent compilation by Walter (1981, 1982) fills two volumes with investigations conducted by more than 20 investigators representing a variety of theoretical orientations.

The European work is also distinctive in the nature of the research paradigms that have been employed. Whereas American studies have been confined almost exclusively to social address models documenting associated differences in the behavior of children (Barker & Schoggen, 1973; Garbarino, 1976; Hollingshead, 1949), European investigations have focused on variations in *socialization processes* arising in different types of communities or neighborhoods defined by their particular physical and social character-istics.

The Family and the School

There is a striking asymmetry in studies of school and family influences on development. For more than 50 years, hundreds of researchers have sought for, and found, evidence for the powerful effect of family characteristics and parent–child interactions on children's performance and behavior in school (e.g., Symonds, 1939; Terman, 1925; Baumrind, 1980). By contrast, studies of influences operating in the opposite direction – that is, of the impact of the school on the child's behavior and development within the family – are both recent and rare. Where today's researchers do find common ground, how-ever, is at the intersection of these two domains; namely, the study of link-ages between home and school, and their effects primarily in the latter re-alm.

Although this area of research is characterized by a lack of precision in both theory and method, nevertheless a pattern of results has emerged that merits the attention of both scholars and practitioners. At the most general level, there are indications that the establishment of cooperative relations and activities between parents and school personnel have a modest but sig-nificant effect on children's school achievement (Becker and Epstein, 1981, 1982; Burns, 1982; Collins, Moles, and Cross, 1982; Epstein, 1983a, 1984; Henderson, 1981; Lightfoot, 1978; McNaughton, Glynn, Robinson, and Quinn, 1983; Medrich, Roizen, Rubin, and Buckley, 1982; Rodick and Heng-geler, 1980; Stewart, Sokol, and Healy, 1981; Tangri and Leitch, 1982). As Henderson (1981) states in a recent review:

Taken together, what is most interesting about the research is that it all points in the same direction. The form of parent involvement does not seem to be critical, so long as it is reasonably well-planned, comprehensive, and long-lasting.

Another aspect of the family-school interface deserves far more research attention than it has received: namely, the study of school influences on fam-ily functioning, including the behavior and development of the child in the home. In addition to the important case study material of Lightfoot (1978) and of Tangri and Leitch (1982), Epstein and her group (Epstein, 1980, 1983a, 1983b, 1983c; Becker and Epstein, 1982) have contributed quantita-tive findings of some interest. Working with a sample of almost 1000 eight-graders, Epstein (1983b, 1983c) examined the joint impact of family and classroom processes on change in pupil's attitudes and their academic achievement during the transition between the last year of middle school and the first year of high school. Children from homes or classrooms affording greater opportunities for communication and decision-making not only exhibited greater initiative and independence after entering high school, but also received higher grades. Family processes were considerably more powerful in producing change than classroom procedures. School influences were nevertheless effective, especially for pupils from families who had not emphasized intergenerational communication in the home or the child's participation in decision-making. The effects of family and school processes were greater than those attributable to socioeconomic status or race.

This study by Epstein illustrates the direction that research on home–school relations might profitably take in the future. In addition, with respect to the narrower domain of parental involvement, perhaps the most important needs are to differentiate between the various forms of this process, and to identify those elements, or combinations thereof, that are most effective in enhancing the power of both the home and the school as contexts of learning and human development.

The Family and the Peer Group

Despite considerable prominence in the 1960s and early 1970s, this area has received relatively little attention during the past decade. For example, a recent research review (Schaffer & Brody, 1981) lists few references after 1975. This state of affairs is somewhat surprising given the provocative nature of the earlier findings. Thus a series of cross-cultural studies (for references see Bronfenbrenner, 1979a, pp. 179–180; Bronfenbrenner & Crouter 1983, pp. 382–383) revealed that peer expectations and pressures can induce patterns of conformity and antisocial behavior, the latter tendency being especially marked in American samples. Moreover, this trend is corroborated by the results of recent investigations in this area by Boehnke et al. (1983), Gold & Petronio (1980), Pulkkinen (1983a, 1983b), and, especially, Jessor (this volume) and Kandel (this volume). The findings recorded in these inquiries suggest that the predominance of peer group pressure over family ties is a major factor in the entrapment of youngsters in juvenile delinquecy and drug abuse. This finding highlights the importance of investigating how families living in different circumstances can influence the nature of their children's peer group experience, how this peer group experience, in turn, can alter the parent's treatment of the child, and how both these processes influence a child's future development. Special priority should be accorded to longitudinal designs that trace alternative pathways from family to peer group, and then from both of these contexts into adult roles in the areas of work, family formation, parenthood, and participation in the social and political life of the community.

The Family and the World of Work

A recent volume prepared by a National Academy of Sciences panel (Kamerman & Hayes, 1982) summarizes most of what is now known in this sphere. In a special chapter devoted to the effects of parental work on children, Bronfenbrenner & Crouter (1982) pointed out that, until very recently, researchers have treated the job situations of mothers and fathers as separate worlds having no relation to each other and, presumably, as leading to rather different results. For mothers, it was the fact of being *employed* that was thought to be damaging to the child, whereas for fathers it was being *unemployed* that was seen as the destructive force. Because of this "division of labor," the principal research findings in each domain are most conveniently summarized under separate headings.

Paternal Employment and Family Life

The hypothesis that the structure and content of activities in the father's job can influence the family's child-rearing values has been explored by Kohn and his group. In his first study, Kohn (1969) demonstrated that working-class men whose jobs typically required compliance with authority tended to hold values that stressed obedience in their children; by contrast, middle-class fathers expected self-direction and independence, the qualities called for by the demands of their job. Occupational values were also reflected in both parents' child-rearing practices. Subsequently, Kohn and Schooler (1973, 1978) examined the nature of work in a finer analysis focusing on the dimension of "occupational self-direction" — the extent to which a job involves complex skills, autonomy, and lack of routinization — and its relation to the worker's "intellectual flexibility" as measured in a series of standardized tests. Using causal modeling techniques with longitudinal data, the investigators demonstrated that the occupational self-direction of a job could affect one's intellectual flexibility 10 years later. This finding was later replicated in a comparative study including samples from both the United States and Poland (Slomezynski, Miller, and Kohn, 1981).

The key question left unresolved in Kohn's own research concerns the last step in the developmental sequence that he posits: Does the opportunity for self-direction in the parent's job, and the intellectual flexibility that it generates, in fact influence parental patterns of child-rearing and thereby affect the development of the child? The one study I have been able to find that bears on this issue did not yield very powerful results. Using data from a sample of several hundred twelfth-graders and their mothers, Morgan, Alwin, and Griffin (1979) found the expected association between father's occupation and mother's child-rearing values. But when these value measures were related to various aspects of the adolescents' academic careers, the results presented a somewhat mixed picture. Neither the students' school grades, academic self-esteem, and expected educational and occupational attainment, not their generalized sense of personal control were affected. The mother's child-rearing values, however, did predict both her child's curriculum placement (measured on a continuum from vocational/commercial courses to college preparation) and the young person's involvement in school activities. The latter finding, however, held only for white students and not for blacks.

The reciprocal influence of the family on the world of work has been clearly documented in a longitudinal study by Mortimer, Lorence, & Kumka (1982). These investigators demonstrated the importance of the family in adult development by comparing the occupational careers of men who had married during the decade following graduation and those who had remained single. The results revealed that the former had experienced greater career stability, higher income and work autonomy, and greater job satisfaction. There was substantial evidence that these findings were not attributable to selection processes.

Maternal Employment and the Family. As documented in three recent reviews (Bronfenbrenner and Crouter, 1982; Hoffman, 1980, 1983), an analysis of research in this sphere reveals a consistent contrast, summarized in the following statement: "By 1980 there had accumulated an appreciable body of evidence indicating that the mother's work outside the home tends to have a salutary effect on girls, but may exert a negative influence on boys" (Bronfenbrenner & Crouter, 1982, pp. 51–52).

The processes underlying this consistent set of findings are illuminated in a study by Bronfenbrenner, Alvarez, and Henderson (1984). The basic data consisted of parents' free descriptions of their 3-year-old children. A systematic content analysis revealed that the most flattering portrait of a daughter was painted by mothers who were working full-time, but this was also the group that portrayed the son in the least favorable terms. A further breakdown by mother's educational status indicated that the enthusiastic view of a daughter in the group with full-time jobs occurred only among those mothers who had some education beyond high school. In the light of both quantitative and qualitative findings, the authors make the following interpretative comment: "The pattern brings to mind the picture of an aspiring professional woman who already sees her three-year-old daughter as an interesting and competent person potentially capable of following in her mother's footsteps" (p. 1366). The most salient feature of the findings for sons was the exceptionally positive description given by mothers working part-time, in contrast to the much lower evaluation offered by those fully employed. The advantages of part-time employment, so far as maternal perceptions are concerned, were appreciably greater for a son than for a daughter. The results of interviews with fathers (conducted separately) revealed the same highly differentiated profile, but in somewhat lower relief.[1]

The preceding comment calls attention to what is perhaps the most serious scientific gap in studies of the family–work interface. I refer to the paucity of studies examining the developmental impact of the joint employment patterns of father and mother. Of particular significance is conflict between the work schedules of the two parents, the hectic atmosphere it may generate in their lives, the resultant impact on the extent and quality of parent–child interaction, and the ultimate consequences for the development of the children of each sex.

The Family and Environmental Change Through the Life Course

An outstanding example of work guided by this paradigm is Elder's longitudinal study of *Children of the Great Depression* (1974). Results from the most recent follow-up of this research are presented elsewhere in this volume. Other research based on life course models have already been discussed under previous headings (e.g., the work of Rutter, Kohn, Mortimer, and Epstein).

Two other examples are especially worthy of note. In a longitudinal study in Finland, Pulkkinen (1982, 1983a, 1983b) examined the influence of environmental stability and change on development from 8 through 20 years of age. Specifically, the "steadiness" vs "unsteadiness" of family living conditions was measured by the occurrence of such events as the number of family moves, changes in day care or school arrangements, extent of parental absence, and altered conditions of parental employment. Greater instability of the family environment was associated with greater submissiveness, aggressiveness, and insecurity among children in later childhood, and with a higher incidence of such behaviors as early sexual activity, excessive smoking and drinking, and delinquency in adolescence and youth, a pattern very similar to that reported by both Jessor (this volume) and Kandel (this volume).

Although the advantages of a chronosystem model are best achieved within the framework of a longitudinal design, important benefits can also be gleaned from cross-sectional studies that include key retrospective data and use appropriate analytic procedures. A case in point is the recent work of Schneewind, Beckman & Engfer (1983). Their sample consisted of 570

---

[1] Regarding the basis for the observed sex differences in the effects of maternal employment, the authors speculate as follows: "One possible explanation draws on the recurrent and generally accepted finding in research on early sex differences (Maccoby and Jacklin, 1974) that male infants tend to be more physically active from birth and hence require more control and supervision. Full-time work may limit opportunities for such necessary monitoring. Viewed from this perspective, the findings suggest that the reported sex difference in effects of maternal employment derive from the cumulative interaction of familial, organismic, and employment factors evolving in a larger socioeconomic context" (p. 1371).

schoolchildren (ages 9–14) from schools in six German *länder*. Data were obtained independently from both the children and their parents. By using a multigenerational path analytic model, the researchers were able to identify the environmental antecedents of two contrasting clusters of children's maladaptive behavior: aggressive and antisocial activity on the one hand, and anxiety and helplessness on the other. Both patterns were influenced by factors outside the child's immediate family, but in each instance the causal path was indirect rather than direct, with the paternal use of corporal punishment serving as a key intervening variable. Parents most likely to apply physical discipline were those who had a lower socioeconomic status, or who themselves had experienced an unhappy childhood. But even here, the influence of parental practices was not direct, but operated principally through effects on parental personality structure, marital conflict, and child-rearing attitudes. It is noteworthy that these findings, obtained from a cross-sectional sample in Germany, are strikingly similar to those reported by Elder et al. (this volume) from a longitudinal study conducted in the United States.

Retrospective and Prospective Views

Despite the diversity of models and materials reviewed in this chapter, it is not difficult to suggest a combination of paradigm properties that offers the greatest promise for future research on the ecology of human development. It may be no easy matter, however, to integrate and implement these components within a single research design.

To begin with the easier task, in the light of the ideas and evidence we have examined an optimal design for research on development in context might well incorporate the following elements:

1. The use of a person-process-context model involving contrasts between at least two settings and between two groups of subjects distinguished by differing personal characteristics.

2. Observations on all three elements in the above model, as well as data on developmental status, obtained at two or more time points.

3. Measures of developmental status that include assessment of both behavioral and experiential function, as well as of the interrelations between these two domains.

It will be observed that the above elements encompass key features not only of a person-process-context model, but also properties of a number of other paradigms presented in the first section of this chapter, in particular the chronosystem, meso- or exosystem, and a developmental outcomes model. It is even more obvious that few investigators will have the time, resources, or, for that matter, the scientific chutzpa to undertake so ambitious an endeavor. To be sure, as we have seen, a number of investigators have already come fairly close to bringing off such an awesome enterprise quite successfully; only one or two of the specified elements were missing.

But the attainment of this comprehensive goal neither can nor should be the measure of the scientific utility of the ideas here presented. Their purpose is not to establish a set of criteria that every researcher should strive to meet, but rather to present an array of promising paradigms that generate a variety of research questions from which an investigator can choose the most attractive and practical alternatives, while at the same time being alerted to the ambiguities of interpretation created by the omission of important elements in the selected design. If this chapter contributes to the achievement of this more attainable goal, it will have served its highest hope.

References

Aug, R. & Bright, T. (1970) A study of wed and unwed motherhood in adolescents and young adults. *Journal of the American Academy of Child Psychiatry, 9,* 577 – 594

Baldwin, A. L. (1947) Changes in parent behavior during pregnancy. *Child Development, 18,* 29 – 39

Baltes, P. B. (1979) Life-span developmental psychology: Some convening observations on history and theory. In P. B. Baltes & O. G. Brim (Eds.), *Life-span development and behavior* (Vol. 2). New York: Academic

Baltes, P. B. & Schaie, K. W. (1973) *Life-span developmental psychology: Personality and socialization.* New York: Academic

Barker, R. G. & Schoggen, P. (1973) *Qualities of community life: Methods of measuring environment and behavior applied to an American and an English town.* San Francisco: Jossey-Bass

Baumrind, D. (1980) New directions in socialization research. *American Psychologist, 35,* 639 – 652

Becker, H. J. & Epstein, J. L. (1981) *Parent involvement: Teacher practices and judgments.* Baltimore, MD: Center for the Social Organization of Schools, Johns Hopkins University

Becker, H. J. & Epstein, J. L. (1982) *Influences on teacher's use of parent involvement at home* (Report No 324). Baltimore, MD: Center for the Social Organization of Schools, Johns Hopkins University

Bell, R. Q. (1968) A reinterpretation of the direction of effects in studies of socialization. *Psychological Review, 75,* 81 – 95

Belle, D. E. (1981, April) *The social network as a source of both stress and support to low-income mothers.* Paper presented at the Biennial Meeting of the Society for Research in Child Development, Boston, Massachusetts

Boehnke, K., Eyferth, K., Kastner, P., Noack, P., Reitzle, M., Silbereisen, R. K., Walper, S., & Zank, S. (1983) *Youth development and substance use.* Paper presented at the Seventh Biennial Meeting of the International Society for the Study of Behavioral Development, Munich, West Germany

Bronfenbrenner, U. (1974) Developmental research, public policy, and the ecology of childhood. *Child Development, 45,* 1 – 5

Bronfenbrenner, U. (1975) Reality and research in the ecology of human development. *Proceedings of the American Philosophical Society, 119,* 439 – 469

Bronfenbrenner, U. (1977a) Toward an experimental ecology of human development. *American Psychologist, 32,* 513 – 531

Bronfenbrenner, U. (1977b) Lewian space and ecological substance. *Journal of Social Issues, 33,* 199 – 212

Bronfenbrenner, U. (1979a) *The ecology of human development: Experiments by nature and design.* Cambridge, MA: Harvard University Press

Bronfenbrenner, U. (1979b) Contexts of child rearing. *American Psychologist, 34,* 844–858

Bronfenbrenner, U. (1981) *Die Ökologie der menschlichen Entwicklung.* Stuttgart: Klett-Cotta

Bronfenbrenner, U. (1984) *The ecology of the family as a context for human development: Research perspectives.* Position paper prepared at the request of the Human Learning and Behavior Branch of the National Institute of Child Health and Human Development as a contribution to the preparation of its Five Year Plan

Bronfenbrenner, U., Alvarez, W. F., & Henderson, C. R. (1984) Working and watching: Maternal employment status, and parents' perceptions of their three-year old children. *Child Development, 55,* 1362–1378

Bronfenbrenner, U. & Crouter, A. C. (1982) Work and family through time and space. In S. B. Kamerman & C. D. Hayes (Eds.), *Families that work: Children in a changing world.* Washington, DC: National Academy

Bronfenbrenner, U. & Crouter, A. C. (1983) The evolution of environmental models in developmental research. In W. Kessen (Ed.) *Handbook of child psychology: Vol. 1. History, theories, and methods* (4th ed). New York: Wiley

Brown, D. W., Bhrolchin, M., & Harris, T. (1975) Social class and psychiatric disturbance among women in urban populations. *Sociology, 9,* 225–254

Burns, J. (1982) *The study of parental involvement in four federal education programs: Executive summary.* Washington, DC: Department of Education, Office of Planning Budget and Evaluation

Chombart de Lauwe, P. H. (1959–1960) *Famille et Habitation* (2 volumes). Paris: Centre National de la Recherche Scientifique

Colletta, N. (1981) Social support and the risk of maternal rejection by adolescent mothers. *The Journal of Psychology, 109,* 191–197

Colletta, N. (1983) At risk for depression: A study of young mothers. *Journal of Genetic Psychology, 142,* 301–310

Colletta, N. D. & Gregg, C. H. (1981) Adolescent mothers' vulnerability to stress. *Journal of Nervous and Mental Diseases, 169,* 50–54

Colletta, N. D. & Lee, D. (1983) The impact of support for Black adolescent mothers. *Journal of Family Issues, 4,* 127–143

Collins, C., Moles, O., & Cross, M. (1982) *The home-school connection: Selected partnership programs in large cities.* Boston, MA: Institute for Responsive Education

Crockenberg, S. B. (1981) Infant irritability, other responsiveness, and social support influences on the security of infant–mother attachment. *Child Development, 52,* 857–865

Crockenberg, S. B. (1984) *Professional support and care of infants by adolescent mothers in England and the United States.* Unpublished manuscript, Department of Psychology, University of California, Davis

Crockenberg, S. B. (in press) English teenage mothers: Attitudes, behavior, and social support. In E. J. Anthony (Ed.), *International year book series of the International Association for Child Psychiatry and Allied Professions*

Crockenberg, S. B. (in press) Support for adolescent mothers during the postnatal period: Theory and research. In Z. Boukydis (Ed.), *Research on support for parents and infants in the postnatal period*

Elder, G. H., Jr. (1974) *Children of the Great Depression.* Chicago, Ill: University of Chicago Press

Epstein, A. (1980) *Assessing the child development information needed by adolescent parents with very young children.* Final report of Grant OCD-90-C-1341. Washington, DC: Office of Child Development, Department of Health, Education and Welfare (ERIC Document Reproduction Service No. ED 183286)

Epstein, J. L. (1983a) *Effects on parents of teacher practices of parent involvement.* (Report No 346). Baltimore, MD: Johns Hopkins University, Center for Social Organization of Schools

Epstein, J. L. (1983b) Longitudinal effects of family–school–person interactions on student outcomes. *Research in Sociology of Education and Socialization, 4,* 101–127

Epstein, J. L. (1983c) Longitudinal study of school and family effects on student development. In S. A. Mednick & M. Harway (Eds.), *Longitudinal research in the United States.* Boston, MA: Nijhoff

Epstein, J. L. (1984) *Single-parents and the schools: The effects of marital status on parent and teacher evaluations.* (Report No 353). Baltimore, MD: Johns Hopkins University, Center for Social Organization of Schools

Furstenberg, F. & Crawford, A. (1978) Family support: Helping teenage mothers to cope. *Family Planning Perspectives, 10,* 322–333

Garbarino, J. (1976) A preliminary study of some ecological correlates of child abuse: The impact of socioeconomic stresses on mothers. *Child Development, 47,* 178–185

Gold, M. & Petronio, R. J. (1980) Delinquent behavior in adolescence. In J. Adelson (Ed.), *Handbook of adolescent psychology.* New York: Wiley

Henderson, A. (1981) *Parent participation – student achievement: The evidence grows.* Columbia, Missouri: National Committee for Citizen Education

Hoffman, L. W. (1980) The effects of maternal employment on the academic attitudes and performance of school-age children. *School Psychology Review, 9,* 319–335

Hoffman, L. W. (1983) Work, family, and the socialization of the child. In R. D. Parke (Ed.), *Review of child development research: Volume 7: The family.* Chicago, Illinois: University of Chicago Press

Hollingshead, A. B. (1949) *Elmtown's youth and Elmtown revisited.* New York: Wiley

Kamerman, S. B. & Hayes, C. D. (Eds.) (1982) *Families that work.* Washington, DC: National Academy

Klineberg, O. (1935) *Negro intelligence in selective migration.* New York: Columbia University Press

Klineberg, O. (1938) The intelligence of migrants. *American Sociological Review, 3,* 218–224

Koel, A. (1984) *Women in the context of remarriage.* Unpublished doctoral dissertation. Ithaca, NY: Cornell University

Kohn, M. L. (1969) *Class and conformity: A study in values.* Homewood, Illinois: Dorsey

Kohn, M. L. & Schooler, C. (1973) Occupational experience and psychological functioning: An assessment of reciprocal effects. *American Sociological Review, 38,* 97–118

Kohn, M. L. & Schooler, C. (1978) The reciprocal effects of substantive complexity of work and intellectual flexibility: A longitudinal assessment. *American Journal of Sociology, 84,* 24–52

Lightfoot, S. L. (1978) *Worlds apart: Relationships between families and school.* New York: Basic Books

Maccoby, E. E. & Jacklin, C. N. (1974). *The psychology of sex differences.* Stanford, CA: Stanford University Press

McNaughton, S., Glynn, T., Robinson, V., & Quinn, M. (1983) *Producing independent reading at school using parents as home-based remedial reading tutors.* Unpublished paper, The Department of Education, University of Auckland, Australia

Medrich, E. A., Roizen, J., Rubin, V., & Buckley, S. (1982) *The serious business of growing up: A study of children's lives outside school.* Berkeley, CA: University of California Press

Meili, R. & Steiner, H. (1965) Eine Untersuchung zum Intelligenzniveau Elfjähriger der deutschen Schweiz. *Schweizerische Zeitschrift für Psychologie und ihre Anwendungen, 24* (1), 23–32

Mercer, R. T., Hackley, K. C., & Bostrom, A. (in press) Social support of teenage mothers. *Birth Defects: Original Article Series*

Morgan, W. R., Alwin, D. F., & Griffin, L. J. (1979) Social origins, parental values, and the transmission of inequality. *American Journal of Sociology, 85,* 156–166

Mortimer, J. T., Lorence, J., & Kumka, D. (1982) Work and family linkages in the transition to adulthood: A panel study of highly-educated men. *Western Psychological Review, 13,* 50–68

Muchow, M. & Muchow, H. H. (1935) *Der Lebensraum des Großstadtkindes.* Hamburg: M. Riegel

Pulkkinen, L. (1982) Self-control and continuity from childhood to late adolescence. In P. Baltes and O. Brim (Eds.), *Life-span development and behavior* (Volume IV, pp 64–102). New York: Academic

Pulkkinen, L. (1983a) Finland: Search of alternatives to aggression. In A. Goldstein and M. Segall (Eds.), *Aggression in global perspective.* New York: Pergamon

Pulkkinen, L. (1983b) Youthful smoking and drinking in a longitudinal perspective. *Journal of Youth and Adolescence, 12* (4), 253–283

Quinton, D. (1980) Family life in the inner city: Myth and reality. In M. Marland (Ed.), *Education for the inner city.* London: Heinemann

Rodick, J. D. & Hennggeler, S. W. (1980) The short-term and long-term amelioration of academic and motivational deficiencies among low-achieving inner-city adolescents. *Child Development, 51,* 1126–1132

Rutter, M. (1980) *Changing youth in a changing society.* Cambridge, MA: Harvard University Press

Rutter, M. (1981) The city and the child. *American Journal of Orthopsychiatry, 51* (4), 610–625

Rutter, M., Cox, A., Tupling, C., Berger, M., & Youle, W. (1975) Attainment and adjustment in two geographical areas. I. The prevalence of psychiatric disorder. *British Journal of Psychiatry, 126,* 493–509

Rutter, M. & Madge, N. (1976) *Cycles of disadvantage.* London: Heinemann

Rutter, M. & Quinton, D. (1977) Psychiatric disorder – ecological factors and concepts of causation. In H. McGurk (Ed.), *Ecological factors in human development.* Amsterdam: North-Holland

Schaffer, D. R. & Brody, G. H. (1981) Parental and peer influences on moral development. In R. W. Henderson (Ed.), *Parent–child interaction.* New York: Academic

Schneewind, K. A., Beckman, M., & Engfer, A. (1983) *Eltern und Kinder.* Stuttgart: Kohlhammer

Schwabe, H. & Bartholomani, F. (1870) Der Vorstellungskreis der Berliner Kinder beim Eintritt in die Schule. In *Berlin und seine Entwickelung: Städtisches Jahrbuch für Volkswirtschaft und Statistik: Vierter Jahrgang.* Berlin: Guttentag

Seaver, W. B. (1973) Effects of naturally induced teacher expectancies. *Journal of Personality and Social Psychology, 28,* 333–342

Slomezynski, K. M., Miller, J., & Kohn, M. (1981) Stratification, work, and values: A Polish-United States Comparison. *American Sociological Review, 46,* 720–744

Stewart, A. J., Sokol, M., & Healy, J. M., Jr. (1981) *The role of the family in mediating the impact of school transitions.* Paper presented at the Biennial Meeting of the Society for Research in Child Development, Boston, MA

Symonds, P. M. (1939) *The psychology of parent–child relationships.* New York: Appleton-Century

Tangri, S. S. & Leitch, M. L. (1982) *Barriers to home-school collaboration: Two case studies in junior high school.* Final Report submitted to the National Institute of Education. Washington, DC: The Urban Institute

Terman, I. M. (1925) *Genetic studies of genius.* Stanford, CA: Stanford University Press

Tietjen, A. M. & Bradley, C. F. (1982) *Social networks, social support and transition to parenthood.* Unpublished paper. University of British Columbia, Vancouver, Division of Family Studies

Tinbergen, N. (1951) *The study of instinct.* London: Oxford

Tulkin, S. R. (1977) Social class differences in maternal and infant behavior. In P. H. Leiderman, A. Rosenfeld, & S. R. Tulkin (Eds.), *Culture and infancy* (pp. 495–537). New York: Academic

Vatter, M. (1981) Intelligenz und regionale Herkunft. Eine Längsschnittstudie im Kanton Bern. In H. Walter (Ed.), *Region und Sozialisation* (Vol. I). Stuttgart: Frommann-Holzboog

Walter, H. (Ed.) (1981) *Region und Sozialisation* (Vol. I) Stuttgart: Frommann-Holzboog

Walter, H. (Ed.) (1982) *Region und Sozialisation* (Vol. II). Stuttgart: Frommann-Holzboog

Wandersman, L. P. & Unger, D. G. (1983) *Interaction of infant difficulty and social support in adolescent mothers.* Paper presented at the Biennial Meeting of the Society for Research in Child Development, Detroit, Michigan

West, D. J. (1982) *Delinquency: Its roots, careers, and prospects.* London: Heinemann Educational

Wheeler, L. R. (1942) A comparative study of the intelligence of East Tennessee mountain children. *Journal of Educational Psychology, 33,* 321 – 334

Wright, S. (1934) The method of path coefficients. *Annals of Mathematical Statistics, 5,* 161 – 215

Author Index

The page numbers in italics refer to the list of references following each chapter.

Subject Index